# The Works of William Cowper

## William Cowper, William Homer, Giovanni Battista Andreini

Cowper
NCF

THE

# WORKS

OF

# WILLIAM COWPER.

COMPRISING

## HIS POEMS,

### CORRESPONDENCE, AND TRANSLATIONS.

WITH

## A LIFE OF THE AUTHOR

BY THE EDITOR,

## ROBERT SOUTHEY, LL.D.

POET LAUREATE, ETC.

ILLUSTRATED WITH FIFTY FINE ENGRAVINGS.

IN EIGHT VOLUMES.
VOL. VII.

## LONDON:
H. G. BOHN, YORK STREET, COVENT GARDEN.
MDCCCLIV.

# THE

# ILIAD OF HOMER,

TRANSLATED BY

# WILLIAM COWPER.

EDITED BY

## ROBERT SOUTHEY, LL.D.

POET LAUREATE, ETC.

ILLUSTRATED WITH ENGRAVINGS ON STEEL, AFTER DRAWINGS

BY W. HARVEY.

LONDON:

HENRY G. BOHN, YORK STREET, COVENT GARDEN.

MDCCCLIV.

# PLATES IN THE SEVENTH VOLUME.

# ADVERTISEMENT.

It is incumbent upon the present Editor to state the reasons which have induced him, between two editions of Cowper's Homer, differing so materially from each other that they might almost be deemed different versions, to prefer the first.

Whoever has perused the Translator's letters must have perceived that he had considered with no ordinary care the scheme of his versification, and that when he resolved upon altering it in a second edition, it was in deference to the opinion of others.

It seems to the Editor that Cowper's own judgement is entitled to more respect than that of any, or all his critics; and that the version which he composed when his faculties were most active and his spirits least subject to depression,—indeed in the happiest part of his life,—ought not to be superseded by a revisal, or rather reconstruction, which was undertaken three years before his death,—not like the first translation as "a pleasant work, an innocent luxury," the cheerful and delightful occupation of hope and ardour and ambition,—but as "a hopeless employment," a task which he gave in "all his miserable days, and often many hours of the night," seeking to beguile the sense of utter wretchedness, by altering as if for the sake of alteration.

The Editor has been confirmed in this opinion by the concurrence of every person with whom he has communicated on the subject. Among others he takes the liberty of mentioning Mr. Cary, whose authority upon such a question is of especial weight, the Translator of Dante being the only one of our countrymen who has ever executed a translation of equal magnitude and not less difficulty, with the same perfect fidelity and admirable skill.

In support of this determination, the case of Tasso may be cited as curiously in point.   The great Italian poet altered his Jerusalem, like Cowper, against his own judgement, in submission to his critics: he made the alteration in the latter years of his life, and in a diseased state of mind ; and he proceeded upon the same prescribed rule of smoothing down his versification, and removing all the elisions.   The consequence has been that the reconstructed poem is utterly neglected, and has rarely, if ever, been reprinted, except in the two great editions of his collected works ; while the original poem has been and continues to be in such demand, that the most diligent bibliographer might vainly attempt to enumerate all the editions through which it has passed.

ROBERT SOUTHEY.

# PREFACE.

---

WHETHER a translation of HOMER may be best executed in blank verse or in rhyme, is a question in the decision of which no man can find difficulty, who has ever duly considered what translation ought to be, or who is in any degree practically acquainted with those very different kinds of versification. I will venture to assert that a just translation of any ancient poet in rhyme, is impossible. No human ingenuity can be equal to the task of closing every couplet with sounds homotonous, expressing at the same time the full sense, and only the full sense of his original. The translator's ingenuity, indeed, in this case, becomes itself a snare, and the readier he is at invention and expedient, the more likely he is to be betrayed into the widest departures from the guide whom he professes to follow. Hence it has happened, that although the public have long been in possession of an English HOMER by a poet whose writings have done immortal honour to his country, the demand of a new one, and especially in blank verse, has been repeatedly and loudly made by some of the best judges and ablest writers of the present day.

I have no contest with my predecessor. None is supposeable between performers on different instruments. Mr. Pope has surmounted all difficulties in his version of HOMER that it was possible to surmount in rhyme. But he was fettered, and his fetters were his choice. Accustomed always to rhyme, he had formed to himself an ear which probably could not be much gratified by verse that wanted it, and determined to encounter even impossibilities, rather than abandon a mode of writing in which he had excelled everybody, for the sake of another to which, unexercised in it as he was, he must have felt strong objections.

I number myself among the warmest admirers of Mr. Pope as an original writer, and I allow him all the merit he can justly claim as the translator of this chief of poets. He has given us the *Tale of Troy divine* in smooth verse, generally in correct and elegant language, and in diction often highly poetical. But his deviations are so many, occasioned chiefly by the cause already mentioned, that, much as he has done, and valuable as his work is on some accounts, it was yet in the humble province of a translator that I thought it possible even for me to follow him with some advantage.

That he has sometimes altogether suppressed the sense of his author, and has not seldom intermingled his own ideas with it, is a remark which, on this occasion, nothing but necessity should have extorted from me. But we differ sometimes so widely in our matter, that unless this remark, invidious as it seems, be premised, I know not how to obviate a suspicion, on the one hand, of careless oversight, or of factitious embellishment on the other. On this head, therefore, the English reader is to be admonished, that the matter found in me, whether he like it or not, is found also in HOMER, and that the matter not found in me, how much soever he may admire it, is found only in Mr. Pope. I have omitted nothing; I have invented nothing.

There is indisputably a wide difference between the case of an original writer in rhyme and a translator. In an original work the author is free; if the rhyme be of difficult attainment, and he cannot find it in one direction, he is at liberty to seek it in another: the matter that will not accommodate itself to his occasions he may discard, adopting such as will. But in a translation no such option is allowable; the sense of the author is required, and we do not surrender it willingly even to the plea of necessity. Fidelity is indeed of the very essence of translation, and the term itself implies it. For which reason, if we suppress the sense of our original, and force into its place our own, we may call our work an *imitation*, if we please, or perhaps a *paraphrase*, but it is no longer the same author only in a different dress, and therefore it is not translation. Should a painter, professing to draw the likeness of a beautiful woman, give her more or fewer features than belong to her, and a general cast of countenance of his own invention, he might be said to have produced a *jeu d'esprit*, a curiosity perhaps in its way, but by no means the lady in question.

It will however be necessary to speak a little more largely to this subject, on which discordant opinions prevail even among good judges.

The free and the close translation have, each, their advocates. But inconveniences belong to both. The former can hardly be true to the original author's style and manner, and the latter is apt to be servile. The one loses his peculiarities, and the other his spirit. Were it possible, therefore, to find an exact medium, a manner so close that it should let slip nothing of the text, nor mingle any thing extraneous with it, and at the same time so free as to have an air of originality, this seems precisely the mode in which an author might be best rendered. I can assure my readers from my own experience, that to discover this very delicate line is difficult, and to proceed by it when found, through the whole length of a poet voluminous as HOMER, nearly impossible. I can only pretend to have endeavoured it.

It is an opinion commonly received, but, like many others, indebted for its prevalence to mere want of examination, that a translator should imagine to himself the style which his author would probably have used, had the language into which he is rendered been his own; a direction which wants nothing but practicability to recommend it. For suppose six persons, equally qualified for the task, employed to translate the same Ancient into their own language, with this rule to guide them. In the event it would be found that each had fallen on a manner different from that of all the rest, and by probable inference it would follow that none had fallen on the right. On the whole, therefore, as has been said, the translation which partakes equally of fidelity and liberality, that is close, but not so close as to be servile, free, but not so free as to be licentious, promises fairest: and my ambition will be sufficiently gratified, if such of my readers as are able, and will take the pains to compare me in this respect with Homer, shall judge that I have in any measure attained a point so difficult.

As to energy and harmony, two grand requisites in a translation of this most energetic and most harmonious of all poets, it is neither my purpose nor my wish, should I be found deficient in either, or in both, to shelter myself under an unfilial imputation of blame to my mother-tongue. Our language is indeed less musical than the Greek, and there is no language with which I am at all acquainted that is not.  But it is musical enough for the purposes of melodious verse, and if it seem to fail, on whatsoever occasion, in energy, the blame is due, not to itself, but to the unskilful manager of it.  For so long as Milton's works, whether his prose or his verse, shall exist, so long there will be abundant proof that no subject, however important, however sublime, can demand greater force of expression than is within the compass of the English language.

I have no fear of judges familiar with Homer in the original. They need not be told that a translation of him is an arduous enterprize, and as such, entitled to some favour.  From these, therefore, I shall expect, and shall not be disappointed, considerable candour and allowance.  Especially *they* will be candid, and I believe that there are many such, who have occasionally tried their own strength in this *bow of Ulysses.* They have not found it supple and pliable, and with me are perhaps ready to acknowledge that they could not always even approach with it the mark of their ambition.  But I would willingly, were it possible, obviate uncandid criticism, because to answer it is lost labour, and to receive it in silence has the appearance of stately reserve, and self-importance.

To those, therefore, who shall be inclined to tell me hereafter that my diction is often plain and unelevated, I reply beforehand that I know it,—that it would be absurd were it otherwise, and that Homer himself stands in the same predicament.  In fact, it is one of his numberless excellencies, and a point in which his judgement never fails him, that he is grand and lofty always in the right place, and knows infallibly how to rise and fall with his subject.  *Big words on small matters* may serve as a pretty exact definition of the burlesque ; an instance of which they will find in the Battle of the Frogs and Mice, but none in the Iliad.

By others I expect to be told that my numbers, though here and there tolerably smooth, are not always such, but have, now and then, an ugly hitch in their gait, ungraceful in itself, and inconvenient to the reader.  To this charge also I plead guilty, but beg leave in alleviation of judgement to add, that my limping lines are not numerous, compared with those that limp not.  The truth is, that not one of them all escaped me, but, such as they are, they were all made such with a wilful intention. In poems of great length there is no blemish more to be feared than sameness of numbers, and every art is useful by which it may be avoided. A line, rough in itself, has yet its recommendations; it saves the ear the pain of an irksome monotony, and seems even to add greater smoothness to others. Milton, whose ear and taste were exquisite, has exemplified in his Paradise Lost the effect of this practice frequently.

Having mentioned Milton, I cannot but add an observation on the similitude of his manner to that of Homer. It is such, that no person familiar with both, can read either without being reminded of the other; and it is in those breaks and pauses, to which the numbers of the English poet are so much indebted both for their dignity and variety, that he chiefly copies the Grecian. But these are graces to which rhyme is not competent; so broken, it loses all its music; of which any person may convince himself by reading a page only of any of our poets anterior to Denham, Waller, and Dryden. A translator of Homer, therefore, seems directed by Homer himself to the use of blank verse, as to that alone in which he can be rendered with any tolerable representation of his manner in this particular. A remark which I am naturally led to make by a desire to conciliate, if possible, some, who, rather unreasonably partial to rhyme, demand it on all occasions, and seem persuaded that poetry in our language is a vain attempt without it. Verse, that claims to be verse in right of its metre only, they judge to be such rather by courtesy than by kind, on an apprehension that it costs the writer little trouble, that he has only to give his lines their prescribed number of syllables, and, so far as the mechanical part is concerned, all is well. Were this true, they would have reason on their side, for the author is certainly best entitled to applause who succeeds against the greatest difficulty, and in verse that calls for the most artificial management in its construction. But the case is not as they suppose. To rhyme, in our language, demands no great exertion of ingenuity, but is always easy to a person exercised in the practice. Witness the multitudes who rhyme, but have no other poetical pretensions. Let it be considered too, how merciful we are apt to be to unclassical and indifferent language for the sake of rhyme, and we shall soon see that the labour lies principally on the other side. Many ornaments of no easy purchase are required to atone for

the absence of this single recommendation. It is not sufficient that the lines of blank verse be smooth in themselves,
they must also be harmonious in the combination. Whereas
the chief concern of the rhymist is to beware that his couplets
and his sense be commensurate, lest the regularity of his
numbers should be (too frequently at least) interrupted. A
trivial difficulty this, compared with those which attend the
poet unaccompanied by his bells. He, in order that he may
be musical, must exhibit all the variations, as he proceeds, of
which ten syllables are susceptible ; between the first syllable
and the last there is no place at which he must not occasionally pause, and the place of the pause must be perpetually
shifted. To effect this variety, his attention must be given, at
one and the same time, to the pauses he has already made in
the period before him, as well as to that which he is about to
make, and to those which shall succeed it. On no lighter
terms than these is it possible that blank verse can be written
which will not, in the course of a long work, fatigue the ear
past all endurance. If it be easier, therefore, to throw five
balls into the air and to catch them in succession, than to sport
in that manner with one only, then may blank verse be more
easily fabricated than rhyme. And if to these labours we add
others equally requisite, a style in general more elaborate than
rhyme requires, farther removed from the vernacular idiom
both in the language itself and in the arrangement of it, we
shall not long doubt which of these two very different species
of verse threatens the composer with most expense of study
and contrivance. I feel it unpleasant to appeal to my own experience, but, having no other voucher at hand, am constrained
to it. As I affirm, so I have found. I have dealt pretty
largely in both kinds, and have frequently written more verses
in a day, with tags, than I could ever write without them.
To what has been here said (which whether it have been said
by others or not, I cannot tell, having never read any modern
book on the subject) I shall only add, that to be poetical without rhyme, is an argument of a sound and classical constitution
in any language.

A word or two on the subject of the following translation,
and I have done.

My chief boast is that I have adhered closely to my original,
convinced that every departure from him would be punished

with the forfeiture of some grace or beauty for which I could substitute no equivalent. The epithets that would consent to an English form I have preserved as epithets; others that would not, I have melted into the context. There are none, I believe, which I have not translated in one way or other, though the reader will not find them repeated so often as most of them are in HOMER, for a reason that need not be mentioned.

Few persons of any consideration are introduced either in the Iliad or Odyssey by their own name only, but their patronymic is given also. To this ceremonial I have generally attended, because it is a circumstance of my author's manner.

HOMER never allots less than a whole line to the introduction of a speaker. No, not even when the speech itself is no longer than the line that leads it. A practice to which, since he never departs from it, he must have been determined by some cogent reason. He probably deemed it a formality necessary to the majesty of his narration. In this article, therefore, I have scrupulously adhered to my pattern, considering these introductory lines as heralds in a procession; important persons, because employed to usher in persons more important than themselves.

It has been my point everywhere to be as little verbose as possible, though at the same time, my constant determination not to sacrifice my author's full meaning to an affected brevity.

In the affair of style, I have endeavoured neither to creep nor to bluster, for no author is so likely to betray his translator into both these faults, as HOMER, though himself never guilty of either. I have cautiously avoided all terms of new invention, with an abundance of which, persons of more ingenuity than judgement have not enriched our language, but incumbered it. I have also everywhere used an unabbreviated fullness of phrase as most suited to the nature of the work, and above all, have studied perspicuity, not only because verse is good for little that wants it, but because HOMER is the most perspicuous of all poets.

In all difficult places I have consulted the best commentators, and where they have differed, or have given, as is often the case, a variety of solutions, I have ever exercised my best judgement, and selected that which appears, at least to myself, the most probable interpretation. On this ground, and on account of the fidelity which I have already boasted, I may venture, I believe, to recommend my work as promising some usefulness to young students of the original.

The passages which will be least noticed, and possibly not at all, except by those who shall wish to find me at a fault, are those which have cost me abundantly the most labour. It is difficult to kill a sheep with dignity in a modern language, to flay and to prepare it for the table, detailing every circumstance of the process. Difficult also, without sinking below the level of poetry, to harness mules to a waggon, particularizing every article of their furniture, straps, rings, staples, and even the tying of the knots that kept all together. HOMER, who writes always to the eye, with all his sublimity and grandeur, has the minuteness of a Flemish painter.

But in what degree I have succeeded in my version either of these passages, and such as these, or of others more buoyant and above-ground, and especially of the most sublime, is now submitted to the decision of the reader, to whom I am ready enough to confess that I have not at all consulted their approbation, who account nothing grand that is not turgid, or elegant that is not bedizened with metaphor.

I purposely decline all declamation on the merits of HOMER, because a translator's praises of his author are liable to a suspicion of dotage, and because it were impossible to improve on those which this author has received already. He has been the wonder of all countries that his works have ever reached, even deified by the greatest names of antiquity, and in some places actually worshipped. And to say truth, were it possible that mere man could entitle himself by preeminence of any kind to divine honours, Homer's astonishing powers seem to have given him the best pretensions.

I cannot conclude without due acknowledgements to the best critic in HOMER I have ever met with, the learned and ingenious Mr. FUSELI. Unknown as he was to me when I entered on this arduous undertaking, (indeed to this moment I have never seen him) he yet voluntarily and generously offered himself as my reviser. To his classical taste and just discernment I have been indebted for the discovery of many blemishes in my own work, and of beauties, which would otherwise have escaped me in the original. But his necessary avocations would not suffer him to accompany me farther than to the latter books of the Iliad, a circumstance which I fear my readers, as well as myself, will regret with too much reason[1].

I have obligations likewise to many friends, whose names, were it proper to mention them here, would do me great honour. They have encouraged me by their approbation, have assisted me with valuable books, and have eased me of almost the whole labour of transcribing.

And now I have only to regret that my pleasant work is ended. To the illustrious Greek I owe the smooth and easy flight of many thousand hours. He has been my companion at home and abroad, in the study, in the garden, and in the field; and no measure of success, let my labours succeed as they may, will ever compensate to me the loss of the innocent luxury that I have enjoyed, as a Translator of HOMER.

[1] Some of the few notes subjoined to my translation of the Odyssey are by Mr. FUSELI, who had a short opportunity to peruse the MS. while the Iliad was printing. They are marked with his initial.

# PREFACE

PREPARED BY MR. COWPER,

FOR A

SECOND EDITION.

SOON after my publication of this work, I began to prepare it
for a second edition, by an accurate revisal of the first. It
seemed to me, that here and there, perhaps, a slight alteration
might satisfy the demands of some, whom I was desirous to
please; and I comforted myself with the reflection, that if I
still failed to conciliate all, I should yet have no cause to account myself in a singular degree unfortunate. To please an
unqualified judge, an author must sacrifice too much; and
the attempt to please an uncandid one were altogether hopeless. In one or other of these classes may be ranged all such
objectors, as would deprive blank verse of one of its principal
advantages, the variety of its pauses; together with all such
as deny the good effect, on the whole, of a line, now and then,
less harmonious than its fellows.

With respect to the pauses, it has been affirmed with an un-
accountable rashness, that Homer himself has given me an
example of verse without them. Had this been true, it would
by no means have concluded against the use of them in an
English version of Homer; because, in one language, and in
one species of metre, that may be musical, which in another
would be found disgusting. But the assertion is totally un-
founded. The pauses in Homer's verse are so frequent and
various, that to name another poet, if pauses are a fault, more
faulty than He, were, perhaps, impossible. It may even be
questioned, if a single passage of ten lines flowing with unin-
terrupted smoothness could be singled out from all the thousands that he has left us. He frequently pauses at the first
word of the line, when it consists of three or more syllables;
not seldom when of two; and sometimes even when of one
only. In this practice he was followed, as was observed in
my Preface to the first Edition, by the Author of the Paradise

Lost. An example inimitable indeed, but which no writer of English heroic verse without rhyme can neglect with impunity.

Similar to this is the objection which proscribes absolutely the occasional use of a line irregularly constructed. When Horace censured Lucilius for his lines *incomposito pede currentes*, he did not mean to say, that he was chargeable with such in some instances, or even in many, for then the censure would have been equally applicable to himself; but he designed by that expression to characterize all his writings. The censure therefore was just; Lucilius wrote at a time when the Roman verse had not yet received its polish, and instead of introducing artfully his rugged lines, and to serve a particular purpose, had probably seldom, and never but by accident, composed a smooth one. Such has been the versification of the earliest poets in every country. Children lisp, at first, and stammer; but, in time, their speech becomes fluent, and, if they are well taught, harmonious.

Homer himself is not invariably regular in the construction of his verse. Had he been so, Eustathius, an excellent critic and warm admirer of Homer, had never affirmed, that some of his lines want a head, some a tail, and others a middle. Some begin with a word that is neither Dactyl nor Spondee, some conclude with a Dactyl, and in the intermediate part he sometimes deviates equally from the established custom. I confess that instances of this sort are rare; but they are surely, though few, sufficient to warrant a sparing use of similar license in the present day.

Unwilling, however, to seem obstinate, in both these particulars, I conformed myself in some measure to these objections, though unconvinced myself of their propriety. Several of the rudest and most unshapely lines I composed anew; and several of the pauses least in use I displaced for the sake of an easier enunciation.—And this was the state of the work after the revisal given it about seven years since.

Between that revisal and the present a considerable time intervened, and the effect of long discontinuance was, that I became more dissatisfied with it myself, than the most difficult to be pleased of all my judges. Not for the sake of a few uneven lines or unwonted pauses, but for reasons far more substantial. The diction seemed to me in many passages either not sufficiently elevated, or deficient in the grace of ease,

and in others I found the sense of the original either not ad-
equately expressed or misapprehended.    Many elisions still
remained unsoftened ; the compound epithets I found not
always happily combined, and the same sometimes too frequently repeated.

There is no end of passages in Homer, which must creep
unless they are lifted; yet in such, all embellishment is out
of the question.    The hero puts on his clothes, or refreshes
himself with food and wine, or he yokes his steed, takes a
journey, and in the evening preparation is made for his repose.
To give relief to subjects prosaic as these without seeming un-
seasonably tumid is extremely difficult.    Mr. Pope much
abridges some of them, and others he omits ; but neither of
these liberties was compatible with the nature of my undertaking.    These, therefore, and many similar to these, have
been new-modelled ; somewhat to their advantage I hope, but
not even now entirely to my satisfaction.    The lines have a
more natural movement, the pauses are fewer and less stately,
the expression as easy as I could make it without meanness,
and these were all the improvements that I could give them.

The elisions, I believe, are all cured, with only one excep-
tion.    An alternative proposes itself to a modern versifier, from
which there is no escape, which occurs perpetually, and which,
choose as he may, presents him always with an evil.    I mean
in the instance of the particle (*the*).    When this particle pre-
cedes a vowel, shall he melt it into the substantive, or leave
the *hiatus* open ? Both practices are offensive to a delicate ear.
The particle absorbed occasions harshness, and the open vowel
a vacuity equally inconvenient.    Sometimes, therefore, to leave
it open, and sometimes to ingraft it into its adjunct seems most
adviseable ; this course Mr. Pope has taken, whose authority
recommended it to me ; though of the two evils I have most
frequently chosen the elision as the least.

Compound epithets have obtained so long in the poetical
language of our country, that I employed them without fear or
scruple. To have abstained from them in a blank verse translation of Homer, who abounds with them, and from whom
our poets probably first adopted them, would have been strange
indeed.    But though the genius of our language favours the
formation of such words almost as much as that of the Greek,
it happens sometimes, that a Grecian compound either cannot

be rendered in English at all, or, at best, but awkwardly. For this reason, and because I found that some readers much disliked them, I have expunged many; retaining, according to my best judgement, the most eligible only, and making less frequent the repetitions even of these.

I know not that I can add anything material on the subject of this last revisal, unless it be proper to give the reason why the Iliad, though greatly altered, has undergone much fewer alterations than the Odyssey. The true reason I believe is this. The Iliad demanded my utmost possible exertions; it seemed to meet me like an ascent almost perpendicular, which could not be surmounted at less cost than of all the labour that I could bestow on it. The Odyssey on the contrary seemed to resemble an open and level country, through which I might travel at my ease. The latter therefore, betrayed me into some negligence, which, though little conscious of it at the time, on an accurate search, I found had left many disagreeable effects behind it.

I now leave the work to its fate. Another may labour hereafter in an attempt of the same kind with more success; but more industriously, I believe, none ever will.

*b* 3

# PREFACE

BY

## J. JOHNSON, LL.D.

**CHAPLAIN TO THE BISHOP OF PETERBOROUGH.**

I HAVE no other pretensions to the honourable name of Editor on this occasion, than as a faithful transcriber of the Manuscript, and a diligent corrector of the Press, which are, doubtless, two of the very humblest employments in that most extensive province. I have wanted the ability to attempt any thing higher; and, fortunately for the Reader, I have also wanted the presumption. What, however, I can do, I will. Instead of critical remark, I will furnish him with anecdote. He shall trace from beginning to end the progress of the following Work; and in proportion as I have the happiness to engage his attention, I shall merit the name of a fortunate Editor.

It was in the darkest season of a most calamitous depression of his spirits, that I was summoned to the house of my inestimable friend the Translator, in the month of January 1794. He had happily completed a revisal of his Homer, and was thinking of the Preface to his new Edition, when all his satisfaction in the one, and whatever he had projected for the other, in a moment vanished from his mind. He had fallen into a deplorable illness; and though the foremost wish of my heart was to lessen the intenseness of his misery, I was utterly unable to afford him any aid.

I had however a pleasing though a melancholy opportunity of tracing his recent footsteps in the Field of Troy, and in the Palace of Ithaca. He had materially altered both the Iliad and Odyssey; and, so far as my ability allowed me to judge, they were each of them greatly improved. He had, also at the request of his bookseller, interspersed the two Poems with copious Notes; for the most part translations of the ancient Scholia, and gleaned, at the cost of many valuable hours, from the pages of Barnes, Clarke, and Villoisson. It has been a constant subject of regret to the admirers of " The Task,"

that the exercise of such marvellous, original powers, should
have been so long suspended by the drudgery of Translation ;
and, in this view, their quarrel with the illustrious Greek will
be, doubtless, extended to his Commentators[1].

During two long years from this most anxious period, the
Translation continued as it was ; and though, in the hope of
its being able to divert his melancholy, I had attempted more
than once to introduce it to its Author, I was every time pain-
fully obliged to desist.   But in the summer of ninety-six, when
he had resided with me in Norfolk twelve miserable months, the
introduction, long wished for, took place.   To my inexpres-
sible astonishment and joy, I surprised him, one morning,
with the Iliad in his hand ; and with an excess of delight, which
I am still more unable to describe, I the next day discovered
that he had been writing.—Were I to mention one of the
happiest moments of my life, it might be that which introduced me to the following lines :—

> Mistaken meanings corrected,
> admonente G. Wakefield.

B. **xxiii.**
L.   429.
>                        that the nave
> Of thy neat wheel seem e'en to grind upon it.

L.   865.
> As when (the North wind freshening) near the bank
> Up springs a fish in air, then falls again
> And disappears beneath the sable flood,
> So at the stroke, he bounded.

L.   1018.
> Thenceforth Tydides o'er his ample shield
> Aim'd and still aim'd to pierce him in the neck.

> Or better thus—

> Tydides, in return, with spear high-poised
> O'er the broad shield, aim'd ever at his neck.

[1] Very few signatures had at this time been affixed to the Notes ; but
I afterward compared them with the Greek, note by note, and endeavoured
to supply the defect ; more especially in the last three Volumes, where
the Reader will be pleased to observe that all the notes without signatures are Mr. Cowper's, and that those marked B. C. V. are respectively
found in the Editions of Homer by Barnes, Clarke, and Villoisson.   But
the employment was so little to the taste and inclination of the Poet,
that he never afterward revised them, or added to their number more than
these which follow :—In the Odyssey, Vol. I. Book xi., the note 32.—Vol.
II. Book xv., the note 13.—The note 10, Book xvi., of that volume, and
the note 14, Book xix. of the same.

Or best of all—

Then Tydeus' son, with spear high-poised above
The ample shield, stood aiming at his neck.

He had written these lines with a pencil, on a leaf at the end of his Iliad ; and when I reflected on the cause which had given them birth, I could not but admire its disproportion to the effect. What the voice of persuasion had failed in for a year, accident had silently accomplished in a single day. The circumstance I allude to was this : I received a copy of the Iliad and Odyssey of Pope, then recently published by the Editor above-mentioned, with illustrative and critical notes of his own. As it commended Mr. Cowper's Translation in the Preface, and occasionally pointed out its merits in the Notes, I was careful to place it in his way ; though it was more from a habit of experiment which I had contracted, than from well-grounded hopes of success. But what a fortunate circumstance was the arrival of this work ! and by what name worthy of its influence shall I call it ? In the mouth of an indifferent person it might be chance ; but in mine, whom it rendered so peculiarly happy, common gratitude requires that it should be Providence.

As I watched him with an indescribable interest in his progress, I had the satisfaction to find, that, after a few mornings given to promiscuous correction, and to frequent perusal of the above-mentioned Notes, he was evidently settling on the sixteenth Book. This he went regularly through, and the fruits of an application so happily resumed were, one day with another, about sixty new lines. But with the end of the sixteenth Book he had closed the corrections of the year. An excursion to the Coast, which immediately followed, though it promised an accession of strength to the body, could not fail to interfere with the pursuits of the mind. It was therefore with much less surprise than regret, that I saw him relinquish the "Tale of Troy Divine."

Such was the prelude to the Last Revisal, which, in the month of January, ninety-seven, Mr. Cowper was persuaded to undertake ; and to a faithful copy, as I trust, of which, I have at this time the honour to conduct the Reader. But it may not be amiss to observe, that with regard to the earlier Books of the Iliad, it was less a revisal of the altered text, than of the text as it stands in the first Edition. For though the interleaved copy was always at hand, and in the multitude of its altered places could hardly fail to offer some things worthy to be preserved, but which the ravages of illness and the lapse of time might have utterly effaced from his mind, I could not often persuade the Translator to consult it. I was therefore induced, in the course of transcribing, to compare the two Revisals as I went along, and to plead for the continuance of the first correction, when it forcibly struck me as better than the last. This, however, but seldom occurred ; and the practice, at length, was completely left off, by his consenting to receive into the number of the Books which were daily laid open before him, the interleaved Copy to which I allude.

At the end of the first six Books of the Iliad, the arrival of Spring brought the usual interruptions of exercise and air, which increased as the Summer advanced to a degree so unfavourable to the progress of Homer, that in the requisite attention to their salutary claims, the Revisal was, at one time, altogether at a stand. Only four Books were added in the course of nine months ; but opportunity returning as the Winter set in, there were added, in less than seven weeks, four more : and thus ended the year ninety-seven.

As the Spring that succeeded was a happier Spring, so it led to a happier Summer. We had no longer air and exercise alone, but exercise and Homer hand in hand. He even followed us thrice to the Sea ; and whether our walks were

> " on the margin of the land,
> O'er the green summit of the" cliffs, " whose base
> Beats back the roaring surge,"
>                     " or on the shore
> Of the untillable and barren Deep,"

they were always within hearing of his magic Song. About the middle of this busy summer, the revisal of the Iliad was brought to a close ; and on the very next day, the 24th of July, the correction of the Odyssey commenced,—a morning rendered memorable by a kind and unexpected visit from the Patroness of that Work, the Dowager Lady Spencer !

It is not my intention to detain the Reader with a progressive account of the Odyssey revised, as circumstantial as that of the Iliad, because it went on smoothly from beginning to end, and was finished in less than eight months.

I cannot deliver these Volumes to the Public without feeling emotions of gratitude towards Heaven, in recollecting how often this corrected Work has appeared to me an instrument of divine mercy, to mitigate the sufferings of my excellent Relation. Its progress in our private hours was singularly medicinal to his mind: may its presentment to the Public prove not less conducive to the honour of the departed Author, who has every claim to my veneration! As a copious Life of the Poet is already in the Press, from the pen of his intimate friend Mr. Hayley, it is unnecessary for me to enter on such extensive commendation of his character, as my own intimacy with him might suggest; but I hope the reader will kindly allow me the privilege of indulging, in some degree, the feelings of my heart, by applying to Him, in the close of this Preface, an expressive verse (borrowed from Homer) which He inscribed Himself, with some little variation, on a Bust of his Grecian Favourite.

'Ὡς τε πατὴρ ᾧ παιδί, καὶ ἔποτε λήσομαι αὐτῶ.

Loved as his Son, in him I early found
A Father, such as I will ne'er forget.

# CONTENTS.

# ILIAD OF HOMER.

## BOOK I.

### ARGUMENT.

The book opens with an account of a pestilence that prevailed in the
Grecian camp, and the cause of it is assigned.  A council is called,
in which fierce altercation takes place between Agamemnon and Achilles.
The latter solemnly renounces the field.  Agamemnon by his heralds
demands Brisëis, and Achilles resigns her.  He makes his complaint to
Thetis, who undertakes to plead his cause with Jupiter.  She pleads
it, and prevails.  The book concludes with an account of what passed
in Heaven on that occasion.

The English reader will be pleased to observe, that by Achaians,
Argives, Danaï, are signified Grecians.   Homer himself having found
these various appellatives both graceful and convenient, it seemed unreasonable that a Translator of him should be denied the same advantage.

ACHILLES sing, O Goddess! Peleus' son;
His wrath pernicious, who ten thousand woes
Caused to Achaia's host, sent many a soul
Illustrious into Hades premature,
And Heroes gave (so stood the will of Jove)          5
To dogs and to all ravening fowls a prey,
When fierce dispute had separated once
The noble Chief Achilles from the son
Of Atreus, Agamemnon, King of men.
    Who them to strife impell'd? What power divine?    10
Latona's son and Jove's.   For He, incensed
Against the King, a foul contagion raised
In all the host, and multitudes destroy'd,
For that the son of Atreus had his priest
Dishonoured, Chryses.   To the fleet he came          15
Bearing rich ransom glorious to redeem

His daughter, and his hands charged with the wreath
And golden sceptre of the God shaft-arm'd.
   His supplication was at large to all
The host of Greece, but most of all to two,         20
The sons of Atreus, highest in command.
   Ye gallant Chiefs, and ye their gallant host,
(So may the Gods who in Olympus dwell
Give Priam's treasures to you for a spoil
And ye return in safety,) take my gifts         25
And loose my child, in honour of the son
Of Jove, Apollo, archer of the skies.
   At once the voice of all was to respect
The priest, and to accept the bounteous price;
But so it pleased not Atreus' mighty son,        30
Who with rude threatenings stern him thence dismiss'd.
   Beware, old man! that at these hollow barks
I find thee not now lingering, or henceforth
Returning, lest the garland of thy God
And his bright sceptre should avail thee nought.        35
I will not loose thy daughter, till old age
Steal on her.   From her native country far,
In Argos, in my palace, she shall ply
The loom, and shall be partner of my bed.
Move me no more.   Begone; hence while thou may'st.    40
   He spake, the old priest trembled and obey'd.
Forlorn he roamed the ocean's sounding shore,
And, solitary, with much prayer his King
Bright-hair'd Latona's son, Phœbus, implored.
   God of the silver bow, who with thy power        45
Encirclest Chrysa, and who reign'st supreme
In Tenedos and Cilla the divine,
Sminthian[1] Apollo! If I e'er adorned
Thy beauteous fame, or on thy altar burn'd
The fat acceptable of bulls or goats,        50
Grant my petition.   With thy shafts avenge
On the Achaian host thy servant's tears.
   Such prayer he made, and it was heard.   The God,
Down from Olympus with his radiant bow
And his full quiver o'er his shoulder slung,        55

[1] So called on account of his having saved the people of Troas from
a plague of mice, sminthos in their language meaning a mouse.

Marched in his anger; shaken as he moved
His rattling arrows told of his approach.
Gloomy he came as night; sat from the ships
Apart, and sent an arrow.  Clang'd the cord
[2] Dread-sounding, bounding on the silver bow.    60
Mules first and dogs he struck, but at themselves
Dispatching soon his bitter arrows keen,
Smote them.   Death-piles on all sides always blazed.
Nine days throughout the camp his arrows flew;
The tenth, Achilles from all parts convened    65
The host in council.   Juno the white-armed,
Moved at the sight of Grecians all around
Dying, imparted to his mind the thought.
The full assembly, therefore, now convened,
Uprose Achilles ardent, and began.    70
    Atrides! Now, it seems, no course remains
For us, but that the seas roaming again,
We hence return; at least if we survive;
But haste, consult we quick some prophet here
Or priest, or even interpreter of dreams,    75
(For dreams are also of Jove,) that we may learn
By what crime we have thus incensed Apollo,
What broken vow, what hecatomb unpaid
He charges on us, and if soothed with steam
Of lambs or goats unblemish'd, he may yet,    80
Be won to spare us, and avert the plague.
    He spake and sat, when Thestor's son arose
Calchas, an augur foremost in his art,
Who all things, present, past, and future knew,
And whom his skill in prophecy, a gift    85
Conferr'd by Phœbus on him, had advanced
To be conductor of the fleet to Troy;
He, prudent, them admonishing, replied.
    Jove-loved Achilles! Would'st thou learn from me
What cause hath moved Apollo to this wrath,    90
The shaft-arm'd King? I shall divulge the cause.
But thou, swear first and covenant on thy part

---

[2] For this singular line the Translator begs to apologize, by pleading
the strong desire he felt to produce an English line, if possible, somewhat
resembling in its effect the famous original one.
     Δεινὴ δὲ κλαγγὴ γένετ' ἀργυρέοιο βιοῖο.

That speaking, acting, thou wilt stand prepared
To give me succour; for I judge amiss,
Or he who rules the Argives, the supreme            95
O'er all Achaia's host, will be incensed.
Woe to the man who shall provoke the King!
For if, to-day, he smother close his wrath,
He harbours still the vengeance and in time
Performs it.   Answer, therefore, wilt thou save me?   100
   To whom Achilles, swiftest of the swift.
What thou hast learn'd in secret from the God,
That speak, and boldly.   By the son of Jove,
Apollo, whom thou, Calchas, seek'st in prayer
Made for the Danaï, and who thy soul               105
Fills with futurity, in all the host
The Grecian lives not, who while I shall breathe,
And see the light of day, shall in this camp
Oppress thee; no, not even if thou name
Him, Agamemnon, sovereign o'er us all.             110
   Then was the seer embolden'd, and he spake.
Nor vow nor hecatomb unpaid on us
He charges, but the wrong done to his priest
Whom Agamemnon slighted when he sought
His daughter's freedom, and his gifts refused.     115
He is the cause.   Apollo for his sake
Afflicts and will afflict us, neither end
Nor intermission of his heavy scourge
Granting, 'till unredeem'd, no price required,
The black-eyed maid be to her father sent,         120
And a whole hecatomb in Chrysa bleed.
Then, not before, the God may be appeased.
   He spake and sat; when Atreus' son arose,
The Hero Agamemnon, throned supreme.
Tempests of black resentment overcharged           125
His heart, and indignation fired his eyes.
On Calchas louring, him he first address'd.
   Prophet of mischief! from whose tongue no note
Of grateful sound to me, was ever heard;
Ill tidings are thy joy, and tidings glad          130
Thou tell'st not, or thy words come not to pass.
And now among the Danaï thy dreams
Divulging, thou pretend'st the Archer-God

For his priest's sake, our enemy, because
I scorn'd his offer'd ransom of the maid     135
Chryséis, more desirous far to bear
Her to my home, for that she charms me more
Than Clytemnestra, my own first espoused,
With whom, in disposition, feature, form,
Accomplishments, she may be well compared.     140
Yet, being such, I will return her hence
If that she go be best.   Perish myself,—
But let the people of my charge be saved!
Prepare ye, therefore, a reward for me,
And seek it instant.   It were much unmeet     145
That I alone of all the Argive host
Should want due recompense, whose former prize
Is elsewhere destined, as ye all perceive.
    To whom Achilles, matchless in the race.
Atrides, glorious above all in rank,     150
And as intent on gain as thou art great,
Whence shall the Grecians give a prize to thee?
The general stock is poor; the spoil of towns
Which we have taken, hath already passed
In distribution, and it were unjust     155
To gather it from all the Greeks again.
But send thou back this Virgin to her God,
And when Jove's favour shall have given us Troy,
A threefold, fourfold share shall then be thine.
    To whom the Sovereign of the host replied.     160
God-like Achilles, valiant as thou art,
Would'st thou be subtle too?   But me no fraud
Shall overreach, or art persuade, of thine.
Would'st thou, that thou be recompensed, and I
Sit meekly down defrauded of my due?     165
And did'st thou bid me yield her? Let the bold
Achaians give me competent amends,
Such as may please me, and it shall be well.
Else, if they give me none, I will command
Thy prize, the prize of Ajax, or the prize     170
It may be of Ulysses to my tent,
And let the loser chafe.   But this concern
Shall be adjusted at convenient time.
Come,—Launch we now into the sacred deep

A bark with lusty rowers well supplied;                    175
Then put on board Chryséis, and with her
The sacrifice required.   Go also one
High in authority, some counsellor,
Idomeneus, or Ajax, or thyself,
Thou most untractable of all mankind;                      180
And seek by rites of sacrifice and prayer
To appease Apollo on our host's behalf.
    Achilles eyed him with a frown, and spake.
Ah! cloathed with impudence as with a cloak,
And full of subtlety, who, thinkest thou—                  185
What Grecian here will serve thee, or for thee
Wage covert war, or open? Me thou know'st
Troy never wronged; I came not to avenge
Harm done to me; no Trojan ever drove
My pastúres, steeds or oxen took of mine,                  190
Or plunder'd of their fruits the golden fields
Of Phthia the deep-soil'd.   She lies remote,
And obstacles are numerous interposed,
Vale-darkening mountains, and the dashing sea.
No, ³ Shameless Wolf! For thy good pleasure sake           195
We came, and, ⁴ Face of flint! to avenge the wrongs
By Menelaus and thyself sustain'd,
On the offending Trojan—service kind,
But lost on thee, regardless of it all.
And now—What now? Thy threatening is to seize              200
Thyself, the just requital of my toils,
My prize hard-earn'd, by common suffrage mine.
I never gain, what Trojan town soe'er
We ransack, half thy booty.   The swift march
And furious onset,—these I largely reap,                   205
But, distribution made, thy lot exceeds
Mine far; while I, with any pittance pleased,
Bear to my ships the little that I win
After long battle, and account it much.
But I am gone, I and my sable barks                        210
(My wiser course) to Phthia, and I judge,
Scorn'd as I am, that thou shalt hardly glean
Without me, more than thou shalt soon consume.
    He ceased, and Agamemnon thus replied.

³ Κυνῶπα. .        ⁴ μεγ' ἀναιδὲς.

Fly, and fly now; if in thy soul thou feel　　　　　215
Such ardour of desire to go—begone!
I woo thee not to stay; stay not an hour
On my behalf, for I have others here
Who will respect me more, and above all
All-judging Jove.　There is not in the host　　　220
King or commander whom I hate as thee,
For all thy pleasure is in strife and blood,
And at all times; yet valour is no ground
Whereon to boast, it is the gift of Heaven.
Go, get ye back to Phthia, thou and thine!　　225
There rule thy Myrmidons.　I need not thee,
Nor heed thy wrath a jot.　But this I say,
Sure as Apollo takes my lovely prize
Chryséis, and I shall return her home
In mine own bark, and with my proper crew,　230
So sure the fair Briséis shall be mine.
I shall demand her even at thy tent.
So shalt thou well be taught, how high in power
I soar above thy pitch, and none shall dare
Attempt, thenceforth, comparison with me.　　235
　　He ended, and the big disdainful heart
Throbbed of Achilles; racking doubt ensued
And sore perplex'd him, whether forcing wide
A passage through them, with his blade unsheathed
To lay Atrides breathless at his foot,　　　　240
Or to command his stormy spirit down.
So doubted he, and undecided yet
Stood drawing forth his faulchion huge; when lo!
Down sent by Juno, to whom both alike
Were dear, and who alike watched over both,　245
Pallas descended.　At his back she stood
To none apparent, save himself alone,
And seized his golden locks.　Startled, he turned,
And instant knew Minerva.　Flashed her eyes
Terrific; whom with accents on the wing　　　250
Of haste, incontinent he questioned thus.
　　Daughter of Jove, why comest thou? that thyself
May'st witness these affronts which I endure
From Agamemnon? Surely as I speak,
This moment, for his arrogance, he dies.　　　255

To whom the blue-eyed Deity.  From heaven
Mine errand is, to soothe, if thou wilt hear,
Thine anger.  Juno the white-arm'd, alike
To him and thee propitious, bade me down:
Restrain thy wrath.  Draw not thy faulchion forth.        260
Retort, and sharply, and let that suffice.
For I foretell thee true.  Thou shalt receive,
Some future day, thrice told, thy present loss
For this day's wrong.  Cease, therefore, and be still.
    To whom Achilles.  Goddess, although much        265
Exasperate, I dare not disregard
Thy word, which to obey is always best.
Who hears the Gods, the Gods hear also him.
    He said; and on his silver hilt the force
Of his broad hand impressing, sent the blade        270
Home to its rest, nor would the counsel scorn
Of Pallas.  She to heaven well-pleased return'd,
And in the mansion of Jove Ægis⁵-armed
Arriving, mingled with her kindred Gods.
But though from violence, yet not from words        275
Abstained Achilles, but with bitter taunt
Opprobrious, his antagonist reproached.
    Oh charged with wine, in stedfastness of face
Dog unabashed, and yet at heart a deer!
Thou never, when the troops have taken arms,        280
Hast dared to take thine also; never thou
Associate with Achaia's Chiefs, to form
The secret ambush.  No.  The sound of war
Is as the voice of destiny to thee.
Doubtless the course is safer far, to range        285
Our numerous host, and if a man have dared
Dispute thy will, to rob him of his prize.
King! over whom? Women and spiritless—
Whom therefore thou devourest; else themselves
Would stop that mouth that it should scoff no more.        290
But hearken.  I shall swear a solemn oath.
By this same sceptre, which shall never bud,
Nor boughs bring forth as once, which having left
Its stock on the high mountains, at what time

---

⁵ The shield of Jupiter, made by Vulcan, and so called from its covering,
which was the skin of the goat that suckled him.

The woodman's axe lopped off its foliage green,                    295
And stript its bark, shall never grow again ;
Which now the judges of Achaia bear,
Who under Jove, stand guardians of the laws,
By this I swear (mark thou the sacred oath)
Time shall be, when Achilles shall be missed ;                    300
When all shall want him, and thyself the power
To help the Achaians, whatsoe'er thy will ;
When Hector at your heels shall mow you down ;
The Hero-slaughtering Hector ! Then thy soul,
Vexation-stung, shall tear thee with remorse,                    305
That thou hast scorn'd, as he were nothing worth,
A Chief, the soul and bulwark of your cause.
    So saying, he cast his sceptre on the ground
Studded with gold, and sat.   On the other side
The son of Atreus all impassion'd stood,                    310
When the harmonious orator arose
Nestor, the Pylian oracle, whose lips
Dropped eloquence—the honey not so sweet.
Two generations past of mortals born
In Pylus, coëtaneous with himself,                    315
He govern'd now the third—amid them all
He stood, and thus, benevolent, began.
    Ah ! what calamity hath fall'n on Greece !
Now Priam and his sons may well exult,
Now all in Ilium shall have joy of heart                    320
Abundant, hearing of this broil, the prime
Of Greece between, in council and in arms.
But be persuaded ; ye are younger both
Than I, and I was conversant of old
With Princes your superiors, yet from them                    325
No disrespect at any time received.
Their equals saw I never ; never shall ;
Exadius, Cœneus, and the God-like son
Of Ægeus, mighty Theseus ; men renown'd
For force superior to the race of man.                    330
Brave Chiefs they were, and with brave foes they fought,
With the rude dwellers on the mountain-heights
The Centaurs, whom with havoc such as fame
Shall never cease to celebrate, they slew.
With these men I consorted erst, what time                    335

From Pylus, though a land from theirs remote,
They called me forth, and such as was my strength,
With all that strength I served them.   Who is he?
What Prince or Chief of the degenerate race
Now seen on earth who might with these compare?          340
Yet even these would listen and conform
To my advice in consultation given,
Which hear ye also; for compliance proves
Oft times the safer and the manlier course.
Thou, Agamemnon! valiant as thou art,                    345
Seize not the maid, his portion from the Greeks,
But leave her his; nor thou, Achilles, strive
With our imperial Chief; for never King
Had equal honour at the hands of Jove
With Agamemnon, or was throned so high.                  350
Say thou art stronger, and art Goddess-born,
How then? His territory passes thine,
And he is Lord of thousands more than thou.
Cease, therefore, Agamemnon; calm thy wrath;
And it shall be mine office to entreat                   355
Achilles also to a calm, whose might
The chief munition is of all our host.
　　To whom the sovereign of the Greeks replied,
The son of Atreus.   Thou hast spoken well,
Old Chief, and wisely.   But this wrangler here—         360
Nought will suffice him but the highest place;
He must controul us all, reign over all,
Dictate to all; but he shall find at least
One here, disposed to question his commands.
If the eternal Gods have made him brave,                 365
Derives he thence a privilege to rail?
　　Whom thus Achilles interrupted fierce.
Could I be found so abject as to take
The measure of my doings at thy lips,
Well might they call me coward through the camp,         370
A vassal, and a fellow of no worth.
Give law to others.   Think not to controul
Me, subject to thy proud commands no more.
Hear yet again! And weigh what thou shalt hear.
I will not strive with thee in such a cause,             375
Nor yet with any man; I scorn to fight

For her, who having given, ye take away.
But I have other precious things on board;
Of those take none away without my leave.
Or if it please thee, put me to the proof                       380
Before this whole assembly, and my spear
Shall stream that moment, purpled with thy blood.
   Thus they long time in opposition fierce
Maintain'd the war of words; and now, at length,
(The grand consult dissolved,) Achilles walked,               385
(Patroclus and the Myrmidons his steps
Attending) to his camp and to his fleet.
But Agamemnon ordered forth a bark,
A swift one, manned with twice ten lusty rowers;
He sent on board the Hecatomb: he placed                      390
Chryseïs with the blooming cheeks, himself,
And to Ulysses gave the freight in charge.
So all embarked, and plough'd their watery way.
Atrides, next, bade purify the host;
The host was purified as he enjoin'd,                          395
And the ablution cast into the sea.
   Then to Apollo, on the shore they slew,
Of the untillable and barren deep,
Whole Hecatombs of bulls and goats, whose steam
Slowly in smoky volumes climbed the skies.                    400
   Thus was the camp employed; nor ceased the while
The son of Atreus from his threats denounced
At first against Achilles, but command
Gave to Talthybius and Eurybates
His heralds, ever faithful to his will.                        405
   Haste—Seek ye both the tent of Peleus' son
Achilles.   Thence lead hither by the hand
Blooming Briseïs, whom if he withhold,
Not her alone, but other spoil myself
Will take in person—He shall rue the hour.                    410
   With such harsh message charged he them dismissed.
They, sad and slow, beside the barren waste
Of Ocean, to the galleys and the tents
Moved of the Myrmidons.   Him there they found
Beneath the shadow of his bark reclined,                      415
Nor glad at their approach.   Trembling they stood,
In presence of the royal Chief awe-struck,

Nor questioned him or spake.   He not the less
Knew well their embassy, and thus began,
　Ye heralds, messengers of Gods and men.　　　　　420
Hail, and draw near! I bid you welcome both.
I blame not you; the fault is his alone
Who sends you to conduct the damsel hence
Briséis.   Go Patroclus, generous friend!
Lead forth, and to their guidance give the maid.　　　425
But be themselves my witnesses before
The blessed Gods, before mankind, before
The ruthless king, should want of me be felt
To save the host from havoc⁶—Oh, his thoughts
Are madness all; intelligence or skill　　　　　430
Forecast or retrospect, how best the camp
May be secured from inroad, none hath he.
　He ended, nor Patroclus disobey'd,
But leading beautiful Briséis forth
Into their guidance gave her; loth she went　　　　435
From whom she loved, and looking oft behind.
Then wept Achilles, and apart from all,
With eyes directed to the gloomy Deep
And arms outstretch'd, his mother suppliant sought.
　Since, mother, though ordain'd so soon to die,　　440
I am thy son, I might with cause expect
Some honour at the Thunderer's hands, but none
To me he shows, whom Agamemnon, Chief
Of the Achaians, hath himself disgraced,
Seizing by violence my just reward.　　　　　445
　So prayed he weeping, whom his mother heard
Within the gulfs of Ocean where she sat
Beside her ancient sire.   From the gray flood
Ascending sudden, like a mist, she came,
Sat down before him, stroked his face, and said.　　450
　Why weeps my son? and what is thy distress?
Hide not a sorrow that I wish to share.
　To whom Achilles, sighing deep, replied.
Why tell thee woes to thee already known?
At Thebes, Eëtion's city we arrived,　　　　　455
Smote, sack'd it, and brought all the spoil away.

⁶ The original is here abrupt, and expresses the precipitancy of the
speaker by a most beautiful aposiopesis.

Just distribution made among the Greeks,
The son of Atreus for his lot received
Blooming Chryséis.   Her, Apollo's priest
Old Chryses followed to Achaia's camp,                         460
That he might loose his daughter.   Ransom rich
He brought, and in his hands the hallow'd wreath
And golden sceptre of the Archer God
Apollo, bore; to the whole Grecian host,
But chiefly to the foremost in command                         465
He sued, the sons of Atreus; then, the rest
All recommended reverence of the Seer,
And prompt acceptance of his costly gifts.
But Agamemnon might not so be pleased,
Who gave him rude dismission; he in wrath                      470
Returning, prayed, whose prayer Apollo heard,
For much he loved him.   A pestiferous shaft
He instant shot into the Grecian host,
And heap'd the people died.   His arrows swept
The whole wide camp of Greece, 'till at the last              475
A Seer, by Phœbus taught, explain'd the cause.
I first advised propitiation.   Rage
Fired Agamemnon.   Rising, he denounced
Vengeance, and hath fulfilled it.   She, in truth,
Is gone to Chrysa, and with her we send                        480
Propitiation also to the King
Shaft-arm'd Apollo.   But my beauteous prize
Briséis, mine by the award of all,
His Heralds, at this moment, lead away.
But thou, wherein thou canst, aid thy own son!                 485
Haste hence to Heaven, and if thy word or deed
Hath ever gratified the heart of Jove,
With earnest suit press him on my behalf.
For I, not seldom, in my father's hall
Have heard thee boasting, how when once the Gods,             490
With Juno, Neptune, Pallas at their head,
Conspired to bind the Thunderer, thou did'st loose
His bands, O Goddess! calling to his aid
The Hundred-handed warrior, by the Gods
Briareus, but by men Ægeon named.                             495
For he in prowess and in might surpassed
His father Neptune, who, enthroned sublime,

Sits second only to Saturnian Jove,
Elate with glory and joy.   Him all the Gods
Fearing from that bold enterprise abstained.          500
Now, therefore, of these things reminding Jove,
Embrace his knees ; entreat him that he give
The host of Troy his succour, and shut fast
The routed Grecians, prisoners in the fleet,
That all may find much solace[7] in their King,      505
And that the mighty sovereign o'er them all,
Their Agamemnon, may himself be taught
His rashness, who hath thus dishonour'd foul
The life itself, and bulwark of his cause.

   To him, with streaming eyes, Thetis replied.    510
Born as thou wast to sorrow, ah, my son !
Why have I rear'd thee ! Would that without tears,
Or cause for tears (transient as is thy life,
A little span) thy days might pass at Troy !
But short and sorrowful the fates ordain             515
Thy life, peculiar trouble must be thine,
Whom, therefore, oh that I had never borne !
But seeking the Olympian hill snow-crown'd,
I will myself plead for thee in the ear
Of Jove, the Thunderer.   Meantime at thy fleet      520
Abiding, let thy wrath against the Greeks
Still burn, and altogether cease from war.
For to the banks of the Oceanus[8],
Where Æthiopia holds a feast to Jove,
He journey'd yesterday, with whom the Gods           525
Went also, and the twelfth day brings them home.
Then will I to his brazen-floor'd abode,
That I may clasp his knees, and much misdeem
Of my endeavour, or my prayer shall speed.

   So saying, she went ; but him she left enraged    530
For fair Brisëis sake, forced from his arms
By stress of power.   Meantime Ulysses came
To Chrysa with the Hecatomb in charge.
Arrived within the haven[9] deep, their sails

---

[7] ἐπαύρωνται.
[8] A name by which we are frequently to understand the Nile in Homer.
[9] The original word (πολυβενθέος) seems to express variety of soundings, an idea probably not to be conveyed in an English epithet.

Furling, they stowed them in the bark below.  535
Then by its tackle lowering swift the mast
Into its crutch, they briskly push'd to land,
Heaved anchors out, and moor'd the vessel fast.
Forth came the mariners, and trod the beach;
Forth came the victims of Apollo next,  540
And, last, Chryséis.   Her Ulysses led
Toward the altar, gave her to the arms
Of her own father, and him thus address'd.
 O Chryses! Agamemnon, King of men,
Hath sent thy daughter home, with whom we bring  545
An Hecatomb on all our host's behalf
To Phœbus, hoping to appease the God
By whose dread shafts the Argives now expire.
 So saying, he gave her to him, who with joy
Received his daughter.   Then, before the shrine  550
Magnificent in order due they ranged
The noble Hecatomb.   Each laved his hands
And took the salted meal, and Chryses made
His fervent prayer with hands upraised on high.
 God of the silver bow, who with thy power  555
Encirclest Chrysa, and who reign'st supreme
In Tenedos, and Cilla the divine!
Thou prov'dst propitious to my first request,
Hast honour'd me, and punished sore the Greeks;
Hear yet thy servant's prayer; take from their host  560
At once the loathsome pestilence away!
 So Chryses prayed, whom Phœbus heard well-pleased;
Then prayed the Grecians also, and with meal
Sprinkling the victims, their retracted necks
First pierced, then flay'd them; the disjointed thighs  565
They, next, invested with the double caul,
Which with crude slices thin they overspread.
The priest burned incense, and libation poured
Large on the hissing brands, while, him beside,
Busy with spit and prong, stood many a youth  570
Trained to the task.   The thighs with fire consumed,
They gave to each his portion of the maw,
Then slashed the remnant, pierced it with the spits,
And managing with culinary skill
The roast, withdrew it from the spits again.  575

Their whole task thus accomplish'd, and the board
Set forth, they feasted, and were all sufficed.
When neither hunger more nor thirst remained
Unsatisfied, boys crown'd the beakers high
With wine delicious, and from right to left                    580
Distributing the cups, served every guest.
Thenceforth the youths of the Achaian race
To song propitiatory gave the day,
Pæans to Phœbus, Archer of the skies,
Chaunting melodious.   Pleased, Apollo heard.                  585
But, when, the sun descending, darkness fell,
They on the beach beside their hawsers slept ;
And, when the day-spring's daughter rosy-palm'd
Aurora look'd abroad, then back they steer'd
To the vast camp.   Fair wind, and blowing fresh,             590
Apollo sent them ; quick they rear'd the mast,
Then spread the unsullied canvass to the gale,
And the wind filled it.   Roared the sable flood
Around the bark, that ever as she went
Dash'd wide the brine, that scudded swift away.               595
Thus reaching soon the spacious camp of Greece,
Their galley they updrew sheer o'er the sands
From the rude surge remote, then propp'd her sides
With scantlings long, and sought their several tents.
    But Peleus' noble son, the speed-renown'd                 600
Achilles, he, his well-built bark beside,
Consumed his hours, nor would in council more,
Where wise men win distinction, or in fight
Appear, to sorrow and heart-withering woe
Abandon'd ; though for battle, ardent, still                  605
He panted, and the shout-resounding field.
But when the twelfth fair morrow streak'd the East,
Then all the everlasting Gods to Heaven
Resorted, with the Thunderer at their head,
And Thetis, not unmindful of her son                         610
From the salt flood emerged, seeking betimes
Olympus and the boundless fields of heaven.
High, on the topmost eminence sublime
Of the deep-fork'd Olympian she perceived
The Thunderer seated, from the Gods apart.                   615
She sat before him, clasped with her left hand

His knees, her right beneath his chin she placed,
And thus the King, Saturnian Jove, implored.
　　Father of all, by all that I have done
Or said that ever pleased thee, grant my suit.　　　　620
Exalt my son, by destiny short-lived
Beyond the lot of others.　　Him with shame
The King of men hath overwhelm'd, by force
Usurping his just meed; thou, therefore, Jove,
Supreme in wisdom, honour him, and give　　　　625
Success to Troy, till all Achaia's sons
Shall yield him honour more than he hath lost!
　　She spake, to whom the Thunderer nought replied,
But silent sat long time.　　She, as her hand
Had grown there, still importunate, his knees　　　　630
Clasp'd as at first, and thus her suit renew'd.
　　Or grant my prayer, and ratify the grant,
Or send me hence, (for thou hast none to fear,)
Plainly refused; that I may know and feel
By how much I am least of all in heaven.　　　　635
　　To whom the cloud-assembler at the last
Spake, deep-distress'd.　　Hard task and full of strife
Thou hast enjoined me; Juno will not spare
For gibe and taunt injurious, whose complaint
Sounds daily in the ears of all the Gods,　　　　640
That I assist the Trojans; but depart,
Lest she observe thee; my concern shall be
How best I may perform thy full desire.
And to assure thee more, I give the sign
Indubitable, which all fear expels　　　　645
At once from heavenly minds.　　Nought, so confirmed
May, after, be reversed or render'd vain.
　　He ceased, and under his dark brows the nod
Vouchsafed of confirmation.　　All around
The Sovereign's everlasting head his curls　　　　650
Ambrosial shook, and the huge mountain reeled.
　　Their conference closed, they parted.　　She, at once,
From bright Olympus plunged into the flood
Profound, and Jove to his own courts withdrew.
Together all the Gods, at his approach,　　　　655
Uprose; none sat expectant till he came,
But all advanced to meet the Eternal Sire.

So on his throne he sat.   Nor Juno him
Not understood ; she, watchful, had observed,
In consultation close with Jove engaged.            660
Thetis, bright-footed daughter of the deep,
And keen the son of Saturn thus reproved.
    Shrewd as thou art, who now hath had thine ear ?
Thy joy is ever such, from me apart
To plan and plot clandestine, and thy thoughts,      665
Think what thou may'st, are always barred to me.
    To whom the father, thus, of heaven and earth.
Expect not, Juno, that thou shalt partake
My counsels at all times, which oft in height
And depth, thy comprehension far exceed,            670
Jove's consort as thou art.   When aught occurs'
Meet for thine ear, to none will I impart
Of Gods or men more free than to thyself.
But for my secret thoughts, which I withhold
From all in heaven beside, them search not thou     675
With irksome curiosity and vain.
    Him answer'd then the Goddess ample-eyed.
What word hath passed thy lips, Saturnian Jove,
Thou most severe ! I never search thy thoughts,
Nor the serenity of thy profound                    680
Intentions trouble ; they are safe from me :
But now there seems a cause.   Deeply I dread
Lest Thetis, silver-footed daughter fair
Of Ocean's hoary Sovereign, here arrived
At early dawn to practise on thee, Jove !           685
I noticed her a suitress at thy knees,
And much misdeem or promise-bound thou stand'st
To Thetis past recall, to exalt her son,
And Greeks to slaughter thousands at the ships.
    To whom the cloud-assembler God, incensed.       690
Ah subtle ! ever teeming with surmise,
And fathomer of my concealed designs,
Thy toil is vain, or (which is worse for thee,)
Shall but estrange thee from mine heart the more.
And be it as thou sayest,—I am well pleased         '695
That so it should be.   Be advised, desist,
Hold thou thy peace.   Else, if my glorious hands
Once reach thee, the Olympian Powers combined

To rescue thee, shall interfere in vain.
   He said,—whom Juno, awful Goddess, heard     700
Appall'd, and mute submitted to his will.
But through the courts of Jove the heavenly Powers
All felt displeasure; when to them arose
Vulcan, illustrious artist, who with speech
Conciliatory interposed to soothe     705
His white-arm'd mother Juno, Goddess dread.
   Hard doom is ours, and not to be endured,
If feast and merriment must pause in heaven
While ye such clamour raise tumultuous here
For man's unworthy sake : yet thus we speed     710
Ever, when evil overpoises good.
But I exhort my mother, though herself
Already warn'd, that meekly she submit
To Jove our father, lest our father chide
More roughly, and confusion mar the feast.     715
For the Olympian Thunderer could with ease
Us from our thrones precipitate, so far
He reigns to all superior.   Seek to assuage
His anger therefore; so shall he with smiles
Cheer thee, nor thee alone, but all in heaven.     720
   So Vulcan, and, upstarting, placed a cup
Full-charged between his mother's hands, and said,
   My mother, be advised, and, though aggrieved,
Yet patient; lest I see thee whom I love
So dear, with stripes chastised before my face,     725
Willing, but impotent to give thee aid.
Who can resist the Thunderer? Me, when once
I flew to save thee, by the foot he seized
And hurl'd me through the portal of the skies.
" From morn to eve I fell, a summer's day,"     730
And dropped, at last, in Lemnos.   There half-dead
The Sintians found me, and with succour prompt
And hospitable, entertained me fallen.
   So He ; then Juno smiled, Goddess white-arm'd,
And smiling still, from his unwonted hand [10]     735

[10] The reader, in order that he may partake with the Gods in the
drollery of this scene, should observe that the crippled and distorted
Vulcan had thrust himself into an office at all other times administered
either by Hebe or Ganymede.

Received the goblet.   He from right to left
Rich nectar from the beaker drawn, alert
Distributed to all the powers divine.
Heaven rang with laughter inextinguishable
Peal after peal, such pleasure all conceived                    740
At sight of Vulcan in his new employ.
    So spent they in festivity the day,
And all were cheered ; nor was Apollo's harp
Silent, nor did the Muses spare to add
Responsive melody of vocal sweets.                             745
But when the sun's bright orb had now declined,
Each to his mansion, wheresoever built
By the lame matchless Architect, withdrew.
Jove also, kindler of the fires of heaven,
His couch descending as at other times                         750
When gentle sleep approach'd him, slept serene,
With golden-sceptred Juno at his side.

# BOOK II.

---

### ARGUMENT.

Jupiter, in pursuance of his purpose to distress the Grecians in answer to
the prayer of Thetis, deceives Agamemnon by a dream. He, in consequence of it, calls a council, the result of which is that the army shall
go forth to battle. Thersites is mutinous, and is chastised by Ulysses.
Ulysses, Nestor, and Agamemnon harangue the people; and preparation is made for battle. An exact account follows of the forces on
both sides.

ALL night both Gods and Chiefs equestrian slept,
But not the Sire of all. He, waking soon,
Mused how to exalt Achilles, and destroy
No few in battle at the Grecian fleet.
This counsel, at the last, as best he chose                    5
And likeliest; to dispatch an evil Dream
To Agamemnon's tent, and to his side
The phantom summoning, him thus addressed.
    Haste, evil Dream! fly to the Grecian fleet,
And, entering royal Agamemnon's tent,                         10
His ear possess thou thus, omitting nought
Of all that I enjoin thee. Bid him arm
His universal host, for that the time
When the Achaians shall at length possess
Wide Ilium, hath arrived. The Gods above                      15
No longer dwell at variance. The request
Of Juno hath prevail'd; now, Woe to Troy!
    So charged, the Dream departed. At the ships
Well-built arriving of Achaia's host,
He Agamemnon, son of Atreus, sought.                          20
Him sleeping in his tent he found, immersed
In soft repose ambrosial. At his head
The shadow stood, similitude exact
Of Nestor, son of Neleus; sage, with whom
In Agamemnon's thought might none compare.                    25
His form assumed, the sacred Dream began.
    O son of Atreus the renown'd in arms

And in the race! Sleep'st thou? It ill behoves,
To sleep all night the man of high employ,
And charged, as thou art, with a people's care.                    30
Now, therefore, mark me well, who, sent from Jove,
Inform thee, that although so far remote,
He yet compassionates and thinks on thee
With kind solicitude.   He bids thee arm
Thine universal host, for that the time                    35
When the Achaians shall at length possess
Wide Ilium, hath arrived.   The Gods above
No longer dwell at variance.   The requests
Of Juno have prevail'd.   Now, woe to Troy
From Jove himself!   Her fate is on the wing.                    40
Awaking from thy dewy slumbers, hold
In firm remembrance all that thou hast heard.
    So spake the Dream, and vanishing, him left
In false hopes occupied and musings vain.
Full sure he thought, ignorant of the plan                    45
By Jove design'd, that day the last of Troy.
Fond thought! For toils and agonies to Greeks
And Trojans both, in many a bloody field
To be endured, the Thunderer yet ordain'd.
Starting he woke, and seeming still to hear                    50
The warning voice divine, with hasty leap
Sprang from his bed, and sat.   His fleecy vest
New-woven he put on, and mantle wide;
His sandals fair to his unsullied feet
He braced, and slung his argent-studded sword.                    55
Then, incorruptible for evermore
The sceptre of his sires he took, with which
He issued forth into the camp of Greece.
    Aurora now on the Olympian heights
Proclaiming stood new day to all in heaven,                    60
When he his clear-voiced heralds bade convene
The Greeks in council.   Went the summons forth
Into all quarters, and the throng began.
First, at the ship of Nestor, Pylian King,
The senior Chiefs for high exploits renown'd                    65
He gather'd, whom he prudent thus address'd.
    My fellow-warriors, hear! A dream from heaven,
Amid the stillness of the vacant night

Approach'd me, semblance close in stature, bulk,
And air, of noble Nestor.   At mine head                    70
The shadow took his stand, and thus he spake.
    Oh son of Atreus the renown'd in arms
And in the race, sleep'st thou ? It ill behoves
To sleep all night the man of high employ,
And charged as thou art with a people's care.            75
Now, therefore, mark me well, who, sent from Jove,
Inform thee, that although so far remote,
He yet compassionates and thinks on thee
With kind solicitude.   He bids thee arm
Thine universal host ; for that the time                     80
When the Achaians shall at length possess
Wide Ilium, hath arrived.   The Gods above
No longer dwell at variance.   The requests
Of Juno have prevail'd.   Now, woe to Troy
From Jove himself ! Her fate is on the wing.           85
Charge this on thy remembrance.   Thus he spake,
Then vanished suddenly, and I awoke.
Haste therefore, let us arm, if arm we may[1],
The warlike sons of Greece ; but first, myself .
Will prove them, recommending instant flight           90
With all our ships, and ye throughout the host
Dispersed, shall, next, encourage all to stay.
    He ceased, and sat ; when in the midst arose
Of highest fame for wisdom, Nestor, King
Of sandy Pylus, who them thus bespake.                   95
    Friends, Counsellors, and Leaders of the Greeks !
Had any meaner Argive told his dream,
We had pronounced it false, and should the more
Have shrunk from battle ; but the dream is his
Who boasts himself our highest in command.           100
Haste, arm we, if we may, the sons of Greece.
    So saying, he left the council ; him, at once,
The sceptred Chiefs, obedient to his voice,
Arising, follow'd ; and the throng began.
As from the hollow rock bees stream abroad,           105
And in succession endless seek the fields,

---

[1] Agamemnon seems to entertain some doubts lest the army should so
resent his treatment of their favourite Achilles, as to be indisposed to serve
him.

Now clustering, and now scattered far and near,
In spring-time, among all the new-blown flowers,
So they to council swarm'd, troop after troop,
Grecians of every tribe, from camp and fleet          110
Assembling orderly o'er all the plain
Beside the shore of Ocean.   In the midst
A kindling rumour, messenger of Jove,
Impell'd them, and they went.   Loud was the din
Of the assembling thousands; groan'd the earth        115
When down they sat, and murmurs ran around.
Nine heralds cried aloud—Will ye restrain
Your clamours, that your heaven-taught Kings may speak?
Scarce were they settled, and the clang had ceased,
When Agamemnon, sovereign o'er them all,              120
Sceptre in hand, arose.   (That sceptre erst
Vulcan with labour forged and to the hand
Consign'd it of the King, Saturnian Jove;
Jove to the vanquisher[2] of Ino's[3] guard.
And he to Pelops; Pelops in his turn,                 125
To royal Atreus; Atreus at his death
Bequeath'd it to Thyestes rich in flocks,
And rich Thyestes left it to be borne
By Agamemnon, symbol of his right
To empire over Argos and her isles)                   130
On that he lean'd, and, rapid, thus began.
     Friends, Grecian Heroes, ministers of Mars!
Ye see me here entangled in the snares
Of unpropitious Jove.   He promised once,
And with a nod confirm'd it, that with spoils         135
Of Ilium laden, we should hence return;
But now, devising ill, he sends me shamed,
And with diminished numbers, home to Greece.
So stands his sovereign pleasure, who hath laid
The bulwarks of full many a city low,                 140
And more shall level, matchless in his might.
That such a numerous host of Greeks as we,
Warring with fewer than ourselves, should find
No fruit of all our toil, (and none appears)
Will make us vile with ages yet to come.              145
For should we now strike truce, till Greece and Troy

------

[2] Mercury.                              [3] Argus.

Might number each her own, and were the Greeks
Distributed in bands, ten Greeks in each,
Our banded decads should exceed so far
Their units, that all Troy could not supply      150
For every ten, a man, to fill us wine ;
So far the Achaians, in my thought, surpass
The native Trojans.   But in Troy are those
Who baffle much my purpose ; aids derived
From other states, spear-arm'd auxiliars, firm      155
In the defence of Ilium's lofty towers.
Nine years have passed us over, nine long years ;
Our ships are rotted, and our tackle marr'd,
And all our wives and little-ones at home
Sit watching our return, while this attempt      160
Hangs still in doubt, for which that home we left.
Accept ye then my counsel.   Fly we swift
With all our fleet back to our native land,
Hopeless of Troy, not yet to be subdued.
  So spake the King, whom all the concourse heard      165
With minds in tumult toss'd ; all, save the few,
Partners of his intent.   Commotion shook
The whole assembly, such as heaves the flood
Of the Icarian Deep, when South and East
Burst forth together from the clouds of Jove.      170
And as when vehement the West-wind falls
On standing corn mature, the loaded ears
Innumerable bow before the gale,
So was the council shaken.   With a shout
All flew toward the ships ; upraised, the dust      175
Stood o'er them ; universal was the cry,
" Now clear the passages, strike down the props,
Set every vessel free, launch, and away !"
Heaven rang with exclamation of the host
All homeward bent, and launching glad the fleet.      180
Then baffled Fate had the Achaians seen
Returning premature, but Juno thus,
With admonition quick to Pallas spake.
  Unconquer'd daughter of Jove Ægis-arm'd !
Ah foul dishonour ! Is it thus at last      185
That the Achaians on the billows borne,
Shall seek again their country, leaving here,

To be the vaunt of Ilium and her King,
Helen of Argos, in whose cause the Greeks
Have numerous perish'd from their home remote?          190
Haste! Seek the mail-arm'd multitude, by force
Detain them of thy soothing speech, ere yét
All launch their oary barks into the flood.

    She spake, nor did Minerva not comply,
But darting swift from the Olympian heights,          195
Reach'd soon Achaia's fleet.    There, she perceived
Prudent as Jove himself, Ulysses; firm
He stood; he touch'd not even with his hand
His sable bark, for sorrow whelm'd his soul.
The Athenæan Goddess azure-eyed          200
Beside him stood, and thus the Chief bespake.

    Laertes' noble son, for wiles renown'd!
Why seek ye, thus precipitate, your ships?
Intend ye flight? And is it thus at last,
That the Achaians on the billows borne,          205
Shall seek again their country, leaving here,
To be the vaunt of Ilium and her King,
Helen of Argos, in whose cause the Greeks
Have numerous perish'd from their home remote?
Delay not.    Rush into the throng; by force          210
Detain them of thy soothing speech, ere yet
All launch their oary barks into the flood.

    She ceased, whom by her voice Ulysses knew,
Casting his mantle from him, which his friend
Eurybates the Ithacensian caught,          215
He ran; and in his course meeting the son
Of Atreus, Agamemnon, from his hand
The everlasting sceptre quick received,
Which bearing, through Achaia's fleet he pass'd.
What King soever, or distinguish'd Greek          220
He found, approaching to his side, in terms
Of gentle sort he stay'd him.    Sir, he cried,
It is unseemly that a man renown'd
As thou, should tremble.    Go—Resume the seat
Which thou hast left, and bid the people sit.          225
Thou know'st not clearly yet the monarch's mind.
He proves us now, but soon he will chastize.
All were not present; few of us have heard

His speech this day in council.  Oh, beware,  
Lest in resentment of this hasty course         230  
Irregular, he let his anger loose.  
Dread is the anger of a King; he reigns  
By Jove's own ordinance, and is dear to Jove.  
    But what plebeian base soe'er he heard  
Stretching his throat to swell the general cry,    235  
He lay'd the sceptre smartly on his back,  
With reprimand severe.  Fellow, he said,  
Sit still; hear others; thy superiors hear.  
For who art thou? A dastard and a drone,  
Of none account in council, or in arms.        240  
By no means may we all alike bear away  
At Ilium; such plurality of Kings  
Were evil.  One suffices.  One, to whom  
The son of politic Saturn hath assign'd  
The sceptre, and inforcement of the laws,    245  
That he may rule us as a monarch ought.  
    With such authority the troubled host  
He sway'd; they, quitting camp and fleet again,  
Rush'd back to council; deafening was the sound  
As when a billow of the boisterous deep     250  
Some broad beach dashes, and the ocean roars.  
    The host all seated, and the benches fill'd,  
Thersites only of loquacious tongue  
Ungovern'd, clamour'd mutinous; a wretch  
Of utterance prompt, but in coarse phrase obscene  255  
Deep learn'd alone, with which to slander Kings.  
Might he but set the rabble in a roar,  
He cared not with what jest; of all from Greece  
To Ilium sent, his country's chief reproach.  
Cross-eyed he was, and halting moved on legs   260  
Ill-pair'd; his gibbous shoulders o'er his breast  
Contracted, pinch'd it; to a peak his head.  
Was moulded sharp, and sprinkled thin with hair  
Of starveling length, flimsy and soft as down.  
Achilles and Ulysses had incurr'd        265  
Most his aversion; them he never spared;  
But now, imperial Agamemnon 'self  
In piercing accents stridulous he charged  
With foul reproach.  The Grecians with contempt

Listen'd, and indignation, while with voice          270
At highest pitch, he thus the monarch mock'd.
 What would'st thou now? Whereof is thy complaint
Now, Agamemnon? Thou hast fill'd thy tents
With treasure, and the Grecians, when they take
A city, choose the loveliest girls for thee.          275
Is gold thy wish? More gold? A ransom brought
By some chief Trojan for his son's release
Whom I, or other valiant Greek may bind?
Or would'st thou yet a virgin, one, by right
Another's claim, but made by force thine own?          280
It was not well, great Sir, that thou shouldst bring
A plague on the Achaians, as of late.
But come, my Grecian sisters, soldiers named
Unfitly, of a sex too soft for war,
Come, let us homeward: let him here digest          285
What he shall gorge, alone; that he may learn
If our assistance profit him or not.
For when he shamed Achilles, he disgraced
A Chief far worthier than himself, whose prize
He now withholds. But tush,—Achilles lacks          290
Himself the spirit of a man; no gall
Hath he within him, or his hand long since
Had stopp'd that mouth[4], that it should scoff no more.
 Thus, mocking royal Agamemnon, spake
Thersites. Instant starting to his side,          295
Noble Ulysses with indignant brows
Survey'd him, and him thus reproved severe.
Thersites! Railer!—peace. Think not thyself,
Although thus eloquent, alone exempt
From obligation not to slander Kings.          300
I deem thee most contemptible, the worst
Of Agamemnon's followers to the war;
Presume not then to take the names revered
Of Sovereigns on thy sordid lips, to asperse
Their sacred character, and to appoint          305
The Greeks a time when they shall voyage home.
How soon, how late, with what success at last
We shall return, we know not: but because

[4] The extremest provocation is implied in this expression, which Thersites quotes exactly as he had heard it from the lips of Achilles.

Achaia's heroes numerous spoils allot
To Agamemnon, Leader of the host,                        310
Thou therefore from thy seat revilest the King.
But mark me.   If I find thee, as even now,
Raving and foaming at the lips again,
May never man behold Ulysses' head
On these my shoulders more, and may my son          315
Prove the begotten of another Sire,
If I not strip thee to that hide of thine
As bare as thou wast born, and whip thee hence
Home to thy galley, sniveling like a boy.
    He ceased, and with his sceptre on the back       320
And shoulders smote him.   Writhing to and fro,
He wept profuse, while many a bloody whelk
Protuberant beneath the sceptre sprang.
Awe-quell'd he sat, and from his visage mean,
Deep-sighing, wiped the rheums.   It was no time     325
For mirth, yet mirth illumined every face,
And laughing, thus they spake.   A thousand acts
Illustrious, both by well-concerted plans
And prudent disposition of the host
Ulysses hath achieved, but this by far               330
Transcends his former praise, that he hath quell'd
Such contumelious rhetoric profuse.
The valiant talker shall not soon, we judge,
Take liberties with royal names again.
    So spake the multitude.   Then, stretching forth   335
The sceptre, city-spoiler Chief, arose
Ulysses.   Him beside, herald in form,
Appeared Minerva.   Silence she enjoined
To all, that all Achaia's sons might hear,
Foremost and rearmost, and might weigh his words,   340
He then his counsel, prudent, thus proposed.
    Atrides! Monarch! The Achaians seek
To make thee ignominious above all
In sight of all mankind.   None recollects
His promise more in steed-famed Argos pledged,      345
Here to abide till Ilium wall'd to heaven
Should vanquish'd sink, and all her wealth be ours.
No—now, like widow'd women, or weak boys,
They whimper to each other, wishing home.

And home, I grant, to the afflicted soul         350
Seems pleasant[5].   The poor seaman from his wife
One month detain'd, cheerless his ship and sad
Possesses, by the force of wintry blasts,
And by the billows of the troubled deep
Fast lock'd in port.   But us the ninth long year     355
Revolving, finds camp'd under Ilium still.
I therefore blame not, if they mourn beside
Their sable barks, the Grecians.   Yet the shame
That must attend us after absence long
Returning unsuccessful, who can bear?         360
Be patient, friends! wait only till we learn
If Calchas truly prophecied, or not;
For well we know, and I to all appeal,
Whom Fate hath not already snatch'd away,
(It seems but yesterday, or at the most        365
A day or two before,) that when the ships
Woe-fraught for Priam, and the race of Troy,
At Aulis met, and we beside the fount
With perfect hecatombs the Gods adored
Beneath the plane-tree, from whose root a stream    370
Ran crystal-clear, there we beheld a sign
Wonderful in all eyes.   A serpent huge,
Tremendous spectacle! with crimson spots
His back all dappled, by Olympian Jove
Himself protruded, from the altar's foot       375
Slipp'd into light, and glided to the tree.
There on the topmost bough, close-cover'd sat
With foliage broad, eight sparrows, younglings all,
Then newly feather'd, with their dam, the ninth.
The little ones lamenting shrill he gorged,       380
While, wheeling o'er his head, with screams the dam
Bewail'd her darling brood.   Her also, next,
Hovering and clamouring, he by the wing
Within his spiry folds drew, and devoured.
All eaten thus, the nestlings and the dam,       385
The God who sent him, signalized him too,
For him Saturnian Jove transform'd to stone.
We wondering stood, to see that strange portent

---

[5] Some for πόνος here read πόθος; which reading I have adopted for the sake both of perspicuity and connexion.

Intrude itself into our holy rites,
When Calchas, instant, thus the sign explain'd.      390
   Why stand ye, Greeks, astonish'd?   Ye behold
A prodigy by Jove himself produced,
An omen, whose accomplishment indeed
Is distant, but whose fame shall never die.
E'en as this serpent in your sight devour'd      395
Eight youngling sparrows, with their dam, the ninth,
So we nine years must war on yonder plain,!
And in the tenth, wide-bulwark'd Troy is ours.
   So spake the seer, and as he spake, is done.
Wait, therefore, brave Achaians! go not hence      400
Till Priam's spacious city be your prize.
   He ceased, and such a shout ensued, that all
The hollow ships the deafening roar return'd
Of acclamation, every voice the speech
Extolling of Ulysses, glorious Chief.      405
   Then Nestor the Gerenian, warrior old,
Arising, spake ; and, by the Gods, he said,
Ye more resemble children inexpert
In war, than disciplined and prudent men.
Where now are all your promises and vows,      410
Councils, libations, right-hand covenants ?
Burn them, since all our occupation here
Is to debate and wrangle, whereof end
Or fruit though long we wait, shall none be found.
But, Sovereign, be not thou appall'd.   Be firm.      415
Relax not aught of thine accustomed sway,
But set the battle forth as thou art wont.
And if there be a  Grecian, here and there,
One [6], adverse to the general voice, let such
Wither alone.   He shall not see his wish      420
Gratified, neither will we hence return
To Argos, ere events shall yet have proved
Jove's promise false or true.   For when we climb'd
Our gallant barks full-charged with Ilium's fate,
Saturnian Jove omnipotent, that day,      425
(Omen propitious !) thunder'd on the right.
Let no man therefore pant for home, till each
Possess a Trojan spouse, and from her lips

[6] Nestor is supposed here to glance at Achilles.

Take sweet revenge for Helen's pangs of heart.
Who then? What soldier languishes and sighs　　430
To leave us? Let him dare to lay his hand
On his own vessel, and he dies the first.
But hear, O King! I shall suggest a course
Not trivial.　Agamemnon! sort the Greeks
By districts and by tribes, that tribe may tribe　　435
Support, and each his fellow.　This performed,
And with consent of all, thou shalt discern
With ease what Chief, what private man deserts,
And who performs his part.　The base, the brave,
Such disposition made, shall both appear;　　440
And thou shalt also know, if heaven or we,
The Gods, or our supineness, succour Troy.
　　To whom Atrides, King of men, replied.
Old Chief! Thou passest all Achaia's sons
In consultation; would to Jove our Sire,　　445
To Athenæan Pallas, and Apollo!
That I had ten such coadjutors, wise
As thou art, and the royal city soon
Of Priam, with her wealth, should all be ours.
But me the son of Saturn, Jove supreme　　450
Himself afflicts, who in contentious broils
Involves me, and in altercation vain.
Thence all that wordy tempest for a girl
Achilles and myself between, and I
The fierce aggressor.　Be that breach but heal'd!　　455
And Troy's reprieve thenceforth is at an end.
Go—take refreshment now that we may march
Forth to our enemies.　Let each whet well
His spear, brace well his shield, well feed his brisk
High-mettled horses, well survey and search　　460
His chariot on all sides, that no defect
Disgrace his bright habiliments of war.
So will we give the day from morn to eve
To dreadful battle.　Pause there shall be none
Till night divide us.　Every buckler's thong　　465
Shall sweat on the toil'd bosom, every hand
That shakes the spear shall ache, and every steed
Shall smoke that whirls the chariot o'er the plain.
Woe then to whom I shall discover here

Loitering among the tents; let him escape   470
My vengeance if he can. The vultures' maw
Shall have his carcase, and the dogs his bones.
 He spake; whom all applauded with a shout
Loud as against some headland cliff the waves
Roll'd by the stormy South o'er rocks that shoot  475
Afar into the deep, which in all winds
The flood still overspreads, blow whence they may.
Arising, forth they rush'd, among the ships
All scatter'd; smoke from every tent arose,
The host their food preparing; next, his God · 480
Each man invoked (of the Immortals him
Whom he preferr'd) with sacrifice and prayer
For safe escape from danger and from death.
But Agamemnon to Saturnian Jove
Omnipotent, an ox of the fifth year   485
Full-flesh'd devoted, and the Princes call'd
Noblest of all the Grecians to his feast.
First, Nestor with Idomeneus the King,
Then either Ajax, and the son he call'd
Of Tydeus, with Ulysses sixth and last,  490
Jove's peer in wisdom. Menelaus went,
Heroic Chief! unbidden, for he knew
His brother's mind with weight of care oppress'd.
The ox encircling, and their hands with meal
Of consecration fill'd, the assembly stood,  495
When Agamemnon thus his prayer preferred.
 Almighty Father! Glorious above all!
Cloud-girt, who dwell'st in heaven thy throne sublime,
Let not the sun go down, till Priam's roof
Fall flat into the flames; till I shall burn  500
His gates with fire; till I shall hew away ·
His hack'd and riven corslet from the breast
Of Hector, and till numerous Chiefs, his friends,
Around him, prone in dust, shall bite the ground.
 So prayed he, but with none effect. The God 505
Received his offering, but to double toil
Doom'd them, and sorrow more than all the past.
 They then, the triturated barley grain,
First duly sprinkling, the sharp steel infix'd
Deep in the victim's neck reversed, then stripp'd 510
s. c.—7.          D

The carcase, and divided at their joint
The thighs, which in the double caul involved
They spread with slices crude, and burn'd with fire
Ascending fierce from billets sere and dry.
The spitted entrails next they o'er the coals          515
Suspended held.   The thighs with fire consumed,
They gave to each his portion of the maw,
Then slash'd the remnant, pierced it with the spits,
And managing with culinary skill
The roast, withdrew it from the spits again.           520
Thus, all their task accomplish'd, and the board
Set forth, they feasted, and were all sufficed.
When neither hunger more nor thirst remain'd
Unsatisfied, Gerenian Nestor spake.
       Atrides! Agamemnon! King of men!               525
No longer waste we time in useless words,
Nor to a distant hour postpone the work
To which heaven calls thee.  Send thine heralds forth.
Who shall convene the Achaians at the fleet,
That we, the Chiefs assembled here, may range,         530
Together, the imbattled multitude,
And edge their spirits for immediate fight.
       He spake, nor Agamemnon not complied.
At once he bade his clear-voiced heralds call
The Greeks to battle.   They the summons loud          535
Gave forth, and at the sound the people throng'd.
Then Agamemnon and the Kings of Greece
Dispatchful drew them into·order just,
With whom Minerva azure-eyed advanced,
The inestimable Ægis on her arm,                       540
Immortal, unobnoxious to decay.
An hundred braids, close twisted, all of gold,
Each valued at an hundred beeves[7], around
Dependent fringed it.   She from side to side
Her eyes cærulean rolled, infusing thirst             545
Of battle endless into every breast.
War won them now, war sweeter now to each
Than gales to waft them over ocean home.
As when devouring flames some forest seize
On the high mountains, splendid from afar             550

       [7] Money stamped with the figure of an ox.

The blaze appears, so, moving on the plain,
The steel-clad host innumerous flash'd to heaven.
And as a multitude of fowls in flocks
Assembled various, geese, or cranes, or swans
Lithe-neck'd, long hovering o'er Cayster's banks     555
On wanton plumes, successive on the mead
Alight at last, and with a clang so loud
That all the hollow vale of Asius rings;
In number such from ships and tents effused,
They cover'd the Scamandrian plain; the earth     560
Rebellow'd to the feet of steeds and men.
They overspread Scamander's grassy vale,
Myriads, as leaves, or as the flowers of spring.
As in the hovel where the peasant milks
His kine in spring-time, when his pails are fill'd,     565
Thick clouds of humming insects on the wing
Swarm all around him, so the Grecians swarm'd
An unsumm'd multitude o'er all the plain,
Bright arm'd, high crested, and athirst for war.
As goat-herds separate their numerous flocks     570
With ease, though fed promiscuous, with like ease
Their leaders them on every side reduced
To martial order glorious; among whom
Stood Agamemnon "with an eye like Jove's,
To threaten or command," like Mars in girth,     575
And with the port of Neptune.   As the bull
Conspicuous among all the herd appears,
For He surpasses all, such Jove ordain'd
That day the son of Atreus, in the midst
Of Heroes, eminent above them all.     580
    Tell me, (for ye are heavenly, and beheld
A scene, whereof the faint report alone
Hath reached our ears, remote and ill-informed,)
Tell me, ye Muses, under whom, beneath
What Chiefs of royal or of humbler note     585
Stood forth the embattled Greeks? The host at large;
*They* were a multitude in number more
Then with ten tongues, and with ten mouths, each mouth
Made vocal with a trumpet's throat of brass,
I might declare, unless the Olympian nine,     590
Jove's daughters, would the chronicle themselves

Indite, of all assembled, under Troy.
I will rehearse the Captains and their fleets.
   Bœotia's sturdy sons Peneleus led,
And Leïtus, whose partners in command       595
Arcesilaus and Prothoenor came,
And Clonius.  Them the dwellers on the rocks
Of Aulis followed, with the hardy clans
Of Hyrie, Schoenos, Scholos, and the hills
Of Eteon; Thespia, Græa, and the plains     600
Of Mycalessus them, and Harma served,
Eleon, Erythræ, Peteon; Hyle them,
Ilesius and Ocalea, and the strength
Of Medeon; Copæ also in their train
Marched, with Eutresis and the mighty men    605
Of Thisbe famed for doves; nor pass unnamed
Whom Coronæa, and the grassy land
Of Haliartus added to the war,
Nor whom Platæa, nor whom Glissa bred,
And Hypothebæ[8], and thy sacred groves    610
To Neptune, dark Onchestus.  Arne claims
A record next for her illustrious sons,
Vine-bearing Arne.  Thou wast also there
Mideia, and thou Nissa; nor be thine
Though last, Anthedon, a forgotten name.    615
These in Bœotia's fair and gallant fleet
Of fifty ships, each bearing o'er the waves
Thrice forty warriors, had arrived at Troy.
   In thirty ships deep-laden with the brave,
Aspledon and Orchomenos had sent      620
Their chosen youth; them ruled a noble pair,
Sons of Astyoche; she, lovely nymph,
Received by stealth, on Actor's stately roof,
The embraces of a God, and bore to Mars
Twins like himself, Ascalaphus the bold,    625
And bold Iälmenus, expert in arms.
   Beneath Epistrophus and Schedius, took
Their destined station on Bœotia's left,
The brave Phocensians; they in forty ships
From Cyparissus came, and from the rocks    630

---

[8] Some say Thebes the less, others, the suburbs of Thebes the greater.
It is certain that Thebes itself sent none.

Of Python, and from Crissa the divine;
From Anemoria, Daulis, Panopeus,
And from Hyampolis, and from the banks
Of the Cephissus, sacred stream, and from
Lilæa, seated at its fountain-head.                    635
    Next from beyond Eubœa's happy isle
In forty ships conveyed, stood forth well armed
The Locrians; dwellers in Augeia some
The pleasant, some of Opoëis possessed,
Some of Calliarus; these Scarpha sent,                 640
And Cynus those; from Bessa came the rest,
From Tarpha, Thronius, and from the brink
Of loud Boagrius; Ajax them, the swift,
Son of Oileus led, not such as he
From Telamon, big-boned and lofty built,               645
But small of limb, and of an humbler crest;
Yet he, competitor had none throughout
The Grecians of what land soe'er, for skill
In ushering to its mark the rapid lance.
    Elphenor brought (Calchodon's mighty son)         650
The Eubœans to the field.   In forty ships
From Histriæa for her vintage famed,
From Chalcis, from Iretria, from the gates
Of maritime Cerinthus, from the heights
Of Dios rock-built citadel sublime,                    655
And from Caristus and from Styra came
His warlike multitudes, all named alike
Abantes, on whose shoulders fell behind
Their locks profuse, and they were eager all
To split the hauberk with the pointed spear.           660
    Nor Athens had withheld her generous sons,
The people of Erectheus.   Him of old
The teeming glebe produced, a wonderous birth!
And Pallas rear'd him: her own unctuous fane
She made his habitation, where with bulls              665
The youth of Athens, and with slaughter'd lambs
Her annual worship celebrate.   Them led
Menestheus, whom, (sage Nestor's self except,
Thrice school'd in all events of human life,)
None rivall'd ever in the just array                   670
Of horse and man to battle.   Fifty ships

Black-prowed, had borne them to the distant war.
    Ajax from Salamis twelve vessels brought,
And where the Athenian band in phalanx stood
Marshall'd compact, there station'd he his powers.                675
    The men of Argos and Tyrintha next,
And of Hermione, that stands retired
With Asine, within her spacious bay ;
Of Epidaurus, crown'd with purple vines,
And of Trœzena, with the Achaian youth                 .          680
Of sea-begirt Ægina, and with thine,
Maseta, and the dwellers on thy coast,
Wave-worn Eïonæ ; these all obeyed
The dauntless Hero Diomede, whom served
Sthenelus, son of Capaneus, a Chief                              685
Of deathless fame, his second in command,
And Godlike man, Euryalus, the son
Of King Mecisteus, Talaüs' son, his third.
But Diomede controll'd them all, and him
Twice forty sable ships their leader own'd.                      690
    Came Agamemnon with a hundred ships,
Exulting in his powers ; more numerous they,
And more illustrious far than other Chief
Could boast, whoever.   Clad in burnish'd brass,
And conscious of pre-eminence, he stood.                         695
He drew his host from cities far renown'd,
Mycenæ, and Corinthus, seat of wealth,
Orneia, and Cleonæ bulwark'd strong,
And lovely Aræthyria ; Sicyon, where
His seat of royal power held at the first                        700
Adrastus : Hyperesia, and the heights
Of Gonoëssa ; Ægium, with the towns
That sprinkle all that far-extended coast,
Pellene also and wide Helice
With all their shores, were number'd in his train.               705
    From hollow Lacedæmon's glen profound,
From Phare, Sparta, and from Messa, still
Resounding with the ring-dove's amorous moan,
From Brysia, from Augeia, from the rocks
Of Laas, from Amycla, Otilus,                                    710
And from the towers of Helos, at whose foot
The surf of Ocean falls, came sixty barks

With Menelaus.   From the monarch's host
The royal brother ranged his own apart,
And panted for revenge of Helen's wrongs,                    715
And of her sighs and tears.   From rank to rank,
Conscious of dauntless might he pass'd, and sent
Into all hearts the fervour of his own.
    Gerenian Nestor in thrice thirty ships
Had brought his warriors; they from Pylus came,             720
From blythe Arene, and from Thryos, built
Fast by the fords of Alpheus, and from steep
And stately Æpy.   Their confederate powers
Sent Amphigenia, Cyparissa veiled
With broad redundance of funereal shades,                   725
Pteleos and Helos, and of deathless fame
Dorion.   In Dorion erst the Muses met
Threïcian Thamyris, on his return
From Eurytus, Oechalian Chief, and hush'd
His song for ever; for he dared to vaunt                    730
That he would pass in song even themselves
The Muses, daughters of Jove Ægis-arm'd.
They, therefore, by his boast incensed, the bard
Struck blind, and from his memory dash'd severe
All traces of his once celestial strains.                   735
    Arcadia's sons, the dwellers at the foot
Of mount Cyllene, where Æpytus sleeps
Intomb'd; a generation bold in fight,
And warriors hand to hand; the valiant men
Of Pheneus, of Orchomenos by flocks                         740
Grazed numberless, of Ripe, Stratia, bleak
Enispe; Mantinea city fair,
Stymphelus and Parrhasia, and the youth
Of Tegea; royal Agapenor these,
Ancæus' offspring, had in sixty ships                       745
To Troy conducted; numerous was the crew,
And skilled in arms, which every vessel brought,
And Agamemnon had with barks himself
Supplied them, for, of inland realms possessed,
They little heeded maritime employs.                        750
    The dwellers in Buprasium, on the shores
Of pleasant Elis, and in all the land
Myrsinus and the Hyrminian plain between,

The rock Olenian, and the Alysian fount;
These all obey'd four Chiefs, and galleys ten      755
Each Chief commanded, with Epeans filled.
Amphimachus and Thalpius govern'd these,
This, son of Cteatus, the other, sprung
From Eurytus, and both of Actor's house.
Diores, son of Amarynceus, those      760
Led on, and, for his godlike form renown'd,
Polyxenus was Chieftain o'er the rest,
Son of Agasthenes, Augeias' son.
    Dulichium, and her sister sacred isles
The Echinades, whose opposite aspect      765
Looks toward Elis o'er the curling waves,
Sent forth their powers with Meges at their head,
Brave son of Phyleus, warrior dear to Jove.
Phyleus in wrath, his father's house renounced,
And to Dulichium wandering, there abode.      770
Twice twenty ships had follow'd Meges forth.
    Ulysses led the Cephallenians bold.
From Ithaca, and from the lofty woods
Of Neritus they came, and from the rocks
Of rude Ægilipa.   Crocylia these,      775
And those Zacynthus own'd; nor yet a few
From Samos, from Epirus join'd their aid,
And from the opposite Ionian shore.
Them, wise as Jove himself, Ulysses led
In twelve fair ships, with crimson prows adorn'd.      780
    From forty ships, Thoas, Andræmon's son,
Had landed his Ætolians; for extinct
Was Meleager, and extinct the house
Of Oeneus all, nor Oeneus self survived;
To Thoas therefore had Ætolia fallen;      785
Him Olenos, Pylene, Chalcis served,
With Pleuro, and the rock-bound Calydon.
    Idomeneus, spear-practised warrior, led
The numerous Cretans.   In twice forty ships
He brought his powers to Troy. The warlike bands      790
Of Cnossus, of Gortyna wall'd around,
Of Lyctus, of Lycastus chalky-white,
Of Phæstus, of Miletus, with the youth
Of Rhytius him obeyed; nor these were all,

But others from her hundred cities Crete                    795
Sent forth, all whom Idomeneus the brave
Commanded, with Meriones in arms
Dread as the God of battles blood-imbrued.
   Nine ships Tlepolemus, Herculean-born,
For courage famed and for superior size,                    800
Fill'd with his haughty Rhodians.   They, in tribes
Divided, dwelt distinct.   Jelyssus these,
Those Lindus, and the rest the shining soil
Of white Camirus occupied.   Him bore
To Hercules, (what time he led the nymphs                   805
From Ephyre, and from Sellea's banks,
After full many a city laid in dust,)
Astyocheia.   In his father's house
Magnificent, Tlepolemus spear-famed
Had scarce up-grown to manhood's lusty prime,              810
When he his father's hoary uncle slew
Lycimnius, branch of Mars.   Then built he ships,
And, pushing forth to sea, fled from the threats
Of the whole house of Hercules.   Huge toil
And many woes he suffer'd, till at length                  815
At Rhodes arriving, in three separate bands
He spread himself abroad.   Much was he loved
Of all-commanding Jove, who bless'd him there,
And shower'd abundant riches on them all.
   Nireus of Syma, with three vessels came;          820
Nireus, Aglæa's offspring, whom she bore
To Charopus the King; Nireus in form,
(The faultless son of Peleus sole except,)
Loveliest of all the Grecians call'd to Troy.
But he was heartless and his men were few.                 825
   Nisyrus, Casus, Crapathus, and Cos
Where reign'd Eurypylus, with all the isles
Calydnæ named, under two valiant Chiefs
Their troops disposed; Phidippus one, and one,
His brother Antiphus, begotten both                        830
By Thessalus, whom Hercules begat.
In thirty ships they sought the shores of Troy.
   The warriors of Pelasgian Argos next,
Of Alus, and Alope, and who held
Trechina, Phthia, and for women fair                       835

Distinguish'd, Hellas; known by various names
Hellenes, Myrmidons, Achæans, them
In fifty ships embark'd, Achilles ruled.
But these were deaf to the hoarse-throated war,
For there was none to draw their battle forth,　　840
And give them just array.　Close in his ships
Achilles, after loss of the bright-hair'd
Brisëis, lay, resentful; her obtained
Not without labour hard, and after sack
Of Thebes and of Lyrnessus, where he slew　　845
Two mighty Chiefs, sons of Evenus both,
Epistrophus and Mynes, her he mourn'd,
And for her sake self-prison'd in his fleet
And idle lay, though soon to rise again.
　From Phylace, and from the flowery fields　　850
Of Pyrrhasus, a land to Ceres given
By consecration, and from Iton green,
Mother of flocks; from Antron by the sea,
And from the grassy meads of Pteleus, came
A people, whom while yet he lived, the brave　　855
Protesilaüs led, but him the earth
Now cover'd dark and drear.　A wife he left,
To rend in Phylace her bleeding cheeks,
And an unfinish'd mansion.　First he died
Of all the Greeks; for as he leap'd to land　　860
Foremost by far, a Dardan struck him dead.
Nor had his troops, though filled with deep regret,
No leader; them Podarces led, a Chief
Like Mars in battle, brother of the slain,
But younger born, and from Iphiclus sprung　　865
Who sprang from Phylacus the rich in flocks.
But him Protesilaüs, as in years,
So also in desert of arms excell'd
Heroic, whom his host, although they saw
Podarces at their head, still justly mourn'd;　　870
For he was fierce in battle, and at Troy
With forty sable-sided ships arrived.
　Eleven galleys, Pheræ on the lake,
And Boebe, and Iölchus, and the vale
Of Glaphyræ supplied with crews robust　　875
Under Eumelus; him Alcestis, praised

For beauty above all her sisters fair,
In Thessaly to King Admetus bore.

    Methone, and Olizon's craggy coast,
With Melibœa and Thaumasia sent          880
Seven ships; their rowers were good archers all,
And every vessel dipped into the wave
Her fifty oars.   Them Philoctetes, skill'd
To draw with sinewy arm the stubborn bow,
Commanded; but he suffering anguish keen          885
Inflicted by a serpent's venom'd tooth,
Lay sick in Lemnos; him the Grecians there
Had left sore-wounded, but were destined soon
To call to dear remembrance whom they left.
Meantime, though sorrowing for his sake, his troops          890
Yet wanted not a Chief; them Medon ruled,
Whom Rhena to the far-famed conqueror bore
Oïleus, fruit of their unsanctioned loves.

    From Tricca, from Ithome rough and rude
With rocks and glens, and from Oechalia, town          895
Of Eurytus Oechalian-born, came forth
Their warlike youth by Podalirius led
And by Machaon, healers both expert
Of all disease, and thirty ships were theirs.

    The men of Ormenus, and from beside          900
The fountain Hyperiea, from the tops
Of chalky Titan, and Asteria's band;
Them ruled Eurypylus, Evæmon's son
Illustrious, whom twice twenty ships obeyed.

    Orthe, Gyrtone, Oloösson white,          905
Argissa and Helone; they their youth
Gave to control of Polypœtes, son
Undaunted of Pirithoüs, son of Jove,
Him, to Pirithoüs, (on the self-same day,
When he the Centaurs punish'd and pursued          910
Sheer to Æthicæ driven from Pelion's heights
The shaggy race) Hippodamia bore.
Nor he alone them led.   With him was join'd
Leonteus dauntless warrior, from the bold
Coronus sprung, who Cæneus call'd his sire.          915
Twice twenty ships awaited their command.

    Guneus from Cyphus twenty and two ships

Led forth; the Enienes him obey'd,
And the robust Perœbi, warriors bold,
And dwellers on Dodona's wintry brow.     920
To these were join'd who till the pleasant fields
Where Titaresius winds; the gentle flood
Pours into Peneus all his limpid stores,
But with the silver-eddied Peneus flows
Unmixt as oil; for Stygian is his stream,     925
And Styx is the inviolable oath.
   Last with his forty ships, Tenthredon's son,
The active Prothoüs came.  From the green banks
Of Peneus his Magnesians far and near
He gather'd, and from Pelion·forest-crown'd.     930
   These were the princes and the Chiefs of Greece.
Say, Muse, who most in personal desert
Excell'd, and whose were the most warlike steeds
And of the noblest strain.  Their hue, their age,
Their height the same, swift as the winds of heaven     935
And passing far all others, were the mares
Which drew Eumelus; on Pierian hills
The heavenly Archer of the silver bow,
Apollo, bred them.  But of men, the chief
Was Telamonian Ajax, while wrath-bound     940
Achilles lay; for he was worthier far,
And more illustrious were the steeds which bore
The noble son of Peleus; but revenge
On Agamemnon leader of the host
Was all his thought, while in his gallant ships     945
Sharp-keel'd to cut the foaming flood, he lay.
Meantime, along the margin of the deep
His soldiers hurled the disk, or bent the bow,
Or to its mark dispatch'd the quivering lance.
Beside the chariots stood the unharness'd steeds     950
Cropping the lotus, or at leisure browzed
On celery wild, from watery freshes gleaned.
Beneath the shadow of the sheltering tent
The chariot stood, while they, the ·charioteers
Roam'd here and there the camp, their warlike lord     955
Regretting sad, and idle for his sake.
   As if a fire had burnt along the ground,
Such seemed their march; earth groan'd their steps beneath;

As when in Arimi, where fame reports
Typhoëus stretch'd, the fires of angry Jove  960
Down darted, lash the ground, so groan'd the earth
Beneath them, for they traversed swift the plain.

And now from Jove, with heavy tidings charged,
Wind-footed Iris to the Trojans came.
It was the time of council, when the throng  965
At Priam's gate assembled, young and old;
Them, standing nigh, the messenger of heaven
Accosted with the voice of Priam's son,
Polites.   He, confiding in his speed
For sure deliverance, posted was abroad  970
On Æsyeta's tomb, intent to watch
When the Achaian host should leave the fleet.
The Goddess in his form thus them address'd.

Oh, ancient Monarch! Ever, evermore
Speaking, debating, as if all were peace:  975
I have seen many a bright-embattled field,
But never one so throng'd as this to-day.
For like the leaves, or like the sands they come
Swept by the winds, to gird the city round.

But Hector! chiefly thee I shall exhort.  980
In Priam's spacious city are allies
Collected numerous, and of nations wide-
Disseminated various are the tongues.
Let every Chief his proper troop command,
And marshal his own citizens to war.  985

She ceased; her Hector heard intelligent,
And quick dissolved the council.   All took arms.
Wide flew the gates; forth rush'd the multitude,
Horsemen and foot, and boisterous stir arose.
In front of Ilium, distant on the plain,  990
Clear all around from all obstruction, stands
An eminence high-raised, by mortal men
Call'd Batiea, but the Gods the tomb
Have named it of Myrinna swift in fight.
Troy and her aids there set the battle forth.  995

Huge Priameian Hector, fierce in arms,
Led on the Trojans; with whom march'd the most
And the most valiant, dexterous at the spear.
Æneas, (on the hills of Ida him

The lovely Venus to Anchises bore,                              1000
A Goddess by a mortal man embraced)
Led the Dardanians ; but not he alone ;
Archilochus with him and Acamas
Stood forth, the offspring of Antenor, each,
And well instructed in all forms of war.                        1005
   Fast by the foot of Ida, where they drank
The limpid waters of Æsepus, dwelt
The Trojans of Zeleia.   Rich were they
And led by Pandarus, Lycaon's son,
Whom Phœbus self graced with the bow he bore.                   1010
   Apæsus, Adrastea, Terie steep,
And Pitueia—them, Amphius clad
In mail thick-woven, and Adrastus, ruled.
They were the sons of the Percosian seer
Merops, expert in the sooth-sayers' art                         1015
Above all other ; he his sons forbad
The bloody fight, but disobedient they
Still sought it, for their destiny prevailed.
   The warriors of Percote, and who dwelt
In Practius, in Arisba, city fair,                              1020
In Sestus, in Abydus, march'd behind
Princely Hyrtacides ; his tawny steeds,
Strong-built and tall, from Selleentes' bank
And from Arisba, had him borne to Troy.
   Hippothous and Pilæus, branch of Mars,             1025
Both sons of Lethus the Pelasgian, they,
Forth from Larissa for her fertile soil
Far-famed, the spear-expert Pelasgians brought.
   The Thracians (all whom Hellespont includes
Within the banks of his swift-racing tide)                      1030
Heroic Acamas and Pirous led.
Euphemus, offspring of Trœzenus, son
Of Jove-protected Ceas, was the Chief
Whom the spear-armed Ciconian band obey'd,
   Pæonia's archers followed to the field                1035
Pyræchmes ; they from Amydon remote
Were drawn, where Axius winds ; broad Axius, stream
Diffused delightful over all the vale.
   Pylæmenes, a Chief of giant might
From the Eneti for forest-mules renowned,                       1040

March'd with his Paphlagonians ; dwellers they
In Sesamus and in Cytorus were,
And by the stream Parthenius ; Cromna these
Sent forth, and those Ægialus on the lip
And margin of the land, and some, the heights     1045
Of Erythini, rugged and abrupt.
     Epistrophus and Odius from the land
Of Alybe, a region far remote,
Where veins of silver wind, led to the field
The Halizonians.   With the Mysians came     1050
Chromis their Chief, and Ennomus ; him skill'd
In augury, but skill'd in vain, his art
Saved not, but by Æacides the swift,
With others in the Xanthus slain, he died.
     Ascanius, lovely youth, and Phorcis, led     1055
The Phrygians from Ascania far remote,
Ardent for battle.   The Mœonian race,
(All those who at the foot of Tmolus dwelt,)
Mesthles and Antiphus, fraternal pair,
Sons of Pylæmenes commanded, both     1060
Of the Gygæan lake in Lydia born.
     Amphimachus and Nastes led to fight
The Carians, people of a barbarous speech,
With the Milesians, and the mountain-race
Of wood-crown'd Phthira, and who dwelt beside     1065
Mæander, or on Mycale sublime.
Them led Amphimachus and Nastes, sons
Renown'd of Nomion.   Like a simple girl
Came forth Amphimachus with gold bedight,
But him his trappings from a woeful death     1070
Saved not, when whirled beneath the bloody tide
To Peleus' stormy son his spoils he left.
     Sarpedon with the noble Glaucus led
Their warriors forth from farthest Lycia, where
Xanthus deep-dimpled rolls his oozy tide.

# BOOK III.

---

## ARGUMENT.

The armies meet. Paris throws out a challenge to the Grecian Princes. Menelaus accepts it. The terms of the combat are adjusted solemnly by Agamemnon on the part of Greece, and by Priam on the part of Troy. The combat ensues, in which Paris is vanquished, whom yet Venus rescues. Agamemnon demands from the Trojans a performance of the covenant.

Now marshall'd all beneath their several chiefs,
With deafening shouts, and with the clang of arms,
The host of Troy advanced. Such clang is heard
Along the skies, when from incessant showers
Escaping, and from winter's cold, the cranes          5
Take wing, and over Ocean speed away;
Woe to the land of dwarfs! prepared, they fly
For slaughter of the small Pygmæan race.
Not so the Greeks; they breathing valour came,
But silent all, and all with faithful hearts          10
On succour mutual to the last, resolved.
As when the south wind wraps the mountain top
In mist the shepherd's dread, but to the thief
Than night itself more welcome, and the eye
Is bounded in its ken to a stone's cast,              15
Such from beneath their footsteps dun and dense
Uprose the dust, for swift they cross the plain.
    When, host to host opposed, full nigh they stood,
Then Alexander[1] in the Trojan van
Advanced was seen, all beauteous as a God;           20
His leopard's skin, his falchion and his bow
Hung from his shoulder; bright with heads of brass
He shook two spears, and challenged to the fight
The bravest Argives there, defying all.
Him, striding haughtily his host before              25
When Menelaus saw, such joy he felt
As hunger-pinch'd the lion feels, by chance

---

[1] Paris, frequently named Alexander in the original.

Conducted to some carcase huge, wild goat,
Or antler'd stag; huntsmen and baying hounds
Disturb not *him*, he gorges in their sight.                    30
So Menelaus at the view rejoiced
Of lovely Alexander, for he hoped
His punishment at hand.   At once, all armed,
Down from his chariot to the ground he leap'd.
   When Godlike Paris him in front beheld                    35
Conspicuous, his heart smote him, and his fate
Avoiding, far within the lines he shrank.
As one, who in some woodland height descrying
A serpent huge, with sudden start recoils,
His limbs shake under him; with cautious step                    40
He slow retires; fear blanches cold his cheeks;
So beauteous Alexander at the sight
Of Atreus' son dishearten'd sore, the ranks
Of haughty Trojans enter'd deep again:
Him Hector eyed, and thus rebuked severe.                    45
   Curst Paris! Fair deceiver! Woman-mad!
I would to all in heaven that thou hadst died
Unborn, at least unmated! happier far
Than here to have incurr'd this public shame!
Well may the Grecians taunt, and laughing loud,                    50
Applaud the champion, slow indeed to fight
And pusillanimous, but wonderous fair.
Wast thou as timid, tell me, when with those
Thy loved companions in that famed exploit,
Thou didst consort with strangers, and convey                    55
From distant lands a warrior's beauteous bride
To be thy father's and his people's curse,
Joy to our foes, but to thyself reproach?
Behold her husband!  Darest thou not to face
The warlike prince?  Now learn how brave a Chief                    60
Thou hast defrauded of his blooming spouse.
Thy lyre, thy locks, thy person, specious gifts
Of partial Venus, will avail thee nought,
Once mixt by Menelaus with the dust.
But we are base ourselves, or long ago,                    65
For all thy numerous mischiefs, thou hadst slept
Secure beneath a coverlet[2] of stone.

          [2] Λάϊνον ἐσσο χιτῶνα.

Then Godlike Alexander thus replied.
Oh Hector, true in temper as the axe ·
Which in the shipwright's hand the naval plank     70
Divides resistless, doubling all his force,
Such is thy dauntless spirit, whose reproach
Perforce I own, nor causeless nor unjust.
Yet let the gracious gifts uncensured pass
Of golden Venus ; man may not reject     75
The glorious bounty by the Gods bestow'd,
Nor follows their beneficence our choice.
But if thy pleasure be that I engage
With Menelaus in decision fierce
Of desperate combat, bid the host of Troy     80
And bid the Grecians sit ; then face to face
Commit us, in the vacant field between,
To fight for Helen and for all her wealth.
Who strongest proves, and conquers, he, of her
And her's possess'd, shall bear them safe away ;     85
While ye (peace sworn and firm accord) shall dwell
At Troy, and these to Argos shall return
And to Achaia praised for women fair.

    He ceased, whom Hector heard with joy ; he moved
Into the middle space, and with his spear     90
Advanced athwart push'd back the Trojan van,
And all stood fast.    Meantime at him the Greeks
Discharged full volley, showering thick around
From bow and sling ; when with a mighty voice
Thus Agamemnon, leader of the host.     95

    Argives ! Be still—shoot not, ye sons of Greece !
Hector bespeaks attention.    Hear the Chief !

    He said, at once the Grecians ceased to shoot,
And all sat silent.    Hector then began.

    Hear me, ye Trojans, and ye Greeks mail-arm'd,     100
While I shall publish in your ears the words
Of Alexander, author of our strife.
Trojans, he bids, and Grecians on the field
Their arms dispose ; while he, the hosts between,
With warlike Menelaus shall in fight     105
Contend for Helen, and for all her wealth.
Who strongest proves, and conquers, he, of her
And her's possest, shall bear them safe away,

And oaths of amity shall bind the rest.
　　He ceased, and all deep silence held, amazed ;　110
When valiant Menelaus thus began.
　　Hear now me also, on whose aching heart
These woes have heaviest fallen.　At last I hope
Decision near, Trojans and Greeks between,
For ye have suffer'd in my quarrel much,　115
And much by Paris, author of the war.
Die he who must, and peace be to the rest.
But ye shall hither bring two lambs, one white,
The other black ; this to the Earth devote,
That to the Sun.　We shall ourselves supply　120
A third for Jove.　Then bring ye Priam forth,
Himself to swear the covenant, (for his sons
Are faithless) lest the oath of Jove be scorn'd.
Young men are ever of unstable mind ;
But when an elder interferes, he views　125
Future and past together, and insures
The compact, to both parties, uninfringed.
　　So Menelaus spake ; and in all hearts
Awaken'd joyful hope that there should end
War's long calamities.　Alighted each,　130
And drew his steeds into the lines.　The field
Glitter'd with arms put off, and side by side,
Ranged orderly, while the interrupted war
Stood front to front, small interval between.
　　Then Hector to the city sent in haste　135
Two heralds for the lambs, and to invite
Priam ; while Agamemnon, royal Chief,
Talthybius to the Grecian fleet dismiss'd
For a third lamb to Jove ; nor he the voice
Of noble Agamemnon disobey'd.　140
　　Iris, ambassadress of heaven, the while,
To Helen came.　Laodice she seem'd,
Loveliest of all the daughters of the house
Of Priam, wedded to Antenor's son,
King Helicaon.　Her she found within.　145
An ample web magnificent she wove,
Inwrought with numerous conflicts for her sake
Beneath the hands of Mars endured by Greeks
Mail-arm'd, and Trojans of equestrian fame.

Swift Iris, at her side, her thus address'd.                    150
   Haste, dearest nymph! a wonderous sight behold!
Greeks brazen-mail'd, and Trojans steed-renown'd,
So lately on the cruel work of Mars
Intent and hot for mutual havoc, sit
Silent, the war hath paused, and on his shield          155
Each leans, his long spear planted at his side.
Paris and Menelaus, warrior bold,
With quivering lances shall contend for thee,
And thou art his who conquers; his for ever.
   So saying, the Goddess into Helen's soul             160
Sweetest desire infused to see again
Her former Lord, her parents, and her home.
At once o'ermantled with her snowy veil
She started forth, and as she went, let fall
A tender tear; not unaccompanied                              165
She went, but by two maidens of her train
Attended, Æthra, Pittheus' daughter fair,
And soft-eyed Clymene.   Their hasty steps
Convey'd them quickly to the Scæan gate.
There Priam, Panthoüs, Clytius, Lampus sat,            170
Thymoetes, Hicetaon, branch of Mars,
Antenor and Ucalegon the wise,
All, elders of the people; warriors erst,
But idle now through age, yet of a voice
Still indefatigable as the fly's[3]                              175
Which perch'd among the boughs sends forth at noon
Through all the grove his slender ditty sweet.
Such sat those Trojan leaders on the tower,
Who, soon as Helen on the steps they saw,
In accents quick, but whisper'd, thus remark'd.        180
   Trojans and Grecians wage, with fair excuse,
Long war for so much beauty.   Oh, how like
In feature to the Goddesses above!
Pernicious loveliness! Ah, hence away,
Resistless as thou art and all divine,                         185
Nor leave a curse to us, and to our sons.
   So they among themselves; but Priam call'd

[3] Not the grasshopper, but an insect well known in hot countries, and
which in Italy is called Cicála. The Grasshopper rests on the ground, but
the favourite abode of the Cicála is in the trees and hedges.

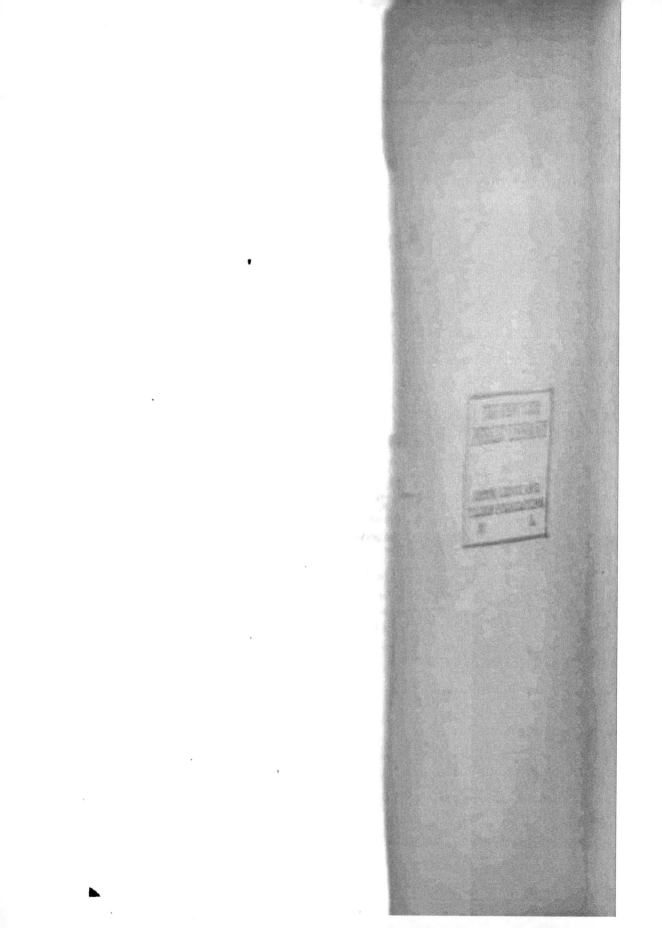

ide.   My daughter dear!
e.   Thou shalt hence discern
thy kindred and thy friends.
on thee.   The Gods have cau
ntable war to Troy.
chaian Chief for bulk
or port.   Taller indeed
he; but with these eyes
dignity, and grace.
Some royal Chief he seems.
len, loveliest of her sex.
ne for ever held
th filial fear beloved!
eath had been my choice,
don, as I did,
atrimonial bliss,
ter, and companions dear,
son.   Yet I alas!
re now, live but to weep.
Thou behold'st the son
non, mighty king,
ious in the throne,
me me now to call him such,
ther once to me.
ient King admiring, said.
ppy was thy birth,
, whom this gallant host
e sons of Greece obey!
gia, in my days of youth,
Phrygians there I saw,
d expert; they were the pow
ygdon, Godlike Chief,
Sangar's stream encamp'd.
em, chosen in that war
d it was her day
man-defying race,
multitudes like these
eeks, I saw not even there.
ng observing next
ed.   My child, declare
by the head he seems

W Harvey

THE FLIGHT OF TROY.

"Such sat those Trojan leaders on the tower,
Who, soon as Helen on the steps they saw,
In accents quick, but whisper'd, thus remark'd."

Fair Helen to his side.   My daughter dear!
Come, sit beside me.   Thou shalt hence discern
Thy former Lord, thy kindred and thy friends.          190
I charge no blame on thee.   The Gods have caused,
Not thou, this lamentable war to Troy.
Name to me yon Achaian Chief for bulk
Conspicuous, and for port.   Taller indeed
I may perceive than he; but with these eyes          195
Saw never yet such dignity, and grace.
Declare his name.   Some royal Chief he seems.
    To whom thus Helen, loveliest of her sex.
My other Sire! by me for ever held
In reverence, and with filial fear beloved!          200
Oh that some cruel death had been my choice,
Rather than to abandon, as I did,
All joys domestic, matrimonial bliss,
Brethren, dear daughter, and companions dear,
A wanderer with thy son.   Yet I alas!          205
Died not, and therefore now, live but to weep.
But I resolve thee.   Thou behold'st the son
Of Atreus, Agamemnon, mighty king,
In arms heroic, gracious in the throne,
And, (though it shame me now to call him such,)          210
By nuptial ties a brother once to me.
    Then him the ancient King admiring, said.
Oh blest Atrides, happy was thy birth,
And thy lot glorious, whom this gallant host
So numerous, of the sons of Greece obey!          215
To vine-famed Phrygia, in my days of youth,
I journey'd; many Phrygians there I saw,
Brave horsemen, and expert; they were the powers
Of Otreus and of Mygdon, Godlike Chief,
And on the banks of Sangar's stream encamp'd.          220
I march'd among them, chosen in that war
Ally of Phrygia, and it was her day
Of conflict with the man-defying race,
The Amazons; yet multitudes like these
Thy bright-eyed Greeks, I saw not even there.          225
    The venerable King observing next
Ulysses, thus enquired.   My child, declare
Him also.   Shorter by the head he seems

Than Agamemnon, Atreus' mighty son,
But shoulder'd broader, and of ampler chest;                230
He hath disposed his armour on the plain,
But like a ram, himself the warrior ranks
Ranges majestic; like a ram full-fleeced
By numerous sheep encompass'd snowy-white.
  To whom Jove's daughter Helen thus replied.      235
In him the son of old Laertes know,
Ulysses; born in Ithaca the rude,
But of a piercing wit, and deeply wise.
  Then answer thus, Antenor sage return'd.
Princess thou hast described him: hither once             240
The noble Ithacan, on thy behalf
Embassador with Menelaus, came:
Beneath my roof, with hospitable fare
Friendly I entertained them.   Seeing then
Occasion opportune, I closely mark'd                      245
The genius and the talents of the Chiefs,
And this I noted well; that when they stood
Amid the assembled counsellors of Troy,
Then Menelaus his advantage show'd,
Who by the shoulders overtopp'd his friend.              250
But when both sat, Ulysses in his air
Had more of state and dignity than he.
In the delivery of a speech address'd
To the full senate, Menelaus used
Few words, but to the matter, fitly ranged,              255
And with much sweetness utter'd; for in loose
And idle play of ostentatious terms
He dealt not, though he were the younger man.
But when the wise Ulysses from his seat
Had once arisen, he would his downcast eyes              260
So rivet on the earth, and with a hand
That seemed untutor'd in its use, so hold
His sceptre, swaying it to neither side,
That hadst thou seen him, thou hadst thought him, sure,
Some chafed and angry idiot, passion-fixt.               265
Yet, when at length, the clear and mellow base
Of his deep voice brake forth, and he let fall
His chosen words like flakes of feather'd snow,
None then might match Ulysses; leisure, then,

Found none to wonder at his noble form.     270
   The third of whom the venerable king
Enquired, was Ajax.—Yon Achaian tall,
Whose head and shoulders tower above the rest
And of such bulk prodigious—who is he?
   Him answer'd Helen, loveliest of her sex.     275
A bulwark of the Greeks. In him thou seest
Gigantic Ajax. Opposite appear
The Cretans, and among the Chiefs of Crete
Stands, like a God, Idomeneus. Him oft
From Crete arrived, was Menelaus wont     280
To entertain; and others now I see,
Achaians, whom I could recall to mind,
And give to each his name; but two brave youths
I yet discern not; for equestrian skill
One famed, and one a boxer never foiled;     285
My brothers; born of Leda; sons of Jove;
Castor and Pollux. Either they abide
In lovely Sparta still, or if they came,
Decline the fight, by my disgrace abash'd,
And the reproaches which have fallen on me.     290
   She said; but they already slept inhumed
In Lacedemon, in their native soil.
   And now the heralds, through the streets of Troy
Charged with the lambs, and with a goat-skin filled
With heart-exhilarating wine prepared     295
For that divine solemnity, return'd.
Idæus in his hand a beaker bore
Resplendent, with its fellow cups of gold,
And thus he summon'd ancient Priam forth.
   Son of Laomedon, arise. The Chiefs     300
Call thee, the Chiefs of Ilium and of Greece.
Descend into the plain. We strike a truce,
And need thine oath to bind it. Paris fights
With warlike Menelaus for his spouse;
Their spears decide the strife. The conqueror wins     305
Helen and all her treasures. We, thenceforth,
(Peace sworn and amity,) shall dwell secure
In Troy, while they to Argos shall return
And to Achaia praised for women fair.
   He spake, and Priam, shuddering, bade his train     310

Prepare his steeds; they sedulous obey'd.
First, Priam mounting, backward stretch'd the reins;
Antenor, next, beside him sat, and through
The Scæan gate they drove into the plain.
Arriving at the hosts of Greece and Troy      315
They left the chariot, and proceeded both
Into the interval between the hosts.
   Then uprose Agamemnon, and uprose
All-wise Ulysses.   Next, the heralds came
Conspicuous forward, expediting each      320
The ceremonial; they the beaker fill'd
With wine, and to the hands of all the kings
Minister'd water.   Agamemnon then
Drawing his dagger which he ever bore
Appendant to his heavy falchion's sheath,      325
Cut off the forelocks of the lambs, of which
The heralds gave to every Grecian Chief
A portion, and to all the Chiefs of Troy.
Then Agamemnon raised his hands, and pray'd.
   Jove, Father, who from Ida stretchest forth      330
Thine arm omnipotent, o'erruling all,
And thou, all-seeing and all-hearing sun,
Ye rivers, and thou conscious earth, and ye
Who under earth on human kind avenge
Severe, the guilt of violated oaths,      335
Hear ye, and ratify what now we swear!
Should Paris slay the hero amber-hair'd,
My brother Menelaus, Helen's wealth
And Helen's self are his, and all our host
Shall home return to Greece; but should it chance      340
That Paris fall by Menelaus' hand,
Then Troy shall render back what she detains,
With such amercement as is meet, a sum
To be remember'd in all future times.
Which penalty should Priam and his sons      345
Not pay, though Paris fall, then here in arms
I will contend for payment of the mulct
My due, till, satisfied, I close the war.
   He said, and with his ruthless steel the lambs
Stretch'd panting all, but soon they ceased to pant,      350
For mortal was the stroke.   Then drawing forth

Wine from the beaker, they with brimming cups
Hail'd the immortal Gods, and pray'd again,
And many a Grecian thus and Trojan spake.
    All-glorious Jove, and ye the powers of heaven,    355
Whoso shall violate this contract first,
So be the brains of them and of their sons
Pour'd out, as we this wine pour on the earth,
And may their wives bring forth to other men!
    So they: but them Jove heard not.   Then arose    360
Priam, the son of Dardanus, and said,
    Hear me, ye Trojans and ye Greeks well-arm'd.
Hence back to wind-swept Ilium I return,
Unable to sustain the sight, my son
With warlike Menelaus match'd in arms.    365
Jove knows, and the immortal Gods, to whom
Of both, this day is preordain'd the last.
    So spake the godlike monarch, and disposed
Within the royal chariot all the lambs;
Then, mounting, check'd the reins; Antenor next    370
Ascended, and to Ilium both return'd.
    First, Hector and Ulysses, noble Chief,
Measured the ground; then taking lots for proof
Who of the combatants should foremost hurl
His spear, they shook them in a brazen casque;    375
Meantime the people raised their hands on high,
And many a Grecian thus and Trojan pray'd.
    Jove, Father, who on Ida seated, seest
And rulest all below, glorious in power!
Of these two champions, to the drear abodes    380
Of Ades him appoint who furnish'd first
The cause of strife between them, and let peace
Oath-bound, and amity unite the rest!
    So spake the hosts; then Hector shook the lots,
Majestic Chief, turning his face aside.    385
Forth sprang the lot of Paris.   They in ranks
Sat all, where stood the fiery steeds of each,
And where his radiant arms lay on the field.
Illustrious Alexander his bright arms
Put on, fair Helen's paramour.   He clasp'd    390
His polish'd greaves with silver studs secured;
His brother's corslet to his breast he bound,

Lycaon's, apt to his own shape and size,
And slung athwart his shoulders, bright emboss'd,
His brazen sword; his massy buckler broad          395
He took, and to his graceful head his casque
Adjusted elegant, which, as he moved,
Its bushy crest waved dreadful; last he seized,
Well fitted to his gripe, his ponderous spear.
Meantime the hero Menelaus made          400
Like preparation, and his arms put on.
    When thus, from all the multitude apart,
Both combatants had arm'd, with eyes that flash'd
Defiance, to the middle space they strode,
Trojans and Greeks between.   Astonishment          405
Seized all beholders.   On the measured ground
Full near they stood, each brandishing on high
His massy spear, and each was fiery wroth.
    First, Alexander his long-shadow'd spear
Sent forth, and on its smooth shield's surface struck          410
The son of Atreus, but the brazen guard
Pierced not, for at the disk, with blunted point
Reflex, his ineffectual weapon stay'd.
Then Menelaus to the fight advanced
Impetuous, after prayer offer'd to Jove.          415
    King over all! now grant me to avenge
My wrongs on Alexander; now subdue
The aggressor under me; that men unborn
May shudder at the thought of faith abused,
And hospitality with rape repaid.          420
    He said, and brandishing his massy spear,
Dismiss'd it.   Through the burnish'd buckler broad
Of Priam's son the stormy weapon flew,
Transpierced his costly hauberk, and the vest
Ripp'd on his flank; but with a sideward bend          425
He baffled it, and baulk'd the dreadful death.
    Then Menelaus drawing his bright blade,
Swung it aloft, and on the hairy crest
Smote him; but shiver'd into fragments small
The falchion at the stroke fell from his hand.          430
Vexation fill'd him; to the spacious heavens
He look'd, and with a voice of woe exclaim'd—
    Jupiter! of all powers by man adored

To me most adverse!   Confident I hoped
Revenge for Paris' treason, but my sword        435
Is shiver'd, and I sped my spear in vain.
    So saying, he sprang on him, and his long crest
Seized fast; then, turning, drew him by that hold
Toward the Grecian host.   The broider'd band
That underbraced his helmet at the chin,        440
Strain'd to his smooth neck with a ceaseless force,
Chok'd him; and now had Menelaus won
Deathless renown, dragging him off the field,
But Venus, foam-sprung Goddess, feeling quick
His peril imminent, snapp'd short the brace     445
Though stubborn, by a slaughter'd[4] ox supplied,
And the void helmet follow'd as he pull'd.
That prize the Hero, whirling it aloft,
Threw to his Greeks, who caught it and secured,
Then with vindictive strides he rush'd again     450
On Paris, spear in hand; but him involved
In mist opaque Venus with ease divine
Snatch'd thence, and in his chamber placed him, fill'd
With scents odorous, spirit-soothing sweets.
Nor stay'd the Goddess, but at once in quest     455
Of Helen went; her on a lofty tower
She found, where many a damsel stood of Troy,
And twitch'd her fragrant robe.   In form she seem'd
An ancient matron, who, while Helen dwelt
In Lacedæmon, her unsullied wool                460
Dress'd for her, faithfullest of all her train.
Like her disguised the Goddess thus began.
    Haste—Paris calls thee—on his sculptured couch,
(Sparkling alike his looks and his attire,)
He waits thy wish'd return.   Thou would'st not dream  465
That he had fought; he rather seems prepared
For dance, or after dance, for soft repose.
    So saying, she tumult raised in Helen's mind.
Yet soon as by her symmetry of neck,
By her love-kindling breasts and luminous eyes  470
She knew the Goddess, her she thus bespake.
    Ah whence, deceitful deity! thy wish

    [4] Because the hide of a beast that dies in health is tougher and fitter
for use than of another that dies diseased.

Now to ensnare me? Would'st thou lure me, say,
To some fair city of Mæonian name
Or Phrygian, more remote from Sparta still?          475
Hast thou some human favourite also there?
Is it because Atrides hath prevailed
To vanquish Paris, and would bear me home
Unworthy as I am, that thou attempt'st ·
Again to cheat me? Go thyself—sit thou          480
Beside him,—for his sake renounce the skies;
Watch him, weep for him; till at length his wife
He deign to make thee, or perchance his slave.
I go not (now to go were shame indeed,)
To dress his couch; nor will I be the jest          485
Of all my sex in Ilium.   Oh! my griefs
Are infinite, and more than I can bear.
     To whom, the foam-sprung Goddess, thus incensed.
Ah wretch! provoke not me; lest in my wrath
Abandoning thee, I not hate thee less          490
Than now I fondly love thee, and beget
Such detestation of thee in all hearts,
Grecian and  Trojan, that thou die abhorr'd.
     The Goddess ceased.   Jove's daughter, Helen, fear'd,
And, in her lucid veil close wrapt around,          495
Silent retired, of all those Trojan dames
Unseen, and Venus led, herself, the way.
Soon then as Alexander's fair abode
They reach'd, her maidens quick their tasks resumed,
And she to her own chamber lofty-roof'd          500
Ascended, loveliest of her sex.   A seat
For Helen, daughter of Jove Ægis-arm'd,
To Paris opposite, the Queen of smiles
Herself disposed; but with averted eyes
She sat before him, and him keen reproach'd.          505
     Thou hast escaped.—Ah would that thou had'st died
By that heroic arm, mine husband's erst!
Thou once didst vaunt thee in address and strength
Superior.   Go then—challenge yet again
The warlike Menelaus forth to fight.          510
But hold.   The hero of the amber locks
Provoke no more so rashly, lest the point
Of his victorious spear soon stretch thee dead.

She ended, to whom Paris thus replied,
Ah Helen, wound me not with taunt severe!  515
Me, Menelaus, by Minerva's aid,
Hath vanquish'd now, who may hereafter, him.
We also have our Gods.  But let us love.
For never since the day when thee I bore
From pleasant Lacedæmon o'er the waves  520
To Cranäe's fair isle, and first enjoy'd
Thy beauty, loved I as I love thee now,
Or felt such sweetness of intense desire.
　　He spake, and sought his bed, whom follow'd soon
Jove's daughter, reconciled to his embrace.  525
　　But Menelaus like a lion ranged
The multitude, enquiring far and near
For Paris lost.  Yet neither Trojan him
Nor friend of Troy could shew, whom, else, through love
None had conceal'd, for him as death itself  530
All hated, but his going none had seen.
　　Amidst them all then spake the King of men.
Trojans, and Dardans, and allies of Troy!
The warlike Menelaus hath prevailed,
As is most plain.  Now therefore bring ye forth  535
Helen with all her treasures, also bring
Such large amercement as is meet, a sum
To be remember'd in all future times.
　　So spake Atrides, and Achaia's host
With loud applause confirm'd the monarch's claim.  540

# BOOK IV.

———

### ARGUMENT.

In a Council of the Gods, a dispute arises between Jupiter and Juno, which
is at last compromised, Jove consenting to dispatch Minerva with a charge
to incite some Trojan to a violation of the truce. Minerva descends for
that purpose, and in the form of Laodocus, a son of Priam, exhorts Pandarus to shoot at Menelaus, and succeeds. Menelaus is wounded, and
Agamemnon having consigned him to the care of Machaon, goes forth
to perform the duties of commander in chief, in the encouragement of
his host to battle. The battle begins.

Now, on the golden floor of Jove's abode  
The Gods all sat consulting; Hebe them,  
Graceful, with nectar served; they pledging each  
His next, alternate quaff'd from cups of gold,  
And at their ease reclined, look'd down on Troy;     5  
When, sudden, Jove essay'd by piercing speech  
Invidious, to enkindle Juno's ire.  
    Two Goddesses on Menelaus' part  
Confederate stand, Juno in Argos known,  
Pallas in Alalcomene[1]; yet they     10  
Sequester'd sit, look on, and are amused.  
Not so smile-loving Venus; she beside  
Her champion station'd, saves him from his fate,  
And at this moment, by her aid, he lives.  
But now, since victory hath proved the lot     15  
Of warlike Menelaus, weigh ye well  
The matter; shall we yet the ruinous strife  
Prolong between the nations, or consent  
To give them peace? should peace your preference win,  
And prove alike acceptable to all,     20  
Stand Ilium, and let Menelaus bear  
Helen of Argos back to Greece again.  
    He ended; Juno and Minerva heard,  
Low-murmuring deep disgust; for side by side  
They forging sat calamity to Troy.     25

[1] A town of that name in Bœotia, where Pallas was particularly worshipped.

Minerva through displeasure against Jove
Nought utter'd, for with rage her bosom boil'd ;
But Juno check'd not hers, who thus replied.
    What word hath pass'd thy lips, Jove most severe !
How? wouldst thou render fruitless all my pains?          30
The sweat that I have pour'd? my steeds themselves
Have fainted while I gather'd Greece in arms
For punishment of Priam and his sons.
Do it.   But small thy praise shall be in heaven.
    Then her the Thunderer answer'd sore displeased.      35
Ah shameless ! how have Priam and his sons
So much transgress'd against thee, that thou burn'st
With ceaseless rage to ruin populous Troy ?
Go, make thine entrance at her lofty gates,
Priam and all his house, and all his host                 40
Alive devour ; then, haply, thou wilt rest ;
Do even as thou wilt, that this dispute
Live not between us a consuming fire
For ever.   But attend ; mark well the word.
When I shall also doom in future time                     45
Some city to destruction, dear to thee,
Oppose me not, but give my fury way
As I give way to thine, not pleased myself,
Yet not unsatisfied, so thou be pleased.
For of all cities of the sons of men,                     50
And which the sun and stars from heaven behold,
Me sacred Troy most pleases, Priam me
Most, and the people of the warrior King.
Nor without cause.   They feed mine altar well ;
Libation there, and steam of savoury scent                55
Fail not, the tribute which by lot is ours.
    Him answer'd, then, the Goddess ample-eyed[2],
Majestic Juno : Three fair cities me,
Of all the earth, most interest and engage,
Mycenæ for magnificence renown'd,                         60
Argos, and Sparta.   Them, when next thy wrath
Shall be inflamed against them, lay thou waste ;
I will not interpose on their behalf ;
Thou shalt not hear me murmur ;. what avail

---

[2] Βοῶπις, constant description of Juno, but not susceptible of literal translation.

Complaint or force against thy matchless arm?                    65
Yet were it most unmeet that even I
Should toil in vain; I also boast a birth
Celestial; Saturn deeply wise, thy Sire,
Is also mine; our origin is one.
Thee I acknowledge Sovereign, yet account          70
Myself entitled by a twofold claim
To veneration both from Gods and men,
The daughter of Jove's sire, and spouse of Jove.
Concession mutual therefore both thyself
Befits and me, whom when the Gods perceive         75
Disposed to peace, they also shall accord.
Come then.—To yon dread field dispatch in haste
Minerva, with command that she incite
The Trojans first to violate their oath
By some fresh insult on the exulting Greeks.       80
    So Juno; nor the sire of all refused,
But in wing'd accents thus to Pallas spake.
    Begone; swift fly to yonder field; incite
The Trojans first to violate their oath
By some fresh insult on the exulting Greeks.       85
    The Goddess heard, and what she wish'd, enjoin'd,
Down-darted swift from the Olympian heights,
In form a meteor, such as from his hand
Not seldom Jove dismisses, beaming bright
And, breaking into stars, an omen sent             90
To mariners, or to some numerous host.
Such Pallas seem'd, and swift descending, dropp'd
Full in the midst between them.   They with awe
That sign portentous and with wonder view'd,
Achaians both and Trojans, and his next            95
The soldier thus bespake.   Now either war
And dire hostility again shall flame,
Or Jove now gives us peace.   Both are from Jove.
    So spake the soldiery; but she the form
Taking of brave Laodocus, the son                  100
Of old Antenor, throughout all the ranks
Sought godlike Pandarus.   Ere long she found
The valiant son illustrious of Lycaon,
Standing encompass'd by his dauntless troops,
Broad-shielded warriors, from Æsepus' stream       105

His followers; to his side the Goddess came,
And in wing'd accents ardent him bespake.
   Brave offspring of Lycaon, is there hope
That thou wilt hear my counsel? darest thou slip
A shaft at Menelaus? much renown          110
Thou shalt and thanks from all the Trojans win,
But most of all, from Paris, prince of Troy.
From him illustrious gifts thou shalt receive
Doubtless, when Menelaus he shall see
The martial son of Atreus by a shaft          115
Subdued of thine, placed on his funeral pile.
Come.   Shoot at Menelaus, glorious Chief!
But vow to Lycian Phœbus bow-renown'd
An hecatomb, all firstlings of the flock,
To fair Zeleia's walls once safe restored.          120
   So Pallas spake, to whom infatuate he
Listening, uncased at once his polish'd bow.
That bow, the laden brows of a wild goat
Salacious had supplied; him on a day
Forth-issuing from his cave, in ambush placed          125
He wounded with an arrow to his breast
Dispatch'd, and on the rock supine he fell.
Each horn had from his head tall growth attain'd,
Full sixteen palms; them shaven smooth the smith
Had aptly join'd, and tipt their points with gold.          130
That bow he strung, then, stooping, planted firm
The nether horn, his comrades bold the while
Screening him close with shields, lest ere the prince
Were stricken, Menelaus, brave in arms,
The Greeks with fierce assault should interpose.          135
He raised his quiver's lid; he chose a dart
Unflown, full-fledged, and barb'd with pangs of death,
He lodged in haste the arrow on the string,
And vow'd to Lycian Phœbus bow-renown'd
An hecatomb, all firstlings of the flock,          140
To fair Zeleia's walls once safe restored.
Compressing next nerve and notch'd arrow-head
He drew back both together, to his pap
Drew home the nerve, the barb home to his bow,
And when the horn was curved to a wide arch,          145
He twang'd it.   Whizz'd the bowstring, and the reed

Leap'd off, impatient for the distant throng.
   Thee, Menelaus, then the blessed Gods
Forgat not ; Pallas huntress of the spoil,
Thy guardian then, baffled the cruel dart.        150
Far as a mother wafts the fly aside
That haunts her slumbering babe, so far she drove
Its course aslant, directing it herself
Against the golden clasps that join'd his belt ;
For there the doubled hauberk interposed.      155
The bitter arrow plunged into his belt ;
It pierced his broider'd belt, stood fixt within
His twisted hauberk, nor the interior quilt,
Though penetrable least to arrow-points
And his best guard, withheld it, but it pass'd    160
That also, and the Hero's skin inscribed.
Quick flowed a sable current from the wound.
   As when a Carian or Mæonian maid
Impurples ivory ordain'd to grace
The cheek of martial steed ; safe stored it lies,   165
By many a Chief desired, but proves at last
The stately trapping of some prince, the pride
Of his high pamper'd steed, nor less his own;
Such, Menelaus, seem'd thy shapely thighs,
Thy legs, thy feet, stained with thy trickling blood.   170
   Shudder'd King Agamemnon when he saw
The blood fast trickling from the wound, nor less
Shudder'd himself the bleeding warrior bold.
But neck and barb observing from the flesh
Extant, he gather'd heart, and lived again.    175
Then royal Agamemnon, sighing, grasp'd
The hand of Menelaus, and while all
Their followers sigh'd around them, thus began.
   I swore thy death, my brother, when I swore
This truce, and set thee forth in sight of Greeks   180
And Trojans, our sole champion ; for the foe
Hath trodden underfoot his sacred oath,
And stained it with thy blood.   But not in vain,
The truce was ratified, the blood of lambs
Poured forth, libation made, and right hands join'd   185
In holy confidence.   The wrath of Jove
May sleep, but will not always ; they shall pay

Dear penalty; their own obnoxious heads
Shall be the mulct, their children and their wives.
For this I know, know surely; that a day                        190
Shall come, when Ilium, when the warlike King
Of Ilium and his host shall perish all.
Saturnian Jove high-throned, dwelling in heaven,
Resentful of this outrage, then shall shake
His storm-clad Ægis over them.   He will;                       195
I speak no fable.   Time shall prove me true.
But, oh my Menelaus, dire distress
Awaits me, if thy close of life be come,
And thou must die.   Then ignominy foul
Shall hunt me back to Argos long-desired;                       200
For then all here will recollect their home,
And, hope abandoning, will Helen yield
To be the boast of Priam, and of Troy.
So shall our toils be vain, and while thy bones
Shall waste these clods beneath, Troy's haughty sons            205
The tomb of Menelaus glory-crown'd
Insulting barbarous, shall scoff at me.
So may Atrides, shall they say, perform
His anger still as he performed it here,
Whither he led an unsuccessful host,                            210
Whence he hath sail'd again without the spoils,
And where he left his brother's bones to rot.
So shall the Trojan speak; then open earth
Her mouth, and hide me in her deepest gulfs!
     But him, the hero of the golden locks                      215
Thus cheer'd.   My brother, fear not, nor infect
With fear the Grecians; the sharp-pointed reed
Hath touch'd no vital part.   The broider'd zone,
The hauberk, and the tough interior quilt,
Work of the armourer, its force repress'd.                      220
     Him answer'd Agamemnon, King of men.
So be it, brother! but the hand of one
Skilful to heal shall visit and shall dress
The wound with drugs of pain-assuaging power.
     He ended, and his noble herald, next,                      225
Bespake, Talthybius.  Haste, call hither quick
The son of Æsculapius, leech renown'd,
The prince Machaon.   Bid him fly to attend

The warlike Chieftain Menelaus ; him
Some archer, either Lycian or of Troy,                     230
A dexterous one, hath stricken with a shaft
To his own glory, and to our distress.
   He spake, nor him the herald disobey'd,
But through the Greeks bright-arm'd his course began
The Hero seeking earnest on all sides                     235
Machaon.   Him, ere long, he station'd saw
Amid the shielded-ranks of his brave band
From steed-famed Tricca drawn, and at his side
With accents ardour-wing'd, him thus address'd.
   Haste, Asclepiades ! The king of men                 240
Calls thee.   Delay not.   Thou must visit quick
Brave Menelaus, Atreus' son, for him
Some archer, either Lycian or of Troy,
A dexterous one, hath stricken with a shaft
To his own glory, and to our distress.                    245
   So saying, he roused Machaon, who his course
Through the wide host began.   Arriving soon
Where wounded Menelaus stood, while all
The bravest of Achaia's host around
The Godlike hero press'd, he strove at once               250
To draw the arrow from his cincture forth,
But, drawing, bent the barbs.   He therefore loosed
His broider'd belt, his hauberk and his quilt,
Work of the armourer, and laying bare
His body where the bitter shaft had plough'd              255
His flesh, he suck'd the wound, then spread it o'er
With drugs of balmy power, given on a time
For friendship's sake by Chiron to his sire.
   While Menelaus thus the cares engross'd
Of all those Chiefs, the shielded powers of Troy          260
'Gan move toward them, and the Greeks again
Put on their armour, mindful of the fight.
Then hadst thou not great Agamemnon seen
Slumbering, or trembling, or averse from war,
But ardent to begin his glorious task.                    265
His steeds, and his bright chariot brass-inlaid
He left ; the snorting steeds Eurymedon,
Offspring of Ptolemy Piraïdes
Detain'd apart ; for him he strict enjoin'd

Attendance near, lest weariness of limbs                    270
Should seize him marshalling his numerous host.
So forth he went, and through the files on foot
Proceeding, where the warrior Greeks he saw
Alert, he roused them by his words the more.

    Argives! abate no spark of all your fire.       275
Jove will not prosper traitors.   Them who first
Transgress'd the truce the vultures shall devour,
But we (their city taken) shall their wives
Lead captive, and their children home to Greece.

    So cheer'd he them.   But whom he saw supine,   280
Or in the rugged work of war remiss,
In terms of anger them he stern rebuked.

    Oh Greeks! The shame of Argos! Arrow-doom'd!
Blush ye not?  Wherefore stand ye thus aghast,
Like fawns which wearied after scouring wide       285
The champaign, gaze and pant, and can no more?
Senseless like them ye stand, nor seek the fight.
Is it your purpose patient here to wait
Till Troy invade your vessels on the shore
Of the grey deep, that ye may trial make           290
Of Jove, if he will prove, himself, your shield?

    Thus, in discharge of his high office, pass'd
Atrides through the ranks, and now arrived
Where, hardy Chief! Idomeneus in front
Of his bold Cretans stood, stout as a boar.         295
The van he occupied, while in the rear
Meriones harangued the most remote.
Them so prepared the King of men beheld
With joyful heart, and thus in courteous terms
Instant the brave Idomeneus address'd.              300

    Thee fighting, feasting, howsoe'er employed,
I most respect, Idomeneus, of all
The well-horsed Danäi; for when the Chiefs
Of Argos, banquetting, their beakers charge
With rosy wine the honourable meed                  305
Of valour, thou alone of all the Greeks
Drink'st not by measure.   No—thy goblet stands
Replenish'd still, and like myself thou know'st
No rule or bound, save what thy choice prescribes.
March.   Seek the foe.   Fight now as heretofore.   310

To whom Idomeneus of Crete replied.
Atrides! all the friendship and the love
Which I have promised will I well perform.
Go; animate the rest, Chief after Chief
Of the Achaians, that the fight begin.                    315
For Troy hath scatter'd to the winds all faith,
All conscience, and for such her treachery foul
Shall have large recompence of death and woe.
   He said, whom Agamemnon at his heart
Exulting, pass'd, and in his progress came               320
Where stood each Ajax; them he found prepared
With all their cloud of infantry behind.
As when the goat-herd on some rocky point
Advanced, a cloud sees wafted o'er the deep
By western gales, and rolling slow along,                325
To him, who stands remote, pitch-black it seems,
And comes with tempest charged; he at the sight
Shuddering, his flock compels into a cave;
So moved the gloomy phalanx, rough with spears,
And dense with shields of youthful warriors bold,        330
Close-following either Ajax to the fight.
   Them also, pleased, the King of men beheld,
And in wing'd accents hail'd them as he pass'd.
   Brave leaders of the mail-clad host of Greece!
I move not you to duty; ye yourselves                     335
Move others, and no lesson need from me.
Jove, Pallas, and Apollo! were but all
Courageous as yourselves, soon Priam's towers
Should totter, and his Ilium storm'd and sack'd
By our victorious bands, stoop to the dust.              340
   He ceased, and still proceeding, next arrived
Where stood the Pylian orator, his band
Marshalling under all their leaders bold
Alastor, Chromius, Pelagon the vast,
Hæmon the prince, and Bias, martial Chief.               345
Chariot and horse he station'd in the front;
His numerous infantry, a strong reserve
Right valiant, in the rear; the worst, and those
In whom he trusted least, he drove between,
That such through mere necessity might act.              350
First to his charioteers he gave in charge

Their duty; bade them rein their horses hard,
Shunning confusion.   Let no warrior, vain
And overweening of his strength or skill,
Start from his rank to dare the fight alone,                    355
Or fall behind it, weakening whom he leaves.
³And if, dismounted from his own, he climb
Another's chariot, let him not affect
Perverse the reins, but let him stand, his spear
Advancing firm, far better so employ'd.                        360
Such was the discipline, in ancient times,
Of our forefathers; by these rules they fought
Successful, and lay'd many a city low.
     So counsell'd them the venerable Chief
Long time expert in arms; him also saw                         365
King Agamemnon with delight, and said,
     Old Chief! ah how I wish that thy firm heart
Were but supported by as firm a knee!
But time unhinges all.   Oh that some youth·
Had thine old age, and thou wast young again!                  370
To whom the valiant Nestor thus replied.
     Atrides, I could also ardent wish
That I were now robust as when I struck
Brave Ereuthalion⁴ breathless to the ground!
But never all their gifts the Gods confer                      375
On man at once; if then I had the force
Of youth, I suffer now the effects of age.
Yet ancient as I am, I will be seen
Still mingling with the charioteers, still prompt
To give them counsel; for to counsel youth                     380
Is the old warrior's province.   Let the green
In years, my juniors, unimpaired by time,
Push with the lance, for they have strength to boast.
     So he, whom Agamemnon joyful heard,

---

³ Diverse interpretations are given of this passage.  I have adopted that
which to me appeared most plausible.  It seems to be a caution against
the mischiefs that might ensue, should the horses be put under the management of a driver with whom they were unacquainted.—The scholium by
Villoison much countenances this solution.        ⁴ Here Nestor only men-
tions the name of Ereuthalion, knowing the present to be an improper time
for story-telling; in the seventh book he relates his fight and victory at
length.   This passage may serve to confute those who charge Nestor with
indiscriminate loquacity.

And passing thence, the son of Peteos found      385
Menestheus, foremost in equestrian fame,
Among the brave Athenians ; near to him
Ulysses held his station, and at hand
The Cephallenians stood, hardy and bold ;
For rumour none of the approaching fight      390
Them yet had reach'd, so recent had the stir
Arisen in either host ; they, therefore, watch'd
Till the example of some other band
Marching, should prompt them to begin the fight.
But Agamemnon, thus, the King of men      395
Them seeing, sudden and severe reproved.
   Menestheus, son of Peteos prince renown'd,
And thou, deviser of all evil wiles !
Adept in artifice ! why stand ye here
Appall'd ? why wait ye on this distant spot      400
'Till others move ? I might expect from you
More readiness to meet the burning war,
Whom foremost I invite of all to share
The banquet, when the Princes feast with me.
There ye are prompt ; ye find it pleasant there      405
To eat your savoury food, and quaff your wine
Delicious, 'till satiety ensue ;
But here ye could be well content to stand
Spectators only, while ten Grecian troops
Should wage before you the wide-wasting war.      410
   To whom Ulysses, with resentful tone
Dark-frowning, thus replied. What words are these
Which have escaped thy lips ; and for what cause,
Atrides, hast thou call'd me slow to fight ?
When we of Greece shall in sharp contest clash      415
With yon steed-tamer Trojans, mark me then ;
Then thou shalt see (if the concerns of war
So nearly touch thee, and thou so incline)
The father of Telemachus, engaged
Among the foremost Trojans. But thy speech      420
Was light as is the wind, and rashly made.
   When him thus moved he saw, the monarch smiled
Complacent, and in gentler terms replied.
   Laertes' noble son, for wiles renown'd !
Short reprimand and exhortation short      425

Suffice for thee, nor did I purpose more.
For I have known thee long, that thou art one
Of kindest nature, and so much my friend
That we have both one heart.   Go therefore thou,
Lead on, and if a word have fallen amiss,                          430
We will hereafter mend it, and may heaven
Obliterate in thine heart its whole effect!
　　He ceased, and ranging still along the line,
The son of Tydeus, Diomede, perceived,
Heroic Chief, by chariots all around                              435
Environ'd, and by steeds, at side of whom
Stood Sthenelus, the son of Capaneus.
Him also, Agamemnon, King of men,
In accents of asperity reproved.
　　Ah, son of Tydeus, Chief of dauntless heart                   440
And of equestrian fame! why standest thou
Appall'd, and peering through the walks of war?
So did not Tydeus.   In the foremost fight
His favourite station was, as they affirm
Who witness'd his exploits; I never saw                           445
Or met him, but by popular report
He was the bravest warrior of his day.
Yet came he once, but not in hostile sort,
To fair Mycenæ, by the Godlike prince
Attended, Polynices, at what time                                 450
The host was called together, and the siege
Was purposed of the sacred city Thebes.
Earnest they sued for an auxiliar band,
Which we had gladly granted, but that Jove
By unpropitious tokens interfered.                                455
So forth they went, and on the reedy banks
Arriving of Asopus, there thy sire
By designation of the Greeks was sent
Ambassador, and enter'd Thebes.   He found
In Eteocles' palace numerous guests,                              460
The sons of Cadmus feasting, among whom,
Although a solitary stranger, stood
Thy father without fear, and challenged forth
Their best to cope with him in manly games.
Them Tydeus vanquish'd easily, such aid                           465
Pallas vouchsafed him.   Then the spur-arm'd race

Of Cadmus was incensed, and fifty youths
In ambush close expected his return.
Them, Lycophontes obstinate in fight,
Son of Autophonus, and Mæon, son                          470
Of Hœmon, Chief of Godlike stature, led.
Those also Tydeus slew ; Mæon except,
(Whom, warned from heaven, he spared, and sent him home
With tidings of the rest,) he slew them all.
Such was Ætolian Tydeus ; who begat                        475
A son in speech his better, not in arms.
  He ended, and his sovereign's awful voice
Tydides reverencing, nought replied ;
But thus the son of glorious Capaneus.
  Atrides, conscious of the truth, speak truth.            480
We with our sires compared, superior praise
Claim justly.   We, confiding in the aid
Of Jove, and in propitious signs from heaven,
Led to the city consecrate to Mars
Our little host, inferior far to theirs,                   485
And took seven-gated Thebes, under whose walls
Our fathers by their own imprudence fell.
Their glory, then, match never more with ours.
  He spake, whom with a frowning brow the brave
Tydides answer'd.   Sthenelus, my friend !                 490
I give thee counsel.   Mark it.   Hold thy peace.
If Agamemnon, who hath charge of all,
Excite his well-appointed host to war,
He hath no blame from me.   For should the Greeks
(Her people vanquish'd) win imperial Troy,                 495
The glory shall be his ; or, if his host
O'erpower'd in battle perish, his the shame.
Come, therefore ; be it ours to rouse at once
To action all the fury of our might.
  He said, and from his chariot to the plain               500
Leap'd ardent ; rang the armour on the breast
Of the advancing Chief ; the boldest heart
Had felt emotion, startled at the sound.
  As when the waves by Zephyrus up-heaved
Crowd fast toward some sounding shore, at first,           505
On the broad bosom of the deep their heads
They curl on high, then breaking on the land

Thunder, and o'er the rocks that breast the flood
Borne turgid, scatter far the showery spray;
So moved the Greeks successive, rank by rank,    510
And phalanx after phalanx, every Chief
His loud command proclaiming, while the rest,
As voice in all those thousands none had been,
Heard mute; and, in resplendent armour clad,
With martial order terrible advanced.    515
Not so the Trojans came. As sheep, the flock
Of some rich man, by thousands in his court
Penn'd close at milking time, incessant bleat,
Loud answering all their bleating lambs without,
Such din from Ilium's wide-spread host arose.    520
Nor was their shout, nor was their accent one,
But mingled languages were heard of men
From various climes. These Mars to battle roused,
Those Pallas azure-eyed; nor Terror thence
Nor Flight was absent, nor insatiate Strife,    525
Sister and mate of homicidal Mars,
Who small at first, but swift to grow, from earth
Her towering crest lifts gradual to the skies.
She, foe alike to both, the brands dispersed
Of burning hate between them, and the woes    530
Enhanced of battle wheresoe'er she pass'd.
    And now the battle join'd. Shield clash'd with shield,
And spear with spear, conflicting corslets rang,
Boss'd bucklers met, and tumult wild arose.
Then, many a yell was heard, and many a shout    535
Loud intermix'd, the slayer o'er the maim'd
Exulting, and the field was drench'd with blood.
As when two winter torrents rolling down
The mountains, shoot their floods through gulleys huge
Into one gulf below, station'd remote    540
The shepherd in the uplands hears the roar;
Such was the thunder of the mingling hosts.
And first, Antilochus a Trojan Chief
Slew Echepolus, from Thalysias sprung,
Contending valiant in the van of Troy.    545
Him smiting on his crested casque, he drove
The brazen lance into his front, and pierced
The bones within; night overspread his eyes,

And in fierce battle, like a tower, he fell.
Him fallen by both feet Calchodon's son 550
Seized, royal Elephenor, leader brave
Of the Abantes, and in haste to strip
His armour, drew him from the fight aside.
But short was that attempt.   Him so employ'd
Dauntless Agenor mark'd, and as he stoop'd, 555
In his unshielded flank a pointed spear
Implanted deep; he languid sunk and died.
So Elephenor fell, for whom arose
Sharp conflict; Greeks and Trojans mutual flew
Like wolves to battle, and man grappled man. 560
Then Telamonian Ajax, in his prime
Of youthful vigour Simöisius slew,
Son of Anthemion.   Him on Simoïs' banks
His mother bore, when with her parents once
She came from Ida down to view the flocks, 565
And thence they named him; but his parents' love
He lived not to requite, in early youth
Slain by the spear of Ajax famed in arms.
For him advancing Ajax at the pap
Wounded; right through his shoulder driven the point 570
Stood forth behind; he fell, and press'd the dust.
So in some spacious marsh the poplar falls
Smooth-skinn'd, with boughs unladen save aloft;
Some chariot-builder with his axe the trunk
Severs, that he may warp it to a wheel 575
Of shapely form; meantime exposed it lies
To parching airs beside the running stream;
Such Simöisius seemed, Anthemion's son,
Whom noble Ajax slew.   But soon at him
Antiphus, son of Priam, bright in arms, 580
Hurl'd through the multitude his pointed spear.
He erred from Ajax, but he pierced the groin
Of Leucus, valiant warrior of the band
Led by Ulysses.   He the body dragg'd
Apart, but fell beside it, and let fall, 585
Breathless himself, the burthen from his hand.
Then burn'd Ulysses' wrath for Leucus slain,
And through the foremost combatants, array'd
In dazzling arms, he rush'd.   Full near he stood,

And, looking keen around him, hurl'd a lance.　　　590
Back fell the Trojans from before the face
Dispersed of great Ulysses.　Not in vain
His weapon flew, but on the field outstretch'd
A spurious son of Priam, from the shores
Call'd of Abydus famed for fleetest mares,　　　595
Democoon; him, for Leucus' sake enraged,
Ulysses through both temples with his spear
Transpierced.　The night of death hung on his eyes,
And sounding on his batter'd arms he fell.
Then Hector and the van of Troy retired;　　　600
Loud shout the Grecians; these draw off the dead,
Those onward march amain, and from the heights
Of Pergamus Apollo looking down
In anger, to the Trojans called aloud.
　　Turn, turn, ye Trojans! face your Grecian foes.　605
They, like yourselves, are vulnerable flesh,
Not adamant or steel.　Your direst dread
Achilles, son of Thetis radiant-hair'd,
Fights not, but sullen in his fleet abides.
　　Such from the citadel was heard the voice　　610
Of dread Apollo.　But Minerva ranged
Meantime, Tritonian progeny of Jove,
The Grecians, rousing whom she saw remiss.
Then Amarynceus' son, Diores, felt
The force of fate, bruised by a rugged rock　　615
At his right heel, which Pirus, Thracian Chief,
The son of Imbrasus of Ænos, threw.
Bones and both tendons in its fall the mass
Enormous crush'd.　He, stretch'd in dust supine,
With palms outspread toward his warrior friends　620
Lay gasping life away.　But he who gave
The fatal blow, Pirus, advancing, urged
Into his navel a keen lance, and shed
His bowels forth; then, darkness veil'd his eyes.
　　Nor Pirus long survived; him through the breast,　625
Above the pap, Ætolian Thoas pierced,
And in his lungs set fast the quivering spear.
Then Thoas swift approach'd, pluck'd from the wound
His stormy spear, and with his falchion bright
Gashing his middle belly, stretch'd him dead.　　630

Yet stripp'd he not the slain, whom with long spears
His Thracians hairy-scalp'd[5] so round about
Encompassed, that though bold and large of limb
Were Thoas, from before them him they thrust
Staggering and reeling in his forced retreat.           635
    They therefore in the dust, the Epean chief
Diores, and the Thracian, Pirus lay
Stretch'd side by side, with numerous slain around.
    Then had Minerva led through all that field
Some warrior yet unhurt, him sheltering safe           640
From all annoyance dread of dart or spear,
No cause of blame in either had he found
That day, so many Greeks and Trojans'press'd,
Extended side by side, the dusty plain.

   [5] 'Ακρόκομοι. They wore only a lock of hair on the crown of the
head.

# BOOK V.

### ARGUMENT.

Diomede is extraordinarily distinguished. He kills Pandarus, who had violated the truce, and wounds first Venus, and then Mars.

THEN Athenæan Pallas on the son
Of Tydeus, Diomede, new force conferr'd
And daring courage, that the Argives all
He might surpass, and deathless fame achieve.
Fires on his helmet, and his shield around                    5
She kindled, bright and steady as the star
Autumnal, which in Ocean newly bathed
Assumes fresh beauty; with such glorious beams
His head encircling and his shoulders broad,
She urged him forth into the thickest fight.                  10
    There lived a man in Troy, Dares his name,
The priest of Vulcan; rich he was and good,
The father of two sons, Idæus this,
That, Phegeus call'd; accomplish'd warriors both.
These, issuing from their phalanx, push'd direct             15
Their steeds at Diomede, who fought on foot.
When now small interval was left between,
First Phegeus his long-shadow'd spear dismiss'd;
But over Diomedes' left shoulder pass'd
The point, innocuous. Then his splendid lance                20
Tydides hurl'd; nor ineffectual flew
The weapon from his hand, but Phegeus pierced
His paps between, and forced him to the ground.
At once, his sumptuous chariot left, down leap'd
Idæus wanting courage to defend                              25
His brother slain; nor had he scaped himself
His louring fate, but Vulcan, to preserve
His ancient priest from unmixt sorrow, snatch'd
The fugitive in darkness wrapt, away.
Then brave Tydides, driving off the steeds,                  30

Consign'd them to his fellow-warriors' care,
That they might lead them down into the fleet.
　The valiant Trojans, when they saw the sons
Of Dares, one beside his chariot slain,
And one by flight preserved, through all their host　　35
Felt consternation.　Then Minerva seized
The hand of fiery Mars, and thus she spake.
　Gore-tainted, homicide, town-battering Mars!
Leave we the Trojans and the Greeks to wage
Fierce fight alone, Jove prospering whom he will,　　40
So shall we not provoke our father's ire.
　She said, and from the fight conducted forth
The impetuous Deity, whom on the side
She seated of Scamander deep-embank'd [1].
　And now the host of Troy to flight inclined　　45
Before the Grecians, and the Chiefs of Greece
Each slew a warrior.　Agamemnon first
Gigantic Odius from his chariot hurl'd,
Chief of the Halizonians.　He to flight
Turn'd foremost, when the monarch in his spine　　50
Between the shoulder-bones his spear infixt,
And urged it through his breast.　Sounding he fell,
And loud his batter'd armour rang around.
　By brave Idomeneus a Lydian died,
Phæstus, from fruitful Tarne sent to Troy,　　55
Son of Mæonian Borus; him his steeds
Mounting, Idomeneus the spear-renown'd
Through his right shoulder pierced; unwelcome night
Involved him; from his chariot down he fell,
And the attendant Cretans stripp'd his arms.　　60
　But Menelaus, son of Atreus slew
With his bright spear Scamandrius, Stropius' son,
A skilful hunter; for Diana him,
Herself, the slaughter of all savage kinds
Had taught, on mountain or in forest bred.　　65
But she, shaft-aiming Goddess, in that hour
Avail'd him not, nor his own matchless skill;
For Menelaus, Atreus son spear-famed,
Him flying wounded in the spine between
His shoulders, and the spear urged through his breast.　　70

[1] 'Ηιόεντι.

Prone on his loud-resounding arms he fell.
   Next, by Meriones Phereclus died,
Son of Harmonides.   All arts that ask
A well-instructed hand his sire had learn'd,
For Pallas dearly loved him.   He the fleet,     75
Prime source of harm to Troy and to himself,
For Paris built, unskill'd to spell aright
The oracles predictive of the woe.
Phereclus fled; Meriones his flight
Outstripping, deep in his posterior flesh     80
A spear infix'd; sliding beneath the bone
It grazed his bladder as it pass'd, and stood
Protruded far before.   Low on his knees
Phereclus sank, and with a shriek expired.
   Pedæus, whom, although his spurious son,     85
Antenor's wife, to gratify her Lord,
Had cherish'd as her own—him Meges slew.
Warlike Phylides[2] following close his flight,
His keen lance drove into his poll, cut sheer
His tongue within, and through his mouth enforced     90
The glittering point.   He, prostrate in the dust,
The cold steel press'd between his teeth and died.
   Eurypylus, Evemon's son, the brave
Hypsenor slew; Dolopion was his sire,
Priest of Scamander, reverenced as a God.     95
In vain before Eurypylus he fled;
He, running, with his falchion lopp'd his arm
Fast by the shoulder; on the field his hand
Fell blood-distained, and destiny severe
With shades of death for ever veil'd his eyes.     100
   Thus strenuous they the toilsome battle waged.
But where Tydides fought, whether in aid
Of Ilium's host, or on the part of Greece,
Might none discern.   For as a winter-flood
Impetuous, mounds and bridges sweeps away;     105
The buttress'd bridge checks not its sudden force,
The firm inclosure of vine-planted fields
Luxuriant, falls before it, finish'd works
Of youthful hinds, once pleasant to the eye,
Now levell'd, after ceaseless rain from Jove;     110

           [2] Meges, son of Phyleus.

So drove Tydides into sudden flight
The Trojans ; phalanx after phalanx fled
Before the terror of his single arm.
  When him Lycaon's son illustrious saw
Scouring the field, and from before his face          115
The ranks dispersing wide, at once he bent
Against Tydides his elastic bow.
The arrow met him in his swift career
Sure-aim'd ; it struck direct the hollow mail
Of his right shoulder, with resistless force           120
Transfix'd it, and his hauberk stain'd with blood.
Loud shouted then Lycaon's son renown'd.
  Rush on, ye Trojans, spur your coursers hard.
Our fiercest foe is wounded, and I deem
His death not distant far, if me the King[3]           125
Jove's son, indeed, from Lycia sent to Troy.
  So boasted Pandarus.   Yet him the dart
Quell'd not.   Retreating, at his coursers' heads
He stood, and to the son of Capaneus
His charioteer and faithful friend he said.            130
  Arise, sweet son of Capaneus, dismount,
And from my shoulder draw this bitter shaft.
  He spake ; at once the son of Capaneus
Descending, by its barb the bitter shaft
Drew forth ; blood spouted through his twisted mail    135
Incontinent, and thus the Hero pray'd.
  Unconquer'd daughter of Jove Ægis-arm'd !
If ever me, propitious, or my sire
Thou hast in furious fight help'd heretofore,
Now aid me also.   Bring within the reach              140
Of my swift spear, Oh grant me to strike through
The warrior who hath check'd my course, and boasts
The sun's bright beams for ever quench'd to me !
  He prayed, and Pallas heard ; she braced his limbs,
She wing'd him with alacrity divine,                   145
And standing at his side, him thus bespake.
  Now Diomede, be bold ! Fight now with Troy.
To thee, thy father's spirit I impart
Fearless ; shield-shaking Tydeus felt the same.
I also from thine eye the darkness purge               150

[3] Apollo.

Which dimm'd thy sight before, that thou may'st know
Both Gods and men ; should, therefore, other God
Approach to try thee, fight not with the powers
Immortal ; but if foam-born Venus come,
Her spare not.   Wound her with thy glittering spear.          155
     So spake the blue-eyed Deity, and went.
Then with the champions in the van again
Tydides mingled ; hot before, he fights
With threefold fury now, nor less enraged
Than some gaunt lion whom o'erleaping light          160
The fold, a shepherd hath but gall'd, not kill'd,
Him irritating more ; thenceforth the swain
Lurks unresisting ; flies the abandon'd flock ;
Heaps slain on heaps he leaves, and with a bound
Surmounting all impediment, escapes ;          165
Such seem'd the valiant Diomede incensed
To fury, mingling with the host of Troy.
     Astynoüs and Hypenor first he slew ;
One with his brazen lance above the pap
He pierced, and one with his huge falchion smote          170
Fast by the key-bone[4], from the neck and spine
His parted shoulder driving at a blow.
     Them leaving, Polyides next he sought
And Abas, sons of a dream-dealing seer,
Eurydamas ; their hoary father's dreams          175
Or not interpreted, or kept concealed,
Them saved not, for by Diomede they died.
Xanthus and Thöon he encounter'd next,
Both sons of Phænops, sons of his old age,
Who other heir had none of all his wealth,          180
Nor hoped another, worn with many years.
Tydides slew them both ; nor aught remain'd
To the old man but sorrow for his sons
For ever lost, and strangers were his heirs.
Two sons of Priam in one chariot borne          185
Echemon next, and Chromius felt his hand
Resistless.   As a lion on the herd
Leaping, while they the shrubs and bushes browze,
Breaks short the neck of heifer or of steer,
So them, though clinging fast and loth to fall,          190

                    [4] Or collar-bone.

Tydides hurl'd together to the ground,
Then stripp'd their splendid armour, and the steeds
Consigned and chariot to his soldiers' care.
    Æneas him discern'd scattering the ranks,
And through the battle and the clash of spears     195
Went seeking Godlike Pandarus; ere long
Finding Lycaon's martial son renown'd,
He stood before him, and him thus address'd.
    Thy bow, thy feather'd shafts, and glorious name
Where are they, Pandarus? whom none of Troy     200
Could equal, whom of Lycia, none excel.
Come.   Lift thine hands to Jove, and at yon Chief
Dispatch an arrow who afflicts the host
Of Ilium thus, conquering where'er he flies,
And who hath slaughter'd numerous brave in arms.     205
But him some Deity I rather deem
Avenging on us his neglected rites,
And who can stand before an angry God?
    Him answer'd then Lycaon's son renown'd.
Brave leader of the Trojans brazen-mail'd,     210
Æneas! By his buckler which I know,
And by his helmet's height, considering too
His steeds, I deem him Diomede the bold;
Yet such pronounce him not, who seems a God.
But if bold Diomede indeed he be     215
Of whom I speak, not without aid from heaven
His fury thus prevails, but at his side
Some God, in clouds enveloped, turns away
From him the arrow to a devious course.
Already, at his shoulder's hollow mail     220
My shaft hath pierced him through, and him I deem'd
Dismiss'd full sure to Pluto ere his time;
But he survives; whom therefore I at last
Perforce conclude some angry Deity.
Steeds have I none or chariot to ascend,     225
Who have eleven chariots in the stands
Left of Lycaon, with fair hangings all
O'ermantled, strong, new finish'd, with their steeds
In pairs beside them, eating winnow'd grain.
Me much Lycaon my old valiant sire     230
At my departure from his palace gates

Persuaded, that my chariot and my steeds
Ascending, I should so conduct my bands
To battle; counsel wise, and ill-refused!
But anxious, lest, (the host in Troy so long     235
Immew'd) my steeds, fed plenteously at home,
Should here want food, I left them, and on foot
To Ilium came, confiding in my bow
Ordain'd at last to yield me little good.
Twice have I shot, and twice I struck the mark,     240
First Menelaus, and Tydides next:
From each I drew the blood, true, genuine blood,
Yet have but more incensed them. In an hour
Unfortunate, I therefore took my bow
Down from the wall that day, when for the sake     245
Of noble Hector, to these pleasant plains
I came, a leader on the part of Troy.
But should I once return, and with these eyes
Again behold my native land, my sire,
My wife, my stately mansion, may the hand,     250
That moment, of some adversary there
Shorten me by the head, if I not snap
This bow with which I charged myself in vain,
And burn the unprofitable tool to dust.
    To whom Æneas, Trojan Chief, replied.     255
Nay, speak not so. For ere that hour arrive
We will, with chariot and with horse, in arms
Encounter him, and put his strength to proof.
Delay not, mount my chariot. Thou shalt see
With what rapidity the steeds of Troy     260
Pursuing or retreating, scour the field.
If after all, Jove purpose still to exalt
The son of Tydeus, these shall bear us safe
Back to the city. Come then. Let us on.
The lash take thou, and the resplendent reins,     265
While I alight for battle, or thyself
Receive them, and the steeds shall be my care.
    Him answer'd then Lycaon's son renown'd.
Æneas! manage thou the reins, and guide
Thy proper steeds. If fly at last we must     270
The son of Tydeus, they will readier draw
Directed by their wonted charioteer.

Else, terrified, and missing thy control,
They may refuse to bear us from the fight,
And Tydeus' son assailing us, with ease                    275
Shall slay us both, and drive thy steeds away.
Rule therefore thou the chariot, and myself
With my sharp spear will his assault receive.
   So saying, they mounted both, and furious drove
Against Tydides.   Them the noble son                      280
Of Capaneus observed, and turning quick
His speech to Diomede, him thus address'd.
   Tydides, Diomede, my heart's delight!
Two warriors of immeasurable force
In battle, ardent to contend with thee,                    285
Come rattling on.   Lycaon's offspring one,
Bow-practised Pandarus; with whom appears
Æneas; he who calls the mighty Chief
Anchises father, and whom Venus bore.
Mount—drive we swift away,—lest borne so far               290
Beyond the foremost battle, thou be slain.
   To whom, dark-frowning, Diomede replied.
Speak not of flight to me, who am disposed
To no such course.   I am ashamed to fly
Or tremble, and my strength is still entire;               295
I cannot mount.   No.   Rather thus, on foot,
I will advance against them.   Fear and dread
Are not for me; Pallas forbids the thought.
One falls, be sure; swift as they are, the steeds
That whirl them on, shall never rescue both.               300
But hear my bidding, and hold fast the word.
Should all-wise Pallas grant me my desire
To slay them both, drive not my coursers hence,
But hook the reins, and seizing quick the pair
That draw Æneas, urge them from the powers                 305
Of Troy away into the host of Greece.
For they are sprung from those which Jove to Tros
In compensation gave for Ganymede;
The Sun himself sees not their like below.
Anchises, King of men, clandestine them                    310
Obtain'd, his mares submitting to the steeds
Of King Laomedon.   Six brought him foals;
Four to himself reserving, in his stalls

He fed them sleek, and two he gave his son :
These, might we win them, were a noble prize.          315
 Thus mutual they conferr'd ; those Chiefs the while,
With swiftest pace approach'd, and first his speech
To Diomede Lycaon's son address'd.
 Heroic offspring of a noble sire,
Brave son of Tydeus! false to my intent          320
My shaft hath harm'd thee little.   I will now
Make trial with my spear, if that may speed.
 He said, and shaking his long-shadow'd spear,
Dismiss'd it.   Forceful on the shield it struck
Of Diomede, transpierced it, and approach'd          325
With threatening point the hauberk on his breast.
Loud shouted Pandarus—Ah nobly thrown !
Home to thy bowels.   Die, for die thou must,
And all the glory of thy death is mine.
 Then answer thus brave Diomede return'd          330
Undaunted.   I am whole.   Thy cast was short.
But ye desist not, as I plain perceive,
Till one at least extended on the plain
Shall sate the God of battles with his blood.
 He said and threw.   Pallas the spear herself          335
Directed ; at his eye fast by the nose
Deep-entering, through his ivory teeth it pass'd,
At its extremity divided sheer
His tongue, and started through his chin below.
He headlong fell, and with his dazzling arms          340
Smote full the plain.   Back flew the fiery steeds
With swift recoil, and where he fell he died.
Then sprang Æneas forth with spear and shield,
That none might drag the body ; lion-like
He stalk'd around it, oval shield and spear          345
Advancing firm, and with incessant cries
Terrific, death denouncing on his foes.
But Diomede with hollow grasp a stone
Enormous seized, a weight to overtask
Two strongest men of such as now are strong,          350
Yet He, alone, wielded the rock with ease.
Full on the hip he smote him, where the thigh
Rolls in its cavity, the socket named.
He crush'd the socket, lacerated wide

Both tendons, and with that rough-angled mass 355
Flay'd all his flesh.   The Hero on his knees
Sank, on his ample palm his weight upbore
Labouring, and darkness overspread his eyes.
　　There had Æneas perish'd, King of men,
Had not Jove's daughter Venus quick perceived 360
His peril imminent, whom she had borne
Herself to Anchises pasturing his herds.
Her snowy arms her darling son around
She threw maternal, and behind a fold
Of her bright mantle screening close his breast 365
From mortal harm by some  brave Grecian's spear,
Stole him with eager swiftness from the fight.
　　Nor then forgat brave Sthenelus his charge
Received from Diomede, but his own steeds
Detaining distant from the boisterous war, 370
Stretch'd tight the reins, and hook'd them fast behind.
The coursers of Æneas next he seized
Ardent, and them into the host of Greece
Driving remote, consign'd them to his care,
Whom far above all others his compeers 375
He loved, Deipylus, his bosom friend
Congenial.   Him he charged to drive them thence
Into the fleet, then, mounting swift his own,
Lash'd after Diomede; he, fierce in arms,
Pursued the Cyprian Goddess, conscious whom, 380
Not Pallas, not Enyo, waster dread
Of cities close-beleaguer'd, none of all
Who o'er the battle's bloody course preside,
But one of softer kind and prone to fear.
When, therefore, her at length, after long chase 385
Through all the warring multitude he reach'd,
With his protruded spear her gentle hand
He wounded, piercing through her thin attire
Ambrosial, by themselves the Graces wrought,
Her inside wrist, fast by the rosy palm. 390
Blood follow'd, but immortal; ichor pure,
Such as the blest inhabitants of heaven
May bleed, nectareous; for the Gods eat not
Man's food, nor slake as he with sable wine
Their thirst, thence bloodless and from death exempt. 395

She, shrieking, from her arms cast down her son,
And Phœbus, in impenetrable clouds
Him hiding, lest the spear of some brave Greek
Should pierce his bosom, caught him swift away.
Then shouted brave Tydides after her—                    400
    Depart, Jove's daughter! fly the bloody field.
Is't not enough that thou beguilest the hearts
Of feeble women? If thou dare intrude
Again into the war, war's very name
Shall make thee shudder, wheresoever heard.              405
    He said, and Venus with excess of pain
Bewilder'd went; but Iris tempest-wing'd
Forth led her through the multitude, oppress'd
With anguish, her white wrist to livid changed.
They came where Mars far on the left retired            410
Of battle sat, his horses and his spear
In darkness veil'd.   Before her brother's knees
She fell, and with entreaties urgent sought
The succour of his coursers golden-rein'd.
    Save me, my brother! Pity me! Thy steeds            415
Give me, that they may bear me to the heights
Olympian, seat of the immortal Gods!
Oh! I am wounded deep; a mortal man
Hath done it, Diomede; nor would he fear
This day in fight the Sire himself of all.              420
    Then Mars his coursers gold-caparison'd
Resign'd to Venus; she, with countenance sad,
The chariot climb'd, and Iris at her side
The bright reins seizing lash'd the ready steeds.
Soon as the Olympian heights, seat of the Gods          425
They reach'd, wing-footed Iris loosing quick
The coursers, gave them large whereon to browse
Ambrosial food; but Venus on the knees
Sank of Dione, who with folded arms
Maternal, to her bosom straining close                  430
Her daughter, stroked her cheek, and thus enquired.
    My darling child! who? which of all the Gods
Hath rashly done such violence to thee
As if convicted of some open wrong?
    Her then the Goddess of love-kindling smiles        435
Venus thus answer'd; Diomede the proud,

Audacious Diomede ; he gave the wound,
For that I stole Æneas from the fight
My son, of all mankind my most beloved ;
Nor is it now the war of Greece with Troy,                440
But of the Grecians with the Gods themselves.
   Then thus Dione, Goddess all divine.
My child ! how hard soe'er thy sufferings seem
Endure them patiently.   Full many a wrong
From human hands profane the Gods endure,                445
And many a painful stroke, mankind from ours.
Mars once endured much wrong, when on a time
Him Otus bound and Ephialtes fast,
Sons of Alöeus, and full thirteen moons
In brazen thraldom held him.   There, at length,         450
The fierce blood-nourished Mars had pined away,
But that Eëribœa, loveliest nymph,
His step-mother, in happy hour disclosed
To Mercury the story of his wrongs ;
He stole the prisoner forth, but with his woes           455
Already worn, languid and fetter-gall'd.
Nor Juno less endured, when erst the bold
Son of Amphytrion with tridental shaft
Her bosom pierced ; she then the misery felt
Of irremediable pain severe.                             460
Nor suffer'd Pluto less, of all the Gods
Gigantic most, by the same son of Jove
Alcides, at the portals of the dead
Transfix'd and fill'd with anguish ; he the house
Of Jove and the Olympian summit sought                  465
Dejected, torture-stung, for sore the shaft
Oppress'd him, into his huge shoulder driven.
But Pæon him not liable to death
With unction smooth of salutiferous balms
Heal'd soon.   Presumptuous, sacrilegious man !          470
Careless what dire enormities he wrought,
Who bent his bow against the powers of heaven !
But blue-eyed Pallas instigated him
By whom thou bleed'st.   Infatuate ! he forgets
That whoso turns against the Gods his arms               475
Lives never long ; he never, safe escaped
From furious fight, the lisp'd caresses hears

Of his own infants prattling at his knees.
Let therefore Diomede beware, lest strong
And valiant as he is, he chance to' meet        480
Some mightier foe than thou, and lest his wife,
Daughter of King Adrastus, the discreet
Ægialea, from portentous dreams
Upstarting, call her family to wail
Her first-espoused, Achaia's proudest boast,    485
Diomede, whom she must behold no more.
    She said, and from her wrist with both hands wiped
The trickling ichor ; the effectual touch
Divine chased all her pains, and she was heal'd.
Them Juno mark'd and Pallas, and with speech   490
Sarcastic pointed at Saturnian Jove
To vex him, blue-eyed Pallas thus began.
    Eternal father! may I speak my thought,
And not incense thee, Jove? I can but judge
That Venus, while she coax'd some Grecian fair   495
To accompany the Trojans whom she loves
With such extravagance, hath heedless stroked
Her golden clasps, and scratch'd her lily hand.
    So she ; then smiled the sire of Gods and men,
And calling golden Venus, her bespake.      500
    War and the tented field, my beauteous child,
Are not for thee.  Thou rather shouldst be found
In scenes of matrimonial bliss.  The toils
Of war to Pallas and to Mars belong.
    Thus they in heaven.  But Diomede the while   505
Sprang on Æneas, conscious of the God
Whose hand o'ershadow'd him, yet even him
Regarding lightly ; for he burn'd to slay
Æneas, and to seize his glorious arms.
Thrice then he sprang impetuous to the deed,   510
And thrice Apollo with his radiant shield
Repulsed him.  But when ardent as a God
The fourth time he advanced, with thundering voice
Him thus the Archer of the skies rebuked. ·
    Think, and retire, Tydides! nor affect    515
Equality with Gods ; for not the same
Our nature is and theirs who tread the ground.
    He spake, and Diomede a step retired,

Not more ; the anger of the Archer-God
Declining slow, and with a sullen awe.                    520
Then Phœbus, far from all the warrior throng
To his own shrine the sacred dome beneath
Of Pergamus, Æneus bore ; there him
Latona and shaft-arm'd Diana heal'd
And glorified within their spacious fane.                 525
Meantime the Archer of the silver bow
A visionary form prepared ; it seem'd
Himself Æneas, and was arm'd as he.
At once, in contest for that airy form,
Grecians and Trojans on each other's breasts              530
The bull-hide buckler batter'd and light targe.

   Then thus Apollo to the warrior God.
Gore-tainted, homicide, town-batterer Mars !
Wilt thou not meet and from the fight withdraw
This man Tydides, now so fiery grown                      535
That he would even cope with Jove himself ?
First Venus' hand he wounded, and assail'd
Impetuous as a God, next, even me.

   He ceased, and on the topmost turret sat
Of Pergamus.   Then all-destroyer Mars                    540
Ranging the Trojan host, rank after rank
Exhorted loud, and in the form assumed
Of Acamas the Thracian leader bold,
The Godlike sons of Priam thus harangued.

   Ye sons of Priam, monarch Jove-beloved !      545
How long permit ye your Achaian foes
To slay the people ?—till the battle rage
(Push'd home to Ilium) at her solid gates ?
Behold—a Chief disabled lies, than whom
We reverence not even Hector more,                        550
Æneas ; fly, save from the roaring storm
The noble Anchisiades your friend.

   He said ; then every heart for battle glow'd ;
And thus Sarpedon with rebuke severe
Upbraiding generous Hector, stern began.                  555

   Where is thy courage, Hector ? for thou once
Hadst courage.   Is it fled ? In other days
Thy boast hath been that without native troops
Or foreign aids, thy kindred and thyself

Alone, were guard sufficient for the town.          560
But none of all thy kindred now appears ;
I can discover none ; they stand aloof
Quaking, as dogs that hear the lion's roar.
We bear the stress, who are but Troy's allies ;
Myself am such, and from afar I came ;          565
For Lycia lies far distant on the banks
Of the deep-eddied Xanthus.   There a wife
I left and infant son, both dear to me,
With plenteous wealth, the wish of all who want.
Yet urge I still my Lycians, and am prompt          570
Myself to fight, although possessing here
Nought that the Greeks can carry or drive hence.
But there stand'st thou, neither employ'd thyself,
Nor moving others to an active part
For all their dearest pledges.   Oh beware !          575
Lest, as with meshes of an ample net,
At one huge draught the Grecians sweep you all,
And desolate at once your populous Troy !
By day, by night, thoughts such as these should still
Thy conduct influence, and from Chief to Chief          580
Of the allies should send thee, praying each
To make firm stand, all bickerings put away.
   So spake Sarpedon, and his reprimand
Stung Hector ; instant to the ground he leap'd
All arm'd, and shaking his bright spears his host          585
Ranged in all quarters animating loud
His legions, and rekindling horrid war.
Then, rolling back, the powers of Troy opposed
Once more the Grecians, whom the Grecians dense
Expected, unretreating, void of fear.          590
   As flies the chaff wide scatter'd by the wind
O'er all the consecrated floor, what time
Ripe Ceres with brisk airs her golden grain
Ventilates, whitening with its husk the ground ;
So grew the Achaians white, a dusty cloud          595
Descending on their arms, which steeds with steeds
Again to battle mingling, with their hoofs
Up-stamp'd into the brazen vault of heaven ;
For now the charioteers turn'd all to fight.
Host toward host with full collected force          600

They moved direct.   Then Mars through all the field
Took wide his range, and overhung the war
With night, in aid of Troy, at the command
Of Phœbus of the golden sword ; for he
Perceiving Pallas from the field withdrawn,      605
Patroness of the Greeks, had Mars enjoin'd
To rouse the spirit of the Trojan host.
Meantime Apollo from his unctuous shrine
Sent forth restored and with new force inspired
Æneas.   He amidst his warriors stood,      610
Who him with joy beheld still living, heal'd,
And all his strength possessing unimpair'd.
Yet no man ask'd him aught.   No leisure now
For question was ; far other thoughts had they ;
Such toils the archer of the silver bow,      615
Wide-slaughtering Mars, and Discord as at first
Raging implacable, for them prepared.
    Ulysses, either Ajax, Diomede,—
These roused the Greeks to battle, who themselves
The force fear'd nothing, or the shouts of Troy,      620
But stedfast stood, like clouds by Jove amass'd
On lofty mountains, while the fury sleeps
Of Boreas, and of all the stormy winds
Shrill-voiced, that chase the vapours when they blow.
So stood the Greeks, expecting firm the approach      625
Of Ilium's powers, and neither fled nor fear'd.
    Then Agamemnon the embattled host
On all sides ranging, cheer'd them.   Now, he cried,
Be steadfast, fellow warriors, now be men !
Hold fast a sense of honour.   More escape      630
Of men who fear disgrace, than fall in fight,
While dastards forfeit life and glory both.
    He said, and hurl'd his spear.   He pierced a friend
Of brave Æneas, warring in the van,
Deicöon son of Pergasus, in Troy      635
Not less esteem'd than Priam's sons themselves,
Such was his fame in foremost fight acquired.
Him Agamemnon on his buckler smote,
Nor stayed the weapon there, but through his belt
His bowels enter'd, and with hideous clang      640

And outcry[5] of his batter'd arms he fell.
　Æneas next two mightiest warriors slew,
Sons of Diocles, of a wealthy sire,
Whose house magnificent in Phæræ stood,
Orsilochus and Crethon.　Their descent          645
From broad-stream'd Alpheus, Pylian flood they drew.
Alpheus begat Orsilochus, a prince
Of numerous powers.　Orsilochus begat
Warlike Diocles.　From Diocles sprang
Twins Crethon and Orsilochus, alike          650
Valiant, and skilful in all forms of war.
Their boyish prime scarce past, they with the Greeks
Embarking, in their sable ships had sail'd
To steed-famed Ilium ; just revenge they sought
For Atreus' sons, but perished first themselves.          655
　As two young lions, in the deep recess
Of some dark forest on the mountain's brow
Late nourish'd by their dam, forth-issuing, seize
The fatted flocks and kine, both folds and stalls
Wasting rapacious, till at length, themselves          660
Deep-wounded perish by the hand of man,
So they, both vanquish'd by Æneas, fell,
And like two lofty pines uprooted, lay.
Them fallen in battle Menelaus saw
With pity moved ; radiant in arms he shook          665
His brazen spear, and strode into the van.
Mars urged him furious on, conceiving hope
Of his death also by Æneas' hand.
　But him the son of generous Nestor mark'd
Antilochus, and to the foremost fight          670
Flew also, fearing lest some dire mischance
The Prince befalling, at one fatal stroke
Should frustrate all the labours of the Greeks.
They hand to hand, and spear to spear opposed,
Stood threatening dreadful onset, when beside          675
The Spartan Chief Antilochus appear'd.
Æneas at the sight of two combined,
Stood not, although intrepid.　They the dead
Thence drawing far into the Grecian host

　[5] Vide Samson to Harapha in the Agonistes.　There the word is used
in the same sense.

To their associates gave the hapless pair, 680
Then, both returning, fought in front again.
    Next, fierce as Mars, Pylæmenes they slew,
Prince of the shielded band magnanimous
Of Paphlagonia.   Him Atrides kill'd
Spear-practised Menelaus, with a lance 685
His throat transpiercing while erect he rode.
Then, while his charioteer, Mydon the brave,
Son of Atymnias, turn'd his steeds to flight,
Full on his elbow-point Antilochus,
The son of Nestor, dash'd him with a stone. 690
The slack reins, white as ivory[6], forsook
His torpid hand and trail'd the dust.   At once
Forth sprang Antilochus, and with his sword
Hew'd deep his temples.   On his head he pitch'd
Panting, and on his shoulders in the sand 695
(For in deep sand he fell) stood long erect,
Till his own coursers spread him in the dust ;
The son of Nestor seized, and with his scourge
Drove them afar into the host of Greece.
    Them Hector through the ranks espying, flew 700
With clamour loud to meet them ; after whom
Advanced in phalanx firm the powers of Troy.
Mars led them, with Enyo terror-clad ;
She by the maddening tumult of the fight
Attended, he, with his enormous spear 705
In both hands brandish'd, stalking now in front
Of Hector, and now following his steps.
    Him Diomede the bold discerning, felt
Himself no small dismay ; and as a man
Wandering he knows not whither, far from home, 710
If chance a rapid torrent to the sea
Borne headlong thwart his course, the foaming flood,
Obstreperous views awhile, then quick retires,
So he, and his attendants thus bespake.
    How oft, my countrymen ! have we admired 715
The noble Hector, skilful at the spear
And unappall'd in fight ? but still hath he
Some God his guard, and even now I view

[6] This is a construction of λευκ' ελεφαντι, given by some of the best
commentators, and that seems the most probable.

In human form Mars moving at his side.
Ye, then, with faces to the Trojans turn'd,  720
Ceaseless retire, and war not with the Gods.
   He ended ; and the Trojans now approach'd.
Then two bold warriors in one chariot borne,
By valiant Hector died, Menesthes, one,
And one, Anchialus.   Them fallen in fight  725
Ajax the vast, touch'd with compassion saw ;
Within small space he stood, his glittering spear
Dismiss'd, and pierced Amphius.   Son was he
Of Selagus, and Pæsus was his home,
Where opulent he dwelt, but by his fate  730
Was led to fight for Priam and his sons.
Him Telamonian Ajax through his belt
Wounded, and in his nether bowels deep
Fix'd his long-shadow'd spear.   Sounding he fell.
Illustrious Ajax running to the slain  735
Prepared to strip his arms, but him a shower
Of glittering weapons keen from Trojan hands
Assail'd, and numerous his broad shield received.
He, on the body planting firm his heel,
Forth drew the polish'd spear, but his bright arms  740
Took not, by darts thick-flying sore annoy'd.
Nor fear'd he little lest his haughty foes,
Spear-arm'd and bold, should compass him around ;
Him, therefore, valiant though he were and huge,
They push'd before them.   Staggering he retired.  745
   Thus toil'd both hosts in that laborious field.
And now his ruthless destiny impell'd .
Tlepolemus, Alcides' son, a Chief
Dauntless and huge, against a Godlike foe
Sarpedon.   They approaching, face to face  750
Stood, son and grandson of high-thundering Jove,
And, haughty, thus Tlepolemus began.
   Sarpedon, leader of the Lycian host,
Thou trembler ! thee what cause could hither urge
A man unskill'd in arms ? They falsely speak  755
Who call thee son of Ægis-bearing Jove,
So far below their might thou fall'st who sprang
From Jove in days of old.   What says report
Of Hercules, (for him I boast my sire,)

s. c.—7.  H

All-daring hero with a lion's heart?                        760
With six ships only, and with followers few,
He for the horses of Laomedon
Lay'd Troy in dust, and widow'd all her streets.
But thou art base, and thy diminish'd powers
Perish around thee; think not that thou camest          765
For Ilium's good, but rather, whatsoe'er
Thy force in fight, to find, subdued by me,
A sure dismission to the gates of hell.
　　To whom the leader of the Lycian band.
Tlepolemus! he ransack'd sacred Troy,                    770
As thou hast said, but for her monarch's fault
Laomedon, who him with language harsh
Requited ill for benefits received,
Nor would the steeds surrender, seeking which
He voyaged from afar.  But thou shalt take              775
Thy bloody doom from this victorious arm,
And, vanquish'd by my spear, shalt yield thy fame
To me, thy soul to Pluto steed-renown'd.
　　So spake Sarpedon, and his ashen beam
Tlepolemus upraised.  Both hurl'd at once               780
Their quivering spears.  Sarpedon's through the neck
Pass'd of Tlepolemus, and show'd beyond
Its ruthless point; thick darkness veil'd his eyes.
Tlepolemus with his long lance the thigh
Pierced of Sarpedon; sheer into his bone                785
He pierced him, but Sarpedon's father, Jove,
Him rescued even on the verge of fate.
　　His noble friends conducted from the field
The godlike Lycian, trailing as he went
The pendant spear, none thinking to extract             790
For his relief the weapon from his thigh,
Through eagerness of haste to bear him thence.
On the other side, the Grecians brazen-mail'd
Bore off Tlepolemus.  Ulysses fill'd
With earnest thoughts tumultuous them observed,         795
Danger-defying Chief! Doubtful he stood
Or to pursue at once the Thunderer's son
Sarpedon, or to take more Lycian lives.
But not for brave Ulysses had his fate
That praise reserved, that he should slay the son       800

Renown'd of Jove; therefore his wavering mind
Minerva bent again the Lycian band.
Then Cœranus, Alastor, Chromius fell,
Alcander, Halius, Prytanis, and brave
Noëmon; nor had these sufficed the Chief          805
Of Ithaca, but Lycians more had fallen,
Had not crest-tossing Hector huge perceived
The havoc; radiant to the van he flew,
Filling with dread the Grecians; his approach
Sarpedon, son of Jove, joyful beheld,          810
And piteous thus address'd him as he came.
    Ah, leave not me, Priamides! a prey
To Grecian hands, but in your city, at least,
Grant me to die : since hither, doom'd, I came
Never to gratify with my return          815
To Lycia, my loved spouse, or infant child.
    He spake ; but Hector unreplying pass'd
Impetuous, ardent to repulse the Greeks
That moment, and to drench his sword in blood.
Then, under shelter of a spreading beech          820
Sacred to Jove, his noble followers placed
The godlike Chief Sarpedon, where his friend
Illustrious Pelagon, the ashen spear
Extracted. Sightless, of all thought bereft,
He sank, but soon revived, by breathing airs          825
Refresh'd, that fann'd him gently from the North.
    Meantime the Argives, although press'd alike
By Mars himself and Hector brazen-arm'd,
Neither to flight inclined, nor yet advanced
To battle, but inform'd that Mars the fight          830
Waged on the side of Ilium, slow retired.
    Whom first, whom last slew then the mighty son
Of Priam, Hector, and the brazen Mars !
First godlike Teuthras, an equestrian Chief,
Orestes, Trechus of Ætolian race,          835
Œnomaüs, Helenus from Œnops' sprung,
And brisk[7] in fight Oresbius ; rich was he,
And covetous of more in Hyla dwelt
Fast by the lake Cephissus, where abode

---

[7] This, according to Porphyrius as quoted by Clarke, is the true mean-ing of αιολομιτρης.

Bœotian Princes numerous, rich themselves          840
And rulers of a people wealth-renown'd.
But Juno, such dread slaughter of the Greeks
Noting, thus, ardent, to Minerva spake.
　　Daughter of Jove invincible! Our word
That Troy shall perish, hath been given in vain     845
To Menelaus, if we suffer Mars
To ravage longer uncontroul'd.　The time
Urges, and need appears that we ourselves
Now call to mind the fury of our might.
　　She spake ; nor blue-eyed Pallas not complied.    850
Then Juno, Goddess dread, from Saturn sprung,
Her coursers gold-caparison'd prepared
Impatient.　Hebe to the chariot roll'd
The brazen wheels, and joined them to the smooth
Steel axle ; twice four spokes divided each          855
Shot from the centre to the verge.　The verge
Was gold by fellies of eternal brass
Guarded, a dazzling show !　The shining naves
Were silver ; silver cords and cords of gold
The seat upbore ; two crescents[8] blazed in front.    860
The pole was argent all, to which she bound
The golden yoke, and in their place disposed
The breast-bands incorruptible of gold ;
But Juno to the yoke, herself, the steeds
Led forth, on fire to reach the dreadful field.      865
　　Meantime, Minerva, progeny of Jove,
On the adamantine floor of his abode
Let fall profuse her variegated robe,
Labour of her own hands.　She first put on
The corslet of the cloud-assembler God,              870
Then arm'd her for the field of woe complete.
She charged her shoulder with the dreadful shield
The shaggy Ægis, bordered thick around
With terror ; there was Discord, Prowess there,
There hot Pursuit, and there the feature grim        875
Of Gorgon, dire Deformity, a sign
Oft borne portentous on the arm of Jove.
Her golden helm, whose concave had sufficed

---

[8] These which I have called crescents, were a kind of hook of a semi-
circular form, to which the reins were occasionally fastened.

The legions of an hundred cities, rough
With warlike ornament superb, she fix'd          880
On her immortal head.   Thus arm'd, she rose
Into the flaming chariot, and her spear
Seized ponderous, huge, with which the Goddess sprung
From an Almighty father, levels ranks
Of heroes, against whom her anger burns.          885
Juno with lifted lash urged quick the steeds ;
At her approach, spontaneous roar'd the wide-
Unfolding gates of heaven ; the heavenly gates
Kept by the watchful Hours, to whom the charge
Of the Olympian summit appertains,          890
And of the boundless ether, back to roll,
And to replace the cloudy barrier dense.
Spurr'd through the portal flew the rapid steeds ;
Apart from all, and seated on the point
Superior of the cloven mount, they found          895
The Thunderer.   Juno the white-arm'd her steeds
There stay'd, and thus the Goddess, ere she pass'd,
Question'd the son of Saturn, Jove supreme.
     Jove, Father, seest thou, and art not incensed,
These ravages of Mars ?   Oh what a field,          900
Drench'd with what Grecian blood ! All rashly spilt,
And in despite of me.   Venus, the while,
Sits, and the Archer of the silver bow
Delighted, and have urged, themselves, to this
The frantic Mars within no bounds confined          905
Of law or order.   But, eternal sire !
Shall I offend thee chasing far away
Mars deeply smitten from the field of war ?
     To whom the cloud-assembler God replied.
Go ! but exhort thou rather to the task          910
Spoil-huntress Athenæan Pallas, him
Accustom'd to chastise with pain severe.
     He spake, nor white-arm'd Juno not obey'd.
She lash'd her steeds ; they readily their flight
Began, the earth and starry vault between.          915
Far as from his high tower the watchmen kens
O'er gloomy ocean, so far at one bound
Advance the shrill-voiced coursers of the Gods.
But when at Troy and at the confluent streams

Of Simoïs and Scamander they arrived,                    920
There Juno, white-arm'd Goddess, from the yoke
Her steeds releasing, them in gather'd shades
Conceal'd opaque, while Simoïs caused to spring
Ambrosia from his bank, whereon they browsed.

 Swift as her pinions waft the dove away          925
They sought the Grecians, ardent to begin:
Arriving where the mightiest and the most
Compass'd equestrian Diomede around,
In aspect lion-like, or like wild boars
Of matchless force, there white-arm'd Juno stood,        930
And in the form of Stentor for his voice
Of brass renown'd, audible as the roar
Of fifty throats, the Grecians thus harangued.

 Oh shame, shame, shame! Argives in form alone,
Beautiful but dishonourable race!                        935
While yet divine Achilles ranged the field,
No Trojan stepp'd from yon Dardanian gates
Abroad; all trembled at his stormy spear;
But now they venture forth, now at your ships
Defy you, from their city far remote.                    940

 She ceased, and all caught courage from the sound.
But Athenæan Pallas eager sought
The son of Tydeus; at his chariot side
She found the Chief cooling his fiery wound
Received from Pandarus; for him the sweat                945
Beneath the broad band of his oval shield
Exhausted, and his arm fail'd him fatigued;
He therefore raised the band and wiped the blood
Coagulate; when o'er his chariot yoke
Her arm the Goddess threw, and thus began.               950

 Tydeus, in truth, begat a son himself
Not much resembling. Tydeus was of size
Diminutive, but had a warrior's heart.
When him I once commanded to abstain
From furious fight (what time he enter'd Thebes          955
Ambassador, and the Cadmeans found
Feasting, himself the sole Achaian there)
And bade him quietly partake the feast,
He, fired with wonted ardour, challenged forth
To proof of manhood the Cadmean youth,                   960

Whom easily, through my effectual aid,
In contest of each kind he overcame.
But thou, whom I encircle with my power,
Guard vigilant, and even bid thee forth
To combat with the Trojans, thou, thy limbs    965
Feelst wearied with the toils of war, or worse,
Indulgest womanish and heartless fear.
Henceforth thou art not worthy to be deem'd
Son of Oenides, Tydeus famed in arms.
   To whom thus valiant Diomede replied.    970
I know thee well, oh Goddess sprung from Jove!
And therefore willing shall, and plain, reply.
Me neither weariness nor heartless fear
Restrains, but thine injunctions which impress
My memory, still, that I should fear to oppose    975
The blessed Gods in fight, Venus except,
Whom in the battle found thou badest me pierce
With unrelenting spear; therefore myself
Retiring hither, I have hither call'd
The other Argives also, for I know    980
That Mars, himself in arms, controuls the war.
   Him answer'd then the Goddess azure-eyed.
Tydides! Diomede, my heart's delight!
Fear not this Mars,[9] nor fear thou other power
Immortal, but be confident in me.    985
Arise.  Drive forth.  Seek Mars; him only seek;
Him hand to hand engage; this fiery Mars
Respect not aught, base implement of wrong
And mischief, shifting still from side to side.
He promised Juno lately and myself    990
That he would fight for Greece, yet now forgets
His promise, and gives all his aid to Troy.
   So saying, she backward by his hand withdrew
The son of Capaneus, who to the ground
Leap'd instant; she, impatient to his place    995
Ascending, sat beside brave Diomede.
Loud groan'd the beechen axle, under weight
Unwonted, for it bore into the fight
An awful Goddess, and the chief of men.
Quick-seizing lash and reins Minerva drove    1000

         [9] Αρεα τονδε.

Direct at Mars.   That moment he had slain
Periphas, bravest of Ætolia's sons,
And huge of bulk ; Ochesius was his sire.
Him Mars the slaughterer had of life bereft
Newly, and Pallas to elude his sight            1005
The helmet fixed of Ades on her head.
Soon as gore-tainted Mars the approach perceived
Of Diomede, he left the giant length
Of Periphas extended where he died,
And flew to cope with Tydeus' valiant son.      1010
Full nigh they came, when Mars on fire to slay
The hero, foremost with his brazen lance
Assail'd him, hurling o'er his horses' heads.
But Athenæan Pallas in her hand
The flying weapon caught and turn'd it wide,    1015
Baffling his aim.   Then Diomede on him
Rush'd furious in his turn, and Pallas plunged
The bright spear deep into his cinctured waist.
Dire was the wound, and plucking back the spear
She tore him.   Bellow'd brazen-throated Mars   1020
Loud as nine thousand warriors, or as ten
Join'd in close combat.   Grecians, Trojans shook
Appall'd alike at the tremendous voice
Of Mars insatiable with deeds of blood.
Such as the dimness is when summer winds        1025
Breathe hot, and sultry mist obscures the sky,
Such brazen Mars to Diomede appear'd
By clouds accompanied in his ascent
Into the boundless ether.   Reaching soon
The Olympian heights, seat of the Gods, he sat  1030
Beside Saturnian Jove ; woe fill'd his heart ;
He show'd fast-streaming from the wound his blood
Immortal, and impatient thus complain'd.
   Jove, Father !   Seest thou these outrageous acts
Unmoved with anger ? Such are day by day        1035
The dreadful mischiefs by the Gods contrived
Against each other, for the sake of man.
Thou art thyself the cause.   Thou hast produced
A foolish daughter petulant, addict
To evil only and injurious deeds ;              1040
There is not in Olympus, save herself,

Who feels not thy controul ;. but she her will
Gratifies ever, and reproof from thee
Finds none, because, pernicious as she is,
She is thy daughter.   She hath now the mind  1045
Of haughty Diomede with madness fill'd
Against the immortal Gods ; first Venus bled ;
Her hand he pierced impetuous, then assail'd,
As if himself immortal, even me,
But me my feet stole thence, or overwhelm'd  1050
Beneath yon heaps of carcases impure,
What had I not sustain'd ? And if at last
I lived, had halted crippled by the sword.
  To whom with dark displeasure Jove replied.
Base and side-shifting traitor ! vex not me  1055
Here sitting querulous ; of all who dwell
On the Olympian heights, thee most I hate
Contentious, whose delight is war alone.
Thou hast thy mother's moods, the very spleen
Of Juno, uncontroulable as she,  1060
Whom even I, reprove her as I may,
Scarce rule by mere commands ; I therefore judge
Thy sufferings a contrivance all her own.
But soft.   Thou art my son whom I begat,
And Juno bare thee.   I cannot endure  1065
That thou shouldst suffer long.   Hadst thou been born
Of other parents thus detestable,
What Deity soe'er had brought thee forth,
Thou shouldst have found long since an humbler sphere.
  He ceased, and to the care his son consign'd  1070
Of Pæon ; he with drugs of lenient powers,
Soon heal'd whom immortality secured
From dissolution.   As the juice from figs
Express'd what fluid was in milk before
Coagulates, stirr'd rapidly around,  1075
So soon was Mars by Pæon's skill restored.
Him Hebe bathed, and with divine attire
Graceful adorn'd ; when at the side of Jove
Again his glorious seat sublime he took.
  Meantime to the abode of Jove supreme  1080
Ascended Juno throughout Argos known
And mighty Pallas ; Mars the plague of man,
By their successful force from slaughter driven.

# BOOK VI.

## ARGUMENT.

The battle is continued. The Trojans being closely pursued, Hector by the advice of Helenus enters Troy, and recommends it to Hecuba to go in solemn procession to the temple of Minerva; she with the matrons goes accordingly. Hector takes the opportunity to find out Paris, and exhorts him to return to the field of battle. An interview succeeds between Hector and Andromache, and Paris, having armed himself in the meantime, comes up with Hector at the close of it, when they sally from the gate together.

THUS was the field forsaken by the Gods.
And now success proved various; here the Greeks
With their extended spears, the Trojans there
Prevail'd alternate, on the champaign spread
The Xanthus and the Simoïs between.                          5
    First Telamonian Ajax, bulwark firm
Of the Achaians, broke the Trojan ranks,
And kindled for the Greeks a gleam of hope,
Slaying the bravest of the Thracian band,
Huge Acamas, Eusoros' son; him first                        10
Full on the shaggy crest he smote, and urged
The spear into his forehead; through his scull
The bright point pass'd, and darkness veil'd his eyes.
But Diomede, heroic Chief, the son
Of Teuthras slew, Axylus. Rich was he,                      15
And in Arisba, (where he dwelt beside
The public road, and at his open door
Made welcome all,) respected and beloved.
But of his numerous guests none interposed
To avert his woeful doom; nor him alone                     20
He slew, but with him also to the shades
Calesius sent, his friend and charioteer.
    Opheltius fell and Dresus, by the hand
Slain of Euryalus, who, next, his arms
On Pedasus and on Æsepus turned                             25
Brethren and twins. Them Abarbarea bore,

A Naiad, to Bucolion, son renown'd
Of King Laomedon, his eldest born,
But by his mother, at his birth, conceal'd.
Bucolion pasturing his flocks, embraced                    30
The lovely nymph ; she twins produced, both whom,
Brave as they were and beautiful, thy son[1]
Mecisteus ! slew, and from their shoulders tore
Their armour.    Dauntless Polypœtes slew
Astyalus.    Ulysses with his spear                        35
Transfixed Pydites, a Percosian Chief,
And Teucer Aretaön ; Nestor's pride
Antilochus, with his bright lance, of life
Bereft Ablerus, and the royal arm
Of Agamemnon, Elatus ; he dwelt                            40
Among the hills of lofty Pedasus,
On Satnio's banks, smooth-sliding river pure.
Phylacus fled, whom Leïtus as swift
Soon smote.    Melanthius at the feet expired
Of the renowned Eurypylus, and, flush'd                    45
With martial ardour, Menelaus seized
And took alive Adrastus.    As it chanced
A thicket his affrighted steeds detain'd
Their feet entangling ; they with restive force
At its extremity snapp'd short the pole,                   50
And to the city, whither others fled,
Fled also.    From his chariot headlong hurl'd,
Adrastus press'd the plain fast by his wheel..
Flew Menelaus, and his quivering spear
Shook over him ; he, life imploring, clasp'd               55
Importunate his knees, and thus exclaim'd.
   Oh, son of Atreus, let me live ! accept
Illustrious ransom ! In my father's house
Is wealth abundant, gold, and brass, and steel
Of truest temper, which he will impart                     60
Till he have gratified thine utmost wish,
Inform'd that I am captive in your fleet.
   He said, and Menelaus by his words
Vanquish'd, him soon had to the fleet dismiss'd
Given to his train in charge, but swift and stern          65
Approaching, Agamemnon interposed. —

                    [1] Euryalus.

Now, brother, whence this milkiness of mind,
These scruples about blood? Thy Trojan friends
Have doubtless much obliged thee.  Die the race!
May none escape us! Neither he who flies,        70
Nor even the infant in his mother's womb
Unconscious.  Perish universal Troy
Unpitied, till her place be found no more!
   So saying, his brother's mind the Hero turn'd,
Advising him aright; he with his hand        75
Thrust back Adrastus, and himself, the King,
His bowels pierced.  Supine Adrastus fell,
And Agamemnon, with his foot the corse
Impressing firm, pluck'd forth his ashen spear.
Then Nestor, raising high his voice, exclaim'd.        80
   Friends, Heroes, Grecians, ministers of Mars!
Let none, desirous of the spoil, his time
Devote to plunder now; now slay your foes,
And strip them when the field shall be your own.
   He said, and all took courage at his word.        85
   Then had the Trojans enter'd Troy again
By the heroic Grecians foul repulsed,
So was their spirit daunted, but the son
Of Priam, Helenus, an augur far
Excelling all, at Hector's side his speech        90
To him and to Æneas thus address'd.
   Hector, and thou, Æneas, since on you
The Lycians chiefly and ourselves depend,
For that in difficult emprize ye show
Most courage; give best counsel; stand yourselves,        95
And, visiting all quarters, cause to stand
Before the city-gates our scatter'd troops,
Ere yet the fugitives within the arms
Be slaughter'd of their wives, the scorn of Greece.
When thus ye shall have rallied every band        100
And roused their courage, weary though we be,
Yet since necessity commands, even here
Will we give battle to the host of Greece.
But, Hector! to the city thou depart;
There charge our mother, that she go direct,        105
With the assembled matrons, to the fane
Of Pallas in the citadel of Troy.

Opening her chambers' sacred doors, of all
Her treasured mantles there, let her select
The widest, most magnificently wrought,　　　　110
And which she values most ; *that* let her spread
On Athenæan Pallas' lap divine.
Twelve heifers of the year yet never touch'd
With puncture of the goad, let her alike
Devote to her, if she will pity Troy,　　　　115
Our wives and little ones, and will avert
The son of Tydeus from these sacred towers,
That dreadful Chief, terror of all our host,
Bravest, in my account, of all the Greeks.
For never yet Achilles hath himself　　　　120
So taught our people fear, although esteem'd
Son of a Goddess.　But this warrior's rage
Is boundless, and his strength past all compare.
　　So Helenus ; nor Hector not complied.
Down from his chariot instant to the ground　　　　125
All arm'd he leap'd, and, shaking his sharp spears,
Through every phalanx pass'd, rousing again
Their courage, and rekindling horrid war.
They, turning, faced the Greeks ; the Greeks repulsed,
Ceased from all carnage, nor supposed they less　　　　130
Than that some Deity, the starry skies
Forsaken, help'd their foes, so firm they stood.
But Hector to the Trojans call'd aloud.
Ye dauntless Trojans and confederate powers
Call'd from afar ! now be ye men, my friends,　　　　135
Now summon all the fury of your might !
I go to charge our senators and wives
That they address the Gods with prayers and vows
For our success, and hecatombs devote.
　　So saying the Hero went, and as he strode　　　　140
The sable hide that lined his bossy shield
Smote on his neck and on his ancle-bone.
　　And now into the middle space between
Both hosts, the son of Tydeus and the son
Moved of Hippolochus, intent alike -　　　　145
On furious combat ; face to face they stood,
And thus heroic Diomede began.
　　Most noble Champion ! who of human kind

Art thou, whom in the man-ennobling fight
I now encounter first? Past all thy peers           .           150
I must esteem thee valiant, who hast dared
To meet my coming, and my spear defy.
Ah! they are sons of miserable sires
Who dare my might; but if a God from heaven
Thou come, behold! I fight not with the Gods.                   155
That war Lycurgus son of Dryas waged,
And saw not many years.   The nurses he
Of brain-disturbing Bacchus down the steep
Pursued of sacred Nyssa; they their wands
Vine-wreathed cast all away, with an ox-goad                    160
Chastised by fell Lycurgus.   Bacchus plunged
Meantime dismay'd into the Deep, where him
Trembling, and at the Hero's haughty threats
Confounded, Thetis in her bosom hid.
Thus by Lycurgus were the blessed powers                        165
Of heaven offended, and Saturnian Jove
Of sight bereaved him, who not long that loss
Survived, for he was curst by all above.
I, therefore, wage no contest with the Gods.
But if thou be of men, and feed on bread                        170
Of earthly growth, draw nigh, that with a stroke
Well-aim'd, I may at once cut short thy days.
    To whom the illustrious Lycian Chief replied.
Why asks brave Diomede of my descent?
For, as the leaves, such is the race of man.                    175
The wind shakes down the leaves, the budding grove
Soon teems with others, and in spring they grow.
So pass mankind.   One generation meets
Its destined period, and a new succeeds.
But since thou seem'st desirous to be taught                    180
My pedigree, whereof no few have heard,
Know that in Argos, in the very lap
Of Argos, for her steed-grazed meadows famed,
Stands Ephyra: there Sisyphus abode,
Shrewdest of human kind; Sisyphus, named                        185
Æolides.   Himself a son begat,
Glaucus, and he Bellerophon, to whom
The Gods both manly force and beauty gave.
Him Prœtus, (for in Argos at that time

Prœtus was sovereign, to whose sceptre Jove          190
Had subjected the land,) plotting his death,
Contrived to banish from his native home.
For fair Anteia, wife of Prœtus, mad
Through love of young Bellerophon, him oft
In secret to illicit joys enticed ;                  195
But she prevail'd not o'er the virtuous mind
Discreet of whom she wooed ! therefore a lie
Framing, she royal Prœtus thus bespake.
    Die thou, or slay Bellerophon, who sought
Of late to force me to his lewd embrace.             200
    So saying, the anger of the King she roused.
Slay him himself he would not, for his heart
Forbad the deed ; him therefore he dismiss'd
To Lycia, charged with tales of dire import
Written in tablets, which he bade him show,          205
That he might perish, to Anteia's sire.
To Lycia then, conducted by the Gods,
He went, and on the shores of Xanthus found
Free entertainment noble at the hands
Of Lycia's potent King.   Nine days complete         210
He feasted him, and slew each day an ox.
But when the tenth day's ruddy morn appear'd,
He asked him then his errand, and to see
Those written tablets from his son-in-law.
The letters seen, he bade him, first, destroy        215
Chimæra, deem'd invincible, divine
In nature, alien from the race of man,
Lion in front, but dragon all behind,
And in the midst a she-goat breathing forth
Profuse the violence of flaming fire.                220
Her, confident in signs from heaven, he slew.
Next, with the men of Solymæ he fought,
Brave warriors far-renown'd, with whom he waged,
In his account, the fiercest of his wars.
And lastly, when in battle he had slain              225
The man-resisting Amazons, the king
Another stratagem at his return
Devised against him, placing close-conceal'd
An ambush for him from the bravest chosen
In Lycia ; but they saw their homes no more ;        230

Bellerophon the valiant slew them all.
The monarch hence collecting, at the last,
His heavenly origin, him there detain'd,
And gave him his own daughter, with the half
Of all his royal dignity and power.                        235
The Lycians also, for his proper use,
Large lot assign'd him of their richest soil,
Commodious for the vine, or for the plough.
And now his consort fair three children bore
To bold Bellerophon ; Isandrus one,                        240
And one, Hippolochus ; his youngest born
Laodamia was for beauty such
That she became a concubine of Jove.
She bore Sarpedon of heroic note.
But when Bellerophon, at last, himself            .          245
Had anger'd all the Gods, feeding on grief
He roam'd alone the Aleian field, exiled
By choice, from every cheerful haunt of man.
Mars, thirsty still for blood, his son destroy'd
Isandrus, warring with the host renown'd                    250
Of Solymæ ; and in her wrath divine
Diana from her chariot golden-rein'd
Laodamia slew.   Myself I boast
Sprung from Hippolochus ; he sent me forth
To fight for Troy, charging me much and oft                 255
That I should outstrip always all mankind
In worth and valour, nor the house disgrace
Of my forefathers, heroes without peer
In Ephyra, and in Lycia's wide domain.
Such is my lineage ; such the blood I boast.                260
    He ceased.   Then valiant Diomede rejoiced.
He pitch'd his spear, and to the Lycian Prince
In terms of peace and amity replied.
    Thou art my own hereditary friend,
Whose noble Grandsire was a guest of mine.                  265
For Oeneus, on a time, full twenty days,
Regaled Bellerophon, and pledges fair
Of hospitality they interchanged.
Oeneus a belt radiant with purple gave
To brave Bellerophon, who in return                         270
Gave him a golden goblet.   Coming forth

I left the kind memorial safe at home.
A child was I when Tydeus went to Thebes,
Where the Achaians perish'd, and of him
Hold no remembrance; but henceforth, my friend,          275
Thine host 'am I in Argos, and thou mine
In Lycia, should I chance to sojourn there.
We will not clash.   Trojans or aids of Troy
No few the Gods shall furnish to my spear,
Whom I may slaughter; and no want of Greeks             280
On whom to prove thy prowess, thou shalt find.
But it were well that an exchange ensued
Between us; take mine armour, give me thine,
That all who notice us may understand
Our patrimonial[2] amity and love.                       285
    So they, and each alighting, hand in hand
Stood lock'd, faith promising and firm accord.
Then Jove of sober judgement.so bereft
Infatuate Glaucus that with Tydeus' son
He barter'd gold for brass, an hundred beeves            290
In value, for the value small of nine.
    But Hector at the Scæan gate and beech
Meantime arrived, to whose approach the wives
And daughters flock'd of Troy, enquiring each
The fate of husband, brother, son, or friend.            295
He bade them all with solemn prayer the Gods
Seek fervent, for that woe was on the wing.
    But when he enter'd Priam's palace, built
With splendid porticoes, and which within
Had fifty chambers lined with polish'd stone,            300
.Contiguous all, where Priam's sons reposed
And his sons' wives, and where, on the other side,
In twelve magnificent chambers also lined
With polish'd marble and contiguous all,
The sons-in-law of Priam lay beside                      305
His spotless daughters, there the mother queen
Seeking the chamber of Laodice,
Loveliest of all her children, as she went
Met Hector.   On his hand she hung and said:
    Why leavest thou, O my son! the dangerous field?    310
I fear that the Achaians (hateful name!)

² Ξεινοι πατρωῖοι.

s. c.—7.                                                   I

Compass the walls so closely, that thou seek'st
Urged by distress the citadel, to lift
Thine hands in prayer to Jove? But pause awhile
Till I shall bring thee wine, that having pour'd      315
Libation rich to Jove and to the powers
Immortal, thou may'st drink and be refresh'd.
For wine is mighty to renew the strength
Of weary man, and weary thou must be
Thyself, thus long defending us and ours.      320
To whom her son majestic thus replied.
    My mother, whom I reverence! cheering wine
Bring none to me, lest I forget my might.
I fear, beside, with unwash'd hands to pour
Libation forth of sable wine to Jove,      325
And dare on none account, thus blood-defiled,
Approach the tempest-stirring God in prayer.
Thou, therefore, gathering all our matrons, seek
The fane of Pallas, huntress of the spoil,
Bearing sweet incense; but from the attire      330
Treasured within thy chamber, first select
The amplest robe, most exquisitely wrought,
And which thou prizest most,—then spread the gift
On Athenæan Pallas' lap divine.
Twelve heifers also of the year, untouch'd      335
With puncture of the goad, promise to slay
In sacrifice, if she will pity Troy,
Our wives and little ones, and will avert
The son of Tydeus from these sacred towers.
That dreadful Chief, terror of all our host.      340
Go then, my mother, seek the hallowed fane
Of the spoil-huntress Deity. I, the while,
Seek Paris, and if Paris yet can hear,
Shall call him forth. But oh that earth would yawn
And swallow him, whom Jove hath made a curse      345
To Troy, to Priam, and to all his house;
Methinks, to see him plunged into the shades
For ever, were a cure for all my woes.
    He ceased; the Queen, her palace entering, charged
Her maidens; they, incontinent, throughout      350
All Troy convened the matrons, as she bade.
Meantime into her wardrobe incense-fumed,

Herself descended; there her treasures lay,
Works of Sidonian women, whom her son
The Godlike Paris, when he cross'd the seas          355
With Jove-begotten Helen, brought to Troy.
The most magnificent, and varied most
With colours radiant, from the rest she chose
For Pallas; vivid as a star it shone,
And lowest lay of all.   Then forth she went,       360
The Trojan matrons all following her steps.
   But when the long procession reach'd the fane
Of Pallas in the heights of Troy, to them
The fair Theano ope'd the portals wide,
Daughter of Cisseus, brave Antenor's spouse.        365
And by appointment public, at that time,
Priestess of Pallas.   All with lifted hands
In presence of Minerva wept aloud.
Beauteous Theano on the Goddess' lap
Then spread the robe, and to the daughter fair      370
Of Jove omnipotent her suit address'd.
   Goddess[3] of Goddesses, our city's shield,
Adored Minerva, hear! oh! break the lance
Of Diomede, and give himself to fall
Prone in the dust before the Scæan gate.            375
So will we offer to thee at thy shrine,
This day twelve heifers of the year, untouch'd
By yoke or goad, if thou wilt pity show
To Troy, and save our children and our wives.
   Such prayer the priestess offer'd, and such prayer  380
All present; whom Minerva heard averse.
But Hector to the palace sped meantime
Of Alexander, which himself had built,
Aided by every architect of name
Illustrious then in Troy.   Chamber it had,         385
Wide hall, proud dome, and on the heights of Troy
Near-neighbouring Hector's house and Priam's stood.
There enter'd Hector, Jove-beloved, a spear
Its length eleven cubits in his hand,
Its glittering head bound with a ring of gold.      390
He found within his chamber whom he sought,
Polishing with exactest care his arms

[3] δῖα θεάων.

Resplendent, shield and hauberk fingering o'er
With curious touch, and tampering with his bow.
Helen of Argos with her female train                            395
Sat occupied, the while, to each in turn
Some splendid task assigning.   Hector fix'd
His eyes on Paris, and him stern rebuked.
     Thy sullen humours, Paris, are ill-timed.
The people perish at our lofty walls ;                          400
The flames of war have compass'd Troy around
And thou hast kindled them ; who yet thyself,
That slackness show'st which in another seen
Thou would'st resent to death.   Haste, seek the field
This moment, lest, the next, all Ilium blaze.                   405
     To whom thus Paris graceful as a God.
Since, Hector, thou hast charged me with a fault,
And not unjustly, I will answer make,
And give thou special heed.   That here I sit,
The cause is sorrow, which I wish'd to soothe                   410
In secret, not displeasure or revenge.
I tell thee also, that even now my wife
Was urgent with me in most soothing terms
That I would forth to battle ; and myself,
Aware that victory oft changes sides,                           415
That course prefer.   Wait, therefore, thou awhile,
'Till I shall dress me for the fight, or go
Thou first, and I will overtake thee soon.
     He ceased, to whom brave Hector answer none
Return'd, when Helen him with lenient speech       .            420
Accosted mild.   My brother ! who in me
Hast found a sister worthy of thy hate,
Authoress of all calamity to Troy,
Oh that the winds, the day when I was born,
Had swept me out of sight, whirl'd me aloft                     425
To some inhospitable mountain-top,
Or plunged me in the deep ; there I had sunk
O'erwhelm'd, and all these ills had never been.
But since the Gods would bring these ills to pass,
I should, at least, some worthier mate have chosen,            430
One not insensible to public shame.
But this, oh this, nor hath nor will acquire
Hereafter, aught which like discretion shews

Or reason, and shall find his just reward.
But enter; take this seat; for who as thou      435
Labours, or who hath cause like thee to rue
The crime, my brother, for which Heaven hath doom'd
Both Paris and my most detested self
To be the burthens of an endless song?
   To whom the warlike Hector huge[4] replied.      440
Me bid not, Helen, to a seat howe'er
Thou wish my stay, for thou must not prevail.
The Trojans miss me, and myself no less
Am anxious to return.   But urge in haste
This loiterer forth; yea, let him urge himself      445
To overtake me ere I quit the town.
For I must home in haste, that I may see
My loved Andromache, my infant boy,
And my domestics, ignorant if e'er
I shall behold them more, or if my fate      450
Ordain me now to fall by Grecian  hands.
   So spake the dauntless hero, and withdrew.
But reaching soon his own well-built abode,
He found not fair Andromache; she stood
Lamenting Hector, with the nurse who bore      455
Her infant, on a turret's top sublime.
He then, not finding his chaste spouse within,
Thus from the portal, of her train enquired.
   Tell me, ye maidens, whither went from home
Andromache the fair?   Went she to see      460
Her female kindred of my father's house,
Or to Minerva's temple, where convened
The bright-hair'd matrons of the city seek
To soothe the awful Goddess? Tell me true.
   To whom his household's governess discreet.      465
Since, Hector, truth is thy demand, receive
True answer.   Neither went she forth to see
Her female kindred of thy father's house,
Nor to Minerva's temple, where convened
The bright-haired matrons of the city seek      470
To soothe the awful Goddess; but she went

---

[4] The bulk of his heroes is a circumstance of which Homer frequently
reminds us by the use of the word μέγας—and which ought, therefore, by
no means to be suppressed.

Hence to the tower of Troy : for she had heard
That the Achaians had prevail'd, and driven
The Trojans to the walls ; she, therefore, wild
With grief, flew thither, and the nurse her steps          475
Attended, with thy infant in her arms.
   So spake the prudent governess ; whose words
When Hector heard, issuing from his door
He backward trod with hasty steps the streets
Of lofty Troy, and having traversed all                    480
The spacious city, when he now approach'd
The Scæan gate, whence he must seek the field,
There, hasting home again his noble wife
Met him, Andromache the rich-endow'd
Fair daughter of Eëtion famed in arms.                     485
Eëtion, who in Hypoplacian Thebes
Umbrageous dwelt, Cilicia's mighty lord,—
His daughter valiant Hector had espoused.
There she encounter'd him, and with herself
The nurse came also, bearing in her arms                   490
Hectorides, his infant darling boy,
Beautiful as a star.   Him Hector called
Scamandrios, but Astyanax[5] all else
In Ilium named him, for that Hector's arm
Alone was the defence and strength of Troy.                495
The father, silent, eyed his babe, and smiled.
Andromache, meantime, before him stood,
With streaming cheeks, hung on his hand, and said.
   Thy own great courage will cut short thy days,
My noble Hector ! neither pitiest thou                     500
Thy helpless infant, or my hapless self,
Whose widowhood is near ; for thou wilt fall
Ere long, assail'd by the whole host of Greece.
Then let me to the tomb, my best retreat
When thou art slain.   For comfort none or joy             505
Can I expect, thy day of life extinct,
But thenceforth, sorrow.   Father I have none ;
No mother.   When Cilicia's city, Thebes
The populous, was by Achilles sack'd,
He slew my father ; yet his gorgeous arms                  510
Stripp'd not through reverence of him, but consumed,

     [5] The name signifies, the *Chief of the city.*

Arm'd as it was, his body on the pile,
And heap'd his tomb, which the Oreades[6],
Jove's daughters, had with elms inclosed around.
My seven brothers, glory of our house,                    515
All in one day descended to the shades ;
For brave Achilles, while they fed their herds
And snowy flocks together, slew them all.
My mother, Queen of the well-wooded realm
Of Hypoplacian Thebes, her hither brought        520
Among his other spoils, he loosed again
At an inestimable ransom-price,
But by Diana[7] pierced, she died at home.
Yet Hector—oh my husband ! I in thee
Find parents, brothers, all that I have lost.        525
Come ! have compassion on us.    Go not hence,
But guard this turret, lest of me thou make
A widow, and an orphan of thy boy.
The city walls are easiest of ascent
At yonder fig-tree ; station there thy powers ;        530
For whether by a prophet warn'd, or taught
By search and observation, in that part
Each Ajax with Idomeneus of Crete,
The sons of Atreus, and the valiant son
Of Tydeus, have now thrice assail'd the town.        535
    To whom the leader of the host of Troy.
    These cares, Andromache, which thee engage,
All touch me also ; but I dread to incur
The scorn of male and female tongues in Troy,
If, dastard-like, I should decline the fight.        540
Nor feel I such a wish.    No.    I have learn'd
To be courageous ever, in the van
Among the flower of Ilium to assert
My glorious father's honour, and my own.
For that the day shall come when sacred Troy,        545
When Priam, and the people of the old
Spear-practised King shall perish, well I know.
But for no Trojan sorrows yet to come
So much I mourn, not e'en for Hecuba,
Nor yet for Priam, nor for all the brave        550

6 Mountain nymphs.
7 Sudden deaths were ascribed either to Diana or Apollo.

Of my own brothers who shall kiss the dust,
As for thyself, when some Achaian Chief
Shall have convey'd thee weeping hence, thy sun
Of peace and liberty for ever set.
Then shalt thou toil in Argos at the loom          555
For a task-mistress, and constrain'd shalt draw
From Hypereïa's fount, or from the fount
Messeïs, water at her proud command.
Some Grecian then, seeing thy tears, shall say—
"This was the wife of Hector, who excell'd          560
All Troy in fight when Ilium was besieged."
Such he shall speak thee, and thy heart, the while,
Shall bleed afresh through want of such a friend
To stand between captivity and thee.
But may I rest beneath my hill of earth          565
Or ere that day arrive! I would not live
To hear thy cries, and see thee torn away.
    So saying, illustrious Hector stretch'd his arms
Forth to his son, but with a scream, the child
Fell back into the bosom of his nurse,          570
His father's aspect dreading, whose bright arms
He had attentive mark'd and shaggy crest
Playing tremendous o'er his helmet's height.
His father and his gentle mother laugh'd[8],
And noble Hector lifting from his head          575
His dazzling helmet, placed it on the ground,
Then kiss'd his boy and dandled him, and thus
In earnest prayer the heavenly powers implored.
    Hear all ye Gods! as ye have given to me,
So also on my son excelling might          580
Bestow, with chief authority in Troy.
And be his record this, in time to come,
When he returns from battle.   Lo! how far
The son excels the sire! May every foe
Fall under him, and he come laden home          585
With spoils blood-stain'd to his dear mother's joy.
    He said, and gave his infant to the arms
Of his Andromache, who him received
Into her fragrant bosom, bitter tears

---

[8] The Scholiast in Villoisson calls it φυσικον τινα και μετριον γελωτα, a natural and moderate laughter.

With sweet smiles mingling; he with pity moved      500
That sight observed, soft touch'd her cheek, and said,
   Mourn not, my loved Andromache, for me
Too much; no man shall send me to the shades
Of Tartarus, ere mine allotted hour,
Nor lives he who can overpass the date      595
By heaven assign'd him, be he base or brave.
Go then, and occupy content at home
The woman's province; ply the distaff, spin
And weave, and task thy maidens.    War belongs
To man; to all men; and of all who first      600
Drew vital breath in Ilium, most to me.
   He ceased, and from the ground his helmet raised
Hair-crested; his Andromache, at once
Obedient, to her home repair'd, but oft
Turn'd as she went, and, turning, wept afresh.      605
No sooner at the palace she arrived
Of havoc-spreading Hector, than among
Her numerous maidens found within, she raised
A general lamentation; with one voice,
In his own house, his whole domestic train      610
Mourn'd Hector, yet alive; for none the hope
Conceived of his escape from Grecian hands,
Or to behold their living master more.
   Nor Paris in his stately mansion long
Delay'd, but, arm'd resplendent, traversed swift      615
The city, all alacrity and joy.
As some stall'd horse high-fed, his stable-cord
Snapt short, beats under foot the sounding plain,
Accustomed in smooth-sliding streams to lave
Exulting; high he bears his head, his mane      620
Undulates o'er his shoulders, pleased he eyes .
His glossy sides, and borne on pliant knees
Shoots to the meadow where his fellows graze;
So Paris, son of Priam, from the heights
Of Pergamus into the streets of Troy,      625
All dazzling as the sun, descended, flush'd
With martial pride, and bounding in his course.
At once he came where noble Hector stood
Now turning, after conference with his spouse,
When godlike Alexander thus began.      630

My hero brother, thou hast surely found
My long delay most irksome.   More dispatch
Had pleased thee more, for such was thy command.
      To whom the warlike Hector thus replied.
No man, judicious, and in feat of arms                  635
Intelligent, would pour contempt on thee,
(For thou art valiant,) wert thou not remiss
And wilful negligent; and when I hear
The very men who labour in thy cause
Reviling thee, I make thy shame my own.                 640
But let us on.   All such complaints shall cease
Hereafter, and thy faults be touch'd no more,
Let Jove but once afford us riddance clear
Of these Achaians, and to quaff the cup
Of liberty, before the living Gods.                     645

# BOOK VII.

### ARGUMENT.

Ajax and Hector engage in single combat.   The Grecians fortify their
camp.

So saying, illustrious Hector through the gates
To battle rush'd, with Paris at his side,
And both were bent on deeds of high renown.
As when the Gods vouchsafe propitious gales
To longing mariners, who with smooth oars          5
Threshing the waves have all their strength consumed,
So them the longing Trojans glad received.
  •At once each slew a Grecian.   Paris slew
Menesthius who in Arna dwelt, the son
Of Areithoüs, club-bearing chief,                  10
And of Philomedusa radiant-eyed.
But Hector wounded with his glittering spear
Eïoneus;  he pierced his neck beneath
His brazen morion's verge, and dead he fell.
Then Glaucus, leader of the Lycian host,           15
Son of Hippolochus, in furious fight
Iphinoüs son of Dexias assail'd,
Mounting his rapid mares, and with his lance
His shoulder pierced;  unhorsed he fell and died.

  Such slaughter of the Grecians in fierce fight   20
Minerva noting, from the Olympian hills
Flew down to sacred Ilium;  whose approach
Marking from Pergamus Apollo flew
To meet her, ardent on the part of Troy.
Beneath the beech they join'd, when first the King, 25
The son of Jove, Apollo, thus began.
  Daughter of Jove supreme!  why hast thou left
Olympus, and with such impetuous speed?
Comest thou to give the Danaï success
Decisive?  For I know that pity none                30

Thou feel'st for Trojans, perish as they may.
But if advice of mine can influence thee
To that which shall be best, let us compose
This day the furious fight, which shall again
Hereafter rage, till Ilium be destroy'd. 35
Since such is Juno's pleasure and thy own.
 Him answer'd then Pallas cærulean-eyed.
Celestial archer! be it so.  I came
Myself so purposing into the field
From the Olympian heights.  But by what means 40
Wilt thou induce the warriors to a pause?
 To whom the King, the son of Jove, replied.
. The courage of equestrian Hector bold
Let us excite, that he may challenge forth
To single conflict terrible some Chief 45
Achaian.  The Achaians brazen-mail'd
Indignant, will supply a champion soon
To combat with the noble Chief of Troy.
 So spake Apollo, and his counsel pleased
Minerva; which when Helenus the seer, 50
Priam's own son, in his prophetic soul
Perceived, approaching Hector, thus he spake.
 Jove's peer in wisdom, Hector, Priam's son!
I am thy brother.  Wilt thou list to me?
Bid cease the battle.  Bid both armies sit. 55
Call first, thyself, the mightiest of the Greeks
To single conflict.  I have heard the voice
Of the Eternal Gods, and well assured
Foretell thee that thy death not now impends.
 He spake, whom Hector heard with joy elate. 60
Before his van striding into the space
Both hosts between, he with his spear transverse
Press'd back the Trojans, and they sat.  Down sat
The well-greaved Grecians also at command
Of Agamemnon; and in shape assumed 65
Of vultures, Pallas and Apollo perch'd
High on the lofty beech sacred to Jove
The father Ægis-arm'd; delighted thence
They view'd the peopled plain horrent around
With shields and helms and glittering spears erect. 70
As when fresh-blowing Zephyrus the flood

Sweeps first, the ocean blackens at the blast,
Such seem'd the plain whereon the Achaians sat
And Trojans, whom between thus Hector spake.
   Ye Trojans, and Achaians brazen-greaved,        75
Attend while I shall speak! Jove high-enthroned
Hath not fulfill'd the truce, but evil plans
Against both hosts, till either ye shall take
Troy's lofty towers, or shall yourselves in flight
Fall vanquish'd at your billow-cleaving barks.       80
With you is all the flower of Greece.   Let him
Whose heart shall move him to encounter sole
Illustrious Hector, from among you all
Stand forth, and Jove be witness to us both.
If he, with his long-pointed lance, of life        85
Shall me bereave, my armour is his prize,
Which he shall hence into your fleet convey;
Not so my body; that he shall resign
For burial to the men and wives of Troy.
But if Apollo make the glory mine,         90
And he fall vanquish'd, him will I despoil,
And hence conveying into sacred Troy
His arms, will in the temple hang them high
Of the bow-bender God, but I will send
His body to the fleet, that him the Greeks       95
May grace with rites funereal.   On the banks
Of wide-spread Hellespont ye shall upraise
His tomb, and as they cleave with oary barks
The sable Deep, posterity shall say—
" It is a warrior's tomb; in ancient days,      100
The Hero died; him warlike Hector slew."
So men shall speak hereafter, and my fame
Who slew him, and my praise, shall never die.
   He ceased, and all sat mute.   His challenge bold
None dared accept, which yet they blush'd to shun,   105
Till Menelaus, at the last, arose
Groaning profound, and thus reproach'd the Greeks.
   Ah boasters! henceforth women—men no more—
Eternal shame, shame infinite is ours,
If none of all  the Grecians dares contend    110
With Hector.   Dastards—deaf to glory's call—
Rot where ye sit! I will myself take arms

Against him, for the gods alone dispose,
At their own pleasure, the events of war.
   He ended, and put on his radiant arms.                    115
Then, Menelaus, manifest appear'd
Thy death, approaching by the dreadful hands
Of Hector, mightier far in arms than thou,
But that the Chiefs of the Achaians all
Upstarting stay'd thee, and himself the King,                    120
The son of Atreus, on thy better hand
Seizing affectionate, thee thus address'd.
   Thou ravest, my royal brother! and art seized
With needless frenzy.   But, however chafed,
Restrain thy wrath, nor covet to contend                    125
With Priameian Hector, whom in fight
All dread, a warrior thy superior far.
Not even Achilles, in the glorious field,
(Though stronger far than thou,) this hero meets
Undaunted.   Go then, and thy seat resume                    130
In thy own band; the Achaians shall for him,
Doubtless, some fitter champion furnish forth.
Brave though he be, and with the toils of war
Insatiable, he shall be willing yet,
Seated on his bent knees, to breathe a while,                    135
Should he escape the arduous brunt severe.
   So saying, the hero by his counsel wise
His brother's purpose alter'd; he complied,
And his glad servants eased him of his arms.
Then Nestor thus the Argive host bespake.                    140
   Great woe, ye Gods! hath on Achaia fallen.
Now may the warlike Peleus, hoary Chief,
Who both with eloquence and wisdom rules
The Myrmidons, our foul disgrace deplore.
With him discoursing, erst of ancient times,                    145
When all your pedigrees I traced, I made
His heart bound in him at the proud report.
But now, when he shall learn how here we sat
Cowering at foot of Hector, he shall oft
His hands uplift to the immortal Gods,                    150
Praying a swift release into the shades.
Jove! Pallas! Phœbus! Oh that I were young
As when the Pylians in fierce fight engaged

The Arcadians spear-expert, beside the stream
Of rapid Celadon! beneath the walls　　　　　155
We fought of Pheia, where the Jardan rolls.
There Ereuthalion, Chief of Godlike form,
Stood forth before his van, and with loud voice
Defied the Pylians.　Arm'd he was in steel
By royal Areïthous whilom worn;　　　　　160
Brave Areïthous, Corynetes[1] named
By every tongue; for that in bow and spear
Nought trusted he, but with an iron mace
The close-embattled phalanx shatter'd wide.
Him by address, not by superior force,　　　　165
Lycurgus vanquish'd, in a narrow pass,
Where him his iron whirl-bat[2] nought avail'd.
Lycurgus stealing on him, with his lance
Transpierced and fix'd him to the soil supine.
Him of his arms, bright gift of brazen Mars,　　　170
He stripp'd, which after, in the embattled field
Lycurgus wore himself, but, growing old,
Surrender'd them to Ereuthalion's use
His armour-bearer, high in his esteem,
And Ereuthalion wore them on the day　　　　175
When he defied our best.　All hung their heads
And trembled; none dared meet him; till at last
With inborn courage warm'd, and nought dismayed,
Though youngest of them all, I undertook
That contest, and, by Pallas' aid, prevail'd.　　　180
I slew the man in height and bulk all men
Surpassing, and much soil he cover'd slain.
Oh for the vigour of those better days!
Then should not Hector want a champion long,
Whose call to combat, ye, although the prime　　185
And pride of all our land, seem slow to hear.
　　He spake reproachful, when at once arose
Nine heroes.　Agamemnon, King of men,
Foremost arose; then Tydeus' mighty son,
With either Ajax in fierce prowess clad;　　　190
The Cretan next, Idomeneus, with whom
Uprose Meriones his friend approved,
Terrible as the man-destroyer Mars.

　　　　[1] The club-bearer.　　　　[2] It is a word used by Dryden.

Evæmon's noble offspring next appear'd
Eurypylus ; Andræmon's son the next　　　　　　195
Thoas ; and last, Ulysses, glorious Chief.
All these stood ready to engage in arms
With warlike Hector, when the ancient King,
Gerenian Nestor, thus his speech resumed.
　　Now cast the lot for all.　Who wins the chance　　200
Shall yield Achaia service, and himself
Serve also, if successful he escape
This brunt of hostile hardiment severe.
　　So Nestor.　They, inscribing each his lot,
Into the helmet cast it of the son　　　　　　205
Of Atreus, Agamemnon.　Then the host
Pray'd all, their hands uplifting, and with eyes
To the wide heavens directed, many said—
　　Eternal sire ! choose Ajax, or the son
Of Tydeus, or the King himself[3] who sways　　210
The sceptre in Mycenæ wealth-renown'd !
　　Such prayer the people made ; then Nestor shook
The helmet, and forth leaped, whose most they wished,
The lot of Ajax.　Throughout all the host
To every chief and potentate of Greece,　　　　215
From right to left the herald bore the lot
By all disown'd ; but when at length he reach'd
The inscriber of the lot, who cast it in,
Illustrious Ajax, in his open palm
The herald placed it, standing at his side.　　220
He, conscious, with heroic joy the lot
Cast at his foot, and thus exclaim'd aloud.
　　My friends ! the lot is mine, and my own heart
Rejoices also ; for I nothing doubt
That noble Hector shall be foil'd by me.　　225
But while I put mine armour on, pray all
In silence to the King Saturnian Jove,
Lest, while ye pray, the Trojans overhear.
Or pray aloud, for whom have we to dread ?
No man shall my firm standing by his strength　　230
Unsettle, or for ignorance of mine
Me vanquish, who, I hope, brought forth and train'd
In Salamis, have, now, not much to learn.

　　　　　　　[3] Agamemnon.

He ended.　They with heaven-directed eyes
The King in prayer address'd, Saturnian Jove.　235
　　Jove! glorious father! who from Ida's height
Controulest all below, let Ajax prove
Victorious, make the honour all his own!
Or, if not less than Ajax, Hector share
Thy love and thy regard, divide the prize　240
Of glory, and let each　achieve renown!
　　Then Ajax put his radiant armour on,
And, arm'd complete, rush'd forward.　As huge Mars
To battle moves the sons of men between
Whom Jove with heart-devouring thirst inspires　245
Of war, so moved huge Ajax to the fight,
Tower of the Greeks, dilating with a smile
His martial features terrible; on feet,
Firm-planted, to the combat he advanced
Stride after stride, and shook his quivering spear.　250
Him viewing, Argos' universal host
Exulted, while a panic loosed the knees
Of every Trojan; even Hector's heart
Beat double, but escape for him remain'd
None now, or to retreat into his ranks　255
Again, from whom himself had challenged forth.
Ajax advancing like a tower his shield
Sevenfold, approach'd.　It was the labour'd work
Of Tychius, armourer of matchless skill,
Who dwelt in Hyla; coated with the hides　260
Of seven high-pamper'd bulls that shield he framed
For Ajax, and the disk plated with brass.
Advancing it before his breast, the son
Of Telamon approach'd the Trojan Chief,
And face to face, him threatening, thus began.　265
　　Now, Hector, prove, by me alone opposed,
What Chiefs the Danaï can furnish forth
In absence of the lion-hearted prince
Achilles, breaker of the ranks of war.
He, in his billow-cleaving barks incensed　270
Against our leader Agamemnon, lies;
But warriors of my measure, who may serve
To cope with thee, we want not; numerous such
Are found amongst us.　But begin to fight.
　　s. c.—7.　　　　　　　　　　　　　　K

To whom majestic Hector fierce in arms.            275
Ajax! heroic leader of the Greeks!
Offspring of Telamon! essay not me
With words to terrify, as I were boy
Or girl unskill'd in war; I am a man
Well exercised in battle, who have shed            280
The blood of many a warrior, and have learn'd,
From hand to hand shifting my shield, to fight
Unwearied; I can make a sport of war,
In standing fight adjusting all my steps
To martial measures sweet, or vaulting light       285
Into my chariot, thence can urge the foe.
Yet in contention with a Chief like thee
I will employ no stratagem, or seek
To smite thee privily, but with a stroke
(If I may reach thee) visible to all.              290
    So saying, he shook, then hurl'd his massy spear
At Ajax, and his broad shield sevenfold
On its eighth surface of resplendent brass
Smote full; six hides the unblunted weapon pierced,
But in the seventh stood rooted.   Ajax, next,     295
Heroic chief, hurl'd his long-shadow'd spear
And struck the oval shield of Priam's son.
Through his bright disk the weapon tempest-driven
Glided, and in his hauberk-rings infixt
At his soft flank, ripp'd wide his vest within.    300
Inclined oblique he 'scaped the dreadful doom.
Then each from other's shield his massy spear
Recovering quick, like lions hunger-pinch'd
Or wild boars irresistible in force,
They fell to close encounter.   Priam's son        305
The shield of Ajax at its centre smote,
But fail'd to pierce it, for he bent his point.
Sprang Ajax then, and meeting full the targe
Of Hector, shock'd him; through it and beyond
He urged the weapon with its sliding edge          310
Athwart his neck, and blood was seen to start.
But still, for no such cause, from battle ceased
Crest-tossing Hector, but retiring, seized
An huge stone angled sharp and black with age
That on the champaign lay. The bull-hide guard     315

Sevenfold of Ajax with that stone he smote
Full on its centre; sang the circling brass.
Then Ajax far an heavier stone upheaved;
He whirled it, and with might immeasurable
Dismiss'd the mass, which with a mill-stone weight          320
Sank through the shield of Hector, and his knees
Disabled; with his shield supine he fell,
But by Apollo raised, stood soon again.
And now, with swords they had each other hewn,
Had not the messengers of Gods and men                     325
The heralds wise, Idæus on the part
Of Ilium, and Talthybius for the Greeks,
Advancing interposed.   His sceptre each
Between them held, and thus Idæus spake.
    My children, cease! prolong not still the fight.        330
Ye both are dear to cloud-assembler Jove,
Both valiant, and all know it.   But the night
Hath fallen, and night's command must be obeyed.
    To him the son of Telamon replied.
Idæus! bid thy master speak as thou.                        335
He is the challenger.   If such his choice,
Mine differs not; I wait but to comply.
    Him answer'd then heroic Hector huge.
Since, Ajax, the immortal powers on thee
Have bulk pre-eminent and strength bestow'd,                340
With such address in battle, that the host
Of Greece hath not thine equal at the spear,
Now let the combat cease.   We shall not want
More fair occasion; on some future day
We will not part till all-disposing heaven                  345
Shall give thee victory, or shall make her mine.
But night hath fallen, and night must be obey'd,
That thou may'st gratify with thy return
The Achaians, and especially thy friends
And thy own countrymen.   I go, no less                     350
To exhilarate in Priam's royal town
Men and robed matrons, who shall seek the Gods
For me, with pious ceremonial due.
But come.   We will exchange, or ere we part,
Some princely gift, that Greece and Troy may say            355
  Hereafter, with soul-wasting rage they fought,

                                          K 2

But parted with the gentleness of friends.
  So saying, he with its sheath and belt a sword
Presented bright-emboss'd, and a bright belt
Purpureal [4] took from Ajax in return.          360
Thus separated, one  the Grecians sought,
And one the Trojans; they when him they saw
From the unconquer'd hands return'd alive
Of Ajax, with delight their Chief received,
And to the city led him, double joy          365
Conceiving all at his unhoped escape.
On the other side, the Grecians brazen-mail'd
To noble Agamemnon introduced
Exulting Ajax, and the King of men
In honour of the conqueror slew an ox         370
Of the fifth year to Jove omnipotent.
Him flaying first, they carved him next and spread
The whole abroad, then, scoring deep the flesh,
They pierced it with the spits, and from the spits,
(Once roasted well) withdrew it all again.         375
Their labour thus accomplish'd, and the board
Furnish'd with plenteous cheer they feasted all
Till all were satisfied; nor Ajax miss'd
The conqueror's meed, to whom the hero-king
Wide-ruling Agamemnon, gave the chine         380
Perpetual, [5] his distinguish'd portion due.
The calls of hunger and of thirst at length
Both well sufficed, thus, foremost of them all
The ancient Nestor, whose advice had oft
Proved salutary, prudent thus began.         385
  Chiefs of Achaia, and thou, chief of all,
Great Agamemnon! Many of our host
Lie slain, whose blood sprinkles, in battle shed,
The banks of smooth Scamander, and their souls
Have journey'd down into the realms of death.        390

[4] This word I have taken leave to coin. The Latins have both substantive and adjective. *Purpura—Purpureus.* We make purple serve both uses; but it seems a poverty to which we have no need to submit, at least in poetry.      [5] The word is here used in the Latin sense of it. Virgil, describing the entertainment given by Evander to the Trojans, says that he regaled them

     Perpetui *tergo bovis et lustralibus extis.*  ÆN. viii.
It means, the whole.

To-morrow, therefore, let the battle pause
As need requires, and at the peep of day
With mules and oxen, wheel ye from all parts
The dead, that we may burn them near the fleet.
So, home to Greece returning, will we give       395
The fathers' ashes to the children's care.
Accumulating next, the pile around,
One common tomb for all, with brisk dispatch
We will upbuild for more secure defence
Of us and of our fleet, strong towers and tall       400
Adjoining to the tomb, and every tower
Shall have its ponderous gate, commodious pass
Affording to the mounted charioteer.
And last, without those towers and at their foot,
Dig we a trench, which compassing around       405
Our camp, both steeds and warriors shall exclude,
And all fierce inroad of the haughty foe.
     So counsell'd he, whom every Chief approved.
In Troy meantime, at Priam's gate beside
The lofty citadel, debate began       410
The assembled senators between, confused,
Clamorous, and with furious heat pursued.
When them Antenor, prudent, thus bespake.
     Ye Trojans, Dardans, and allies of Troy,
My counsel hear! Delay not. Instant yield       415
To the Atridæ, hence to be convey'd,
Helen of Greece with all that is her own.
For charged with violated oaths we fight,
And hope I none conceive that aught by us
Design'd shall prosper, unless so be done.       420
     He spake and sat; when from his seat arose
Paris, fair Helen's noble paramour,
Who thus with speech impassion'd quick replied.
     Antenor! me thy counsel hath not pleased;
Thou could'st have framed far better; but if this       425
Be thy deliberate judgement, then the Gods
Make thy deliberate judgement nothing worth.
But I will speak myself. Ye Chiefs of Troy,
I tell you plain. I will not yield my spouse.
But all her treasures to our house convey'd       430
From Argos, those will I resign, and add

Still other compensation from my own.
   Thus Paris said and sat; when like the Gods
Themselves in wisdom, from his seat uprose
Dardanian Priam, who them thus address'd.                    435
   Trojans, Dardanians, and allies of Troy!
I shall declare my sentence; hear ye me.
Now let the legions, as at other times,
Take due refreshment; let the watch be set,
And keep ye vigilant guard.   At early dawn                  440
We will dispatch Idæus to the fleet,
Who shall inform the Atridæ of this last
Resolve of Paris, author of the war.
Discreet Idæus also shall propose
A respite (if the Atridæ so incline)                         445
From war's dread clamour, while we burn the dead.
Then will we clash again, till heaven at length
Shall part us, and the doubtful strife decide.
   He ceased, whose voice the assembly pleased, obey'd.
Then, troop by troop, the army took repast,                  450
And at the dawn Idæus sought the fleet;
He found the Danaï, servants of Mars,
Beside the stern of Agamemnon's ship
Consulting; and amid the assembled Chiefs
Arrived, with utterance clear them thus address'd.           455
   Ye sons of Atreus, and ye Chiefs, the flower
Of all Achaia! Priam and the Chiefs
Of Ilium, bade me to your ear impart
(If chance such embassy might please your ear)
The mind of Paris, author of the war.                        460
The treasures which on board his ships he brought
From Argos home, (oh, had he perish'd first!)
He yields them with addition from his own.
Not so the consort of the glorious prince
Brave Menelaus; her, (although in Troy                       465
All counsel otherwise,) he still detains.
Thus too I have in charge.   Are ye inclined
That the dread-sounding clamours of the field
Be caused to cease, till we shall burn the dead?
Then will we clash again, 'till heaven at length             470
Shall part us, and the doubtful strife decide.
   So spake Idæus, and all silent sat;

Till at the last brave Diomede replied.
   No.    We will none of Paris' treasures now,
Nor even Helen's self.    A child may see           475
Destruction winging swift her course to Troy.
   He said.    The admiring Greeks with loud applause
All praised the speech of warlike Diomede,
And answer thus the King of men return'd.
   Idæus! thou hast witness'd the resolve         480
Of the Achaian Chiefs, whose choice is mine.
But for the slain, I shall not envy them
A funeral pile; the spirit fled, delay
Suits not.    Last rites cannot too soon be paid.
Burn them.    And let high-thundering Jove attest     485
Himself mine oath, that war shall cease the while.
   So saying, he to all the Gods upraised
His sceptre, and Idæus homeward sped
To sacred Ilium.    The Dardanians there
And Trojans, all assembled, his return        490
Expected anxious.    He amid them told
Distinct his errand, when, at once dissolved,
The whole assembly rose, these to collect
The scatter'd bodies, those to gather wood;
While on the other side, the Greeks arose       495
As sudden, and all issuing from the fleet
Sought fuel, some, and, some, the scatter'd dead.
   Now from the gently-swelling flood profound
The sun arising, with his earliest rays
In his ascent to heaven smote on the fields,      500
When Greeks and Trojans met.    Scarce could the slain
Be clear distinguish'd, but they cleansed from each
His clotted gore with water, and warm tears
Distilling copious, heaved them to the wains.
But wailing none was heard, for such command     505
Had Priam issued; therefore heaping high
The bodies, silent and with sorrowing hearts
They burn'd them, and to sacred Troy return'd.
The Grecians also, on the funeral pile
The bodies heaping sad, burn'd them with fire     510
Together, and return'd into the fleet.
   Then, ere the peep of dawn, and while the veil
Of night, though thinner, still o'erhung the earth,

Achaians, chosen from the rest, the pile
Encompass'd.   With a tomb (one tomb for all)                    515
They crown'd the spot adust, and to the tomb
(For safety of their fleet and of themselves)
Strong fortress added of high wall and tower,
With solid gates affording egress thence
Commodious to the mounted charioteer ;                          520
Deep foss and broad they also dug without,
And planted it with piles.   So toil'd the Greeks.
    The Gods, that mighty labour, from beside
The Thunderer's throne with admiration view'd,
When Neptune, shaker of the shores began.                       525
    Eternal father ! is there on the face
Of all the boundless earth one mortal man
Who will, in times to come, consult with heaven ?
See'st thou yon height of wall, and yon deep trench
With which  the Grecians have their fleet inclosed,             530
And, careless of our blessing, hecatomb
Or invocation have presented none ?
Far as the day-spring shoots herself abroad,
So far the glory of this work shall spread,
While Phœbus and myself, who, toiling hard,                     535
Built walls for King Laomedon, shall see
Forgotten all the labour of our hands.
    To whom, indignant, thus high-thundering Jove.
Oh thou, who shakest the solid earth at will,
What hast thou spoken ? An inferior power,                      540
A god of less sufficiency than thou,
Might be allowed some fear from such a cause.
Fear not.   Where'er the morning shoots her beams,
Thy glory shall be known ; and when the Greeks
Shall seek their country through the waves again,               545
Then break this bulwark down, submerge it whole,
And spreading deep with sand the spacious shore
As at the first, leave not a trace behind.
    Such conference held the Gods ; and now the sun
Went down, and, that great work perform'd, the Greeks     550
From tent to tent slaughter'd the fatted ox
And ate their evening cheer.   Meantime arrived
Large fleet with Lemnian wine ; Euneus, son
Of Jason and Hypsipile, that fleet

From Lemnos freighted, and had stow'd on board     555
A thousand measures from the rest apart
For the Atridæ; but the host at large
By traffic were supplied; some barter'd brass,
Others bright steel; some purchased wine with hides,
These with their cattle, with their captives those,     560
And the whole host prepared a glad regale.
All night the Grecians feasted, and the host
Of Ilium, and all night deep-planning Jove
Portended dire calamities to both,
Thundering tremendous!—Pale was every cheek;     565
Each pour'd his goblet on the ground, nor dared
The hardiest drink, 'till he had first perform'd
Libation meet to the Saturnian King
Omnipotent; then, all retiring, sought
Their couches, and partook the gift of sleep.     570

# BOOK VIII.

---

### ARGUMENT.

Jove calls a council, in which he forbids all interference of the Gods between the Greeks and Trojans. He repairs to Ida, where having consulted the scales of destiny, he directs his lightning against the Grecians. Nestor is endangered by the death of one of his horses. Diomede delivers him. In the chariot of Diomede they both hasten to engage Hector, whose charioteer is slain by Diomede. Jupiter again interposes by his thunders, and the whole Grecian host, discomfited, is obliged to seek refuge within the rampart. Diomede, with others, at sight of a favourable omen sent from Jove in answer to Agamemnon's prayer, sallies. Teucer performs great exploits, but is disabled by Hector. Juno and Pallas set forth from Olympus in aid of the Grecians, but are stopped by Jupiter, who reascends from Ida, and in heaven foretells the distresses which await the Grecians.

Hector takes measures for the security of Troy during the night, and prepares his host for an assault to be made on the Grecian camp in the morning.

THE saffron-mantled morning now was spread
O'er all the nations, when the Thunderer Jove,
On the deep-fork'd Olympian topmost height
Convened the Gods in council, amid whom
He spake himself; they all attentive heard.          5
   Gods! Goddesses! Inhabitants of heaven!
Attend; I make my secret purpose known.
Let neither God nor Goddess interpose
My counsel to rescind, but with one heart
Approve it that it reach, at once, its end.          10
Whom I shall mark soever from the rest
Withdrawn, that he may Greeks or Trojans aid,
Disgrace shall find him; shamefully chastised
He shall return to the Olympian heights,
Or I will hurl him deep into the gulfs          15
Of gloomy Tartarus, where Hell shuts fast
Her iron gates, and spreads her brazen floor,
As far below the shades, as earth from heaven.

There shall he learn how far I pass in might
All others; which if ye incline to doubt,                         20
Now prove me.   Let ye down the golden chain
From heaven, and at its nether links pull all
Both Goddesses and Gods.   But me your King,
Supreme in wisdom, ye shall never draw
To earth from heaven, toil adverse as ye may.          25
Yet I, when once I shall be pleased to pull,
The earth itself, itself the sea, and you
Will lift with ease together, and will wind
The chain around the spiry summit sharp
Of the Olympian, that all things upheaved          30
Shall hang in the mid heaven.   So far do I,
Compared with all who live, transcend them all.
     He ended, and the Gods long time amazed
Sat silent, for with awful tone he spake;
But at the last Pallas blue-eyed began.          35
     Father! Saturnian Jove! of Kings supreme!
We know thy force resistless; but our hearts
Feel not the less, when we behold the Greeks
Exhausting all the sorrows of their lot.
If thou command, we, doubtless, will abstain          40
From battle, yet such counsel to the Greeks
Suggesting still, as may in part effect
Their safety, lest thy wrath consume them all.
     To whom with smiles answer'd cloud-gatherer Jove.
Fear not, my child! stern as my accent was,          45
I forced a frown—no more.   For in mine heart
Nought feel I but benevolence to thee.
     He said, and to his chariot join'd his steeds
Swift, brazen-hoof'd, and maned with wavy gold;
He put on golden raiment, his bright scourge          50
Of gold receiving rose into his seat,
And lash'd his steeds; they not unwilling flew
Midway the earth between and starry heaven.
To spring-fed Ida, mother of wild beasts,
He came, where stands in Gargarus his shrine          55
Breathing fresh incense! there the Sire of all
Arriving, loosed his coursers, and around
Involving them in gather'd clouds opaque,
Sat on the mountain's head, in his own might
Exulting, with the towers of Ilium all          60

Beneath his eye, and the whole fleet of Greece.
  In all their tents, meantime, Achaia's sons
Took short refreshment, and for fight prepared.
On the other side, though fewer, yet constrain'd
By strong necessity, throughout all Troy,            65
In the defence of children and of wives
Ardent, the Trojans panted for the field.
Wide flew the city-gates; forth rush'd to war
Horsemen and foot, and tumult wild arose.
They met, they clash'd; loud was the din of spears   70
And bucklers on their bosoms brazen-mail'd
Encountering, shields in opposition firm
Met bossy shields, and tumult wild arose [1].
  There many a shout and many a dying groan
Were heard, the slayer and the maim'd aloud          75
Clamouring, and the earth was drench'd with blood.
'Till sacred morn had brighten'd into noon,
The vollied weapons on both sides their task
Perform'd effectual, and the people fell.
But when the sun had climb'd the middle skies,       80
The Sire of all then took his golden scales;
Doom against doom he weigh'd, the eternal fates
In counterpoise, of Trojans and of Greeks.
He raised the beam; low sank the heavier lot
Of the Achaians; the Achaian doom                    85
Subsided, and the Trojan struck the skies.
  Then roar'd his thunders from the summit hurl'd
Of Ida, and his vivid lightnings flew
Into Achaia's host.   They at the sight
Astonish'd stood; fear whiten'd every cheek.         90
Idomeneus dared not himself abide
That shock, nor Agamemnon stood, nor stood
The heroes Ajax, ministers of Mars.
Gerenian Nestor, guardian of the Greeks,
Alone fled not, nor he by choice remain'd,           95
But by his steed retarded, which the mate
Of beauteous Helen, Paris, with a shaft
Had stricken where the forelock grows, a part
Of all most mortal.   Tortured by the wound
Erect he rose, the arrow in his brain,              100
And writhing furious, scared his fellow steeds.

[1] In the repetition of this expression, the translator follows the original.

Meantime, while, strenuous, with his falchion's edge
The hoary warrior stood slashing the reins,
Through multitudes of fierce pursuers borne
On rapid wheels, the dauntless charioteer,          105
Approach'd him, Hector.   Then, past hope, had died
The ancient King, but Diomede discern'd
His peril imminent, and with a voice
Like thunder, called Ulysses to his aid.
 Laertes' noble son, for wiles renown'd!          110
Art thou too fugitive, and turn'st thy back
Like the base multitude?   Ah! fear a lance
Implanted ignominious in thy spine.
Stop—Nestor dies.   Fell Hector is at hand.
 So shouted Diomede, whose summons loud,          115
Ulysses yet heard not, but, passing, flew
With headlong haste to the Achaian fleet.
Then, Diomede, unaided as he was,
Rush'd ardent to the vaw-ward, and before
The steeds of the Neleian sovereign old          120
Standing, in accents wing'd, him thus address'd.
 Old Chief! these youthful warriors are too brisk
For thee, press'd also by encroaching age.
Thy servant too is feeble, and thy steeds
Are tardy.   Mount my chariot.   Thou shalt see          125
With what rapidity the steeds of Troy,
Pursuing or retreating, scour the field.
I took them from that terror of his foes,
Æneas.   Thine to our attendants leave,
While these against the warlike powers of Troy          130
We push direct; that Hector's self may know
If my spear rage not furious as his own.
 He said, nor the Gerenian Chief refused.
Thenceforth their servants, Sthenelus and good
Eurymedon, took charge of Nestor's steeds,          135
And they the chariot of Tydides both
Ascended; Nestor seized the reins, plied well
The scourge, and soon they met.   Tydides hurl'd
At Hector first, while rapid he advanced;
But missing Hector, wounded in the breast          140
Eniopeus his charioteer, the son
Of brave Thebæus, managing the steeds.

He fell ; his fiery coursers, at the sound
Startled, recoil'd, and where he fell he died.
Deep sorrow for his charioteer o'erwhelm'd                    145
The mind of Hector ; yet, although he mourn'd
He left him, and another sought as brave.
Nor wanted long his steeds a charioteer,
For finding soon the son of Iphitus,
Bold Archeptolemus, he bade him mount                         150
His chariot, and the reins gave to his hand.
Then deeds of bloodiest note should have ensued,
Penn'd had the Trojans been, as lambs, in Troy,
But for quick succour of the sire of all.
Thundering, he downward hurl'd his candent bolt              155
To the horse-feet of Diomede ; dire fumed
The flaming sulphur, and both horses drove
Under the axle, belly to the ground.
Forth flew the splendid reins from Nestor's hand,
And thus to Diomede, appall'd, he spake.                     160
    Back to the fleet, Tydides ! Can'st not see
That Jove ordains not, now, the victory thine ?
The son of Saturn glorifies to-day
This Trojan, and, if such his will, can make
The morrow ours ; but vain it is to thwart                   165
The mind of Jove, for he is Lord of all.
    To him the valiant Diomede replied.
Thou hast well said, old warrior ! but the pang
That wrings my soul, is this.   The public ear
In Ilium shall from Hector's lips be told—                   170
I drove Tydides—fearing me he fled.
So shall he vaunt, and may the earth her jaws
That moment opening swallow me alive !
    Him answer'd the Gerenian warrior old.
What saith the son of Tydeus, glorious Chief?                175
Should Hector so traduce thee as to call
Thee base and timid, neither Trojan him
Nor Dardan would believe, nor yet the wives
Of numerous shielded warriors brave of Troy,
Widow'd by thy unconquerable arm.                            180
    So saying, he through the fugitives his steeds
Turn'd swift to flight.   Then Hector and his host
With clamour infinite their darts woe-wing'd
Shower'd after them, and Hector, mighty Chief

Majestic, from afar, thus call'd aloud.　　　　185
　Tydides! thee the Danaï swift-horsed
Were wont to grace with a superior seat,
The mess of honour, and the brimming cup,
But now will mock thee.　Thou art woman now.
Go, timorous girl! Thou never shalt behold　　　190
Me flying, climb our battlements, or lead
Our women captive.　I will slay thee first.
　He ceased.　Then Diomede in dread suspense
Thrice purposed, turning, to withstand the foe,
And thrice in thunder from the mountain-top　　195
Jove gave the signal of success to Troy,
When Hector thus the Trojans hail'd aloud.
　Trojans and Lycians, and close-warring sons
Of Dardanus, oh summon all your might,
Now, now be men! I know that from his heart　　200
Saturnian Jove glory and bright success
For me prepares, but havoc for the Greeks.
Fools! they shall find this wall which they have raised
Too weak to check my course, a feeble guard
Contemptible ; · such also is the trench ;　　　205
My steeds shall slight it with an easy leap.
But when ye see me in their fleet arrived,
Remember fire.　Then bring me flaming brands
That I may burn their galleys, and themselves
Slaughter beside them, struggling in the smoke.　210
　He spake, and thus encouraged next his steeds.
Xanthus! Podargus! and ye generous pair
Æthon and glossy Lampus! now requite
Mine, and the bounty of Andromache,
Far-famed Eëtion's daughter ; she your bowl　　215
With corn fresh-flavour'd and with wine full oft
Hath mingled, your refreshment seeking first
Ere mine, who have a youthful husband's claim.
Now follow! now be swift ; that we may seize
The shield of Nestor, bruited to the skies　　　220
As golden all, trappings and disk alike.
Now from the shoulders of the equestrian Chief
Tydides tear we off his splendid mail,
The work of Vulcan.　May we take but these,
I have good hope that, ere this night be spent,　225
The Greeks shall climb their galleys and away.

So vaunted he, but Juno with disdain
His proud boast heard, and shuddering in her throne,
Rock'd the Olympian; turning then toward
The Ocean's mighty sovereign, thus she spake.          230
    Alas! earth-shaking sovereign of the waves,
Feel'st thou no pity of the perishing Greeks?
Yet Greece, in Helice, with gifts nor few
Nor sordid, and in Ægæ, honours thee,
Whom therefore thou shouldst prosper.   Would we all   235
Who favour Greece associate to repulse
The Trojans, and to check loud-thundering Jove,
On Ida seated he might lour alone.
    To whom the sovereign, shaker of the shores,
Indignant.   Juno! rash in speech! what word          240
Hath 'scaped thy lips? never, with my consent,
Shall we, the powers subordinate, in arms
With Jove contend.   He far excels us all.
    So they.   Meantime, the trench and wall between[2],
The narrow interval with steeds was fill'd            245
Close throng'd and shielded warriors.   There immew'd
By Priameian Hector, fierce as Mars,
They stood, for Hector had the help of Jove.
And now with blazing fire their gallant barks
He had consumed, but Juno moved the mind              250
Of Agamemnon, vigilant himself,
To exhortation of Achaia's host.
Through camp and fleet the monarch took his way,
And, his wide robe imperial in his hand,
High on Ulysses' huge black galley stood,             255
The central ship conspicuous; thence his voice
Might reach the most remote of all the line
At each extreme, where Ajax had his tent
Pitch'd, and Achilles, fearless of surprise.
Thence, with loud voice, the Grecians thus he hail'd.  260
    Oh shame to Greece! Warriors in shew alone!
Where is your boasted prowess? Ye profess'd
Vain-glorious erst in Lemnos, while ye fed

---

[2] None daring to keep the field, and all striving to enter the gates together, they obstructed their own passage, and were, of course, compelled
into the narrow interval between the foss and rampart.
    But there are different opinions about the space intended.  See Vil-
loisson.

Plenteously on the flesh of beeves full-grown,
And crown'd your beakers high, that ye would face 265
Each man a hundred Trojans in the field—
Ay, twice a hundred,—yet are all too few·
To face one Hector now; nor doubt I aught
But he shall soon fire the whole fleet of Greece.
Jove! Father! what great sovereign ever felt 270
Thy frowns as I? Whom hast thou shamed as me?·
Yet I neglected not, through all the course
Of our disasterous voyage (in the hope
That we should vanquish Troy) thy sacred rites,
But where I found thine altar, piled it high 275
With fat and flesh of bulls, on every shore.
But oh, vouchsafe to us, that we at least
Ourselves, deliver'd, may escape the sword,
Nor let their foes thus tread the Grecians down!
 He said. The eternal father pitying saw 280
His tears, and for the monarch's sake preserved
The people. Instant, surest of all signs,
He sent his eagle; in his pounces strong
A fawn he bore, fruit of the nimble hind,
Which fast beside the beauteous altar raised 285
To Panomphæan[3] Jove sudden he dropp'd.
 They, conscious, soon, that sent from Jove he came,
More ardent sprang to fight. Then none of all
Those numerous Chiefs could boast that he outstripp'd
Tydides, urging forth beyond the foss 290
His rapid steeds, and rushing to the war.
He, foremost far, a Trojan slew, the son
Of Phradmon, Ageläus; as he turn'd
His steeds to flight, him turning with his spear
Through back and bosom Diomede transpierced, 295
And with loud clangor of his arms he fell.
Then, royal Agamemnon pass'd the trench
And Menelaus; either Ajax, then,
Clad with fresh prowess both; them follow'd, next,
Idomeneus, with his heroic friend 300
In battle dread as homicidal Mars,
Meriones; Evæmon's son renown'd
Succeeded, bold Eurypylus; and ninth
Teucer, wide-straining his impatient bow.

  [3] To Jove the source of all oracular information.

He under covert fought of the broad shield          305
Of Telamonian Ajax; Ajax high
Upraised his shield; the hero from beneath
Took aim, and whom his arrow struck, he fell;
Then close as to his mother's side a child
For safety creeps, Teucer to Ajax' side          310
Retired, and Ajax shielded him again.
Whom then slew Teucer first, illustrious Chief?
Orsilochus, and Ophelestes, first,
And Ormenus he slew, then Dætor died,
Chromius and Lycophontes brave in fight          315
With Amopaon Polyæmon's son,
And Melanippus.   These, together heap'd,
All fell by Teucer on the plain of Troy.
The Trojan ranks thinn'd by his mighty bow
The King of armies Agamemnon saw          320
Well-pleased, and him approaching, thus began.
    Brave Telamonian Teucer, oh, my friend,
Thus shoot, that light may visit once again
The Danaï, and Telamon rejoice!
Thee Telamon within his own abode          325
Rear'd although spurious; mount him, in return,
Although remote, on glory's heights again.
I tell thee, and the effect shall follow sure,
Let but the Thunderer and Minerva grant
The pillage of fair Ilium to the Greeks,          330
And I will give to thy victorious hand,
After my own, the noblest recompense,
A tripod or a chariot with its steeds,
Or some fair captive to partake thy bed.
    To whom the generous Teucer thus replied.          335
Atrides! glorious monarch! wherefore me
Exhortest thou to battle? who myself
Glow with sufficient ardour, and such strength
As heaven affords me spare not to employ.
Since first we drove them back, with watchful eye          340
Their warriors I have mark'd; eight shafts my bow
Hath sent long-barb'd, and every shaft, well-aim'd,
The body of some Trojan youth robust
Hath pierced, but still yon ravening wolf escapes.
    He said, and from the nerve another shaft          345
Impatient sent at Hector; but it flew

Devious, and brave Corgythion struck instead.
Him beautiful Castianira, brought
By Priam from Æsyma, nymph of form
Celestial, to the King of Ilium bore.                350
As in the garden, with the weight surcharged
Of its own fruit, and drench'd by vernal rains
The poppy falls oblique, so he his head
Hung languid, by his helmet's weight depress'd.
Then Teucer yet an arrow from the nerve            355
Dispatch'd at Hector, with impatience fired
To pierce him; but again his weapon err'd
Turn'd by Apollo, and the bosom struck
Of Archeptolemus, his rapid steeds
To battle urging, Hector's charioteer.             360
He fell, his fiery coursers at the sound
Recoil'd, and lifeless where he fell he lay.
Deep sorrow for his charioteer the mind
O'erwhelm'd of Hector, yet he left the slain,
And seeing his own brother nigh at hand,           365
Cebriones, him summon'd to the reins,
Who with alacrity that charge received.
Then Hector, leaping with a dreadful shout
From his resplendent chariot, grasp'd a stone,
And rush'd on Teucer, vengeance in his heart.      370
Teucer had newly fitted to the nerve
An arrow keen selected from the rest,
And warlike Hector, while he stood the cord
Retracting, smote him with that rugged rock
Just where the key-bone interposed divides         375
The neck and bosom, a most mortal part.
It snapp'd the bow-string, and with numbing force
Struck dead his hand; low on his knees he dropp'd,
And from his opening grasp let fall the bow.
Then not unmindful of a brother fallen             380
Was Ajax, but, advancing rapid, stalk'd
Around him, and his broad shield interposed,
Till brave Alaster and Mecisteus, son
Of Echius, friends of Teucer, from the earth
Upraised and bore him groaning to the fleet.       385
And now again fresh force Olympian Jove
Gave to the Trojans; right toward the foss
They drove the Greeks, while Hector in the van

Advanced, death menacing in every look.
    As some fleet hound close-threatening flank or haunch  390
Of boar or lion, oft as he his head
Turns flying, marks him with a steadfast eye,
So Hector chased the Grecians, slaying still
The hindmost of the scatter'd multitude.
But when, at length, both piles and hollow foss  395
They had surmounted, and no few had fallen
By Trojan hands, within their fleet they stood
Imprison'd, calling each to each, and prayer
With lifted hands, loud offering to the Gods.
With Gorgon looks, meantime, and eyes of Mars,  400
Hector impetuous his mane-tossing steeds
From side to side before the rampart drove,
When white-arm'd Juno pitying the Greeks,
In accents wing'd her speech to Pallas turn'd.
    Alas, Jove's daughter! shall not we at least  405
In this extremity of their distress
Care for the Grecians by the fatal force
Of this one Chief destroy'd? I can endure
The rage of Priameïan Hector now
No longer; such dire mischiefs he hath wrought.  410
    Whom answer'd thus Pallas, cærulean-eyed.
—And Hector had himself long since his life
Resign'd and rage together, by the Greeks
Slain under Ilium's walls, but Jove, my sire,
Mad counsels executing and perverse,  415
Me counterworks in all that I attempt,
Nor aught remembers how I saved ofttimes
His son enjoin'd full many a task severe
By King Eurystheus; to the Gods he wept,
And me Jove sent in haste to his relief.  420
But had I then foreseen what now I know,
When through the adamantine gates he pass'd
To bind the dog of hell, by the deep floods
Hemm'd in of Styx, he had return'd no more.
But Thetis wins him now; her will prevails,  425
And mine he hates; for she hath kiss'd his knees
And grasp'd his beard, and him in prayer implored
That he would honour her heroic son
Achilles, city-waster prince renown'd.
'Tis well,—the day shall come when Jove again  430

Shall call me darling, and his blue-eyed maid
As heretofore ;—but thou thy steeds prepare,
While I, my father's mansion entering, arm
For battle.   I would learn by trial sure,
If Hector Priam's offspring famed in fight      435
(Ourselves appearing in the walks of war)
Will greet us gladly.   Doubtless at the fleet
Some Trojan also, shall to dogs resign
His flesh for food, and to the fowls of heaven.
    So counsell'd Pallas, nor the daughter dread     440
Of mighty Saturn, Juno, disapproved,
But busily and with dispatch prepared
The trappings of her coursers golden-rein'd.
Meantime, Minerva progeny of Jove,
On the adamantine floor of his abode      445
Let fall profuse her variegated robe,
Labour of her own hands.   She first put on
The corslet of the cloud assembler God,
Then arm'd her for the field of woe, complete.
Mounting the fiery chariot, next she seized     450
Her ponderous spear, huge, irresistible,
With which Jove's aweful daughter levels ranks
Of heroes against whom her anger burns.
Juno with lifted lash urged on the steeds.
At their approach, spontaneous roar'd the wide-     455
Unfolding gates of heaven; the heavenly gates
Kept by the watchful Hours, to whom the charge
Of the Olympian summit appertains,
And of the boundless ether, back to roll,
And to replace the cloudy barrier dense.     460
Spurr'd through the portal flew the rapid steeds.
Which when the Eternal Father from the heights
Of Ida saw, kindling with instant ire
To golden-pinion'd Iris thus he spake.
    Haste, Iris, turn them thither whence they came,    465
Me let them not encounter ; honour small
To them, to me, should from that strife accrue.
Tell them, and the effect shall sure ensue,
That I will smite their steeds, and they shall halt
Disabled, break their chariot, dash themselves     470
Headlong, and ten whole years shall not efface
The wounds by my avenging bolts impress'd.

So shall my blue-eyed daughter learn to dread
A father's anger; but for the offence
Of Juno, I resent it less; for she                                   475
Clashes[4] with all my counsels from of old.
   He ended: Iris with a tempest's speed
From the Idæan summit soar'd at once
To the Olympian; at the open gates
Exterior of the mountain many-valed                                  480
She stayed them, and her coming thus declared.
   Whither, and for what cause? What rage is this?
Ye may not aid the Grecians; Jove forbids;
The son of Saturn threatens, if ye force
His wrath by perseverance into act,                                  485
That he will smite your steeds, and they shall halt
Disabled, break your chariot, dash yourselves
Headlong, and ten whole years shall not efface
The wounds by his avenging bolts impress'd.
So shall his blue-eyed daughter learn to dread                       490
A father's anger; but for the offence
Of Juno, he resents it less; for she
Clashes with all his counsels from of old.
But thou, Minerva, if thou dare indeed
Lift thy vast spear against the breast of Jove,                      495
Incorrigible art and dead to shame.
   So saying, the rapid Iris disappear'd,
And thus her speech to Pallas Juno turn'd.
   Ah Pallas, progeny of Jove! henceforth
No longer, in the cause of mortal men,                               500
Contend we against Jove.  Perish or live
Grecians or Trojans as he wills; let him
Dispose the order of his own concerns,
And judge between them, as of right he may.
   So saying, she turn'd the coursers; them the Hours    505
Released, and to ambrosial mangers bound,
Then thrust their chariot to the luminous wall.
They, mingling with the Gods, on golden thrones
Dejected sat, and Jove from Ida borne
Reach'd the Olympian heights, seat of the Gods.                      510
His steeds the glorious King of Ocean loosed,
And thrust the chariot, with its veil o'erspread,

   [4] Ενικλᾳν.—The word is here metaphorical, and expresses, in its primary use, the breaking of a spear against a shield.

Into its station at the altar's side.
Then sat the Thunderer on his throne of gold
Himself, and the huge mountain shook.   Meantime          515
Juno and Pallas, seated both apart,
Spake not or question'd him.   Their mute reserve
He noticed, conscious of the cause, and said.
    Juno and Pallas, wherefore sit ye sad?
Not through fatigue by glorious fight incurr'd          520
And slaughter of the Trojans whom ye hate.
Mark now the difference.   Not the Gods combined
Should have constrained *me* back, till all my force,
Superior as it is, had fail'd, and all
My fortitude.   But ye, ere ye beheld          525
The wonders of the field, trembling retired,
And ye did well—Hear what had else befallen.
My bolts had found you both, and ye had reach'd,
In your own chariot borne, the Olympian height,
Seat of the blest Immortals, never more.          530
    He ended; Juno and Minerva heard
Low murmuring deep disgust, and side by side
Devising sat calamity to Troy.
Minerva, through displeasure against Jove,
Nought utter'd, for her bosom boil'd with rage;          535
But Juno check'd not hers, who thus replied.
    What word hath pass'd thy lips, Jove most severe!
We know thy force resistless; yet our hearts
Feel not the less when we behold the Greeks
Exhausting all the sorrows of their lot.          540
If thou command, we doubtless will abstain
From battle, yet such counsel to the Greeks
Suggesting still, as may in part affect
Their safety, lest thy wrath consume them all.
    Then answer, thus, cloud-gatherer Jove return'd.          545
Look forth, imperial Juno, if thou wilt,
To-morrow at the blush of earliest dawn,
And thou shalt see Saturn's almighty son
The Argive host destroying far and wide.
For Hector's fury shall admit no pause          550
Till he have roused Achilles, in that day
When at the ships, in perilous streights, the hosts
Shall wage fierce battle for Patroclus slain.
Such is the voice of fate.   But as for thee—

Withdraw thou to the confines of the abyss          555
Where Saturn and Iäpetus retired,
Exclusion sad endure from balmy airs
And from the light of morn, hell-girt around,
I will not call thee thence.   No.   Should thy rage
Transport thee thither, there thou may'st abide,          560
There sullen nurse thy disregarded spleen
Obstinate as thou art, and void of shame.
 He ended ; to whom Juno nought replied.
And now the radiant sun in Ocean sank,
Drawing night after him o'er all the earth ;          565
Night, undesired by Troy, but to the Greeks
Thrice welcome for its interposing gloom
 Then Hector on the river's brink fast by
The Grecian fleet, where space he found unstrew'd
With carcases, convened the Chiefs of Troy.          570
They, there dismounting, listen'd to the words
Of Hector Jove-beloved ; he grasp'd a spear
In length eleven cubits, bright its head
Of brass, and collar'd with a ring of gold.
He lean'd on it, and ardent thus began.          575
 Trojans, Dardanians, and allies of Troy !
I hoped, this evening, (every ship consumed,
And all the Grecians slain,) to have return'd
To wind-swept Ilium.   But the shades of night
Have interven'd, and to the night they owe,          580
In chief, their whole fleet's safety and their own.
Now, therefore, as the night enjoins, all take
Needful refreshment.   Your high-mettled steeds
Release, lay food before them, and in haste
Drive hither from the city fatted sheep          585
And oxen ; bring ye from your houses bread,
Make speedy purchase of heart-cheering wine,
And gather fuel plenteous ; that all night,
E'en till Aurora, daughter of the morn,
Shall look abroad, we may with many fires          590
Illume the skies ; lest even in the night,
Launching, they mount the billows and escape.
Beware that they depart not unannoy'd,
But, as he leaps on board, give each a wound
With shaft or spear, which he shall nurse at home.          595
So shall the nations fear us, and shall vex

With ruthless war Troy's gallant sons no more.
Next, let the heralds, ministers of Jove,
Loud notice issue, that the boys well-grown,
And ancients silver-hair'd on the high towers          600
Built by the Gods, keep watch ; on every hearth
In Troy, let those of the inferior sex
Make sprightly blaze, and place ye there a guard
Sufficient, lest in absence of the troops
An ambush enter, and surprise the town.                605
Act thus, ye dauntless Trojans ; the advice
Is wholesome, and shall serve the present need,
And so much for the night ; ye shall be told
The business of the morn when morn appears.
It is my prayer to Jove and to all heaven              610
(Not without hope) that I may hence expel
These dogs, whom Ilium's unpropitious fates
Have wafted hither in their sable barks.
But we will also watch this night, ourselves,
And, arming with the dawn, will at their ships         615
Give them brisk onset.   Then shall it appear
If Diomede the brave shall me compel
Back to our walls, or I, his arms blood-stain'd,
Torn from his breathless body, bear away.
To-morrow, if he dare but to abide                     620
My lance, he shall not want occasion meet
For show of valour.   But much more I judge
That the next rising sun shall see him slain
With no few friends around him.   Would to heaven!
I were as sure to 'scape the blight of age,            625
And share their honours with the Gods above,
As comes the morrow fraught with woe to Greece.
  So Hector, whom his host with loud acclaim
All praised.   Then each his sweating steeds released,
And rein'd them safely at his chariot-side.            630
And now from Troy provision large they brought,
Oxen, and sheep, with store of wine and bread,
And fuel much was gather'd.   ⁵Next, the Gods
With sacrifice they sought, and from the plain

  ⁵ The following lines, to the end of this paragraph, are a translation
of some which Barnes has here inserted from the second Alcibiades of
Plato.

Upwafted by the winds the smoke aspired          635
Savoury, but unacceptable to those
Above ; such hatred in their hearts they bore
To Priam, to the people of the brave
Spear-practised Priam, and to sacred Troy.
   Big with great purposes and proud they sat,     640
Not disarray'd, but in fair form disposed
Of even ranks , and watch'd their numerous fires.
As when around the clear bright moon, the stars
Shine in full splendour, and the winds are hush'd,
The groves, the mountain-tops, the headland-heights   645
Stand all apparent, not a vapour streaks
The boundless blue, but ether open'd wide
All glitters, and the shepherd's heart is cheer'd ;
So numerous seem'd those fires the bank between
Of Xanthus, blazing, and the fleet of Greece,      650
In prospect all of Troy ; a thousand fires,
Each watch'd by fifty warriors seated near.
The steeds beside the chariots stood, their corn
Chewing, and waiting till the golden-throned
Aurora should restore the light of day.          655

# BOOK IX.

## ARGUMENT.

By advice of Nestor, Agamemnon sends Ulysses, Phœnix, and Ajax to the tent of Achilles with proposals of reconciliation. They execute their commission, but without effect. Phœnix remains with Achilles; Ulysses and Ajax return.

So watch'd the Trojan host ; but thoughts of flight,
Companions of chill fear, from heaven infused,
Possess'd the Grecians ; every leader's heart
Bled, pierced with anguish insupportable.
As when two adverse winds blowing from Thrace, 5
Boreas and Zephyrus, the fishy Deep
Vex sudden, all around, the sable flood
High curl'd, flings forth the salt weed on the shore,
Such tempest rent the mind of every Greek.
    Forth stalk'd Atrides with heart-riving woe 10
Transfixt ; he bade his heralds call by name
Each Chief to council, but without the sound
Of proclamation ; and that task himself
Among the foremost sedulous perform'd.
The sad assembly sat ; when weeping fast 15
As some deep[1] fountain pours its rapid stream
Down from the summit of a lofty rock,
King Agamemnon in the midst arose,
And, groaning, the Achaians thus address'd.
    Friends, counsellors and leaders of the Greeks ! 20
In dire perplexity Saturnian Jove
Involves me, cruel ; he assured me erst,
And solemnly, that I should not return
Till I had wasted wall-encircled Troy ;

---

[1] In the original the word is—μελανυδρος—dark-watered,—and it is rendered—*deep*—by the best interpreters, because deep waters have a blackish appearance. Δνοφερον ὑδωρ is properly water that runs with rapidity ; water—μετα δονησεως φερομενον.—See Villoisson.

But now (ah fraudulent and foul reverse!)                25
Commands me back inglorious to the shores
Of distant Argos, with diminish'd troops.
So stands the purpose of almighty Jove,
Who many a citadel hath laid in dust,
And shall hereafter, matchless in his power.            30
Haste therefore.   My advice is, that we all
Fly with our fleet into our native land,
For wide-built Ilium shall not yet be ours.
    He ceased, and all sat silent; long the sons
Of Greece, o'erwhelm'd with sorrow, silent sat,        35
When thus, at last, bold Diomede began.
    Atrides! foremost of the Chiefs I rise
To controvert thy purpose ill-conceived,
And with such freedom as the laws, O King!
Of consultation and debate allow.                      40
Hear patient.   Thou hast been thyself the first
Who e'er reproach'd me in the public ear
As one effeminate and slow to fight ;
How truly, let both young and old decide,
The son of wily Saturn hath to thee                    45
Given, and refused ; he placed thee high in power,
Gave thee to sway the sceptre o'er us all,
But courage gave thee not, his noblest gift.
Art thou in truth persuaded that the Greeks
Are pusillanimous, as thou hast said?                  50
If thy own fears impel thee to depart,
Go thou, the way is open ; numerous ships,
Thy followers from Mycenæ, line the shore.
But we, the rest, depart not, 'till the spoil
Of Troy reward us.   Or if all incline                 55
To seek again their native home, fly all ;
Myself and Sthenelus will persevere
Till Ilium fall, for with the Gods we came.
    He ended ; all the admiring sons of Greece
With shouts the warlike Diomede extoll'd,              60
When thus equestrian Nestor next began.
    Tydides, thou art eminently brave
In fight, and all the princes of thy years
Excell'st in council.   None of all the Greeks
Shall find occasion just to blame thy speech           65

Or to gainsay; yet thou hast fallen short.
What wonder? Thou art young; and were myself
Thy father, thou should'st be my latest-born.
Yet when thy speech is to the Kings of Greece,
It is well framed and prudent.   Now attend!                70
Myself will speak, who have more years to boast
Than thou hast seen, and will so closely scan
The matter, that Atrides, our supreme,
Himself shall have no cause to censure *me*.
He is a wretch, insensible and dead                        75
To all the charities of social life,
Whose pleasure is in civil broils alone².
But night is urgent, and with night's demands
Let all comply.   Prepare we now repast,
And let the guard be stationed at the trench               80
Without the wall; the youngest shall supply
That service; next, Atrides, thou begin
(For thou art here supreme) thy proper task.
Banquet the elders; it shall not disgrace
Thy sovereignty; but shall become thee well.               85
Thy tents are filled with wine which day by day
Ships bring from Thrace; accommodation large
Hast thou, and numerous is thy menial train.
Thy many guests assembled, thou shalt hear
Our counsel, and shalt choose the best; great need         90
Have all Achaia's sons, now, of advice
Most prudent; for the foe, fast by the fleet
Hath kindled numerous fires, which who can see
Unmoved?   This night shall save us or destroy.

He spake, whom all with full consent approved.             95
Forth rush'd the guard well-arm'd! first went the son
Of Nestor, Thrasymedes, valiant Chief;
Then, sons of Mars, Ascalaphus advanced,
And brave Iälmenus; whom follow'd next
Deipyrus, Aphareus, Meriones,                             100
And Lycomedes, Creon's son renown'd.
Seven were the leaders of the guard, and each

² The observation seems made with a view to prevent such a reply
from Agamemnon to Diomede as might give birth to new dissensions,
while it reminds him indirectly of the mischiefs that had already attended
his quarrel with Achilles.

An hundred spearmen headed, young and bold.
Between the wall and trench their seat they chose,
There kindled fires, and each his food prepared.          105
    Atrides, then, to his pavilion led
The thronging Chiefs of Greece, and at his board
Regaled them; they with readiness and keen
Dispatch of hunger shared the savoury feast,
And when nor thirst remain'd nor hunger more             110
Unsated, Nestor then, arising first,
Whose counsels had been ever wisest deem'd,
Warm for the public interest, thus began.
    Atrides! glorious sovereign! King of men!
Thou art my first and last, proem and close,             115
For thou art mighty, and to thee are given
From Jove the sceptre and the laws in charge,
For the advancement of the general good.
Hence, in peculiar, both to speak and hear
Become thy duty, and the best advice,                    120
By whomsoever offer'd, to adopt
And to perform, for thou art judge alone.
I will promulge the counsel which to me
Seems wisest; such, that other Grecian none
Shall give thee better; neither is it new,               125
But I have ever held it since the day
When, most illustrious! thou wast pleased to take
By force the maid Briseïs from the tent
Of the enraged Achilles; not, in truth,
By my advice, who did dissuade thee much;                130
But thou complying with thy princely wrath,
Hast shamed an Hero whom themselves the Gods
Delight to honour, and his prize detain'st.
Yet even now contrive we, although late,
By lenient gifts liberal, and by speech                  135
Conciliatory, to assuage his ire.
    Then answer'd Agamemnon, King of men.
Old Chief! there is no falsehood in thy charge;
I have offended, and confess the wrong.
The warrior is alone an host, whom Jove                  140
Loves as he loves Achilles, for whose sake
He hath Achaia's thousands thus subdued.
But if the impulse of a wayward mind

Obeying, I have err'd, behold me, now,
Prepared to soothe him with atonement large          145
Of gifts inestimable, which by name
I will propound in presence of you all.
Seven tripods, never sullied yet with fire;
Of gold ten talents; twenty cauldrons bright;
Twelve coursers, strong, victorious in the race;          150
No man possessing prizes such as mine
Which they have won for me, shall feel the want
Of acquisitions splendid, or of gold.
Seven virtuous female captives will I give
Expert in arts domestic, Lesbians all,          155
Whom, when himself took Lesbos, I received
My chosen portion, passing womankind
In perfect loveliness of face and form.
These will I give, and will with these resign
Her whom I took, Briseïs, with an oath          160
Most solemn, that unconscious as she was
Of my embraces, such I yield her his.
All these I give him now; and if at length
The Gods vouchsafe to us to overturn
Priam's great city, let him heap his ships          165
With gold and brass, entering and choosing first
When we shall share the spoil.   Let him beside
Choose twenty from among the maids of Troy,
Helen except, loveliest of all their sex.
And if once more, the rich milk-flowing land          170
We reach of Argos, he shall there become
My son-in-law, and shall enjoy like state
With him whom I in all abundance rear,
My only son Orestes.   At my home
I have three daughters; let him hence conduct          175
To Phthia, her whom he shall most approve.
Chrysothemis shall be his bride, or else
Laodice; or if she please him more,
Iphianassa; and from him I ask
No dower, myself will such a dower bestow          180
As never father on his child before.
Seven fair well-peopled cities I will give;
Cardamyle and Enope, and rich
In herbage, Hira; Pheræ stately-built,

And for her depth of pasturage renown'd        185
Antheia; proud Æpeia's lofty towers,
And Pedasus impurpled dark with vines.
All these are maritime, and on the shore
They stand of Pylus, by a race possess'd
Most rich in flocks and herds, who tributes large,    190
And gifts presenting to his sceptred hand,
Shall hold him high in honour as a God.
These will I give him if from wrath he cease.
Let him be overcome.   Pluto alone
Is found implacable and deaf to prayer,        195
Whom therefore of all Gods men hate the most.
My power is greater, and my years than his
More numerous, therefore let him yield to me.
   To him Gerenian Nestor thus replied.
Atrides! glorious sovereign! King of men!     200
No sordid gifts, or to be view'd with scorn,
Givest thou the Prince Achilles.   But away!
Send chosen messengers, who shall the son
Of Peleus, instant, in his tent address.
Myself will choose them, be it theirs to obey.    205
Let Phœnix lead, Jove loves him.   Be the next
Huge Ajax; and the wise Ulysses third.
Of heralds, Odius and Eurybates
Shall them attend.   Bring water for our hands;
Give charge that every tongue abstain from speech   210
Portentous, and propitiate Jove by prayer.
   He spake, and all were pleased.   The heralds pour'd
Pure water on their hands; attendant youths
The beakers crown'd, and wine from right to left
Distributed to all.   Libation made,       215
All drank, and in such measure as they chose,
Then hasted forth from Agamemnon's tent.
Gerenian Nestor at their side them oft
Instructed, each admonishing by looks
Significant, and motion of his eyes,       220
But most Ulysses, to omit no means
By which Achilles likeliest might be won.
Along the margin of the sounding Deep
They pass'd, to Neptune, compasser of earth,
Preferring vows ardent with numerous prayers,   225

That they might sway with ease the mighty mind
Of fierce Æacides.   And now they reach'd
The station where his Myrmidons abode.
Him solacing they found his heart with notes
Struck from his silver-framed harmonious lyre ;          230
Among the spoils he found it when he sack'd
Eëtion's city ; with that lyre his cares
He sooth'd and glorious heroes were his theme.
Patroclus silent sat, and he alone,
Before him, on Æacides intent,                           235
Expecting still when he should cease to sing.
The messengers advanced (Ulysses first)
Into his presence ; at the sight, his harp
Still in his hand, Achilles from his seat
Started astonish'd ; nor with less amaze               · 240
Patroclus also, seeing them, arose.
Achilles seized their hands, and thus he spake.
     Hail friends ! ye all are welcome.   Urgent cause
Hath doubtless brought you, whom I dearest hold,
(Though angry still,) of all Achaia's host.               245
     So saying, he introduced them, and on seats
Placed them with purple arras overspread,
Then thus bespake Patroclus standing nigh.
     Son of Menætius ! bring a beaker more
Capacious, and replenish it with wine                    250
Diluted³ less ; then give to each his cup ;
For dearer friends than these who now arrive
My roof beneath, or worthier, have I none.
     He ended, and Patroclus quick obey'd
Whom much he loved.   Achilles, then, himself           255
Advancing near the fire an ample⁴ tray,
Spread goats' flesh on it, with the flesh of sheep
And of a fatted brawn ; of each a chine.      `

³ I have given this sense to the word Ζωροτερον—on the authority of
the Venetian Scholium, though some contend that it should be translated
—*quickly*.   Achilles, who had reproached Agamemnon with intemperate
drinking, was, himself, more addicted to music than to wine.

⁴ It is not without authority that I have thus rendered κρειον μεγα.
Homer's banquets are never stewed or boiled ; it cannot therefore signify
a kettle.   It was probably a kitchen table, dresser, or tray, on which the
meat was prepared for the spit.   Accordingly we find that this very meat
was spitted afterward.—See Schaufelbergerus.

Automedon attending held them fast,
While with sharp steel Achilles from the bone          260
Sliced thin the meat, then pierced it with the spits.
Meantime the godlike Menætiades
Kindled fierce fire, and when the flame declined,
Raked wide the embers, laid the meat to roast,
And taking sacred salt from the hearth-side          265
Where it was treasured, shower'd it o'er the feast.
When all was finish'd, and the board set forth,
Patroclus furnish'd it around with bread
In baskets, and Achilles served the guests.
Beside the tent-wall, opposite he sat          270
To the divine Ulysses! first he bade
Patroclus make oblation; he consign'd
The consecrated morsel to the fire,
And each, at once, his savoury mess assail'd.
When neither edge of hunger now they felt          275
Nor thirsted longer, Ajax with a nod
Made sign to Phœnix, which Ulysses mark'd,
And charging high his cup, drank to his host.
    Health to Achilles! hospitable cheer
And well prepared, we want not at the board          280
Of royal Agamemnon, or at thine,
For both are nobly spread; but dainties now,
Or plenteous boards, are little our concern.
Oh godlike Chief! tremendous ills we sit
Contemplating with fear, doubtful if life          285
Or death, with the destruction of our fleet,
Attend us, unless thou put on thy might.
For lo! the haughty Trojans, with their friends
Call'd from afar, at the fleet-side encamp,
Fast by the wall, where they have kindled fires          290
Numerous, and threaten that no force of ours
Shall check their purposed inroad on the ships.
Jove grants them favourable signs from heaven,
Bright lightnings; Hector glares revenge, with rage
Infuriate, and by Jove assisted, heeds          295
Nor God nor man, but prays the morn to rise
That he may hew away our vessel-heads,
Burn all our fleet with fire, and at their sides
Slay the Achaians struggling in the smoke.

Horrible are my fears lest these his threats          300
The Gods accomplish, and it be our doom
To perish here, from Argos far remote.
Up, therefore! if thou canst, and now at last
The weary sons of all Achaia save
From Trojan violence.   Regret, but vain,          305
Shall else be thine hereafter, when no cure
Of such great ill, once suffer'd, can be found.
Thou therefore, seasonably kind, devise
Means to preserve from such disasterous fate
The  Grecians.   Ah, my friend! when Peleus thee          310
From Phthia sent to Agamemnon's aid,
On that same day he gave thee thus in charge.
" Juno, my son, and Pallas, if they please,
Can make thee valiant; but thy own big heart
Thyself restrain.   Sweet manners win respect.          315
Cease from pernicious strife, and young and old
Throughout the host shall honour thee the more."
Such was thy father's charge, which thou, it seems,
Remember'st not.   Yet even now thy wrath
Renounce; be reconciled; for princely gifts          320
Atrides gives thee if thy wrath subside.
Hear, if thou wilt, and I will tell thee all,
How vast the gifts which Agamemnon made
By promise thine, this night within his tent.
Seven tripods never sullied yet with fire;          325
Of gold ten talents; twenty cauldrons bright;
Twelve steeds strong-limb'd, victorious in the race;
No man possessing prizes such as those
Which they have won for him, shall feel the want
Of acquisitions splendid, or of gold.          330
Seven virtuous female captives he will give,
Expert in arts domestic, Lesbians all,
Whom when thou conquer'dst Lesbos, he received
His chosen portion, passing woman-kind
In perfect loveliness of face and form.          335
These will he give, and will with these resign
Her whom he took, Briseïs, with an oath
Most solemn, that unconscious as she was
Of his embraces, such he yields her back.
All these he gives thee now! and if at length          340

The Gods vouchsafe to us to overturn
Priam's great city, thou shalt heap thy ships
With gold and brass, entering and choosing first,
When we shall spare the spoil; and shalt beside
Choose twenty from among the maids of Troy,    345
Helen except, loveliest of all their sex.
And if once more the rich milk-flowing land
We reach of Argos, thou shalt there become
His son-in-law, and shalt enjoy like state
With him, whom he in all abundance rears,    350
His only son Orestes.   In his house
He hath three daughters; thou may'st home conduct
To Phthia, her whom thou shalt most approve.
Chrysothemis shall be thy bride; or else
Laodice; or if she please thee more    355
Iphianassa; and from thee he asks
No dower; himself will such a dower bestow
As never father on his child before.
Seven fair well-peopled cities will he give;
Cardamyle and Enope; and rich    360
In herbage, Hira; Pheræ stately built,
And for her depth of pasturage renown'd,
Antheia; proud Æpeia's lofty towers,
And Pedasus impurpled dark with vines.
All these are maritime, and on the shore    365
They stand of Pylus, by a race possess'd
Most rich in flocks and herds, who tribute large
And gifts presenting to thy sceptred hand,
Shall hold thee high in honour as a God.
These will he give thee, if thy wrath subside.    370
   But should'st thou rather in thine heart the more
Both Agamemnon and his gifts detest,
Yet oh compassionate the afflicted host
Prepared to adore thee.   Thou shalt win renown
Among the Grecians that shall never die.    375
Now strike at Hector.  He is here;—himself
Provokes thee forth; madness is in his heart,
And in his rage he glories that our ships
Have hither brought no Grecian brave as he.
   Then thus Achilles matchless in the race.    380
Laertes' noble son, for wiles renown'd!

I must with plainness speak my fixt resolve
Unalterable ; lest I hear from each
The same long murmur'd melancholy tale.
For I abhor the man, not more the gates          385
Of hell itself, whose words belie his heart.
So shall not mine.   My judgement undisguised
Is this ; that neither Agamemnon me
Nor all the Greeks shall move ; for ceaseless toil
Wins here no thanks ; one recompense awaits      390
The sedentary and the most alert,
The brave and base in equal honour stand,
And drones and heroes fall unwept alike.
I after all my labours, who exposed
My life continual in the field, have earn'd       395
No very sumptuous prize.   As the poor bird
Gives to her unfledged brood a morsel gain'd
After long search, though wanting it herself,
So I have worn out many sleepless nights,
And waded deep through many a bloody day          400
In battle for their wives[5].   I have destroy'd
Twelve cities with my fleet, and twelve, save one,
On foot contending in the fields of Troy.
From all these cities, precious spoils I took
Abundant, and to Agamemnon's hand                405
Gave all the treasure.   He within his ships
Abode the while, and having all received,
Little distributed, and much retained ;
He gave, however, to the Kings and Chiefs
A portion, and they keep it.   Me alone           410
Of all the Grecian host he hath despoil'd ;
My bride, my soul's delight is in his hands,
And let him, couch'd with her, enjoy his fill
Of dalliance.   What sufficient cause, what need
Have the Achaians to contend with Troy?           415
Why hath Atrides gather'd such an host,
And led them hither ? Was't not for the sake
Of beauteous Helen ? And of all mankind
Can none be found who love their proper wives
But the Atridæ ? There is no good man            420

[5] Dacier observes, that he pluralizes the one wife of Menelaus through
the impetuosity of his spirit.

Who loves not, guards not and with care provides
For his own wife, and, though in battle won,
I loved the fair Briseïs at my heart.
But having dispossess'd me of my prize
So foully, let him not essay me now,                                    425
For I am warn'd, and he shall not prevail.
With thee and with thy peers let him advise,
Ulysses! how the fleet may likeliest 'scape
Yon hostile fires! full many an arduous task
He hath accomplish'd without aid of mine ;                              430
So hath he now this rampart and the trench
Which he hath digg'd around it, and with stakes
Planted contiguous—puny barriers all
To Hero-slaughtering Hector's force opposed.
While I the battle waged, present myself                                435
Among the Achaians, Hector never fought
Far from his walls, but to the Scæan gate
Advancing and the beech-tree, there remain'd
Once, on that spot he met me, and my arm
Escaped with difficulty even there.                                     440
But since I feel myself not now inclined
To fight with noble Hector, yielding first
To Jove due worship, and to all the Gods,
To-morrow will I launch, and give my ships
Their lading.   Look thou forth at early dawn,                          445
And, if such spectacle delight thee aught,
Thou shalt behold me cleaving with my prows
The waves of Hellespont, and all my crews
Of lusty rowers, active in their task,
So shall I reach (if Ocean's mighty God                                 450
Prosper my passage) Phthia the deep-soil'd
On the third day.   I have possessions there,
Which hither roaming in an evil hour
I left abundant.   I shall also hence
Convey much treasure, gold and burnish'd brass,                        455
And glittering steel, and women passing fair
My portion of the spoils.   But he, your King,
The prize he gave, himself, himself resumed,
And taunted at me.   Tell him my reply,
And tell it him aloud, that other Greeks                                460
May indignation feel like me, if arm'd

Always in impudence, he seek to wrong
Them also.    Let him not henceforth presume,
Canine and hard in aspect though he be,
To look me in the face.    I will not share          465
His counsels, neither will I aid his works.
Let it suffice him, that he wrong'd me once,
Deceived me once, henceforth his glozing arts
Are lost on me.    But let him rot in peace
Crazed as he is, and by the stroke of Jove          470
Infatuate.    I detest his gifts, and him
So honour, as the thing which mòst I scorn.
And would he give me twenty times the worth
Of this his offer, all the treasured heaps
Which he possesses, or shall yet possess,           475
All that Orchomenos within her walls,
And all that opulent Egyptian Thebes
Receives, the city with an hundred gates,
Whence twenty thousand chariots rush to war,
And would he give me riches as the sands,           480
And as the dust of earth, no gifts from him
Should soothe me, till my soul were first avenged
For all the offensive licence of his tongue.
I will not wed the daughter of your Chief,
Of Agamemnon.    Could she vie in charms           485
With golden Venus, had she all the skill
Of blue-eyed Pallas, even so endow'd
She were no bride for me.    No.    He may choose
From the Achaians some superior Prince,
One more her equal.    Peleus, if the Gods          490
Preserve me, and I safe arrive at home,
Himself, ere long, shall mate me with a bride.
In Hellas and in Phthia may be found
Fair damsels many, daughters of the Chiefs
Who guard our cities; I may choose of them,        495
And make the loveliest of them all my own.
There, in my country, it hath ever been
My dearest purpose, wedded to a wife
Of rank convenient, to enjoy in peace
Such wealth as ancient Peleus hath acquired.       500
For life in my account, surpasses far
In value, all the treasures which report

Ascribed to populous Ilium ere the Greeks
Arrived, and while the city yet had peace;
Those also which Apollo's marble shrine          505
In rocky Pytho boasts.   Fat flocks and beeves
May be by force obtain'd, tripods and steeds
Are bought or won, but if the breath of man
Once overpass its bounds, no force arrests
Or may constrain the unbodied spirit back.          510
Me, as my silver-footed mother speaks
Thetis, a twofold consummation waits.
If still with battle I encompass Troy,
I win immortal glory, but all hope
Renounce of my return.   If I return          515
To my beloved country, I renounce
The illustrious meed of glory, but obtain
Secure and long immunity from death.
And truly I would recommend to all
To voyage homeward, for the fall as yet          520
Ye shall not see of Ilium's lofty towers,
For that the Thunderer with uplifted arm
Protects her, and her courage hath revived.
Bear ye mine answer back, as is the part
Of good ambassadors, that they may frame          525
Some likelier plan, by which both fleet and host
May be preserved; for, my resentment still
Burning, this project is but premature.
Let Phœnix stay with us, and sleep this night
Within my tent, that, if he so incline,          .530
He may to-morrow in my fleet embark,
And hence attend me; but I leave him free.
     He ended; they astonish'd at his tone
(For vehement he spake) sat silent all,
Till Phœnix, aged warrior, at the last          535
Gush'd into tears, (for dread his heart o'erwhelm'd
Lest the whole fleet should perish,) and replied.
     If thou indeed have purposed to return,
Noble Achilles! and such wrath retain'st
That thou art altogether fixt to leave          540
The fleet a prey to desolating fires,
How then, my son! shall I at Troy abide
Forlorn of thee?   When Peleus, hoary Chief,

Sent thee to Agamemnon, yet a child,
Unpractised in destructive fight, nor less          545
Of councils ignorant, the schools in which
Great minds are form'd, he bade me to the war
Attend thee forth, that I might teach thee all,
Both elocution and address in arms.
Me therefore shalt thou not with my consent          550
Leave here, my son ! no, not would Jove himself
Promise me, reaping smooth this silver beard,
To make me downy-cheek'd as in my youth ;
Such as when erst from Hellas beauty-famed
I fled, escaping from my father's wrath          555
Amyntor, son of Ormenus, who loved
A beauteous concubine, and for her sake
Despised his wife and persecuted me.
My mother suppliant at my knees, with prayer
Perpetual importuned me to embrace          560
The damsel first, that she might loathe my sire.
I did so ; and my father soon possess'd
With hot suspicion of the fact, let loose
A storm of imprecation, in his rage
Invoking all the Furies to forbid          565
That ever son of mine should press his knees.
Tartarian Jove[6] and dread Persephone[7]
Fulfill'd his curses ; with my pointed spear
I would have pierced his heart, but that my wrath
Some Deity assuaged, suggesting oft          570
What shame and obloquy I should incur,
Known as a parricide through all the land.
At length, so treated, I resolved to dwell
No longer in his house.   My friends, indeed,
And all my kindred compass'd me around          575
With much entreaty, wooing me to stay ;
Oxen and sheep they slaughter'd, many a plump
Well-fatted brawn extended in the flames,
And drank the old man's vessels to the lees.
Nine nights continual at my side they slept,          580
While others watch'd by turns, nor were the fires
Extinguish'd ever, one, beneath the porch
Of the barr'd hall, and one that from within

[6] Pluto.                    [7] Proserpine.

The vestibule illumed my chamber door.
But when the tenth dark night at length arrived, 585
Sudden the chamber doors bursting I flew
That moment forth, and unperceived alike
By guards and menial women, leap'd the wall.
Through spacious Hellas flying thence afar,
I came at length to Phthia the deep-soil'd, 590
Mother of flocks, and to the royal house
Of Peleus; Peleus with a willing heart
Receiving, loved me as a father loves
His only son, the son of his old age,
Inheritor of all his large demesnes. 595
He made me rich; placed under my controul
A populous realm, and on the skirts I dwelt
Of Phthia, ruling the Dolopian race.
Thee from my soul, thou semblance of the Gods,
I loved, and all-illustrious as thou art, 600
Achilles! such I made thee. For with me,
Me only, would'st thou forth to feast abroad,
Nor would'st thou taste thy food at home, 'till first
I placed thee on my knees, with my own hand
Thy viands carved and fed thee, and the wine 605
Held to thy lips; and many a time, in fits
Of infant frowardness, the purple juice
Rejecting thou hast deluged all my vest,
And fill'd my bosom. Oh, I have endured
Much, and have also much perform'd for thee, 610
Thus purposing, that since the Gods vouchsaf'd
No son to me, thyself should'st be my son,
Godlike Achilles! who should'st screen perchance
From a foul fate my else unshelter'd age.
Achilles! bid thy mighty spirit down. 615
Thou should'st not be thus merciless; the Gods,
Although more honourable, and in power
And virtue thy superiors, are themselves
Yet placable; and if a mortal man
Offend them by transgression of their laws, 620
Libation, incense, sacrifice, and prayer,
In meekness offer'd turn their wrath away.
Prayers are Jove's daughters, wrinkled[8], lame, slant-eyed,

[8] Wrinkled—because the countenance of a man driven to prayer by

Which though far distant, yet with constant pace
Follow Offence.  Offence robust of limb,                    625
And treading firm the ground, outstrips them all,
And over all the earth before them runs
Hurtful to man.   They, following, heal the hurt.
Received respectfully when they approach,
They help us, and our prayers hear in return.               630
But if we slight, and with obdurate heart
Resist them, to Saturnian Jove they cry
Against us, supplicating that Offence
May cleave to us for vengeance of the wrong.
Thou, therefore, O Achilles! honour yield                   635
To Jove's own daughters, vanquish'd, as the brave
Have ofttimes been, by honour paid to Thee.
For came not Agamemnon as he comes
With gifts in hand, and promises of more
Hereafter ; burn'd his anger still the same,                640
I would not move thee to renounce thy own,
And to assist us, howsoe'er distress'd.
But now, not only are his present gifts
Most liberal, and his promises of more
Such also, but these Princes he hath sent                   645
Charged with entreaties, thine especial friends,
And chosen for that cause, from all the host.
Slight not their embassy, nor put to shame
Their intercession.   We confess that once
Thy wrath was unreproveable and just.                       650
Thus we have heard the heroes of old times
Applauded oft, whose anger, though intense,
Yet left them open to the gentle sway
Of reason and conciliatory gifts.
I recollect an ancient history,                             655
Which, since all here are friends, I will relate.
The brave Ætolians and Curetes met
Beneath the walls of Calydon, and fought

a consciousness of guilt is sorrowful and dejected.   Lame—because it
is a remedy to which men recur late, and with reluctance.   And slant-
eyed—either because, in that state of humiliation, they fear to lift their
eyes to heaven, or are employed in taking a retrospect of their past mis-
conduct.

The whole allegory, considering *when* and *where* it was composed, forms
a very striking passage.

With mutual slaughter; the Ætolian powers
In the defence of Calydon the fair,      660
And the Curetes, bent to lay it waste:
That strife Diana of the golden throne
Kindled between them, with resentment fired
That Oeneus had not in some fertile spot
The first fruits of his harvest set apart      665
To her; with hecatombs he entertained
All the Divinities of heaven beside,
And her alone, daughter of Jove supreme,
Or through forgetfulness, or some neglect,
Served not; omission careless and profane!      670
She, progeny of Jove, Goddess shaft-arm'd,
A savage boar bright-tusk'd in anger sent,
Which haunting Oeneus' fields much havoc made.
Trees numerous on the earth in heaps he cast
Uprooting them, with all their blossoms on.      675
But Meleager, Oeneus' son, at length
Slew him, the hunters gathering and the hounds
Of numerous cities; for a boar so vast
Might not be vanquish'd by the power of few,
And many to their funeral piles he sent.      680
Then raised Diana clamorous dispute,
And contest hot between them, all alike,
Curetes and Ætolians fierce in arms
The boar's head claiming, and his bristly hide.
So long as warlike Meleager fought,      685
Ætolia prosper'd, nor with all their powers
Could the Curetes stand before the walls.
But when resentment once had fired the heart
Of Meleager, which hath tumult oft
Excited in the breasts of wisest men,      690
(For his own mother had his wrath provoked
Althæa) thenceforth with his wedded wife
He dwelt, fair Cleopatra, close retired.
She was Marpessa's daughter, whom she bore
To Idas, bravest warrior in his day      695
Of all on earth. He fear'd not 'gainst the King
Himself Apollo, for the lovely nymph
Marpessa's sake, his spouse, to bend his bow.
Her, therefore, Idas and Marpessa named

Thenceforth Alcyone, because the fate                          700
Of sad Alcyone Marpessa shared,
And wept like her, by Phœbus forced away.
Thus Meleager, tortured with the pangs
Of wrath indulged, with Cleopatra dwelt,
Vex'd that his mother curs'd him; for, with grief             705
Frantic, his mother importuned the Gods
To avenge her slaughter'd brothers* on his head.
Oft would she smite the earth, while on her knees
Seated, she fill'd her bosom with her tears,
And call'd on Pluto and dread Proserpine                      710
To slay her son; nor vain was that request,
But by implacable Erynnis heard
Roaming the shades of Erebus.   Ere long
The tumult and the deafening din of war
Roar'd at the gates, and all the batter'd towers             715
Resounded.   Then the elders of the town
Dispatch'd the high-priests of the Gods to plead
With Meleager for his instant aid,
With strong assurances of rich reward.
Where Calydon afforded fattest soil                          720
They bade him choose to his own use a farm
Of fifty measured acres, vineyard half,
And half of land commodious for the plough.
Him Oeneus also, warrior grey with age,
Ascending to his chamber, and his doors                      725
Smiting importunate, with earnest prayers
Assay'd to soften, kneeling to his son.
Nor less his sisters woo'd him to relent,
Nor less his mother; but in vain; he grew
Still more obdurate.   His companions last,                  730
The most esteem'd and dearest of his friends,
The same suit urged, yet he persisted still
Relentless, nor could even they prevail.
But when the battle shook his chamber-doors
And the Curetes climbing the high towers                     735
Had fired the spacious city, then with tears
The beauteous Cleopatra, and with prayers
Assail'd him; in his view she set the woes

* She had five brothers: Iphiclus, Polyphontes, Phanes, Eurypylus, Plexippus.

Numberless of a city storm'd,—the men
Slaughter'd, the city burnt to dust, the chaste                         740
Matrons with all their children dragg'd away.
That dread recital roused him, and at length
Issuing, he put his radiant armour on.
Thus Meleager, gratifying first
His own resentment from a fatal day                        ·         745
Saved the Ætolians, who the promised gift
Refused him, and his toils found no reward.
But thou my son, be wiser; follow thou
No dæmon who would tempt thee to a course
Like his; occasion more propitious far                              750
Smiles on thee now, than if the fleet were fired.
Come, while by gifts invited, and receive
From all the host, the honours of a God;
For should'st thou, by no gifts induced, at last
Enter the bloody field, although thou chase                         755
The Trojans hence, yet less shall be thy praise.
    Then thus Achilles, matchless in the race.
Phœnix, my guide, wise, noble and revered!
I covet no such glory! the renown
Ordain'd by Jove for me, is to resist                               760
All importunity to quit my ships
While I have power to move, or breath to draw.
Hear now, and mark me well.   Cease thou from tears.
Confound me not, pleading with sighs and sobs
In Agamemnon's cause; O love not Him,                              765
Lest I renounce thee, who am now thy friend.
Assist me rather, as thy duty bids,
Him to afflict, who hath afflicted me,
So shalt thou share my glory and my power.
These shall report as they have heard, but here                    770
Rest thou this night, and with the rising morn
We will decide, to stay or to depart.
    He ceased, and silent, by a nod enjoin'd
Patroclus to prepare an easy couch
For Phœnix, anxious to dismiss the rest                            775
Incontinent; when Ajax, godlike son
Of Telamon, arising, thus began.
    Laertes' noble son, for wiles renown'd!
Depart we now; for I perceive that end

Or fruit of all our reasonings shall be none.                  780
It is expedient also that we bear
Our answer back (unwelcome as it is)
With all dispatch, for the assembled Greeks
Expect us.   Brave Achilles shuts a fire
Within his breast ; the kindness of his friends,             785
And the respect peculiar by ourselves
Shown to him, on his heart work no effect.
Inexorable man ! others accept
Even for a brother slain, or for a son
Due compensation ; the delinquent dwells               790
Secure at home, and the receiver, soothed
And pacified, represses his revenge.
But thou, resentful of the loss of one,
One virgin (such obduracy of heart
The Gods have given thee) can'st not be appeased.        795
Yet we assign thee seven in her stead,
The most distinguish'd of their sex, and add
Large gifts beside.   Ah then, at last relent !
Respect thy roof; we are thy guests ; we come
Chosen from the multitude of all the Greeks,             800
Beyond them all ambitious of thy love. ·
    To whom Achilles, swiftest of the swift.
My noble friend, offspring of Telamon !
Thou seem'st sincere, and I believe thee such.
But at the very mention of the name                      805
Of Atreus' son, who shamed me in the sight
Of all Achaia's host, bearing me down
As I had been some vagrant at his door,
My bosom boils.   Return ye and report
Your answer.   I no thought will entertain               810
Of crimson war, till the illustrious son
Of warlike Priam, Hector, blood-embrued,
Shall in their tents the Myrmidons assail
Themselves, and fire my fleet.   At my own ship,
And at my own pavilion, it may chance                    815
That even Hector's violence shall pause.
    He ended ; they from massy goblets each
Libation pour'd, and to the fleet their course
Resumed direct, Ulysses at their head.
Patroclus then his fellow warriors bade,                 820

And the attendant women, spread a couch
For Phœnix; they the couch, obedient, spread
With fleeces, with rich arras, and with flax
Of subtlest woof.   There hoary Phœnix lay
In expectation of the sacred dawn.                    825
Meantime Achilles in the interior tent,
With beauteous Diomeda by himself
From Lesbos brought, daughter of Phorbas, lay.
Patroclus opposite reposed, with whom
Slept charming Iphis; her, when he had won      830
The lofty towers of Scyros, the divine
Achilles took, and on his friend bestow'd.
   But when those Chiefs at Agamemnon's tent
Arrived, the Greeks on every side arose
With golden cups welcoming their return.          835
All question'd them, but Agamemnon first.
   Oh worthy of Achaia's highest praise,
And her chief ornament, Ulysses, speak!
Will he defend the fleet? or his big heart
Indulging wrathful, doth he still refuse?           840
   To whom renown'd Ulysses thus replied.
Atrides, Agamemnon, King of men!
He, his resentment quenches not, or will,
But burns with wrath the more, thee and thy gifts
Rejecting both.   He bids thee with the Greeks     845
Consult·by what expedient thou may'st save
The fleet and people, threatening that himself
Will at the peep of day launch all his barks,
And counselling, beside, the general host
To voyage homeward, for that end as yet           850
Of Ilium wall'd to heaven, ye shall not find,
Since Jove the Thunderer with uplifted arm
Protects her, and her courage hath revived.
Thus speaks the Chief, and Ajax is prepared,
With the attendant heralds, to report               855
As I have said.   But Phœnix in the tent
Sleeps of Achilles, who his stay desired,
That on the morrow, if he so incline,
The hoary warrior may attend him hence
Home to his country, but he leaves him free.      860
   He ended.   They astonish'd at his tone

(For vehement he spake) sat silent all.
Long silent sat the afflicted sons of Greece,
When thus the mighty Diomede began.
    Atrides, Agamemnon, King of men !    865
Thy supplications to the valiant son
Of Peleus, and the offer of thy gifts
Innumerous, had been better far withheld.
He is at all times haughty, and thy suit
Hath but increased his haughtiness of heart    870 ·
Past bounds : but let him stay, or let him go
As he shall choose.  He will resume the fight
When his own mind shall prompt him, and the Gods
Shall urge him forth.   Now follow my advice.
Ye have refresh'd your hearts with food and wine,    875⁻
Which are the strength of man ; take now repose,
And when the rosy-finger'd morning fair,
Shall shine again, set forth without delay
The battle, horse and foot, before the fleet,
And where the foremost fight, fight also thou.    880
    He ended ; all the Kings applauded warm
His counsel, and the dauntless tone admired
Of Diomede.   Then, due libation made,
Each sought his tent, and took the gift of sleep.

# BOOK X.

### ARGUMENT.

Diomede and Ulysses enter the Trojan host by night, and slay Rhesus.

ALL night, the leaders of the host of Greece
Lay sunk in soft repose, all, save the Chief,
The son of Atreus ; him from thought to thought
Roving solicitous, no sleep relieved.
As when the spouse of beauteous Juno, darts          5
His frequent fires, designing heavy rain
Immense or hail storm, or field-whitening snow,
Or else wide-throated war calamitous,
So frequent were the groans by Atreus' son
Heaved from his inmost heart, trembling with dread.   10
For cast he but his eye toward the plain
Of Ilium, there, astonish'd, he beheld
The city fronted with bright fires, and heard
Pipes, and recorders, and the hum of war ;
But when again the Grecian fleet he view'd,           15
And thought on his own people, then his hair
Uprooted elevating to the Gods,
He from his generous bosom groan'd again.
At length he thus resolved ; of all the Greeks
To seek Neleian Nestor first, with whom               20
He might, perchance, some plan for the defence
Of the afflicted Danaï devise.
Rising, he wrapp'd his tunic to his breast,
And to his royal feet unsullied bound
His sandals ; o'er his shoulders, next, he threw      25
Of amplest size a lion's tawny skin
That swept his footsteps, dappled o'er with blood,
Then took his spear.   Meantime not less appall'd
Was Menelaus, on whose eyelids sleep

Sat not, lest the Achaians for his sake                    30
O'er many waters borne, and now intent
On glorious deeds, should perish all at Troy.
With a pard's spotted hide his shoulders broad
He mantled over; to his head he raised
His brazen helmet, and with vigorous hand               35
Grasping his spear, forth issued to arouse
His brother, mighty sovereign of the host,
And by the Grecians like a God revered.
He found him at his galley's stern, his arms
Assuming radiant; welcome he arrived                    40
To Agamemnon, whom he thus address'd.
    Why arm'st thou, brother? Would'st thou urge abroad
Some trusty spy into the Trojan camp?
I fear lest none so hardy shall be found
As to adventure, in the dead still night,               45
So far, alone; valiant indeed were he!
    To whom great Agamemnon thus replied.
Heaven-favour'd Menelaus! We have need,
Thou and myself, of some device well-framed,
Which both the Grecians and the fleet of Greece         50
May rescue, for the mind of Jove hath changed,
And Hector's prayers alone now reach his ear.
I never saw, nor by report have learn'd
From any man, that ever single chief
Such aweful wonders in one day perform'd                55
As he with ease against the Greeks, although
Nor from a Goddess sprung nor from a God.
Deeds he hath done, which, as I think, the Greeks
Shall deep and long lament, such numerous ills
Achaia's host hath at his hands sustain'd.              60
But haste, begone, and at their several ships
Call Ajax and Idomeneus; I go
To exhort the noble Nestor to arise,
That he may visit, if he so incline,
The chosen band who watch, and his advice              65
Give them; for him most prompt they will obey,
Whose son, together with Meriones,
Friend of Idomeneus, controuls them all,
Entrusted by ourselves with that command.
    Him answer'd Menelaus bold in arms.                 70

N 2

Explain thy purpose.—Would'st thou that I wait
Thy coming, there, or thy commands to both
Given, that I incontinent return?
   To whom the Sovereign of the host replied.
There stay; lest striking into different paths                75
(For many passes intersect the camp)
We miss each other; summon them aloud
Where thou shalt come; enjoin them to arise;
Call each by his hereditary name,
Honouring all.   Beware of manners proud,                    80
For we ourselves must labour, at our birth
By Jove ordain'd to suffering and to toil.
   So saying, he his brother thence dismiss'd
Instructed duly, and, himself, his steps
Turned to the tent of Nestor.   Him he found                 85
Amid his sable galleys in his tent
Reposing soft, his armour at his side,
Shield, spears, bright helmet, and the broider'd belt
Which, when the Senior arm'd led forth his host
To fight, he wore; for he complied not yet                   90
With the encroachments of enfeebling age.
He raised his head, and on his elbow propp'd,
Questioning Agamemnon, thus began.
   But who art thou, who thus alone, the camp
Roamest, amid the darkness of the night,                     95
While other mortals sleep?   Comest thou abroad
Seeking some friend or soldier of the guard?
Speak—come not nearer mute.   What is thy wish?
   To whom the son of Atreus, King of men.
Oh Nestor, glory of the Grecian name,                        100
Offspring of Neleus! thou in me shalt know
The son of Atreus, Agamemnon, doom'd
By Jove to toil, while life shall yet inform
These limbs, or I shall draw the vital air.
I wander thus, because that on my lids                       105
Sweet sleep sits not, but war and the concerns
Of the Achaians occupy my soul.
Terrible are the fears which I endure
For these my people; such as supersede
All thought; my bosom can no longer hold                     110
My throbbing heart, and tremors shake my limbs.

But if thy mind, more capable, project
Aught that may profit us (for thee it seems
Sleep also shuns) arise, and let us both
Visit the watch, lest, haply, overtoil'd                    115
They yield to sleep, forgetful of their charge.
The foe is posted near, and may intend
(None knows his purpose) an assault by night.
   To him Gerenian Nestor thus replied.
Illustrious Agamemnon, King of men!                         120
Deep-planning Jove the imaginations proud
Of Hector will not ratify, nor all
His sanguine hopes effectuate; in his turn
He also (fierce Achilles once appeased)
Shall trouble feel, and, haply, more than we.               125
But with all readiness I will arise
And follow thee, that we may also rouse
Yet others; Diomede the spear-renown'd,
Ulysses, the swift Ajax, and the son
Of Phyleus, valiant Meges.  It were well                    130
Were others also visited and call'd,
The Godlike Ajax, and Idomeneus,
Whose ships are at the camp's extremest bounds.
But though I love thy brother and revere,
And though I grieve e'en thee, yet speak I must,            135
And plainly censure him, that thus he sleeps
And leaves to thee the labour, who himself
Should range the host, soliciting the Chiefs
Of every band, as utmost need requires.
   Him answer'd Agamemnon, King of men.            140
Old warrior, times there are, when I could wish
Myself thy censure of him, for in act
He is not seldom tardy and remiss.
Yet is not sluggish indolence the cause,
No, nor stupidity, but he observes                          145
Me much, expecting till I lead the way.
But he was foremost now, far more alert
This night than I, and I have sent him forth
Already, those to call whom thou hast named.
But let us hence, for at the guard I trust                  150
To find them, since I gave them so in charge.
   To whom the brave Gerenian Chief replied.

Him none will censure, or his will dispute,
Whom he shall waken and exhort to rise.
   So saying, he bound his corslet to his breast,    155
His sandals fair to his unsullied feet,
And fastening by its clasps his purple cloak
Around him, double and of shaggy pile,
Seized, next, his sturdy spear headed with brass,
And issued first, into the Grecian fleet.    160
There, Nestor, brave Gerenian, with a voice
Sonorous roused the Godlike counsellor
From sleep, Ulysses; the alarm came o'er
His startled ear, forth from his tent he sprang
Sudden, and of their coming, quick, enquired.    165
   Why roam ye thus the camp and fleet alone
In darkness? by what urgent need constrain'd?
   To whom the hoary Pylian thus replied.
Laertes' noble son, for wiles renown'd!
Resent it not, for dread is our distress.    170
Come, therefore, and assist us to convene
Yet others, qualified to judge if war
Be most expedient, or immediate flight.
   He ended, and regaining, quick, his tent,
Ulysses slung his shield, then coming forth    175
Join'd them.   The son of Tydeus first they sought.
Him sleeping arm'd before his tent they found,
Encompass'd by his friends also asleep;
His head each rested on his shield, and each
Had planted on its nether point[1] erect    180
His spear beside him; bright their polish'd heads,
As Jove's own lightning glitter'd from afar.
Himself, the Hero slept.   A wild bull's hide
Was spread beneath him, and on arras tinged
With splendid purple lay his head reclined.    185
Nestor, beside him standing, with his heel
Shook him, and urgent, thus the Chief reproved.
   Awake Tydides! wherefore givest the night
Entire to balmy slumber?   Hast not heard
How on the rising ground beside the fleet    190

---

[1] Σαυρωτηρ—seems to have been a hollow iron with a point, fitted to
the obtuse end of the spear for the purpose of planting that end of it in
the ground.  It might probably be taken off at pleasure.

The Trojans sit, small interval between?
   He ceased; then upsprang Diomede alarm'd
Instant, and in wing'd accents thus replied.
   Old wakeful Chief! thy toils are never done.
Are there not younger of the sons of Greece,        195
Who ranging in all parts the camp, might call
The Kings to council?   But no curb controuls
Or can abate activity like thine.
   To whom Gerenian Nestor in return.
My friend! thou hast well spoken. I have sons,     200
And they are well deserving; I have here
A numerous people also, one of whom
Might have sufficed to call the Kings of Greece.
But such occasion presses now the host
As hath not oft occurr'd: the overthrow       205
· Complete, or full deliverance of us all,
In balance hangs, poised on a razor's edge.
But haste, and if thy pity of my toils
Be such, since thou art younger, call, thyself,
Ajax the swift, and Meges to the guard.      210
   Then Diomede a lion's tawny skin
Around him wrapp'd, dependent to his heels,
And, spear in hand, set forth.   The Hero call'd
Those two, and led them whither Nestor bade.
   They, at the guard arrived, not sleeping found   215
The captains of the guard, but sitting all
In vigilant posture with their arms prepared.
As dogs that, careful watch the fold by night,
Hearing some wild beast in the woods, which hounds
And hunters with tumultuous clamour drive    220
Down from the mountain top, all sleep forego;
So, sat not on their eyelids gentle sleep
That dreadful night, but constant to the plain
At every sound of Trojan feet they turn'd.
The old Chief joyful at the sight, in terms     225
Of kind encouragement them thus address'd.
   So watch, my children! and beware that sleep
Invade none here lest all become a prey.
   So saying, he traversed with quick pace the trench
By every Chief whom they had thither call'd    230
Attended, with whom Nestor's noble son

Went, and Meriones, invited both
To join their consultation.   From the foss
Emerging, in a vacant space they sat,
Unstrew'd with bodies of the slain, the spot                235
Whence furious Hector, after slaughter made
Of numerous Greeks, night falling, had returned.
There seated, mutual converse close they held,
And Nestor, brave Gerenian, thus began.
  Oh friends ! hath no Achaian here such trust         240
In his own prowess, as to venture forth
Among yon haughty Trojans ? He, perchance,
Might on the borders of their host surprise
Some wandering adversary, or might learn
Their consultations whether they propose                    245
Here to abide in prospect of the fleet,
Or, satiate with success against the Greeks
So signal, meditate retreat to Troy.
These tidings gain'd, should he at last return
Secure, his recompence will be renown                       250
Extensive as the heavens, and fair reward.
From every leader of the fleet, his gift
Shall be a sable[2] ewe, and sucking lamb,
Rare acquisition ! and at every board
And sumptuous banquet, he shall be a guest.                 255
  He ceased, and all sat silent, when at length
The mighty son of Tydeus thus replied.
  Me, Nestor, my courageous heart incites
To penetrate into the neighbour host
Of enemies ; but went some other Chief                      260
With me, far greater would my comfort prove,
And I should dare the more.   Two going forth,
One quicker sees than other, and suggests
Prudent advice ; but he who singly goes,
Mark whatsoe'er he may, the occasion less                   265
Improves, and his expedients soon exhausts.
  He ended, and no few willing arose
To go with Diomede.   Servants of Mars
Each Ajax willing stood ; willing as they
Meriones ; most willing Nestor's son ;                      270

---

[2] *Sable*, because the expedition was made by night, and *each with a lamb*,
as typical of the fruit of their labours.

Willing the brother of the Chief of all,
Nor willing less Ulysses to explore
The host of Troy, for he possess'd a heart
Delighted ever with some bold exploit.
 Then Agamemnon, King of men, began.   275
Now Diomede, in whom my soul delights!
Choose whom thou wilt for thy companion; choose
The fittest here; for numerous wish to go.
Leave not through deference to another's rank,
The more deserving, nor prefer a worse,   280
Respecting either pedigree or power.
 Such speech he interposed, fearing his choice
Of Menelaus; then, renown'd in arms
The son of Tydeus, rising, spake again.
 Since, then, ye bid me my own partner choose 285
Free from constraint, how can I overlook
Divine Ulysses, whose courageous heart
With such peculiar cheerfulness endures
Whatever toils, and whom Minerva loves?
Let *Him* attend me, and through fire itself  290
We shall return; for none is wise as he.
 To him Ulysses, hardy Chief, replied.
Tydides! neither praise me much, nor blame,
For these are Grecians in whose ears thou speak'st,
And know me well. But let us hence! the night 295
Draws to a close; day comes apace; the stars
Are far advanced; two portions have elapsed
Of darkness, but the third is yet entire.
 So they; then each his dreadful arms put on.
To Diomede, who at the fleet had left   300
His own, the dauntless Thrasymedes gave
His shield and sword two-edged, and on his head
Placed, crestless, unadorn'd his bull-skin casque.
It was a stripling's helmet, such as youths
Scarce yet confirm'd in lusty manhood, wear.  305
Meriones with quiver, bow and sword
Furnish'd Ulysses, and his brows enclosed
In his own casque of hide with many a thong
Well braced within; guarded it was without
With boar's teeth ivory-white inherent firm  310
On all sides, and with woollen head-piece lined.

That helmet erst Autolycus'[a] had brought
From Eleon, city of Amyntor son
Of Hormenus, where he the solid walls
Bored through, clandestine, of Amyntor's house.          315
He on Amphidamas the prize bestow'd
In Scandia ; from Amphidamas it pass'd
To Molus as an hospitable pledge ;
He gave it to Meriones his son,
And now it guarded shrewd Ulysses' brows.                320
Both clad in arms terrific, forth they sped,
Leaving their fellow Chiefs, and as they went
An heron, by command of Pallas, flew
Close on the right beside them ; darkling they
Discern'd him not, but heard his clanging plumes.        325
Ulysses in the favourable sign
Exulted, and Minerva thus invoked.
    Oh hear me, daughter of Jove Ægis-arm'd !
My present helper in all streights, whose eye
Marks all my ways, oh with peculiar care                 330
Now guard me, Pallas ! grant that after toil
Successful, glorious, such as long shall fill
With grief the Trojans, we may safe return
And with immortal honours to the fleet.
    Valiant Tydides, next, his prayer preferr'd.         335
Hear also me, Jove's offspring by the toils
Of war invincible ! me follow now
As my heroic father erst to Thebes
Thou followedst, Tydeus ; by the Greeks dispatch'd
Ambassador, he left the mail-clad host                   340
Beside Asopus, and with terms of peace
Entrusted, enter'd Thebes ; but by thine aid
Benevolent, and in thy strength, perform'd
Returning, deeds of terrible renown.
Thus, now, protect me also ! In return                   345
I vow an offering at thy shrine, a young
Broad-fronted heifer, to the yoke as yet
Untamed, whose horns I will incase with gold.
    Such prayer they made, and Pallas heard well pleased.
Their orisons ended to the daughter dread                350
Of mighty Jove, lion-like they advanced
    [a] Autolycus was grandfather of Ulysses by the mother's side.

Through shades of night, through carnage, arms and blood.
 Nor Hector to his gallant host indulged
Sleep, but convened the leaders ; leader none
Or senator of all his host he left                    355
Unsummon'd, and his purpose thus promulged.
 Where is the warrior who for rich reward,
Such as shall well suffice him, will the task
Adventurous, which I propose, perform ?
A chariot with two steeds of proudest height,         360
Surpassing all in the whole fleet of Greece,
Shall be his portion, with immortal praise,
Who shall the well-appointed ships approach
Courageous, there to learn if yet a guard
As heretofore, keep them, or if subdued               365
Beneath us, the Achaians flight intend,
And worn with labour have no will to watch.
 So Hector spake, but answer none return'd.
There was a certain Trojan, Dolon named,
Son of Humedes herald of the Gods,                    370
Rich both in gold and brass, but in his form
Unsightly ; yet the man was swift of foot,
Sole brother of five sisters ; he his speech
To Hector and the Trojans thus address'd.
 My spirit, Hector, prompts me, and my mind       375
Endued with manly vigour, to approach
Yon gallant ships, that I may tidings hear.
But come.   For my assurance, lifting high
Thy sceptre, swear to me, for my reward,
The horses and the brazen chariot bright              380
Which bear renown'd Achilles o'er the field.
I will not prove an useless spy, nor fall
Below thy best opinion ; pass I will
Their army through, 'till I shall reach the ship
Of Agamemnon, where the Chiefs, perchance,            385
Now sit consulting, or to fight, or fly.
 Then raising high his sceptre, Hector sware.
Know, Jove himself, Juno's high-thundering spouse !
That Trojan none shall in that chariot ride
By those steeds drawn, save Dolon ; on my oath        390
I make them thine ; enjoy them evermore.
 He said, and falsely sware, yet him assured.

Then Dolon, instant, o'er his shoulder slung
His bow elastic, wrapp'd himself around
With a grey wolf-skin, to his head a casque          395
Adjusted, coated o'er with ferret's felt,
And seizing his sharp javelin, from the host
Turn'd right toward the fleet, but was ordain'd
To disappoint his sender, and to bring
No tidings thence.   The throng of Trojan steeds     400
And warriors left, with brisker pace he moved,
When brave Ulysses his approach perceived,
And thus to Diomede his speech address'd.
    Tydides! yonder man is from the host;
Either a spy he comes, or with intent                405
To spoil the dead.   First, freely let him pass
Few paces, then pursuing him with speed,
Seize on him suddenly; but should he prove
The nimbler of the three, with threatening spear
Enforce him from his camp toward the fleet,          410
Lest he elude us, and escape to Troy.
    So they; then, turning from the road oblique,
Among the carcases each lay'd him down.
Dolon, suspecting nought, ran swiftly by.
⁴But when such space was interposed as mules         415
Plough in a day,(for mules the ox surpass
Through fallows deep drawing the ponderous plough)
Both ran toward him.   Dolon at the sound
Stood; for he hoped some Trojan friends at hand
From Hector sent to bid him back again.              420
But when within spear's cast, or less they came,
Knowing them enemies he turn'd to flight
Incontinent, whom they as swift pursued.
As two fleet hounds sharp fang'd, train'd to the chace,
Hang on the rear of flying hind or hare,             425
And drive her, never swerving from the track,
Through copses close; she screaming scuds before;
So Diomede and dread Ulysses him
·Chased constant, intercepting his return.

⁴ Commentators here are extremely in the dark, and even Aristarchus
seems to have attempted an explanation in vain.—The Translator does not
pretend to have ascertained the distance intended, but only to have given a
distance suited to the occasion.

And now, fast-fleeing to the ships, he soon          430
Had reach'd the guard, but Pallas with new force
Inspired Tydides, lest a meaner Greek
Should boast that he had smitten Dolon first,
And Diomede win only second praise.
He poised his lifted spear, and thus exclaim'd.          435
    Stand! or my spear shall stop thee.   Death impends
At every step; thou can'st not 'scape me long.
    He said, and threw his spear, but by design,
Err'd from the man.   The polish'd weapon swift
O'er-glancing his right shoulder, in the soil          440
Stood fixt, beyond him.   Terrified he stood,
Stammering, and sounding through his lips the clash
Of chattering teeth, with visage deadly wan.
They panting rush'd on him, and both his hands
Seized fast; he wept, and suppliant them bespake.          445
    Take me alive, and I will pay the price
Of my redemption.   I have gold at home,
Brass also, and bright steel, and when report
Of my captivity within your fleet
Shall reach my father, treasures he will give          450
Not to be told, for ransom of his son.
    To whom Ulysses politic replied.
Take courage; entertain no thought of death.
But haste! this tell me, and disclose the truth.
Why thus toward the ships comest thou alone          455
From yonder host, by night, while others sleep?
To spoil some carcase? or from Hector sent
A spy of all that passes in the fleet?
Or by thy curiosity impell'd?
    Then Dolon, his limbs trembling, thus replied.          460
To my great detriment, and far beyond
My own design, Hector trepann'd me forth,
Who promised me the steeds of Peleus' son
Illustrious, and his brazen chariot bright.
He bade me, under night's fast-flitting shades          465
Approach our enemies, a spy, to learn
If still as heretofore, ye station guards
For safety of your fleet, or if subdued
Completely, ye intend immediate flight,
And worn with labour, have no will to watch.          470

To whom Ulysses, smiling, thus replied.
Thou hadst, in truth, an appetite to gifts
Of no mean value, coveting the steeds
Of brave Æacides, but steeds are they
Of fiery sort, difficult to be ruled                            475
By force of mortal man, Achilles' self
Except, whom an immortal mother bore.
But tell me yet again ; use no disguise ;
Where left'st thou, at thy coming forth, your Chief,
The valiant Hector? where hath he disposed              480
His armour battle-worn, and where his steeds?
What other quarters of your host are watch'd?
Where lodge the guard, and what intend ye next?
Still to abide in prospect of the fleet?
Or well-content that ye have thus reduced              485
Achaia's host, will ye retire to Troy?
   To whom this answer Dolon straight returned
Son of Eumedes.   With unfeigning truth
Simply and plainly will I utter all.
Hector, with all the Senatorial Chiefs,                   490
Beside the tomb of sacred Ilius sits
Consulting, from the noisy camp remote.
But for the guards, Hero! concerning whom
Thou hast enquired, there is no certain watch
And regular appointed o'er the camp ;                    495
The native[5] Trojans (for *they* can no less)
Sit sleepless all, and each his next exhorts
To vigilance ; but all our foreign aids,
Who neither wives nor children hazard here,
Trusting the Trojans for that service, sleep.            500
   To whom Ulysses, ever wise, replied.
How sleep the strangers, and allies?—apart?
Or with the Trojans mingled?—I would learn.
   So spake Ulysses ; to whom Dolon thus,
Son of Eumedes.   I will all unfold,                      505
And all most truly.   By the sea are lodged
The Carians, the Pæonians arm'd with bows,
The Leleges, with the Pelasgian band,
And the Caucones.   On the skirts encamp

---

[5] Ὄσσαι γαρ Τρωων πυρος εσχαραι—As many as are owners of hearths,
—that is to say, all who are householders here, or natives of the city.

Of Thymbra, the Mæonians crested high,       510
The Phrygian horsemen, with the Lycian host,
And the bold troop of Mysia's haughty sons.
But wherefore these enquiries, thus minute?
For if ye wish to penetrate the host,
These who possess the borders of the camp       515
Farthest removed of all, are Thracian powers
Newly arrived; among them Rhesus sleeps,
Son of Eïoneus, their Chief and King.
His steeds I saw, the fairest by these eyes
Ever beheld, and loftiest; snow itself       520
They pass in whiteness, and in speed the winds.
With gold and silver all his chariot burns,
And he arrived in golden armour clad
Stupendous! little suited to the state
Of mortal man—fit for a God to wear!       525
Now, either lead me to your gallant fleet,
Or, where ye find me, leave me straightly bound
Till ye return, and, after trial made,
Shall know if I have spoken false or true.
    But him brave Diomede with aspect stern       530
Answer'd. Since, Dolon! thou art caught, although
Thy tidings have been good, hope not to live;
For should we now release thee and dismiss,
Thou wilt revisit yet again the fleet
A spy or open foe; but smitten once       535
By this death-dealing arm, thou shalt return
To render mischief to the Greeks no more.
    He ceased, and Dolon would have stretch'd his hand
Toward his beard, and pleaded hard for life,
But with his faulchion, rising to the blow,       540
On the mid-neck he smote him, cutting sheer
Both tendons with a stroke so swift, that ere
His tongue had ceased, his head was in the dust.
They took his helmet clothed with ferret's felt,
Stripp'd off his wolf-skin, seized his bow and spear,       545
And brave Ulysses lifting in his hand
The trophy to Minerva, pray'd and said:
    Hail Goddess; these are thine! for thee of all
Who in Olympus dwell, we will invoke
First to our aid. Now also guide our steps,       550

Propitious, to the Thracian tents and steeds.
  He ceased, and at arm's-length the lifted spoils
Hung on a tamarisk; but mark'd the spot,
Plucking away with hand-full grasp the reeds
And spreading boughs, lest they should seek the prize    555
Themselves in vain, returning ere the night,
Swift traveller, should have fled before the dawn.
Thence, o'er the bloody champaign strew'd with arms
Proceeding, to the Thracian lines they came.
They, wearied, slept profound; beside them lay,    560
In triple order regular arranged,
Their radiant armour, and their steeds in pairs.
Amid them Rhesus slept, and at his side
His coursers, to the outer chariot-ring
Fasten'd secure.  Ulysses saw him first,    565
And, seeing, mark'd him out to Diomede.
  Behold the man, Tydides!  Lo! the steeds
By Dolon specified whom we have slain.
Be quick.  Exert thy force.  Arm'd as thou art,
Sleep not.  Loose thou the steeds, or slaughter thou    570
The Thracians, and the steeds shall be my care.
  He ceased; then blue-eyed Pallas with fresh force
Invigour'd Diomede.  From side to side
He slew; dread groans arose of dying men
Hewn with the sword, and the earth swam with blood.    575
As if he find a flock unguarded, sheep
Or goats, the lion rushes on his prey,
With such unsparing force Tydides smote
The men of Thrace, till he had slaughter'd twelve;
And whom Tydides with his faulchion struck    580
Laertes' son dragg'd by his feet abroad,
Forecasting that the steeds might pass with ease,
Nor start, as yet uncustom'd to the dead.
But when the son of Tydeus found the King,
Him also panting forth his last, last breath,    585
He added to the twelve; for at his head
An evil dream that night had stood, the form
Of Diomede, by Pallas' art devised.
Meantime, the bold Ulysses loosed the steeds,
Which, to each other rein'd, he drove abroad,    590
Smiting them with his bow, (for of the scourge

He thought not in the chariot-seat secured,)
And as he went, hiss'd, warning Diomede.
But he, projecting still some hardier deed,
Stood doubtful, whether by the pole to draw          595
The chariot thence, laden with gorgeous arms,
Or whether heaving it on high, to bear
The burthen off, or whether yet to take
More Thracian lives; when him with various thoughts
Perplex'd, Minerva, drawing near, bespake.          600
    Son of bold Tydeus! think on thy return
To yonder fleet, lest thou depart constrain'd.
Some other God may rouse the powers of Troy.
    She ended, and he knew the voice divine.
At once he mounted.   With his bow the steeds          605
Ulysses plyed, and to the ships they flew.
    Nor look'd the bender of the silver bow,
Apollo, forth in vain, but at the sight
Of Pallas following Diomede incensed,
Descended to the field where numerous most          610
He saw the Trojans, and the Thracian Chief
And counsellor, Hippocoön aroused,
Kinsman of Rhesus, and renown'd in arms.
He, starting from his sleep, soon as he saw
The spot deserted where so lately lay          615
Those fiery coursers, and his warrior friends
Gasping around him, sounding loud the name
Of his loved Rhesus.   Instant, at the voice,
Wild stir arose and clamorous uproar
Of fast-assembling Trojans.   Deeds they saw—          620
Terrible deeds, and marvellous perform'd,
But not their authors—they had sought the ships.
    Meantime arrived where they had slain the spy
Of Hector, there Ulysses, dear to Jove,
The coursers stay'd, and, leaping to the ground,          625
The son of Tydeus in Ulysses' hands
The arms of Dolon placed foul with his blood,
Then vaulted light into his seat again.
He lash'd the steeds, they, not unwilling, flew
To the deep-bellied barks, as to their home          630
First Nestor heard the sound, and thus he said.
    Friends! Counsellors! and leaders of the Greeks!

s. c.—7.                                        o

False shall I speak, or true?—but speak I must.
The echoing sound of hoofs alarms my ear.
Oh, that Ulysses, and brave Diomede                         635
This moment might arrive drawn into camp
By Trojan steeds! But ah, the dread I feel!
Lest some disaster have for ever quell'd
In yon rude host those noblest of the Greeks!
   He had not ended, when themselves arrived.      640
Both quick dismounted; joy at their return
Fill'd every bosom; each with kind salute
Cordial, and right-hand welcome greeted them,
And first Gerenian Nestor thus enquired.
   Oh Chief by all extoll'd, glory of Greece,      645
Ulysses! how have ye these steeds acquired?
In yonder host? or met ye as ye went
Some God who gave them to you? for they show
A lustre dazzling as the beams of day.
Old as I am, I mingle yet in fight                          650
With Ilium's sons,—lurk never in the fleet—
Yet saw I at no time, or have remark'd
Steeds such as these; which therefore I believe
Perforce, that ye have gained by gift divine;
For cloud-assembler Jove, and azure-eyed                    655
Minerva, Jove's own daughter, love you both.
   To whom Ulysses, thus, discreet, replied.
Neleian Nestor, glory of the Greeks!
A God, so willing, could have given us steeds
Superior, for their bounty knows no bounds.                 660
But, venerable Chief! these which thou seest
Are Thracians new-arrived.   Their master lies
Slain by the valiant Diomede, with twelve
The noblest of his warriors at his side.
A thirteenth[6] also, at small distance hence                665
We slew, by Hector and the Chiefs of Troy
Sent to inspect the posture of our host.
   He said; then, high in exultation, drove
The coursers o'er the trench, and with him pass'd
The glad Achaians; at the spacious tent                     670

[6] Homer did not here forget himself, though some have altered ρις
to τετρακαιδεκατον.—Rhesus for distinction sake is not numbered with
his people.—See Villoisson *in loco.*

Of Diomede arrived, with even thongs
They tied them at the cribs where stood the steeds
Of Tydeus' son, with winnow'd wheat supplied.
Ulysses in his bark the gory spoils
Of Dolon placed, designing them a gift                    675
To Pallas.   Then, descending to the sea,
Neck, thighs, and legs from sweat profuse they cleansed,
And, so refresh'd and purified, their last
Ablution in bright tepid baths perform'd.
Each thus completely laved, and with smooth oil           680
Anointed, at the well-spread board they sat,
And quaff'd, in honour of Minerva, wine
Delicious, from the brimming beaker drawn.

# BOOK XI.

AURORA from Tithonus' side arose
With light for heaven and earth, when Jove dispatch'd
Discord, the fiery signal in her hand
Of battle bearing, to the Grecian fleet.
High on Ulysses' huge black ship she stood            5
The centre of the fleet, whence all might hear,
The tent of Telamon's huge son between,
And of Achilles ; for confiding they
In their heroic fortitude, their barks
Well-poised had station'd utmost of the line.         10
There standing, shrill she sent a cry abroad
Among the Achaians, such as thirst infused
Of battle ceaseless into every breast.
All deem'd, at once, war sweeter, than to seek
Their native country through the waves again.         15
Then with loud voice Atrides bade the Greeks
Gird on their armour, and himself his arms
Took radiant.   First around his legs he clasp'd
His shining greaves with silver studs secured,
Then bound his corslet to his bosom, gift             20
Of Cynyras long since ; for rumour loud
Had Cyprus reached of an Achaian host
Assembling, destined to the shores of Troy,
Wherefore, to gratify the king of men,

He made the splendid ornament his own.                          25
Ten rods of steel cœrulean all around
Embraced it, twelve of gold, twenty of tin ;
Six[1] spiry serpents their uplifted heads
Cœrulean darted at the wearer's throat,
Splendour diffusing as the various bow                          30
Fix'd by Saturnian Jove in showery clouds,
A sign to mortal men.   He slung his sword
Athwart his shoulders ; dazzling bright it shone
With gold emboss'd, and silver was the sheath
Suspended graceful in a belt of gold.                           35
His massy shield o'ershadowing him whole,
High-wrought and beautiful, he next assumed.
Ten circles bright of brass around its field
Extensive, circle within circle, ran ;
The central boss was black, but hemm'd about                    40
With twice ten bosses of resplendent tin.
There, dreadful ornament ! the visage dark
Of Gorgon scowl'd, border'd by Flight and Fear.
The loop was silver, and a serpent form
Cœrulean over all its surface twined,                           45
Three heads erecting on one neck, the heads
Together wreath'd into a stately crown.
His helmet quatre-crested,[2] and with studs
Fast rivetted around he to his brows
Adjusted, whence tremendous waved his crest                     50
Of mounted hair on high.   Two spears he seized
Ponderous, brass-pointed, and that flash'd to heaven.
Sounds[3] like clear thunder, by the spouse of Jove
And by Minerva raised to extol the King
Of opulent Mycenæ, roll'd around.                               55
At once each bade his charioteer his steeds
Hold fast beside the margin of the trench

---

[1] Τρεις ἑκατερθ',—Three on a side.   This is evidently the proper
punctuation, though it differs from that of all the editions that I have
seen.   I find it nowhere but in the *Venetian Scholium.*

[2] Quâtre-crested.   So I have rendered τετραφαληρον, which literally
signifies having four cones.   The cone was a tube into which the crest
was inserted.   The word quâtre-crested may need a precedent for its
justification, and seems to have a sufficient one in the cinque-spotted
cowslip of Shakspeare.           [3] This seems the proper import of
εγδουπησαν.   Jupiter is called εριγδουπος.

In orderly array ; the foot all arm'd
Rush'd forward, and the clamour of the host
Rose infinite into the dawning skies.                      60
First, at the trench, the embattled infantry[4]
Stood ranged ; the chariots followed close behind ;
Dire was the tumult by Saturnian Jove
Excited and from ether down he shed
Blood-tinctured dews among them, for he meant              65
That day to send full many a warrior bold
To Pluto's dreary realm, slain premature.
   Opposite, on the rising-ground, appear'd
The Trojans ; them majestic Hector led,
Noble Polydamas, Æneas raised                              70
To Godlike honours in all Trojan hearts,
And Polybus, with whom Antenor's sons
Agenor, and young Acamas advanced.
Hector the splendid orb of his broad shield
Bore in the van, and as a comet now                        75
Glares through the clouds portentous, and again,
Obscured by gloomy vapours, disappears,
So Hector, marshalling his host, in front
Now shone, now vanish'd in the distant rear.
All-cased he flamed in brass, and on the sight             80
Flash'd as the lightnings of Jove Ægis-arm'd.
As reapers, toiling opposite, lay bare
Some rich man's furrows, while the sever'd grain,
Barley or wheat, sinks as the sickle moves,
So Greeks and Trojans springing into fight                 85
Slew mutual ; foul retreat alike they scorn'd,
Alike in fierce hostility their heads
Both bore aloft, and rush'd like wolves to war.
Discord, spectatress terrible, that sight
Beheld exulting ; she, of all the Gods,                    90
Alone was present ; not a Power beside
There interfered, but each his bright abode
Quiescent occupied wherever built
Among the windings of the Olympian heights ;
Yet blamed they all the storm-assembler King              95
Saturnian, for his purposed aid to Troy.

[4] The Translator follows Clarke in this interpretation of a passage to
us not very intelligible.

The eternal father reck'd not; he, apart,
Seated in solitary pomp, enjoy'd
His glory, and from on high the towers survey'd
Of Ilium and the fleet of Greece, the flash     100
Of gleaming arms, the slayer and the slain.
    While morning lasted, and the light of day
Increased, so long the weapons on both sides
Flew in thick vollies, and the people fell.
But, what time his repast the woodman spreads     105
In some umbrageous vale, his sinewy arms
Wearied with hewing many a lofty tree,
And his wants satisfied, he feels at length
The pinch of appetite to pleasant food,
Then was it, that encouraging aloud     110
Each other, in their native virtue strong,
The Grecians through the phalanx burst of Troy.
Forth sprang the monarch first; he slew the Chief
Bianor, nor himself alone, but slew
Oïleus also driver of his steeds.     115
Oïleus, with a leap alighting, rush'd
On Agamemnon; he his fierce assault
Encountering, with a spear met full his front.
Nor could his helmet's ponderous brass sustain
That force, but both his helmet and his scull     120
It shatter'd, and his martial rage repress'd.
The King of men, stripping their corslets, bared
Their shining breasts, and left them. Isus, next,
And Antiphus he flew to slay, the sons
Of Priam both, and in one chariot borne,     125
This spurious, genuine that. The bastard drove,
And Antiphus, a warrior high-renown'd,
Fought from the chariot; them Achilles erst
Feeding their flocks on Ida had surprized
And bound with osiers, but for ransom loosed.     130
Of these, imperial Agamemnon, first
Above the pap pierced Isus; next, he smote
Antiphus with his sword beside the ear,
And from his chariot cast him to the ground.
Conscious of both, their glittering arms he stripp'd,     135
For he had seen them when from Ida's heights
Achilles led them to the Grecian fleet.

As with resistless fangs the lion breaks
The young in pieces of the nimble hind,
Entering her lair, and takes ther feeble lives ;            140
She, though at hand, can yield them no defence,
But through the thick wood, wing'd with terror, starts
Herself away, trembling at such a foe ;
So them the Trojans had no power to save,
Themselves all driven before the host of Greece.            145
Next, on Pisandrus, and of dauntless heart
Hippolochus he rush'd ; they were the sons
Of brave Antimachus, who with rich gifts
By Paris bought, inflexible withheld
From Menelaus still his lovely bride.            150
His sons, the monarch, in one chariot borne
Encounter'd ; they (for they had lost the reins)
With trepidation and united force
Essay'd to check the steeds ; astonishment
Seized both ; Atrides with a lion's rage            155
Came on, and from the chariot thus they sued.
    Oh spare us ! son of Atreus, and accept
Ransom immense.    Antimachus our sire
Is rich in various treasure, gold and brass,
And temper'd steel, and, hearing the report            160
That in Achaia's fleet his sons survive,
He will requite thee with a glorious price.
    So they, with tears and gentle terms the King
Accosted, but no gentle answer heard.
    Are ye indeed the offspring of the Chief            165
Antimachus, who when my brother once
With Godlike Laertiades your town
Enter'd ambassador, his death advised
In council, and to let him forth no more ?
Now rue ye both the baseness of your sire.            170
    He said, and from his chariot to the plain
Thrust down Pisandrus, piercing with keen lance
His bosom, and supine he smote the field.
Down leap'd Hippolochus, whom on the ground
He slew ; cut sheer his hands, and lopp'd his head,            175
And roll'd it like a mortar[5] through the ranks.
He left the slain, and where he saw the field

                    [5] ολμος.

With thickest battle cover'd, thither flew
By all the Grecians follow'd bright in arms.
The scatter'd infantry constrained to fly,      180
Fell by the infantry; the charioteers,
While with loud hoofs their steeds the dusty soil
Excited, o'er the charioteers their wheels
Drove brazen-fellied, and the King of men
Incessant slaughtering, called his Argives[6] on.      185
As when fierce flames some ancient forest seize,
From side to side in flakes the various wind
Rolls them, and to the roots devour'd, the trunks
Fall prostrate under fury of the fire,
So under Agamemnon fell the heads      190
Of flying Trojans. Many a courser proud
The empty chariots through the paths of war
Whirl'd rattling, of their charioteers deprived;
They breathless press'd the plain, now fitter far
To feed the vultures than to cheer their wives.      195
   Conceal'd, meantime, by Jove, Hector escaped
The dust, darts, deaths, and tumult of the field,
And Agamemnon to the swift pursuit
Call'd loud the Grecians. Through the middle plain
Beside the sepulchre of Ilus, son      200
Of Dardanus, and where the fig-tree stood,
The Trojans flew, panting to gain the town,
While Agamemnon pressing close the rear,
Shout after shout terrific sent abroad,
And his victorious hands reek'd, red with gore.      205
But at the beech-tree and the Scæan gate
Arrived, the Trojans halted, waiting there
The rearmost fugitives; they o'er the field
Came like a herd, which in the dead of night
A lion drives; all fly, but one is doom'd      210
To death inevitable; her with jaws
True to their hold he seizes, and her neck
Breaking, embowels her, and laps the blood;
So, Atreus' royal son, the hindmost still
Slaying, and still pursuing, urged them on.      215

  [6] The Grecians at large are indiscriminately called Danaï. Argives,
and Achaians, in the original. The Phthians in particular—Hellenes.
They were the troops of Achilles.

Many supine, and many prone, the field
Press'd, by the son of Atreus in their flight
Dismounted; for no weapon raged as his.
But now, at last, when he should soon have reach'd
The lofty walls of Ilium, came the Sire          220
Of Gods and men descending from the skies,
And on the heights of Ida fountain-fed,
Sat arm'd with thunders.   Calling to his foot
Swift Iris golden-pinion'd, thus he spake.
    Iris! away.   Thus speak in Hector's ears.          225
While yet he shall the son of Atreus see
Fierce warring in the van, and mowing down
The Trojan ranks, so long let him abstain
From battle, leaving to his host the task
Of bloody contest furious with the Greeks.          230
But soon as Atreus' son by spear or shaft
Wounded shall climb his chariot, with such force
I will endue Hector, that he shall slay
Till he have reach'd the ships, and till, the sun
Descending, sacred darkness cover all.          235
    He spake, nor rapid Iris disobey'd
Storm-wing'd embassadress, but from the heights
Of Ida stoop'd to Ilium.   There she found
The son of royal Priam by the throng
Of chariots and of steeds compass'd about.          240
She, standing at his side, him thus bespake.
    Oh, son of Priam! as the Gods discreet!
I bring thee counsel from the Sire of all.
While yet thou shalt the son of Atreus see
Fierce warring in the van, and mowing down          245
The warrior ranks, so long he bids thee pause
From battle, leaving to thy host the task
Of bloody contest furious with the Greeks.
But soon as Atreus' son, by spear or shaft
Wounded, shall climb his chariot, Jove will then          250
Endue thee with such force, that thou shalt slay
Till thou have reach'd the ships, and till, the sun
Descending, sacred darkness cover all.
    So saying, swift-pinion'd Iris disappear'd.
Then Hector from his chariot at a leap          255
Came down all arm'd, and, shaking his bright spears,

Ranged every quarter, animating loud
The legions, and rekindling horrid war.
Back roll'd the Trojan ranks, and faced the Greeks;
The Greeks their host to closer phalanx drew;   260
The battle was restored, van fronting van
They stood, and Agamemnon into fight
Sprang foremost, panting for superior fame.
 Say now, ye Nine, who on Olympus dwell!
What Trojan first, or what ally of Troy   265
Opposed the force of Agamemnon's arm?
Iphidamas, Antenor's valiant son,
Of loftiest stature, who in fertile Thrace
Mother of flocks was nourish'd. Cisseus him
His grandsire, father of Theano praised   270
For loveliest features, in his own abode
Rear'd yet a child, and when at length he reach'd
The measure of his glorious manhood firm
Dismiss'd him not, but, to engage him more,
Gave him his daughter. Wedded, he his bride  275
As soon deserted, and with galleys twelve
Following the rumour'd voyage of the Greeks,
The same course steer'd; but at Percope moor'd,
And marching thence, arrived on foot at Troy.
He first opposed Atrides. They approach'd.  280
The spear of Agamemnon wander'd wide;
But him Iphidamas on his broad belt
Beneath the corslet struck, and, bearing still
On his spear-beam, enforced it; but ere yet
He pierced the broider'd zone, his point impress'd  285
Against the silver, turn'd, obtuse as lead.
Then royal Agamemnon in his hand
The weapon grasping, with a lion's rage
Home drew it to himself, and from his gripe
Wresting it, with his faulchion keen his neck  290
Smote full, and stretch'd him lifeless at his foot.
So slept Iphidamas among the slain;
Unhappy! from his virgin bride remote,
Associate with the men of Troy in arms
He fell, and left her beauties unenjoy'd.  295
He gave her much, gave her an hundred beeves,
And sheep and goats a thousand from his flocks

Promised, for numberless his meadows ranged ;
But Agamemnon, son of Atreus, him
Slew and despoil'd, and through the Grecian host            300
Proceeded, laden with his gorgeous arms.
Coön that sight beheld, illustrious Chief,
Antenor's eldest born, but with dim eyes
Through anguish for his brother's fall.   Unseen
Of noble Agamemnon, at his side                              305
He cautious stood, and with a spear his arm,
Where thickest flesh'd, below his elbow, pierced,
Till opposite the glittering point appear'd.
A thrilling horror seized the King of men
So wounded ; yet though wounded so, from fight             310
He ceased not, but on Coön rush'd, his spear
Grasping, well-thriven growth[7] of many a wind.
He by the foot drew off Iphidamas,
His brother, son of his own sire, aloud
Calling the Trojan leaders to his aid,                      315
When him so occupied with his keen point
Atrides pierced his bossy shield beneath.
Expiring on Iphidamas he fell
Prostrate, and Agamemnon lopp'd his head.
Thus, under royal Agamemnon's hand,                         320
Antenor's sons their destiny fulfill'd,
And to the house of Ades journey'd both.
Through other ranks of warriors then he pass'd,
Now with his spear, now with his faulchion arm'd,
And now with missile force of massy stones,                 325
While yet his warm blood sallied from the wound.
But when the wound grew dry, and the blood ceased,
Anguish intolerable undermined
Then all the might of Atreus' royal son.
As when a labouring woman's arrowy throes                   330
Seize her intense, by Juno's daughters dread
The birth-presiding Ilithyæ deep
Infixt, dispensers of those pangs severe ;
So, anguish insupportable subdued
Then all the might of Atreus' royal son.                    335
Up-springing to his seat, instant he bade
His charioteer drive to the hollow barks,

[7] Ανεμοτρεφες—literally—wind-nourished.

Heart-sick himself with pain; yet, ere he went,
With voice loud-echoing hail'd the Danaï.
 Friends! counsellors and leaders of the Greeks!  340
Now drive, yourselves, the battle from your ships.
For me the Gods permit not to employ
In fight with Ilium's host the day entire.
 He ended, and the charioteer his steeds
Lash'd to the ships; they not unwilling flew,  345
Bearing from battle the afflicted King
With foaming chests and bellies grey with dust.
Soon Hector, noting his retreat, aloud
Call'd on the Trojans and allies of Troy.
 Trojans and Lycians, and close-fighting sons  350
Of Dardanus! oh summon all your might;
Now, now be men! Their bravest is withdrawn!
Glory and honour from Saturnian Jove
On me attend; now full against the Greeks
Drive all your steeds, and win a deathless name.  355
 He spake—and all drew courage from his word.
As when his hounds bright-tooth'd some hunter cheers
Against the lion or the forest-boar,
So Priameïan Hector cheer'd his host
Magnanimous against the sons of Greece,  360
Terrible as gore-tainted Mars. Among
The foremost warriors, with success elate
He strode, and flung himself into the fight
Black as a storm which sudden from on high
Descending, furrows deep the gloomy flood.  365
 Then whom slew Priameïan Hector first,
Whom last, by Jove, that day, with glory crown'd?
Assæus, Dolops, Orus, Agelaüs,
Autonoüs, Hipponoüs, Æsymnus,
Opheltius and Opites first he slew,  370
All leaders of the Greeks, and, after these,
The people. As when whirlwinds of the West
A storm encounter from the gloomy South,
The waves roll multitudinous, and the foam
Upswept by wandering gusts fills all the air,  375
So Hector swept the Grecians. Then defeat
Past remedy and havoc had ensued,
Then had the routed Grecians, flying, sought

Their ships again, but that Ulysses thus
Summon'd the brave Tydides to his aid. 380
 Whence comes it, Diomede, that we forget
Our wonted courage? Hither, O my friend!
And, fighting at my side, ward off the shame
That must be ours, should Hector seize the fleet.
 To whom the valiant Diomede replied. 385
I will be firm; trust me thou shalt not find
Me shrinking; yet small fruit of our attempts
Shall follow, for the Thunderer, not to us,
But to the Trojan, gives the glorious day.
 The Hero spake, and from his chariot cast 390
Thymbræus to the ground pierced through the pap,
While by Ulysses' hand his charioteer
Godlike Molion, fell. The warfare thus
Of both for ever closed, them there they left,
And plunging deep into the warrior-throng 395
Troubled the multitude. As when two boars
Turn desperate on the close-pursuing hounds,
So they, returning on the host of Troy,
Slew on all sides, and overtoil'd with flight
From Hector's arm, the Greeks meantime respired. 400
Two warriors, next, their chariot and themselves
They took, plebeians brave, sons of the seer
Percosian Merops in prophetic skill
Surpassing all; he both his sons forbad
The mortal field, but disobedient they 405
Still sought it, for their destiny prevail'd.
Spear-practised Diomede of life deprived
Both these, and stripp'd them of their glorious arms,
While by Ulysses' hand Hippodamus
Died and Hypeirochus. And now the son 410
Of Saturn, looking down from Ida, poised
The doubtful war, and mutual deaths they dealt.
Tydides plunged his spear into the groin
Of the illustrious son of Pæon, bold
Agastrophus. No steeds at his command 415
Had he, infatuate! but his charioteer
His steeds detain'd remote, while through the van
Himself on foot rush'd madly till he fell.
But Hector through the ranks darting his eye

Perceived, and with ear-piercing cries advanced          420
Against them, follow'd by the host of Troy.
The son of Tydeus, shuddering, his approach
Discern'd, and instant to Ulysses spake.
  Now comes the storm! This way the mischief rolls!
Stand and repulse the Trojan.   Now be firm.          425
  He said, and hurling his long-shadow'd beam
Smote Hector.   At his helmet's crown he aim'd,
Nor err'd, but brass encountering brass, the point
Glanced wide, for he had cased his youthful brows
In triple brass, Apollo's glorious gift.          430
Yet with rapidity at such a shock
Hector recoil'd into the multitude
Afar, where sinking to his knees, he lean'd
On his broad palm, and darkness veil'd his eyes.
But while Tydides follow'd through the van          435
His stormy spear, which in the distant soil
Implanted stood, Hector his scatter'd sense
Recovering, to his chariot sprang again,
And, diving deep into his host, escaped.
The noble son of Tydeus, spear in hand,          440
Rush'd after him, and as he went, exclaim'd.
  Dog! thou hast now escaped; but, sure the stroke
Approach'd thee nigh, well-aim'd.   Once more thy prayers
Which ever to Apollo thou prefer'st
Entering the clash of battle, have prevail'd,          445
And he hath rescued thee.   But well beware
Our next encounter, for if also me
Some God befriend, thou diest.   Now will I seek
Another mark, and smite whom next I may.
  He spake, and of his armour stripp'd the son          450
Spear-famed of Pæon.   Meantime Paris, mate
Of beauteous Helen, drew his bow against
Tydides; by a pillar of the tomb
Of Ilus, ancient senator revered,
Conceal'd he stood, and while the Hero loosed          455
His corslet from the breast of Pæon's son
Renown'd, and of his helmet and his targe
Despoil'd him; Paris, arching quick his bow,
No devious shaft dismiss'd, but his right foot
Pierced through the sole, and fix'd it to the ground.          460

Transported from his ambush forth he leap'd
With a loud laugh, and, vaunting, thus exclaim'd :
   Oh shaft well shot! it galls thee.   Would to heaven
That it had pierced thy heart, and thou hadst died !
So had the Trojans respite from their toils          465
Enjoy'd, who, now, shudder at sight of thee
Like she-goats when the lion is at hand.
   To whom, undaunted, Diomede replied.
Archer shrew-tongued ! spie-maiden ! man of curls ![8]
Should'st thou in arms attempt me face to face,      470
Thy bow and arrows should avail thee nought.
Vain boaster ! thou hast scratch'd my foot,—no more—
And I regard it as I might the stroke
Of a weak woman or a simple child.
The weapons of a dastard and a slave          475
Are ever such.   More terrible are mine,
And whom they pierce, though slightly pierced, he dies.
His wife her cheeks rends inconsolable,
His babes are fatherless, his blood the glebe
Incarnadines, and where he bleeds and rots       480
More birds of prey than women haunt the place.
   He ended, and Ulysses, drawing nigh,
Shelter'd Tydides ; he behind the Chief
Of Ithaca sat drawing forth the shaft,
But pierced with agonizing pangs the while.      485
Then, climbing to his chariot-seat, he bade
Sthenelus hasten to the hollow ships,
Heart-sick with pain.   And now alone was seen
Spear-famed Ulysses ; not an Argive more
Remain'd, so universal was the rout,          490
And groaning, to his own great heart he said.
   Alas ! what now awaits me ? if, appall'd
By multitudes, I fly, much detriment ;
And if alone they intercept me here,
Still more ; for Jove hath scatter'd all the host.    495
Yet why these doubts ? for know I not of old

---

[8] In the original—κέρα αγλαέ.—All that I pretend to know of this expression is that it is ironical, and may relate either to the head-dress of Paris, or to his archership.  To translate it is impossible : to paraphrase it in a passage of so much emotion, would be absurd.  I have endeavoured to supply its place by an appellation in point of contempt equal.

That only dastards fly, and that the voice
Of honour bids the famed in battle stand,
Bleed they themselves, or cause their foes to bleed ?
   While busied in such thought he stood, the ranks   500
Of Trojans fronted with broad shields, enclosed
The hero with a ring, hemming around
Their own destruction.   As when dogs, and swains
In prime of manhood, from all quarters rush
Around a boar, he from his thicket bolts,   505
The bright tusk whetting in his crooked jaws :
They press him on all sides, and from beneath
Loud gnashings hear, yet, firm, his threats defy ;
Like them the Trojans on all sides assail'd
Ulysses dear to Jove.   First with his spear   510
He sprang impetuous on a valiant chief,
Whose shoulder with a downright point he pierced,
Deïopites ; Thoön next he slew,
And Ennomus, and from his coursers' backs
Alighting quick, Chersidamas ; beneath   515
His bossy shield the gliding weapon pass'd
Right through his navel ; on the plain he fell
Expiring, and with both hands clench'd the dust.
Them slain he left, and Charops wounded next,
Brother of Socus, generous Chief, and son   520
Of Hippasus ; brave Socus to the aid
Of Charos flew, and, godlike, thus began.
   Illustrious chief, Ulysses! strong to toil
And rich in artifice !   Or boast to-day
Two sons of Hippasus, brave warriors both,   525
Of armour and of life bereft by thee,
Or to my vengeful spear resign thy own !
   So saying, Ulysses' oval disk he smote.
Through his bright disk the stormy weapon flew,
Transpierced his twisted mail, and from his side   530
Drove all the skin, but to his nobler parts
Found entrance none, by Pallas turn'd aslant.
Ulysses, conscious of his life untouch'd,
Retired a step from Socus, and replied.
   Ah hapless youth ; thy fate is on the wing ;   535
Me thou hast forced indeed to cease a while
From battle with the Trojans, but I speak
   S. C.—7.                       P

Thy death at hand ; for vanquish'd by my spear,
This self-same day thou shalt to me resign
Thy fame, thy soul to Pluto steed-renown'd.          540
    He ceased ; then Socus turn'd his back to fly,
But, as he turn'd, his shoulder-blades between
He pierced him, and the spear urged through his breast.
On his resounding arms he fell, and thus
Godlike Ulysses gloried in his fall.                 545
    Ah, Socus, son of Hippasus, a chief
Of fame equestrian ! swifter far than thou
Death follow'd thee, and thou hast not escaped.
Ill-fated youth ! thy parents' hands thine eyes
Shall never close, but birds of ravenous maw         550
Shall tear thee, flapping thee with frequent wing,
While me the noble  Grecians shall entomb !
    So saying, the valiant Socus' spear he drew
From his own flesh, and through his bossy shield.
The weapon drawn, forth sprang the blood, and left   555
His spirit faint.    Then Ilium's dauntless sons,
Seeing Ulysses' blood, exhorted glad
Each other, and, with force united, all
Press'd on him.    He, retiring, summon'd loud
His followers.    Thrice, loud as a mortal may,      560
He call'd, and valiant Menelaus thrice
Hearing the voice, to Ajax thus remark'd.
    Illustrious son of Telamon !    The voice
Of Laertiades comes o'er my ear
With such a sound, as if the hardy chief,            565
Abandon'd of his friends, were overpower'd
By numbers intercepting his retreat.
Haste ! force we quick a passage through the ranks.
His worth demands our succour, for I fear
Lest sole conflicting with the host of Troy,         570
Brave as he is, he perish, to the loss
Unspeakable and long regret of Greece.
    So saying, he went, and Ajax, godlike Chief,
Follow'd him.    At the voice arrived, they found
Ulysses Jove-beloved compass'd about                 575
By Trojans, as the lynxes in the hills,
Adust for blood, compass an antler'd stag
Pierced by an archer ; while his blood is warm

And his limbs pliable, from him he 'scapes ;
But when the feather'd barb hath quell'd his force,		580
In some dark hollow of the mountain's side,
The hungry troop devour him ; chance, the while,
Conducts a lion thither, before whom
All vanish, and the lion feeds alone ;
So swarm'd the Trojan powers, numerous and bold,		585
Around Ulysses, who with wary skill
Heroic combated his evil day.
But Ajax came cover'd with his broad shield
That seem'd a tower, and at Ulysses' side
Stood fast ; then fled the Trojans wide-dispersed,		590
And Menelaus led him by the hand
Till his own chariot to his aid approach'd.
But Ajax, springing on the Trojans, slew
Doryclus, from the loins of Priam sprung,
But spurious.   Pandocus he wounded next,		595
Then wounded Pyrasus, and after him
Pylartes and Lysander.   As a flood
Runs headlong from the mountains to the plain
After long showers from Jove ; many a dry oak
And many a pine the torrent sweeps along,		600
And, turbid, shoots much soil into the sea,
So, glorious Ajax troubled wide the field,
Horse and man slaughtering, whereof Hector yet
Heard not ; for on the left of all the war
He fought beside Scamander, where around		605
Huge Nestor, and Idomeneus the brave,
Most deaths were dealt, and loudest roar'd the fight.
There Hector toil'd, feats wonderful of spear
And horsemanship  achieving, and the lines
Of many a phalanx desolating wide.		610
Nor even then had the bold Greeks retired,
But that an arrow triple-barb'd, dispatch'd
By Paris, Helen's mate, against the Chief
Machaon warring with distinguish'd force,
Pierced his right shoulder.   For his sake alarm'd,		615
The valour-breathing Grecians fear'd, lest he
In that disasterous field should also fall.
At once, Idomeneus of Crete approach'd
The noble Nestor, and him thus bespake.

Arise, Neleian Nestor! Pride of Greece!                    620
Ascend thy chariot, and Machaon placed
Beside thee, bear him, instant, to the fleet.
For one, so skill'd in medicine, and to free
The inherent barb, is worth a multitude.
 He said, nor the Gerenian hero old            625
Aught hesitated, but into his seat
Ascended, and Machaon, son renown'd
Of Æsculapius, mounted at his side.
He lash'd the steeds, they not unwilling sought
The hollow ships, long their familiar home.               630
 Cebriones, meantime the charioteer
Of Hector, from his seat the Trojan ranks
Observing sore discomfited, began.
 Here are we busied, Hector! on the skirts
Of roaring battle, and meantime I see               635
Our host confused, their horses and themselves
All mingled. ·Telamonian Ajax there
Routs them; I know the hero by his shield.
Haste, drive we thither, for the carnage most
Of horse and foot conflicting furious, there            640
Rages, and infinite the shouts arise.
 He said, and with shrill-sounding scourge the steeds
Smote ample-maned; they, at the sudden stroke
Through both hosts whirl'd the chariot, shields and men
Trampling; with blood the axle underneath            645
All redden'd, and the chariot-rings with drops
From the horse-hoofs, and from the fellied wheels.
Full on the multitude he drove, on fire
To burst the phalanx, and confusion sent
Among the Greeks, for nought[9] he shunn'd the spear.     650
All quarters else with faulchion or with lance,
Or with huge stones he ranged, but cautious shunn'd
The encounter of the Telamonian Chief.
 But the eternal father throned on high
With fear fill'd Ajax; panic-fixt he stood,            655
His seven-fold shield behind his shoulder cast,

 [9] This interpretation of—μινυνθα δε χαζετο δυρος—is taken from the
Scholium by Villoisson. It differs from those of Clarke, Eustathius, and
another Scholiast quoted by Clarke, but seems to suit the context much
better than either.

And hemm'd by numbers, with an eye askant,
Watchful retreated.   As a beast of prey
Retiring, turns and looks, so he his face
Turn'd oft, retiring slow, and step by step.                    660
As when the watch-dogs and assembled swains
Have driven a tawny lion from the stalls,
Then, interdicting him his wish'd repast,
Watch all the night, he, famish'd, yet again
Comes furious on, but speeds not, kept aloof                    665
By frequent spears from daring hands, but more
By flash of torches, which, though fierce, he dreads,
Till, at the dawn, sullen he stalks away;
So from before the Trojans Ajax stalk'd
Sullen, and with reluctance slow retired,                    670
His brave heart trembling for the fleet of Greece.
As when (the boys o'erpower'd) a sluggish ass,
On whose tough sides they have spent many a staff,
Enters the harvest, and the spiry ears.
Crops persevering; with their rods the boys                    675
Still ply him hard, but all their puny might
Scarce drives him forth when he hath browzed his fill,
So, there, the Trojans and their foreign aids
With glittering lances keen huge Ajax urged,
His broad shield's centre smiting.   He, by turns,                    680
With desperate force the Trojan phalanx dense
Facing, repulsed them, and by turns he fled,
But still forbad all inroad on the fleet.
Trojans and Greeks between, alone, he stood
A bulwark.  Spears from daring hands dismiss'd                    685
Some, piercing his broad shield, there planted stood,
While others, in the midway falling, spent
Their disappointed rage deep in the ground.
    Eurypylus, Evæmon's noble son,
Him seeing, thus, with weapons overwhelm'd                    690
Flew to his side, his glittering lance dismiss'd,
And Apisaon, son of Phausias, struck
Under the midriff; through his liver pass'd
The ruthless point, and, falling, he expired.
Forth sprang Eurypylus to seize the spoil;                    695
Whom soon as godlike Alexander saw
Despoiling Apisaon of his arms,

Drawing incontinent his bow, he sent
A shaft to his right thigh ; the brittle reed
Snapp'd, and the rankling barb stuck fast within.　　700
Terrified at the stroke, the wounded Chief
To his own band retired, but, as he went,
With echoing voice call'd on the Danaï—
　　Friends ! Counsellors, and leaders of the Greeks !
Turn ye and stand, and from his dreadful lot　　705
Save Ajax whelm'd with weapons ; 'scape, I judge,
He cannot from the roaring fight, yet oh
Stand fast around him ; save, if save ye may,
Your champion huge, the Telamonian Chief !
　　So spake the wounded warrior.　They at once　　710
With sloping bucklers, and with spears erect,
To his relief approach'd.　Ajax with joy
The friendly phalanx join'd, then turn'd and stood.
　　Thus burn'd the embattled field as with the flames
Of a devouring fire.　Meantime afar　　715
From all that tumult the Neleian mares
Bore Nestor, foaming as they ran, with whom
Machaon also rode, leader revered.
Achilles mark'd him passing ; for he stood
Exalted on his huge ship's lofty stern,　　720
Spectator of the toil severe, and flight
Deplorable of the defeated Greeks.
He call'd his friend Patroclus.　He below
Within his tent the sudden summons heard
And sprang like Mars abroad, all unaware　　725
That in that sound he heard the voice of fate.
Him first Menœtius' gallant son address'd.
　　What would Achilles ? Wherefore hath he call'd ?
To whom Achilles swiftest of the swift :
　　Brave Menœtiades ! my soul's delight !　　730
Soon will the Grecians now my knees surround
Suppliant, by dread extremity constrain'd.
But fly Patroclus, haste, oh dear to Jove !
Enquire of Nestor, whom he hath convey'd
From battle, wounded ? Viewing him behind,　　735
I most believed him Æsculapius' son
Machaon, but the steeds so swiftly pass'd
My galley, that his face escaped my note.

He said, and prompt to gratify his friend,
Forth ran Patroclus through the camp of Greece.          740
    Now when Neleian Nestor to his tent
Had brought Machaon, they alighted both,
And the old hero's friend Eurymedon
Released the coursers.   On the beach awhile
Their tunics sweat-imbued in the cool air               745
They ventilated, facing full the breeze,
Then on soft couches in the tent reposed.
Meantime, their beverage Hecamede mix'd,
The old King's bright-hair'd captive, whom he brought
From Tenedos, what time Achilles sack'd                750
The city, daughter of the noble Chief
Arsinoüs, and selected from the rest
For Nestor, as the honourable meed
Of counsels always eminently wise.
She, first, before them placed a table bright,         755
With feet cœrulean; thirst-provoking sauce
She brought them also in a brazen tray,
Garlick and honey new, and sacred meal.
Beside them, next, she placed a noble cup
Of labour exquisite, which from his home               760
The ancient King had brought with golden studs
Embellish'd; it presented to the grasp
Four ears; two golden turtles, perch'd on each,
Seem'd feeding, and two turtles[10] form'd the base.
That cup once fill'd, all others must have toil'd       765
To move it from the board, but it was light
In Nestor's hand; he lifted it with ease.
The graceful virgin in that cup a draught
Mix'd for them, Pramnian wine and savoury cheese
Of goat's milk, grated with a brazen rasp,             770
Then sprinkled all with meal.  The draught prepared,
She gave it to their hand; they, drinking, slaked
Their fiery thirst, and with each other sat
Conversing friendly, when the Godlike youth
By brave Achilles sent, stood at the door.             775

[10] I have interpreted the very ambiguous words δυω δ' ὑπο πυθμενες
ἠσαν according to Athenæus as quoted by Clarke, and his interpretation
of them is confirmed by the Scholium in the Venetian edition of the Iliad,
lately published by Villoisson.

Him seeing, Nestor from his splendid couch
Arose, and by the hand leading him in,
Entreated him to sit, but that request
Patroclus, on his part refusing, said,
   Oh venerable King! no seat is here         780
For me, nor may thy courtesy prevail.
He is irascible, and to be fear'd
Who bade me ask what Chieftain thou hast brought
From battle, wounded; but untold I learn;
I see Machaon, and shall now report         785
As I have seen; oh ancient King revered!
Thou know'st Achilles fiery, and propense
Blame to impute even where blame is none.
   To whom the brave Gerenian thus replied.
Why feels Achilles for the wounded Greeks    790
Such deep concern? He little knows the height
To which our sorrows swell. Our noblest lie
By spear or arrow wounded in the fleet.
Diomede, warlike son of Tydeus, bleeds,
Gall'd by a shaft; Ulysses, glorious Chief,    795
And Agamemnon[11] suffer by the spear;
Eurypylus is shot into the thigh,
And here lies still another newly brought
By me from fight, pierced also by a shaft.
What then? How strong soe'er to give them aid   800
Achilles feels no pity of the Greeks.
Waits he till every vessel on the shore
Fired, in despite of the whole Argive host,
Be sunk in its own ashes, and ourselves
All perish, heaps on heaps? For in my limbs   805
No longer lives the agility of my youth.
Oh, for the vigour of those days again,
When Elis, for her cattle which we took,
Strove with us, and Itymoneus I slew,
Brave offspring of Hypirochus; he dwelt   810
In Elis, and while I the pledges drove,
Stood for his herd, but fell among the first
By a spear hurl'd from my victorious arm.

---

[11] It would have suited the dignity of Agamemnon's rank to have mentioned *his* wound first; but Nestor making this recital to the *friend of Achilles* names him slightly, and without any addition.

Then fled the rustic multitude, and we
Drove off abundant booty from the plain,      815
Herds fifty of fat beeves, large flocks of goats
As many, with as many sheep and swine,
And full thrice fifty mares of brightest hue,
All breeders, many with their foals beneath.
All these, by night returning safe, we drove      820
Into Neleian Pylus, and the heart
Rejoiced of Neleus, in a son so young
A warrior, yet enrich'd with such a prize.
At early dawn the heralds summon'd loud
The citizens, to prove their just demands      825
On fruitful Elis, and the assembled Chiefs
Division made, (for numerous were the debts
Which the Epeans, in the weak estate
Of the unpeopled Pylus, had incurr'd;
For Hercules, few years before, had sack'd[12]      830
Our city, and our mightiest slain.   Ourselves
The gallant sons of Neleus, were in all
Twelve youths, of whom myself alone survived;
The rest all perish'd; whence presumptuous grown,
The brazen-mail'd Epeans wrong'd us oft).      835
An herd of beeves my father for himself
Selected, and a numerous flock beside,
Three hundred sheep, with shepherds for them all.
For he a claimant was of large arrears
From sacred Elis.   Four unrivall'd steeds      840
With his own chariot to the games he sent,
That should contend for the appointed prize
A tripod; but Augeias, King of men,
Detain'd the steeds, and sent the charioteer
Defrauded home.   My father, therefore, fired      845
At such foul outrage both of deeds and words,
Took much, and to the Pylians gave the rest
For satisfaction of the claims of all.
While thus we busied were in these concerns,
And in performance of religious rites      850
Throughout the city, came the Epeans arm'd,

[12] It is said that the Thebans having war with the people of Orchomenos, the Pylians assisted the latter, for which cause Hercules destroyed their city.—See Scholium per Villoisson.

Their whole vast multitude both horse and foot
On the third day ; came also clad in brass
The two Molions, inexpert as yet
In feats of arms, and of a boyish age.                           855
There is a city on a mountain's head,
Fast by the banks of Alpheus, far remote,
The utmost town which sandy Pylus owns,
Named Thryoëssa, and, with ardour fired
To lay it waste, that city they besieged.                        860
Now when their host had traversed all the plain,
Minerva from Olympus flew by night
And bade us arm ; nor were the Pylians slow
To assemble, but impatient for the fight.
Me, then, my father suffer'd not to arm,                         865
But hid my steeds, for he supposed me raw
As yet, and ignorant how war is waged.
Yet, even thus, unvantaged and on foot,
Superior honours I that day acquired
To theirs who rode, for Pallas led me on                         870
Herself to victory.   There is a stream
Which at Arena falls into the sea,
Named Minuëius ; on that river's bank
The Pylian horsemen waited day's approach,
And thither all our foot came pouring down.                      875
The flood divine of Alpheus thence we reach'd
At noon, all arm'd complete ; there, hallow'd rites
We held to Jove omnipotent, and slew
A bull to sacred Alpheus, with a bull
To Neptune, and an heifer of the herd                            880
To Pallas ; then, all marshall'd as they were,
From van to rear our legions took repast,
And at the river's side slept on their arms.
Already the Epean host had round
Begirt the city, bent to lay it waste,                           885
A task which cost them, first, both blood and toil.
For when the radiant sun on the green earth
Had risen, with prayer to Pallas and to Jove,
We gave them battle.   When the Pylian host
And the Epeans thus were close engaged,                          890
I first a warrior slew, Mulius the brave,
And seized his coursers.   He the eldest-born

Of King Augeias' daughters had espoused
The golden Agamede ; not an herb
The spacious earth yields but she knew its powers.          895
Him, rushing on me, with my brazen lance
I smote, and in the dust he fell ; I leap'd
Into his seat, and drove into the van.
A panic seized the Epeans when they saw
The leader of their horse o'erthrown, a Chief          900
Surpassing all in fight.   Black as a cloud
With whirlwind fraught, I drove impetuous on,
Took fifty chariots, and at side of each
Lay two slain warriors, with their teeth the soil
Grinding, all vanquish'd by my single arm.          905
I had slain also the Molions, sons
Of Actor, but the Sovereign of the deep
Their own authentic sire, in darkness dense
Involving both, convey'd them safe away.
Then Jove a victory of prime renown          910
Gave to the Pylians ; for we chased and slew
And gather'd spoil o'er all the champaign spread
With scatter'd shields, till we our steeds had driven
To the Buprasian fields laden with corn,
To the Olenian rock, and to a town          915
In fair Colona situate, and named
Alesia.   There it was that Pallas turn'd
Our people homeward ; there I left the last
Of all the slain, and he was slain by me.
Then drove the Achaians from Buprasium home          920
Their coursers fleet, and Jove, of Gods above,
Received most praise, Nestor of men below.
Such once was I.   But brave Achilles shuts
His virtues close, an unimparted store ;
Yet even he shall weep, when all the host,          925
His fellow-warriors once, shall be destroy'd.
But recollect, young friend ! the sage advice
Which when thou camest from Phthia to the aid
Of Agamemnon, on that selfsame day
Menœtius gave thee.   We were present there,          930
Ulysses and myself, both in the house,
And heard it all ; for to the house we came
Of Peleus in our journey through the land

Of fertile Greece, gathering her states to war.
We found thy noble sire Menœtius there,          935
Thee and Achilles ; ancient Peleus stood
To Jove the Thunderer offering in his court
Thighs of an ox, and on the blazing rites
Libation pouring from a cup of gold.
While ye on preparation of the feast          940
Attended both, Ulysses and myself
Stood in the vestibule ; Achilles flew
Toward us, introduced us by the hand,
And, seating us, such liberal portion gave
To each, as hospitality requires.          945
Our thirst, at length, and hunger both sufficed,
I, foremost speaking, ask'd you to the wars,
And ye were eager both, but from your sires
Much admonition, ere ye went, received.
Old Peleus charged Achilles to aspire          950
To highest praise, and always to excel.
But thee, thy sire Menœtius thus advised.
" My son ! Achilles boasts the nobler birth,
But thou art elder ; He in strength excels
Thee far ; Thou, therefore, with discretion rule          955
His inexperience ; thy advice impart
With gentleness ; instruction wise suggest
Wisely, and thou shalt find him apt to learn."
So thee thy father taught, but, as it seems,
In vain.   Yet even now essay to move          960
Warlike Achilles ; if the Gods so please,
Who knows but that thy reasons may prevail
To rouse his valiant heart ? men rarely scorn
The earnest intercession of a friend.
But if some prophecy alarm his fears,          965
And from his Goddess mother he have aught
Received, who may have learnt the same from Jove,
Thee let him send at least, and order forth
With thee the Myrmidons ; a dawn of hope
Shall thence, it may be, on our host arise.          970
And let him send thee to the battle clad
In his own radiant armour ; Troy, deceived
By such resemblance, shall abstain perchance
From conflict, and the weary Greeks enjoy

Short respite; it is all that war allows.                    975
Fresh as ye are, ye, by your shouts alone,
May easily repulse an army spent
With labour from the camp and from the fleet.
    Thus Nestor, and his mind bent to his words.
Back to Æacides through all the camp                         980
He ran; and when, still running, he arrived
Among Ulysses' barks, where they had fix'd
The forum, where they minister'd the laws,
And had erected altars to the Gods,
There him Eurypylus, Evæmon's son,                           985
Illustrious met, deep-wounded in his thigh,
And halting back from battle.   From his head
The sweat, and from his shoulders ran profuse,
And from his perilous wound the sable blood
Continual stream'd; yet was his mind composed.              990
Him seeing, Menœtiades the brave
Compassion felt, and, mournful, thus began.
    Ah hapless senators and Chiefs of Greece!
Left ye your native country that the dogs
Might fatten on your flesh at distant Troy?                  995
But tell me, Hero! say, Eurypylus!
Have the Achaians power still to withstand
The enormous force of Hector, or is this
The moment when his spear must pierce us all?
    To whom Eurypylus, discreet, replied.                   1000
Patroclus, dear to Jove! there is no help,
No remedy.   We perish at our ships.
The warriors, once most strenuous of the Greeks,
Lie wounded in the fleet by foes whose might
Increases ever.   But thyself afford                        1005
To me some succour; lead me to my ship;
Cut forth the arrow from my thigh; the gore
With warm ablution cleanse, and on the wound
Smooth unguents spread, the same as by report
Achilles taught thee; taught, himself, their use           1010
By Chiron, Centaur, justest of his kind.
For Podalirius and Machaon both
Are occupied.   Machaon, as I judge,
Lies wounded in his tent, needing like aid
Himself, and Podalirius in the field                        1015

Maintains sharp conflict with the sons of Troy.
  To whom Menœtius' gallant son replied.
Hero! Eurypylus! how shall we act
In this perplexity? what course pursue?
I seek the brave Achilles, to whose ear      1020
I bear a message from the ancient Chief
Gerenian Nestor, guardian of the Greeks.
Yet will I not, even for such a cause,
My friend! abandon thee in thy distress.
  He ended, and his arms folding around      1025
The warrior bore him thence into his tent.
His servant, on his entrance, spread the floor
With hides, on which Patroclus at his length
Extended him, and with his knife cut forth
The rankling point; with tepid lotion, next,      1030
He cleansed the gore, and with a bitter root
Bruised small between his palms, sprinkled the wound.
At once, the anodyne his pains assuaged,
The wound was dried within, and the blood ceased.

# BOOK XII.

---

## ARGUMENT.

The Trojans assail the ramparts, and Hector forces the gates.

So was Menœtius' valiant son employ'd
Healing Eurypylus.   The Greeks, meantime,
And Trojans with tumultuous fury fought.
Nor was the foss ordain'd long time to exclude
The host of Troy, nor yet the rampart built          5
Beside it for protection of the fleet ;
For hecatomb the Greeks had offer'd none,
Nor prayer to heaven, that it might keep secure
Their ships with all their spoils.   The mighty work
As in defiance of the Immortal Powers               10
Had risen, and could not therefore long endure.
While Hector lived, and while Achilles held
His wrathful purpose ; while the city yet
Of royal Priam was unsack'd, so long
The massy structure stood ; but when the best        15
And bravest of the Trojan host were slain,
And of  the  Grecian heroes, some had fallen
And some survived, when Priam's towers had blazed
In the tenth year, and to their native shores
The  Grecians  with their ships, at length return'd,  20
Then Neptune, with Apollo leagued, devised
Its ruin ; every river that descends
From the Idæan heights into the sea
They brought against it, gathering all their force,
Rhesus, Caresus, Rhodius, the wide-branch'd          25
Heptaporus, Æsepus, Granicus,
Scamander's sacred current, and thy stream
Simöis, whose banks with helmets and with shields
Were strew'd, and Chiefs of  origin divine ;
All these with refluent course Apollo drove           30

Nine days against the rampart, and Jove rain'd
Incessant, that the Grecian wall wave-whelm'd
Through all its length might sudden disappear.
Neptune with his tridental mace, himself,
Led them, and beam and buttress to the flood          35
Consigning, laid by the laborious Greeks,
Swept the foundation, and the level bank
Of the swift-rolling Hellespont restored.
The structure thus effaced, the spacious beach
He spread with sand as at the first; then bade          40
Subside the streams, and in their channels wind
With limpid course, and pleasant as before.
   Apollo thus and Neptune, from the first,
Design'd its fall; but now the battle raved
And clamours of the warriors all around          45
The strong-built turrets, whose assaulted planks
Rang, while the Grecians, by the scourge of Jove
Subdued, stood close within their fleet immured,
At Hector's phalanx-scattering force appall'd.
He, as before, with whirlwind fury fought.          50
As when the boar or lion fiery-eyed
Turns short, the hunters and the hounds among,
The close-imbattled troop him firm oppose,
And ply him fast with spears; he no dismay
Conceives or terror in his noble heart,          55
But by his courage falls; frequent he turns
Attempting bold the ranks, and where he points
Direct his onset, there the ranks retire;
So, through the concourse on his rolling wheels
Borne rapid, Hector animated loud          60
His fellow-warriors to surpass the trench.
But not his own swift-footed steeds would dare
That hazard; standing on the dangerous brink
They neigh'd aloud, for by its breadth the foss
Deterr'd them; neither was the effort slight          65
To leap that gulf, nor easy the attempt
To pass it through; steep were the banks profound
On both sides, and with massy piles acute
Thick-planted, interdicting all assault.
No courser to the rapid chariot braced          70
Had enter'd there with ease; yet strong desires

Possess'd the infantry of that emprize,
And thus Polydamas the ear address'd
Of dauntless Hector, standing at his side.
　　Hector, and ye the leaders of our host,　　　75
Both Trojans and allies! rash the attempt
I deem, and vain, to push our horses through,
So dangerous is the pass; rough is the trench
With pointed stakes, and the Achaian wall
Meets us beyond.　No chariot may descend　　　80
Or charioteer fight there; straight are the bounds,
And incommodious, and his death were sure.
If Jove, high-thundering Ruler of the skies,
Will succour Ilium, and nought less intend
Than utter devastation of the Greeks,　　　85
I am content; now perish all their host
Inglorious, from their country far remote.
But should they turn, and should ourselves be driven
Back from the fleet impeded and perplex'd
In this deep foss, I judge that not a man,　　　90
'Scaping the rallied Grecians, should survive,
To bear the tidings of our fate to Troy.
Now, therefore, act we all as I advise.
Let every charioteer his coursers hold
Fast-rein'd beside the foss, while we on foot,　　　95
With order undisturb'd and arms in hand,
Shall follow Hector.　If destruction borne
On wings of destiny this day approach
The　Grecians, they will fly our first assault.
　　So spake Polydamas, whose safe advice　　　100
Pleased Hector; from his chariot to the ground
All arm'd he leap'd, nor would a Trojan there
(When once they saw the Hero on his feet)
Ride into battle, but, unanimous
Descending with a leap, all trod the plain.　　　105
Each gave command that at the trench his steeds
Should stand detain'd in orderly array;
Then, suddenly, the parted host became
Five bands, each following its appointed chief.
The bravest and most numerous, and whose hearts　　　110
Wish'd most to burst the barrier and to wage
The battle at the ships, with Hector march'd

And with Polydamas, whom follow'd, third,
Cebriones; for Hector had his steeds
Consign'd and chariot to inferior care.     115
Paris, Alcathoüs, and Agenor led
The second band, and, sons of Priam both,
Deïphobus and Helenus, the third;
With them was seen partner of their command,
The Hero Asius; from Arisba came     120
Asius Hyrtacides, to battle drawn
From the Selleïs banks by martial steeds
Hair'd fiery-red and of the noblest size.
The fourth, Anchises' mighty son controul'd,
Æneas; under him Antenor's sons,     125
Archilochus and Acamas, advanced,
Adept in all the practice of the field.
Last came the glorious powers in league with Troy
Led by Sarpĕdon; he with Glaucus shared
His high controul, and with the warlike Chief     130
Asteropæus; for of all his host
Them bravest he esteem'd, himself except
Superior in heroic might to all.
And now, (their shields adjusted each to each)
With dauntless courage fired, right on they mov'd     135
Against the Grecians; nor expected less
Than that beside their sable ships, the host
Should self-abandon'd fall an easy prey.
    The Trojans, thus, with their confederate powers,
The counsel of the accomplish'd Prince pursued,     140
Polydamas, one Chief alone except,
Asius Hyrtacides. He scorn'd to leave
His charioteer and coursers at the trench,
And drove toward the fleet. Ah, madly brave!
His evil hour was come; he was ordain'd     145
With horse and chariot and triumphant shout
To enter wind-swept Ilium never more.
Deucalion's offspring, first, into the shades
Dismiss'd him; by Idomeneus he died.
Leftward he drove furious, along the road     150
By which the steeds and chariots of the Greeks
Return'd from battle; in that track he flew,
Nor found the portals by the massy bar

Secured, but open for reception safe
Of fugitives, and to a guard consign'd.                    155
Thither he drove direct, and in his rear
His band shrill-shouting follow'd, for they judged
The Greeks no longer able to withstand
Their foes, but sure to perish in the camp.
Vain hope! for in the gate two Chiefs they found          160
Lapithæ-born, courageous offspring each
Of dauntless father; Polypœtes, this,
Sprung from Pirithöus; that, the warrior bold
Leonteus, terrible as gore-tainted Mars.
These two, defenders of the lofty gates,                  165
Stood firm before them.   As when two tall oaks
On the high mountains day by day endure
Rough wind and rain, by deep-descending roots
Of hugest growth fast-founded in the soil;
So they, sustain'd by conscious valour, saw,             170
Unmoved, high towering Asius on his way,
Nor fear'd him aught, nor shrank from his approach.
Right on toward the barrier, lifting high
Their season'd bucklers and with clamour loud
The band advanced, King Asius at their head,             175
With whom Iämenus, expert in arms,
Orestes, Thöon, Acamas the son
Of Asius, and Oenamäus, led them on.
Till now, the warlike pair, exhorting loud
The Grecians to defend the fleet, had stood              180
Within the gates; but soon as they perceived
The Trojans swift advancing to the wall,
And heard a cry from all the flying Greeks,
Both sallying, before the gates they fought
Like forest-boars, which hearing in the hills            185
The crash of hounds and huntsmen nigh at hand,
With start oblique lay many a saplin flat
Short-broken by the root, nor cease to grind
Their sounding tusks, till by the spear they die;
So sounded on the breasts of those brave Two             190
The smitten brass; for resolute they fought,
Embolden'd by their might who kept the wall,
And trusting in their own; they, in defence
Of camp and fleet and life, thick battery hurl'd

Of stones precipitated from the towers ;                        195
Frequent as snows they fell, which stormy winds,
Driving the gloomy clouds, shake to the ground,
Till all the fertile earth lies cover'd deep.
Such volley pour'd the Greeks, and such return'd
The Trojans ; casques of hide, arid and tough,               200
And bossy shields rattled, by such a storm
Assail'd of millstone masses from above.
Then Asius, son of Hyrtacus, a groan
Indignant uttered ; on both thighs he smote
With disappointment furious, and exclaim'd,                   205
    Jupiter ! even thou art false become,
And altogether such.   Full sure I deem'd
That not a Grecian Hero should abide
One moment force invincible as ours,
And lo ! as wasps ring-straked[1], or bees that build        210
Their dwellings in the highway's craggy side
Leave not their hollow home, but fearless wait
The hunter's coming, in their brood's defence,
So these, although two only, from the gates
Move not, or will, till either seized or slain.              215
    So Asius spake, but speaking so, changed not
The mind of Jove on Hector's glory bent.
Others, as obstinate, at other gates
Such deeds performed, that to enumerate all
Were difficult, unless to power divine.                       220
For fierce the hail of stones from end to end
Smote on the barrier ; anguish fill'd the Greeks,
Yet, by necessity constrain'd, their ships
They guarded still ; nor less the Gods themselves,
Patrons of Greece, all sorrow'd at the sight.                225
    At once the valiant Lapithæ began
Terrible conflict, and Pirithous' son
Brave Polypætes through his helmet pierced
Damasus ; his resplendent point the brass
Sufficed not to withstand ; entering, it crush'd             230
The bone within, and mingling all his brain
With his own blood, his onset fierce repress'd.
Pylon and Ormenus he next subdued.

---

[1] The word is of scripture use : see Gen. ch. xxx. where it describes
the cattle of Jacob.

Meantime Leonteus, branch of Mars, his spear
Hurl'd at Hippomachus, whom through his belt          235
He pierced ; then drawing forth his faulchion keen,
Through all the multitude he flew to smite
Antiphates, and with a downright stroke
Fell'd him.   Iämenus and Menon next
He slew, with brave Orestes, whom he heap'd,          240
All three together, on the fertile glebe.
    While them the Lapithæ of their bright arms
Despoil'd, Polydamas and Hector stood
(With all the bravest youths and most resolved
To burst the barrier and to fire the fleet)          245
Beside the foss, pondering the event.
For, while they press'd to pass, they spied a bird
Sublime in air, an eagle.   Right between
Both hosts he soar'd (the Trojan on his left)
A serpent bearing in his pounces clutch'd          250
Enormous, dripping blood, but lively still
And mindful of revenge ; for from beneath
The eagle's breast, updarting fierce his head,
Fast by the throat he struck him ; anguish-sick
The eagle cast him down into the space          255
Between the hosts, and, clanging loud his plumes,
As the wind bore him, floated far away.
Shudder'd the Trojans viewing at their feet
The spotted serpent ominous, and thus
Polydamas to dauntless Hector spake.          260.
    Ofttimes in council, Hector, thou art wont
To censure me, although advising well ;
Nor ought the private citizen, I confess,
Either in council or in war to indulge
Loquacity, but ever to employ          265
All his exertions in support of thine.
Yet hear my best opinion once again.
Proceed we not in our attempt against
The Grecian fleet.   For if in truth the sign
Respect the host of Troy ardent to pass,          270
Then, as the eagle soar'd both hosts between,
With Ilium's on his left, and clutch'd a snake
Enormous, dripping blood, but still alive,
Which yet he dropp'd suddenly, ere he reach'd

His eyry, or could give it to his young,                    275
So we, although with mighty force we burst
Both gates and barrier, and although the Greeks
Should all retire, shall never yet the way
Tread honourably back by which we came.
No.   Many a Trojan shall we leave behind             280
Slain by the Grecians in their fleet's defence.
An augur skill'd in omens would expound
This omen thus, and faith would win from all.
    To whom, dark-louring, Hector thus replied.
Polydamas! I like not thy advice ;                          285
Thou couldst have framed far better ; but if this
Be thy deliberate judgement, then the Gods
Make thy deliberate judgement nothing worth,
Who bidd'st me disregard the Thunderer's firm
Assurance to myself announced[2], and make          290
The wild inhabitants of air my guides,
Which I alike despise, speed they their course
With right-hand flight toward the ruddy East,
Or leftward down into the shades of eve.
Consider *we* the will of Jove alone,                        295
Sovereign of heaven and earth.   Omens abound,
But the best omen is our country's cause.
Wherefore should fiery war *thy* soul alarm?
For were we slaughter'd, one and all, around
The fleet of Greece, *thou* need'st not fear to die,      300
Whose courage never will thy flight retard.
But if thou shrink thyself, or by smooth speech
Seduce one other from a soldier's part,
Pierced by this spear incontinent thou diest.
    So saying he led them, who with deafening roar      305
Follow'd him.   Then, from the Idæan hills
Jove hurl'd a storm which wafted right the dust
Into the fleet ; the spirits too he quell'd
Of the Achaians, and the glory gave
To Hector and his host ; they, trusting firm              310
In signs from Jove, and in their proper force,
Assay'd the barrier ; from the towers they tore
The galleries, cast the battlements to ground,
And the projecting buttresses adjoin'd

[2] Alluding to the message delivered to him from Jupiter by Iris.

To strengthen the vast work, with bars upheaved.     315
All these, with expectation fierce to break
The rampart, down they drew; nor yet the Greeks
Gave back, but, fencing close with shields the wall,
Smote from behind them many a foe beneath.
Meantime from tower to tower the Ajaces moved     320
Exhorting all, with mildness some, and some
With harsh rebuke, whom they observed through fear
Declining base the labours of the fight.
      Friends! Argives! warriors of whatever rank!
Ye who excel, and ye of humbler note!     325
And ye the last and least! (for such there are,
All have not magnanimity alike,)
Now have we work for all, as all perceive.
Turn not, retreat not to your ships, appall'd
By sounding menaces, but press the foe;     330
Exhort each other, and e'en now perchance
Olympian Jove, by whom the lightnings burn,
Shall grant us to repulse them, and to chase
The routed Trojans to their gates again.
      So they vociferating to the Greeks,     335
Stirr'd them to battle.   As the feathery snows
Fall frequent, on some wintry day, when Jove
Hath risen to shed them on the race of man,
And show his arrowy stores; he lulls the winds,
Then shakes them down continual, covering thick     340
Mountain tops, promontories, flowery meads,
And cultured valleys rich; the ports and shores
Receive it also of the hoary Deep,
But there the waves bound it, while all beside
Lies whelm'd beneath Jove's fast-descending shower,     345
So thick, from side to side, by Trojans hurl'd
Against the Greeks, and by the Greeks return'd
The stony vollies flew; resounding loud
Through all its length the battered rampart roar'd.
Nor yet had Hector and his host prevail'd     350
To burst the gates, and break the massy bar
Had not all-seeing Jove Sarpedon moved
His son, against the Greeks, furious as falls
The lion on some horned herd of beeves.
At once his polish'd buckler he advanced     355
With leafy brass o'erlaid; for with smooth brass

The forger of that shield its oval disk
Had plated, and with thickest hides throughout
Had lined it, stitch'd with circling wires of gold.
That shield he bore before him, firmly grasp'd      360
He shook two spears, and with determined strides
March'd forward.   As the lion mountain-bred,
After long fast, by impulse of his heart
Undaunted urged, seeks resolute the flock
Even in the shelter of their guarded home;      365
He finds, perchance, the shepherds arm'd with spears,
And all their dogs awake, yet cannot leave
Untried the fence, but either leaps it light,
And entering tears the prey, or in the attempt
Pierced by some dexterous peasant, bleeds himself;      370
So high his courage to the assault impell'd
Godlike Sarpedon, and him fired with hope
To break the barrier; when to Glaucus thus,
Son of Hippolochus his speech he turn'd.

Why, Glaucus, is the seat of honour ours,      375
Why drink we brimming cups, and feast in state?
Why gaze they all on us as we were Gods
In Lycia, and why share we pleasant fields
And spacious vineyards, where the Xanthus winds?
Distinguish'd thus in Lycia, we are call'd      380
To firmness here, and to encounter bold
The burning battle, that our fair report
Among the Lycians may be blazon'd thus—
No dastards are the potentates who rule
The bright-arm'd Lycians; on the fatted flock      385
They banquet, and they drink the richest wines,
But they are also valiant, and the fight
Wage dauntless in the vaward of us all.
Oh Glaucus, if escaping safe the death
That threats us here, we also could escape      390
Old age, and to ourselves secure a life
Immortal, I would neither in the van
Myself expose, nor would encourage thee
To tempt the perils of the glorious field.
But since a thousand messengers of fate      395
Pursue us close, and man is born to die—
E'en let us on; the prize of glory yield,
If yield we must, or wrest it from the foe.

He said, nor cold refusal in return
Received from Glaucus, but toward the wall                    400
Their numerous Lycian host both led direct.
Menestheus, son of Peteos, saw appall'd
Their dread approach, for to his tower they bent
Their threatening march.   An eager look he cast
On the embodied Greeks, seeking some Chief                    405
Whose aid might turn the battle from his van :
He saw, where never sated with exploits
Of war, each Ajax fought, near whom his eye
Kenn'd Teucer also, newly from his tent ;
But vain his efforts were with loudest call                    410
To reach their ears, such was the deafening din
Upsent to Heaven, of shields and crested helms,
And of the batter'd gates ; for at each gate
They thundering stood, and urged alike at each
Their fierce attempt by force to burst the bars.                    415
To Ajax therefore he at once dispatch'd
An herald, and Thöotes thus enjoin'd.
    My noble friend, Thöotes ! with all speed
Call either Ajax ; bid them hither both ;
Far better so ; for havoc is at hand.                    420
The Lycian leaders, ever in assault
Tempestuous, bend their force against this tower
My station.   But if also there they find
Laborious conflict pressing them severe,
At least let Telamonian Ajax come,                    425
And Teucer with his death-dispensing bow.
    He spake, nor was Thöotes slow to hear ;
Beside the rampart of the mail-clad Greeks
Rapid he flew, and, at their side arrived,
To either Ajax, eager, thus began.                    430
    Ye leaders of the well-appointed Greeks,
The son of noble Peteos calls ; he begs
With instant suit, that ye would share his toils,
However short your stay ; the aid of both
Will serve him best, for havoc threatens there.                    435
The Lycian leaders, ever in assault
Tempestuous, bend their force toward the tower
His station.   But if also here ye find
Laborious conflict pressing you severe,

At least let Telamonian Ajax come,　　　　　　440
And Teucer with his death-dispensing bow.
　　He spake, nor his request the towering son
Of Telamon denied, but quick his speech
To Ajax Oïliades address'd.
　　Ajax! abiding here, exhort ye both　　　　445
(Heroic Lycomedes and thyself)
The Greeks to battle.　Thither I depart
To aid our friends, which service once perform'd
Duly, I will incontinent return.
　　So saying, the Telamonian Chief withdrew,　450
With whom went Teucer, son of the same sire,
Pandion also, bearing Teucer's bow.
Arriving at the turret given in charge
To the bold Chief Menestheus, and the wall
Entering, they found their friends all sharply tried.　455
Black as a storm the senators renown'd
And leaders of the Lycian host assail'd
Buttress and tower, while opposite the Greeks
Withstood them, and the battle-shout began.
First, Ajax, son of Telamon, a friend　　　460
And fellow-warrior of Sarpedon slew,
Epicles.　With a marble fragment huge
That crown'd the battlement's interior side,
He smote him.　No man of our puny race,
Although in prime of youth, had with both hands　465
That weight sustain'd; but he the cumberous mass
Uplifted high, and hurl'd it on his head.
It burst his helmet, and his batter'd skull
Dash'd from all form.　He from the lofty tower
Dropp'd downright, with a diver's plunge, and died.　470
But Teucer wounded Glaucus with a shaft,
Son of Hippolochus; he, climbing, bared
His arm, which Teucer, marking, from the wall
Transfix'd it, and his onset fierce repress'd;
For with a backward leap Glaucus withdrew　475
Sudden and silent, cautious lest the Greeks
Seeing him wounded should insult his pain.
Grief seized, at sight of his retiring friend,
Sarpedon, who forgat not yet the fight,
But piercing with his lance Alcmaon, son　　480

Of Thestor, suddenly revulsed the beam,
Which following, Alcmaon to the earth
Fell prone, with clangor of his brazen arms.
Sarpedon, then, strenuous with both hands
Tugg'd, and down fell the battlement entire;          485
The wall, dismantled at the summit, stood
A ruin, and wide chasm was open'd through.
Then Ajax him and Teucer at one time
Struck both; an arrow struck from Teucer's bow
The belt that cross'd his bosom, by which hung          490
His ample shield; yet lest his son should fall
Among the ships, Jove turn'd the death aside.
But Ajax, springing to his thrust, a spear
Drove through his shield.   Sarpedon at the shock
With backward step short interval recoil'd,          495
But not retired, for in his bosom lived
The hope of glory still, and looking back
On all his Godlike Lycians, he exclaim'd,
    Oh Lycians! where is your heroic might?
Brave as I boast myself, I feel the task          500
Arduous, through the breach made by myself
To win a passage to the ships, alone.
Follow me all—Most labourers, most dispatch[3].
    So he; at whose sharp reprimand abash'd
The embattled host to closer conflict moved,          505
Obedient to their counsellor and King.
On the other side the Greeks within the wall
Made firm the phalanx, seeing urgent need;
Nor could the valiant Lycians through the breach
Admittance to the Grecian fleet obtain,          510
Nor, since they first approach'd it, had the Greeks
With all their efforts, thrust the Lycians back.
But as two claimants of one common field,
Each with his rod of measurement in hand,
Dispute the boundaries, litigating warm          515
Their right in some small portion of the soil,
So they, divided by the barrier, struck
With hostile rage the bull-hide bucklers round,
And the light targets on each other's breast.

[3] πλεόνων δέ τοι ἔργον ἀμεῖνον. — This is evidently proverbial, for which reason I have given it that air in the translation.

Then many a wound the ruthless weapons made. 520
Pierced through the unarm'd back, if any turn'd,
He died, and numerous even through the shield.
The battlements from end to end with blood
Of Grecians and of Trojans on both sides
Were sprinkled; yet no violence could move 525
The stubborn Greeks, or turn their powers to flight.
So hung the war in balance, as the scales
Held by some woman scrupulously just,
A spinner; wool and weight she poises nice,
Hard-earning slender pittance for her babes, 530
Such was the poise in which the battle hung,
Till Jove himself superior fame, at length,
To Priamëian Hector gave, who sprang
First through the wall.   In lofty sounds that reach'd
Their utmost ranks, he call'd on all his host, 535
    Now press them, now ye Trojans steed-renown'd
Rush on! break through the Grecian rampart, hurl
At once devouring flames into the fleet.
    Such was his exhortation; they his voice
All hearing, with close-order'd ranks direct 540
Bore on the barrier, and upswarming show'd
On the high battlement their glittering spears.
But Hector seized a stone; of ample base
But tapering to a point, before the gate
It stood.   No two men, mightiest of a land 545
(Such men as now are mighty) could with ease
Have heaved it from the earth up to a wain;
He swung it easily alone; so light
The son of Saturn made it in his hand.
As in one hand with ease the shepherd bears 550
A ram's fleece home, nor toils beneath the weight,
So Hector, right toward the planks of those
Majestic folding-gates, close-jointed, firm
And solid, bore the stone.   Two bars within
Their corresponding force combined transverse 555
To guard them, and one bolt secured the bars.
He stood fast by them, parting wide his feet
For 'vantage sake, and smote them in the midst.
He burst both hinges; inward fell the rock
Ponderous, and the portals roar'd; the bars 560

Endured not, and the planks, riven by the force
Of that huge mass, flew scatter'd on all sides.
In leap'd the godlike Hero at the breach,
Gloomy as night in aspect, but in arms
All-dazzling, and he grasp'd two quivering spears.          565
Him entering with a leap the gates, no force
Whate'er of opposition had repress'd,
Save of the Gods alone.   Fire fill'd his eyes;
Turning, he bade the multitude without
Ascend the rampart; they his voice obey'd;          570
Part climb'd the wall, part pour'd into the gate;
The Grecians to their hollow galleys flew
Scatter'd, and tumult infinite arose.

# BOOK XIII.

### ARGUMENT.

Neptune engages on the part of the Grecians. The battle proceeds. Deiphobus advances to combat, but is repulsed by Meriones, who losing his spear, repairs to his tent for another. Teucer slays Imbrius, and Hector Amphimachus. Neptune, under the similitude of Thoas, exhorts Idomeneus. Idomeneus having armed himself in his tent, and going forth to battle, meets Meriones. After discourse held with each other, Idomeneus accommodates Meriones with a spear, and they proceed to battle. Idomeneus slays Othryoneus, and Asius. Deiphobus assails Idomeneus, but, his spear glancing over him, kills Hypsenor. Idomeneus slays Alcathoüs, son-in-law of Anchises. Deiphobus and Idomeneus respectively summon their friends to their assistance, and a contest ensues for the body of Alcathoüs.

WHEN Jove to Hector and his host had given
Such entrance to the fleet, to all the woes
And toils of unremitting battle there
He them abandon'd, and his glorious eyes
Averting, on the land look'd down remote                   5
Of the horse-breeding Thracians, of the bold
Close-fighting Mysian race, and where abide
On milk sustain'd, and blest with length of days,
The Hippemolgi, justest of mankind.
No longer now on Troy his eyes he turn'd,                  10
For expectation none within his breast
Survived, that God or Goddess would the Greeks
Approach with succour, or the Trojans more.
    Nor Neptune, sovereign of the boundless Deep,
Look'd forth in vain; he on the summit sat                 15
Of Samothracia forest-crown'd, the stir
Admiring thence and tempest of the field;
For thence appear'd all Ida, thence the towers
Of lofty Ilium, and the fleet of Greece.
There sitting from the deeps uprisen, he mourn'd           20
The vanquish'd Grecians, and resentment fierce
Conceived and wrath against all-ruling Jove.

Arising sudden, down the rugged steep
With rapid strides he came ; the mountains huge
And forests under the immortal feet                          25
Trembled of Ocean's Sovereign as he strode.
Three strides he made, the fourth convey'd him home
To Ægæ.   At the bottom of the abyss,
There stands magnificent his golden fane,
A dazzling incorruptible abode.                              30
Arrived, he to his chariot join'd his steeds
Swift, brazen-hoof'd, and maned with wavy gold ;
Himself attiring next in gold, he seized
His golden scourge, and to his seat sublime
Ascending, o'er the billows drove ; the whales              35
Leaving their caverns, gambol'd on all sides
Around him, not unconscious of their King ;
He swept the surge that tinged not as he pass'd
His axle, and the sea parted for joy.
His bounding coursers to the Grecian fleet                  40
Convey'd him swift.   There is a spacious cave
Deep in the bottom of the flood, the rocks
Of Imbrus rude and Tenedos between ;
There Neptune, shaker of the shores, his steeds
Station'd secure ; he loosed them from the yoke,            45
Gave them ambrosial food, and bound their feet
With golden tethers not to be untied
Or broken, that unwandering they might wait
Their Lord's return, then sought the Grecian host.
The Trojans, tempest-like or like a flame,                  50
Now, following Priameïan Hector, all
Came furious on and shouting to the skies.
Their hope was to possess the fleet, and leave
Not an Achaian of the host unslain.
But earth-encircler Neptune from the gulf                   55
Emerging, in the form and with the voice
Loud-toned of Calchas, roused the Argive ranks
To battle—and his exhortation first
To either Ajax turn'd, themselves prepared.
    Ye heroes Ajax !  your accustomed force                 60
Exert, oh !  think not of disastrous flight,
And ye shall save the people.   Nought I fear
Fatal elsewhere, although Troy's haughty sons

Have pass'd the barrier with so fierce a throng
Tumultuous; for the Grecians brazen-greaved 65
Will check them there.   Here only I expect
And with much dread some dire event forebode,
Where Hector, terrible as fire, and loud
Vaunting his glorious origin from Jove,
Leads on the Trojans.   Oh that from on high 70
Some God would form the purpose in your hearts
To stand yourselves firmly, and to exhort
The rest to stand! so should ye chase him hence
All ardent as he is, and even although
Olympian Jove himself his rage inspire. 75
  So Neptune spake, compasser of the earth,
And, with his sceptre smiting both, their hearts
Fill'd with fresh fortitude; their limbs the touch
Made agile, wing'd their feet and nerved their arms.
Then, swift as stoops a falcon from the point 80
Of some rude rock sublime, when he would chase
A fowl of other wing along the meads,
So started Neptune thence, and disappear'd.
Him, as he went, swift Oïliades
First recognized, and, instant, thus his speech 85
To Ajax, son of Telamon, address'd.
  Since, Ajax, some inhabitant of heaven
Exhorts us, in the prophet's form to fight,
(For prophet none or augur we have seen;
This was not Calchas; as he went I mark'd 90
His steps and knew him; Gods are known with ease.)
I feel my spirit in my bosom fired
Afresh for battle; lightness in my limbs,
In hands and feet a glow unfelt before.
  To whom the son of Telamon replied. 95
I also with invigorated hands
More firmly grasp my spear, my courage mounts,
A buoyant animation in my feet
Bears me along, and I am all on fire
To cope with Priam's furious son, alone. 100
  Thus they, with martial transport to their souls
Imparted by the God, conferr'd elate.
Meantime the King of Ocean roused the Greeks,
Who in the rear, beside their gallant barks

Some respite sought.　They, spent with arduous toil,　　105
Felt not alone their weary limbs unapt
To battle, but their hearts with grief oppress'd,
Seeing the numerous multitude of Troy
Within the mighty barrier; sad they view'd
That sight, and bathed their cheeks with many a tear,　110
Despairing of escape.　But Ocean's Lord
Entering among them, soon the spirit stirr'd
Of every valiant phalanx to the fight.
Teucer and Leïtus, and famed in arms
Peneleus, Thoas and Deipyrus,　　　　　115
Meriones, and his compeer renown'd,
Antilochus; all these in accents wing'd
With fierce alacrity the God address'd.
　　Oh shame, ye Grecians! vigorous as ye are
And in life's prime, to your exertions most　　120
I trusted for the safety of our ships.
If *ye* renounce the labours of the field,
Then hath the day arisen of our defeat
And final ruin by the powers of Troy.
Oh! I behold a prodigy, a sight　　　　125
Tremendous, deem'd impossible by me,
The Trojans at our ships! the dastard race
Fled once like fleetest hinds the destined prey
Of lynxes, leopards, wolves; feeble and slight
And of a nature indisposed to war　　　　130
They rove uncertain; so the Trojans erst
Stood not, nor to Achaian prowess dared
The hindrance of a moment's strife oppose.
But now, Troy left afar, even at our ships
They give us battle, through our leader's fault　135
And through the people's negligence, who fill'd
With fierce displeasure against *him*, prefer
Death at their ships, to war in their defence.
But if the son of Atreus, our supreme,
If Agamemnon, have indeed transgress'd　　140
Past all excuse, dishonouring the swift
Achilles, ye at least the fight decline
Blame-worthy, and with no sufficient plea.
But heal we speedily the breach; brave minds
Easily coalesce.　It is not well　　　　145
　　s. o.—7.　　　　　　　　　　　　　　R

That thus your fury slumbers, for the host
Hath none illustrious as yourselves in arms.
I can excuse the timid if he shrink,
But am incensed at *you*.   My friends beware!
Your tardiness will prove ere long the cause               150
Of some worse evil.   Let the dread of shame
Affect your hearts; oh tremble at the thought
Of infamy! Fierce conflict hath arisen,
Loud shouting Hector combats at the ships
Nobly, hath forced the gates and burst the bar.           155
　　With such encouragement those Grecian chiefs
The King of Ocean roused.   Then, circled soon
By many a phalanx either Ajax stood,
Whose order Mars himself arriving there
Had praised, or Pallas, patroness of arms.                160
For there the flower of all expected firm
Bold Hector and his host; spear crowded spear,
Shield, helmet, man, press'd helmet, man and shield[1];
The hairy crests of their resplendent casques
Kiss'd close at every nod, so wedged they stood:          165
No spear was seen but in the manly grasp
It quiver'd, and their every wish was war.
The powers of Ilium gave the first assault
Embattled close; them Hector led himself
Right on, impetuous as a rolling rock                     170
Destructive; torn by torrent waters off
From its old lodgement on the mountain's brow,
It bounds, it shoots away; the crashing wood
Falls under it; impediment or check
None stays its fury, till the level found,                175
There, settling by degrees, it rolls no more;
So after many a threat that he would pass
Easily through the Grecian camp and fleet
And slay to the sea-brink, when Hector once
· Had fallen on those firm ranks, standing, he bore       180
Vehement on them; but by many a spear
Urged and bright faulchion, soon, reeling, retired,
And call'd vociferous on the host of Troy.
　　Trojans, and Lycians, and close-fighting sons
Of Dardanus, oh stand! not long the Greeks                185

[1] For this admirable line the Translator is indebted to Mr. Fuseli.

Will me confront, although embodied close
In solid phalanx ; doubt it not ; my spear
Shall chase and scatter them, if Jove, in truth,
High-thundering mate of Juno, bid me on.
　　So saying he roused the courage of them all,　　190
Foremost of whom advanced, of Priam's race
Deiphobus, ambitious of renown.
Tripping he came with shorten'd steps[2], his feet
Sheltering behind his buckler ; but at him
Aiming, Meriones his splendid lance　　　　195
Dismiss'd, nor err'd ; his bull-hide targe he struck
But ineffectual ; where the hollow wood
Receives the inserted brass, the quivering beam
Snapp'd ; then, Deiphobus his shield afar
Advanced before him, trembling at a spear　　200
Hurl'd by Meriones.　He, moved alike
With indignation for the victory lost
And for his broken spear, into his band
At first retired, but soon set forth again
In progress through the Achaian camp, to fetch　　205
Its fellow-spear within his tent reserved.
　　The rest all fought, and dread the shouts arose
On all sides.　Telamonian Teucer, first,
Slew valiant Imbrius, son of Mentor, rich
In herds of sprightly steeds.　He ere the Greeks　　210
Arrived at Ilium, in Pedæus dwelt,
And Priam's spurious daughter had espoused
Medesicasta.　But the barks well-oar'd
Of Greece arriving, he return'd to Troy,
Where he excell'd the noblest, and abode　　215
With Priam, loved and honour'd as his own.
Him Teucer pierced beneath his ear, and pluck'd
His weapon home ; he fell as falls an ash
Which on some mountain visible afar,
Hewn from its bottom by the woodman's axe,　　220
With all its tender foliage meets the ground.
So Imbrius fell ; loud rang his armour bright
With ornamental brass, and Teucer flew
To seize his arms, whom hasting to the spoil

[2] A fitter occasion to remark on this singular mode of approach in
battle, will present itself hereafter.

Hector with his resplendent spear assail'd ;                    225
He, marking opposite its rapid flight,
Declined it narrowly and it pierced the breast,
As he advanced to battle, of the son
Of Cteatus of the Actorian race,
Amphimachus ; he, sounding, smote the plain,          230
And all his batter'd armour rang aloud.
Then Hector swift approaching, would have torn
The well-forged helmet from the brows away
Of brave Amphimachus ; but Ajax hurl'd
Right forth at Hector hasting to the spoil                     235
His radiant spear ; no wound the spear impress'd,
For he was arm'd complete in burnish'd brass
Terrific ; but the solid boss it pierced
Of Hector's shield, and with enormous force
So shock'd him, that retiring he resign'd               240
Both bodies[3], which the Grecians dragg'd away.
Stichius and Menestheus, leaders both
Of the Athenians, to the host of Greece
Bore off Amphimachus, and, fierce in arms
The Ajaces, Imbrius.   As two lions bear              245
Through thick entanglement of boughs and brakes
A goat snatch'd newly from the peasants' dogs,
Upholding high their prey above the ground,
So either Ajax terrible in fight,
Upholding Imbrius high, his brazen arms                 250
Tore off, and Oïliades his head
From his smooth neck dissevering in revenge
For slain Amphimachus, through all the host
Sent it with swift rotation like a globe,
Till in the dust at Hector's feet it fell.                    255
　　Then anger fill'd the heart of Ocean's King,
His grandson[4] slain in battle ; forth he pass'd
Through the Achaian camp and fleet, the Greeks
Rousing, and meditating woe to Troy.
It chanced that brave Idomeneus return'd            260
That moment from a Cretan at the knee
Wounded, and newly borne into his tent ;
His friends had borne him off, and when the Chief
Had given him into skilful hands, he sought

[3] The bodies of Imbrius and Amphimachus.　　[4] Amphimachus.

The field again, still coveting renown.     265
Him therefore, meeting him on his return,
Neptune bespake, but with the borrow'd voice
Of Thoas, offspring of Andræmon, King
In Pleuro and in lofty Calydon,
And honour'd by the Ætolians as a God.     270
    Oh counsellor of Crete! our threats denounced
Against the towers of Troy, where are they now?
    To whom the leader of the Cretans, thus,
Idomeneus.   For aught that I perceive
Thoas! no Grecian is this day in fault!     275
For we are all intelligent in arms,
None yields by fear oppress'd, none lull'd by sloth
From battle shrinks, but such the pleasure seems
Of Jove himself, that we should perish here
Inglorious, from our country far remote.     280
But, Thoas! (for thine heart was ever firm
In battle, and thyself art wont to rouse
Whom thou observ'st remiss) now also fight
As erst, and urge each leader of the host.
    Him answered, then, the Sovereign of the Deep.     285
Return that Grecian never from the shores
Of Troy, Idomeneus! but may the dogs
Feast on him, who shall this day intermit
Through wilful negligence his force in fight!
But haste, take arms and come; we must exert     290
All diligence, that, being only two,
We yet may yield some service.   Union much
Emboldens even the weakest, and our might
Hath oft been proved on warriors of renown.
    So Neptune spake, and, turning, sought again     295
The toilsome field.   Ere long, Idomeneus
Arriving in his spacious tent, put on
His radiant armour, and, two spears in hand,
Set forth like lightning which Saturnian Jove
From bright Olympus shakes into the air,     300
A sign to mortal men, dazzling all eyes;
So beam'd the Hero's armour as he ran.
But him not yet far distant from his tent
Meriones, his fellow-warrior met,
For he had left the fight, seeking a spear,     305

When thus the brave Idomeneus began.
　Swift son of Molus! chosen companion dear!
Wherefore, Meriones, hast thou the field
Abandon'd? Art thou wounded? Bring'st thou home
Some pointed mischief in thy flesh infixt?　　　　　310
Or comest thou sent to me, who of myself
The still tent covet not, but feats of arms?
　To whom Meriones discreet replied.
Chief leader of the Cretans, brazen-mail'd
Idomeneus! if yet there be a spear　　　　　315
Left in thy tent, I seek one; for I broke
The spear, even now, with which erewhile I fought,
Smiting the shield of fierce Deiphobus.
　Then answer thus the Cretan Chief return'd,
Valiant Idomeneus. If spears thou need,　　　　　320
Within my tent, leaning against the wall,
Stand twenty spears and one, forged all in Troy,
Which from the slain I took; for distant fight
Me suits not; therefore in my tent have I
Both spears and bossy shields, with brazen casques　　　325
And corslets bright that smile against the sun.
　Him answer'd, then, Meriones discreet.
I also, at my tent, and in my ship
Have many Trojan spoils, but they are hence
Far distant. I not less myself than thou　　　　　330
Am ever mindful of a warrior's part,
And when the din of glorious arms is heard,
Fight in the van. If other Greeks my deeds
Know not, at least I judge them known to thee.
　To whom the leader of the host of Crete　　　　　335
Idomeneus. I know thy valour well,
Why speakest thus to me? Chose we this day
An ambush forth of all the bravest Greeks,
(For in the ambush is distinguish'd best
The courage; there the timorous and the bold　　　340
Plainly appear; the dastard changes hue
And shifts from place to place, nor can he calm
The fears that shake his trembling limbs, but sits
Low-crouching on his hams, while in his breast
Quick palpitates his death-foreboding heart,　　　　345
And his teeth chatter; but the valiant man

His posture shifts not ; no excessive fears
Feels he, but seated once in ambush, deems
Time tedious till the bloody fight begin ;)
Even there, thy courage should no blame incur.                350
For should'st thou, toiling in the fight, by spear
Or faulchion bleed, not on thy neck behind
Would fall the weapon, or thy back annoy,
But it would meet thy bowels or thy chest
While thou didst rush into the clamorous van.                355
But haste—we may not longer loiter here
As children prating, lest some sharp rebuke
Reward us.   Enter quick, and from within
My tent provide thee with a nobler spear.
　　Then, swift as Mars, Meriones produced                360
A brazen spear of those within the tent
Reserved, and kindling with heroic fire
Follow'd Idomeneus.   As gory Mars
By Terror follow'd, his own dauntless son
Who quells the boldest heart, to battle moves ;               365
From Thrace against the Ephyri they arm,
Or hardy Phlegyans, and by both invoked,
Hear and grant victory to which they please ;
Such, bright in arms Meriones, and such
Idomeneus advanced, when foremost thus                370
Meriones his fellow-chief bespake.
　　Son of Deucalion ! where inclinest thou most
To enter into battle ?   On the right
Of all the host ? or through the central ranks ?
Or on the left ? for nowhere I account                375
The Greeks so destitute of force as there.
　　Then answer thus Idomeneus return'd
Chief of the Cretans.   Others stand to guard
The middle fleet ; there either Ajax wars,
And Teucer, noblest archer of the Greeks,                380
Nor less in stationary fight approved.
Bent as he is on battle, they will task
And urge to proof sufficiently the force
Of Priameian Hector ; burn his rage
How fierce soever, he shall find it hard,                385
With all his thirst of victory, to quell
Their firm resistance, and to fire the fleet,

Let not Saturnian Jove cast down from heaven
Himself a flaming brand into the ships.
High towering Telamonian Ajax yields                            390
To no mere mortal by the common gift
Sustain'd of Ceres, and whose flesh the spear
Can penetrate, or rocky fragment bruise;
In standing fight Ajax would not retire
Even before that breaker of the ranks                           395
Achilles, although far less swift than He.
But turn we to the left, that we may learn
At once, if glorious death, or life be ours.
   Then, rapid as the God of war, his course
Meriones toward the left began,                                 400
As he enjoin'd.   Soon as the Trojans saw
Idomeneus advancing like a flame,
And his compeer Meriones in arms
All-radiant clad, encouraging aloud
From rank to rank each other, on they came                      405
To the assault combined.   Then soon arose
Sharp contest on the left of all the fleet.
As when shrill winds blow vehement, what time
Dust deepest spreads the ways, by warring blasts
Upborne a sable cloud stands in the air,                        410
Such was the sudden conflict; equal rage
To stain with gore the lance ruled every breast.
Horrent with quivering spears the fatal field
Frown'd on all sides; the brazen flashes dread
Of numerous helmets, corslets furbish'd bright,                 415
And shields refulgent meeting, dull'd the eye,
And turn'd it dark away.   Stranger indeed
Were he to fear, who could that strife have view'd
With heart elate, or spirit unperturb'd.
   Two mighty sons of Saturn adverse parts             420
Took in that contest, purposing alike
To many a valiant Chief sorrow and pain.
Jove, for the honour of Achilles, gave
Success to Hector and the host of Troy,
Not for complete destruction of the Greeks                      425
At Ilium, but that glory might redound
To Thetis thence, and to her dauntless son.
On the other side, the King of Ocean risen

Secretly from the hoary Deep, the host
Of Greece encouraged, whom he grieved to see          430
Vanquish'd by Trojans, and with anger fierce
Against the Thunderer burn'd on their behalf.
Alike from one great origin divine
Sprang they, but Jove was elder, and surpass'd
In various knowledge; therefore when he roused        435
Their courage, Neptune traversed still the ranks
Clandestine, and in human form disguised.
Thus, these Immortal Two, straining the cord
Indissoluble of all-wasting war,
Alternate measured with it either host,               440
And loosed the joints of many a warrior bold.
Then, loud exhorting (though himself with age
Half grey,) the Achaians, into battle sprang
Idomeneus, and scatter'd, first, the foe,
Slaying Othryoneus, who, by the lure                  445
Of martial glory drawn, had left of late
Cabesus.   He Priam's fair daughter woo'd
Cassandra, but no nuptial gift vouchsafed[5]
To offer, save a sounding promise proud
To chase, himself, however resolute                   450
The Grecian host, and to deliver Troy.
To him assenting, Priam, ancient King,
Assured to him his wish, and in the faith
Of that assurance confident, he fought.
But brave Idomeneus his splendid lance                455
Well-aim'd dismissing, struck the haughty Chief,
Pacing elate the field; his brazen mail
Endured not; through his bowels pierced, with clang
Of all his arms he fell, and thus with joy
Immense exulting, spake Idomeneus.                    460
    I give thee praise, Othryoneus! beyond
All mortal men, if truly thou perform
Thy whole big promise to the Dardan king,
Who promised thee his daughter.   Now, behold,
We also promise: doubt not the effect.                465
We give into thy arms the most admired
Of Agamemnon's daughters, whom ourselves
Will hither bring from Argos, if thy force

_____
[5] It was customary for the suitor to pay the dower.

With ours uniting, thou wilt rase the walls
Of populous Troy. Come—follow me ; that here     470
Among the ships we may adjust the terms
Of marriage, for we take not scanty dower.
   So saying, the Hero dragg'd him by his heel
Through all the furious fight. His death to avenge
Asius on foot before his steeds advanced,     475
For them, where'er he moved, his charioteer
Kept breathing ever on his neck behind.
With fierce desire the heart of Asius burn'd
To smite Idomeneus, who with his lance
Him reaching first, pierced him beneath the chin     480
Into his throat, and urged the weapon through.
He fell, as some green poplar falls, or oak,
Or lofty pine, by naval artists hewn
With new-edged axes on the mountain's side.
So, his teeth grinding, and the bloody dust     485
Clenching, before his chariot and his steeds
Extended, Asius lay. His charioteer
(All recollection lost) sat panic-stunn'd,
Nor dared for safety turn his steeds to flight.
Him bold Antilochus right through the waist     490
Transpierced ; his mail sufficed not, but the spear
Implanted in his midmost bowels stood.
Down from his seat magnificent he fell
Panting, and young Antilochus the steeds
Drove captive thence into the host of Greece.     495
Then came Deiphobus by sorrow urged
For Asius, and, small interval between,
Hurl'd at Idomeneus his glittering lance ;
But he, foreseeing its approach, the point
Eluded, cover'd whole by his round shield     500
Of hides and brass by double belt sustain'd,
And it flew over him, but on his targe
Glancing, elicited a tinkling sound.
Yet left it not in vain his vigorous grasp,
But pierced the liver of Hypsenor, son     505
Of Hippasus ; he fell incontinent,
And measureless exulting in his fall
Deiphobus with mighty voice exclaim'd.
   Not unavenged lies Asius ; though he seek

Hell's iron portals, yet shall he rejoice,     510
For I have given him a conductor home.
    So he, whose vaunt the Greeks indignant heard;
But of them all to anger most he roused
Antilochus, who yet his breathless friend[6]
Left not, but, hasting, fenced him with his shield,     515
And brave Alastor with Mecisteus son
Of Echius, bore him to the hollow ships
Deep-groaning both, for of their band was he.
Nor yet Idomeneus his warlike rage
Remitted aught, but persevering strove     520
Either to plunge some Trojan in the shades,
Or fall himself, guarding the fleet of Greece.
Then slew he brave Alcathoüs the son
Of Æsyeta, and the son-in-law
Of old Anchises, who to him had given     525
The eldest-born of all his daughters fair,
Hippodamia; dearly loved was she
By both her parents in her virgin state[7],
For that in beauty she surpass'd, in works
Ingenious, and in faculties of mind     530
All her coevals; wherefore she was deem'd
Well worthy of the noblest prince of Troy.
Him in that moment, Neptune by the arm
Quell'd of Idomeneus, his radiant eyes
Dimming, and fettering his proportioned limbs.     535
All power of flight or to elude the stroke
Forsook him, and while motionless he stood
As stands a pillar tall or towering oak,
The hero of the Cretans with a spear
Transfix'd his middle chest.   He split the mail     540
Erewhile his bosom's faithful guard; shrill rang
The shiver'd brass; sounding he fell; the beam
Implanted in his palpitating heart
Shook to its topmost point, but, its force spent,
At last, quiescent, stood.   Then loud exclaim'd     545
Idomeneus, exulting in his fall.
    What thinks Deiphobus? seems it to thee,

---

[6] Hypsenor.     [7] This seems to be the meaning of ἐν μεγάρῳ,
an expression similar to that of Demosthenes in a parallel case—ἔτι
ἔνδον οὖσαν.—See Schaufelbergerus.

Vain boaster, that, three warriors slain for one,
We yield thee just amends? else, stand thyself
Against me; learn the valour of a Chief        550
The progeny of Jove; Jove first begat
Crete's guardian, Minos, from which Minos sprang
Deucalion, and from famed Deucalion, I;
I, sovereign of the numerous race of Crete's
Extensive isle, and whom my galleys brought    555
To these your shores at last, that I might prove
Thy curse, thy father's, and a curse to Troy.
   He spake; Deiphobus uncertain stood
Whether, retreating, to engage the help
Of some heroic Trojan, or himself             560
To make the dread experiment alone.
At length, as his discreeter course, he chose
To seek Æneas; him he found afar
Station'd, remotest of the host of Troy,
For he resented evermore his worth            565
By Priam[8] recompensed with cold neglect.
Approaching him, in accents wing'd he said.
   Æneas! Trojan Chief! If e'er thou lov'dst
Thy sister's husband, duty calls thee now
To prove it. Haste—defend with me the dead    570
Alcathoüs, guardian of thy tender years,
Slain by Idomeneus the spear-renown'd.
   So saying, he roused his spirit, and on fire
To combat with the Cretan, forth he sprang.
But fear seized not Idomeneus as fear         575
May seize a nursling boy; resolved he stood
As in the mountains, conscious of his force,
The wild boar waits a coming multitude
Of boisterous hunters to his lone retreat;
Arching his bristly spine he stands, his eyes  580
Beam fire, and whetting his bright tusks, he burns
To drive, not dogs alone, but men to flight;
So stood the royal Cretan, and fled not,
Expecting brave Æneas; yet his friends
He summon'd, on Ascalaphus his eyes           585

[8] He is said to have been jealous of him on account of his great popularity, and to have discountenanced him, fearing a conspiracy in his favour to the prejudice of his own family.—See Villoisson.

Fastening, on Aphareus, Deipyrus,
Meriones, and Antilochus, all bold
In battle, and in accents wing'd exclaim'd.
    Haste ye, my friends ! to aid me, for I stand
Alone, nor undismay'd the coming wait       590
Of swift Æneas, nor less brave than swift,
And who possesses fresh his flower of youth,
Man's prime advantage ; were we match'd in years
As in our spirits, either he should earn
At once the meed of deathless fame, or I.      595
    He said ; they all unanimous approach'd,
Sloping their shields, and stood.   On the other side
His aids Æneas call'd, with eyes toward
Paris, Deiphobus, Agenor, turn'd,
His fellow-warriors bold ; them follow'd all   600
Their people as the pastured flock the ram
To water, by the shepherd seen with joy ;
Such joy Æneas felt, seeing, so soon,
That numerous host attendant at his call.
Then, for Alcathoüs, into contest close     605
Arm'd with long spears they rush'd ; on every breast
Dread rang the brazen corslet, each his foe
Assailing opposite ; but two, the rest
Surpassing far, terrible both as Mars,
Æneas and Idomeneus, alike       610
Panted to pierce each other with the spear.
Æneas, first, cast at Idomeneus,
But, warn'd, he shunn'd the weapon, and it pass'd.
Quivering in the soil Æneas' lance
Stood, hurl'd in vain, though by a forceful arm.   615
Not so the Cretan ; at his waist he pierced
Oenomaüs, his hollow corslet clave,
And in his midmost bowels drench'd the spear ;
Down fell the Chief, and dying, clench'd the dust.
Instant, his massy spear the King of Crete   620
Pluck'd from the dead, but of his radiant arms
Despoil'd him not, by numerous weapons urged ;
For now, time-worn, he could no longer make
Brisk sally, spring to follow his own spear,
Or shun another, or by swift retreat     625
Vanish from battle, but the evil day

Warded in stationary fight alone.
At him retiring, therefore, step by step
Deiphobus, who had with bitterest hate
Long time pursued him, hurl'd his splendid lance,          630
But yet again erroneous, for he pierced
Ascalaphus instead, offspring of Mars ;
Right through his shoulder flew the spear ; he fell
Incontinent, and dying, clench'd the dust.
But tidings none the brazen-throated Mars               635
Tempestuous yet received, that his own son
In bloody fight had fallen, for on the heights
Olympian over-arch'd with clouds of gold
He sat, where sat the other Powers divine,
Prisoners together of the will of Jove.                 640
Meantime, for slain Ascalaphus arose
Conflict severe ; Deiphobus his casque
Resplendent seized, but swift as fiery Mars
Assailing him, Meriones his arm
Pierced with a spear, and from his idle hand            645
Fallen, the casque sonorous struck the ground.
Again, as darts the vulture on his prey,
Meriones assailing him, the lance
Pluck'd from his arm, and to his band retired.
Then, casting his fraternal arms around                 650
Deiphobus, him young Polites led
From the hoarse battle to his rapid steeds
And his bright chariot in the distant rear,
Which bore him back to Troy, languid and loud-
Groaning, and bleeding from his recent wound.           655
Still raged the war, and infinite arose
The clamour.   Aphareus, Caletor's son,
Turning to face Æneas, in his throat
Instant the Hero's pointed lance received.
With head reclined, and bearing to the ground           660
Buckler and helmet with him, in dark shades
Of soul-divorcing death involved, he fell.
Antilochus, observing Thoön turn'd
To flight, that moment pierced him ; from his back
He ripp'd the vein which through the trunk its course   665
Winds upward to the neck ; that vein he ripp'd
All forth ; supine he fell, and with both hands

Extended to his fellow warriors, died.
Forth sprang Antilochus to strip his arms,
But watch'd, meantime, the Trojans, who in crowds          670
Encircling him, his splendid buckler broad
Smote oft, but none with ruthless point prevail'd
Even to inscribe the skin of Nestor's son,
Whom Neptune, shaker of the shores, amid
Innumerable darts kept still secure.          675
Yet never from his foes he shrank, but faced
From side to side, nor idle slept his spear,
But with rotation ceaseless turn'd and turn'd
To every part, now levell'd at a foe
Far-distant, at a foe, now, near at hand.          680
Nor he, thus occupied, unseen escaped
By Asius' offspring Adamas, who close
Advancing, struck the centre of his shield.
But Neptune azure-hair'd so dear a life
Denied to Adamas, and render'd vain          685
The weapon; part within his disk remain'd
Like a seer'd stake, and part fell at his feet.
Then Adamas, for his own life alarm'd,
Retired, but as he went, Meriones
Him reaching with his lance, the shame between          690
And navel pierced him, where the stroke of Mars
Proves painful most to miserable man.
There enter'd deep the weapon; down he fell,
And in the dust lay panting as an ox
Among the mountains pants by peasants held          695
In twisted bands, and dragg'd perforce along;
So panted dying Adamas, but soon
Ceased, for Meriones, approaching, pluck'd
The weapon forth, and darkness veil'd his eyes.
Helenus, with his heavy Thracian blade          700
Smiting the temples of Deipyrus,
Dash'd off his helmet; from his brows remote
It fell, and wandering roll'd, till at his feet
Some warrior found it, and secured; meantime
The sightless shades of death him wrapp'd around.          705
Grief at that spectacle the bosom fill'd
Of valiant Menelaus; high he shook
His radiant spear, and threatening him, advanced

On royal Helenus, who ready stood
With his bow bent. They met; impatient, one,    710
To give his pointed lance its rapid course,
And one, to start his arrow from the nerve.
The arrow of the son of Priam struck
Atrides' hollow corslet, but the reed
Glanced wide. As vetches or as swarthy beans    715
Leap from the van and fly athwart the floor,
By sharp winds driven, and by the winnower's force,
So from the corslet of the glorious Greek
Wide-wandering flew the bitter shaft away.
But Menelaus the left-hand transpierced    720
Of Helenus, and with the lance's point
Fasten'd it to his bow; shunning a stroke
More fatal, Helenus into his band
Retired, his arm dependent at his side,
And trailing, as he went, the ashen beam;    725
There, bold Agenor from his hand the lance
Drew forth, then folded it with softest wool
Around, sling-wool, and borrow'd from the sling
Which his attendant into battle bore.
Then sprang Pisander on the glorious Chief    730
The son of Atreus, but his evil fate
Beckon'd him to his death in conflict fierce,
Oh Menelaus, mighty Chief! with thee.
And now they met, small interval between.
Atrides hurl'd his weapon, and it err'd.    735
Pisander with his spear struck full the shield
Of glorious Menelaus, but his force
Resisted by the stubborn buckler broad
Fail'd to transpierce it, and the weapon fell
Snapp'd at the neck. Yet, when he struck, the heart    740
Rebounded of Pisander, full of hope.
But Menelaus, drawing his bright blade,
Sprang on him, while Pisander from behind
His buckler drew a brazen battle-axe
By its long haft of polish'd olive-wood,    745
And both Chiefs struck together. He the crest
That crown'd the shaggy casque of Atreus' son
Hew'd from its base, but Menelaus him
In his swift onset smote full on the front

Above his nose : sounded the shatter'd bone,                750
And his eyes both fell bloody at his feet.
Convolved with pain he lay ; then, on his breast
Atrides setting fast his heel, tore off
His armour, and exulting thus began.
    So shall ye leave at length  the Grecian fleet,    755
Traitors, and never satisfied with war !
Nor want ye other guilt, dogs and profane !
But me have injured also, and defied
The hot displeasure of high-thundering Jove
The Hospitable, who shall waste in time,                    760
And level with the dust your lofty Troy.
I wrong'd not you, yet bore ye far away
My youthful bride who welcomed you, and stole
My treasures also,  and ye now are bent
To burn Achaia's gallant fleet with fire                    765
And slay her Heroes ; but your furious thirst
Of battle shall hereafter meet a check.
Oh, Father Jove ! Thee wisest we account
In heaven or earth, yet from thyself proceed
All these calamities, who favour show'st                    770
To this flagitious race the Trojans, strong
In wickedness alone, and whose delight
In war and bloodshed never can be cloy'd.
All pleasures breed satiety, sweet sleep,
Soft dalliance, music, and the graceful dance,              775
Though sought with keener appetite by most
Than bloody war ; but Troy still covets blood.
    So spake the royal Chief, and to his friends
Pisander's gory spoils consigning, flew
To mingle in the foremost fight again.                      780
Him, next, Harpalion, offspring of the King
Pylæmenes assailed ; to Troy he came
Following his sire, but never thence return'd.
He, from small distance, smote the central boss
Of Menelaus' buckler with his lance,                        785
But wanting power to pierce it, with an eye
Of cautious circumspection, lest perchance
Some spear should reach him, to his band retired.
But him retiring with a brazen shaft
Meriones pursued ; swift flew the dart                      790

To his right buttock, slipp'd beneath the bone,
His bladder grazed, and started through before.
There ended his retreat; sudden he sank
And like a worm lay on the ground, his life
Exhaling in his fellow-warrior's arms,                    795
And with his sable blood soaking the plain.
Around him flock'd his Paphlagonians bold,
And in his chariot placed drove him to Troy,
With whom his father went, mourning with tears
A son, whose death he never saw avenged.                  800
    Him slain with indignation Paris view'd,
For he, with numerous Paphlagonians more,
His guest had been, he, therefore, in the thirst
Of vengeance, sent a brazen arrow forth.
There was a certain Greek, Euchenor, son                  805
Of Polyides the soothsayer, rich
And brave in fight, and who in Corinth dwelt.
He, knowing well his fate, yet sail'd to Troy.
For Polyides oft, his reverend sire,
Had prophecied that he should either die                  810
By some dire malady at home, or, slain
By Trojan hands, amid the fleet of Greece.
He, therefore, shunning the reproach alike
Of the Achaians, and that dire disease,
Had joined the Grecian host; him Paris pierced            815
The ear and jaw beneath; life at the stroke
Left him, and darkness overspread his eyes.
    So raged the battle like devouring fire.
But Hector dear to Jove not yet had learn'd,
Nor aught surmised the havoc of his host                  820
Made on the left, where victory crown'd well-nigh
The Grecians animated to the fight
By Neptune seconding himself their arms.
He, where he first had started through the gate
After dispersion of the shielded Greeks                   825
Compact, still persevered. The galleys there
Of Ajax and Protesilaüs stood
Updrawn above the hoary Deep; the wall
Was there of humblest structure, and the steeds
And warriors there conflicted furious most.               830

The Epeans there and Iäonians' robed-
Prolix, the Phthians[10], Locrians, and the bold
Bœotians check'd the terrible assault
Of Hector, noble Chief, ardent as flame,
Yet not repulsed him. Chosen Athenians form'd 835
The van, by Peteos' son, Menestheus, led,
Whose high command undaunted Bias shared,
Phidas, and Stichius. The Epean host
Under Amphion, Dracius, Meges, fought.
Podarces brave in arms the Phthians ruled, 840
And Medon (Medon was by spurious birth
Brother of Ajax Oïliades,
And for his uncle's death, whom he had slain,
The brother of Oïleus' wife abode
In Phylace; but from Iphiclus sprang 845
Podarces;) these all station'd in the front
Of Phthias' hardy sons, together strove
With the Bœotians for the fleet's defence.
Ajax the swift swerved never from the side
Of Ajax son of Telamon a step, 850
But as in some deep fallow two black steers
Labour combined, dragging the ponderous plough,
The briny sweat around their rooted horns
Oozes profuse; they, parted as they toil
Along the furrow, by the yoke alone, 855
Cleave to its bottom sheer the stubborn glebe,
So, side by side, they persevering fought.
The son of Telamon a people led
Numerous and bold, who, when his bulky limbs
Fail'd overlabour'd, eased him of his shield. 860
Not so attended by his Locrians fought
Oïleus' valiant son; pitch'd battle them
Suited not, unprovided with bright casques
Of hairy crest, with ashen spears, and shields
Of ample orb; for, trusting in the bow 865

---

9 The Iäonians were a distinct people from the Ionians, and according
to the Scholium, separated from them by a pillar bearing on opposite
sides the name of each.—See Barnes. See also Villoisson.

10 The people of Achilles were properly called the Phthiotæ; whereas
the Phthians belonged to Protesiläus and Philoctetes.—See Eustathius,
as quoted by Clarke.

And twisted sling alone, they came to Troy,
And broke with shafts and volley'd stones the ranks.
Thus occupying, clad in burnish'd arms,
The van, these Two with Hector and his host
Conflicted, while the Locrians from behind                870
Vex'd them with shafts, secure ; nor could the men
Of Ilium stand, by such a shower confused.
Then, driven with dreadful havoc thence, the foe
To wind-swept Ilium had again retired,
Had not Polydamas, at Hector's side                     875
Standing, the dauntless Hero thus address'd.
   Hector ! Thou ne'er canst listen to advice ;
But think'st thou, that if heaven in feats of arms
Give thee pre-eminence, thou must excel
Therefore in council also all mankind ?                 880
No.   All-sufficiency is not for thee.
To one, superior force in arms is given,
Skill, to another, in the graceful dance,
Sweet song and powers of music to a third,
And to a fourth loud-thundering Jove imparts           885
Wisdom, which profits many, and which saves
Whole cities oft, though reverenced but by few.
Yet hear ; I speak as wisest seems to me.
War, like a fiery circle, all around
Environs thee ; the Trojans, since they pass'd          890
The bulwark, either hold themselves aloof,
Or, wide dispersed among the galleys, cope
With numbers far superior to their own.
Retiring, therefore, summon all our Chiefs
To consultation on the sum of all,                      895
Whether (should heaven so prosper us) to rush
Impetuous on the gallant barks of Greece,
Or to retreat secure ; for much I dread
Lest the Achaians punctually refund
All yesterday's arrear, since yonder Chief[11]          900
Insatiable with battle still abides
Within the fleet, nor longer, as I judge,
Will rest a mere spectator of the field.
   So spake Polydamas, whose safe advice
Pleased Hector ; from his chariot down he leap'd        905

[11] Achilles.

All arm'd, and in wing'd accents thus replied.
    Polydamas! here gather all the Chiefs;
I haste into the fight, and my commands
Once issued there, incontinent return.
    He ended, and conspicuous as the height     910
Of some snow-crested mountain, shouting ranged
The Trojans and confederates of Troy.
They swift around Polydamas, brave son
Of Panthus, at the voice of Hector, ran.
Himself with hasty strides the front, meantime,     915
Of battle roam'd, seeking from rank to rank
Asius Hyrtacides, with Asius' son
Adamas, and Deiphobus, and the might
Of Helenus, his royal brother bold.
Them neither altogether free from hurt     920
He found, nor living all.   Beneath the sterns
Of the Achaian ships some slaughter'd lay
By Grecian hands; some stricken by the spear
Within the rampart sat, some by the sword.
But leftward of the woeful field he found,     925
Ere long, bright Helen's paramour his band
Exhorting to the fight.   Hector approach'd,
And him, in fierce displeasure, thus bespake.
    Curst Paris, specious, fraudulent and lewd!
Where is Deiphobus, and where the might     930
Of royal Helenus? Where Adamas
Offspring of Asius, and where Asius, son
Of Hyrtacus, and where Othryoneus?
Now lofty Ilium from her topmost height
Falls headlong, now is thy own ruin sure.     935
    To whom the Godlike Paris thus replied.
Since Hector! thou art pleased with no just cause
To censure me, I may decline, perchance,
Much more the battle on some future day,
For I profess some courage, even I.     940
Witness our constant conflict with the Greeks
Here, on this spot, since first led on by thee
The host of Troy waged battle at the ships.
But those our friends of whom thou hast enquired
Are slain, Deiphobus alone except     945
And royal Helenus, who in the hand

Bear each a wound inflicted by the spear,
And have retired ; but Jove their life preserved.
Come now—conduct us whither most thine heart
Prompts thee, and thou shalt find us ardent all          950
To face like danger ; what we can, we will,
The best and most determined can no more.
   So saying, the Hero sooth'd his brother's mind.
Then moved they both toward the hottest war
Together, where Polydamas the brave,                     955
Phalces, Cebriones, Orthæus fought,
Palmys and Polyphœtes, godlike Chief,
And Morys and Ascanius, gallant sons
Both of Hippotion.   They at Troy arrived
From fair Ascania the preceding morn,                    960
In recompense for aid[12] by Priam lent
Erewhile to Phrygia, and, by Jove impell'd,
Now waged the furious battle side by side.
The march of these at once, was as the sound
Of mighty winds from deep-hung thunder-clouds            965
Descending ; clamorous the blast and wild
With Ocean mingles ! many a billow, then,
Upridged rides turbulent the sounding flood,
Foam-crested, billow after billow driven,
So moved the host of Troy, rank after rank               970
Behind their Chiefs, all dazzling bright in arms.
Before them Priameian Hector strode
Fierce as gore-tainted Mars, and his broad shield
Advancing came, heavy with hides, and thick-
Plated with brass ; his helmet on his brows              975
Refulgent shook, and in its turn he tried
The force of every phalanx, if perchance
Behind his broad shield pacing he might shake
Their stedfast order ; but he bore not down
The spirit of the firm Achaian host.                     980
Then Ajax striding forth, him, first, defied.
   Approach.   Why temptest thou the Greeks to fear ?
No babes are we in aught that appertains
To arms, though humbled by the scourge of Jove.
Thou cherishest the foolish hope to burn                 985

---

[12] This according to Eustathius, is the import of ἀμοιβοὶ.—See Iliad
III.—in which Priam relates an expedition of his into that country.

Our fleet with fire ; but even we have hearts
Prepared to guard it, and your populous Troy,
By us dismantled and to pillage given,
Shall perish sooner far.   Know this thyself
Also ; the hour is nigh when thou shalt ask                990
In prayer to Jove and all the Gods of heaven,
That speed more rapid than the falcon's flight
May wing thy coursers, while, exciting dense
The dusty plain, they whirl thee back to Troy.
 While thus he spake, sublime on the right-hand       995
An eagle soar'd ; confident in the sign
The whole Achaian host with loud acclaim
Hail'd it.   Then glorious Hector thus replied.
 Brainless and big, what means this boast of thine,
Earth-cumberer Ajax? Would I were the son               1000
As sure, for ever, of almighty Jove
And Juno, and such honour might receive
Henceforth as Pallas and Apollo share,
As comes this day with universal woe
Fraught for the Grecians, among whom thyself            1005
Shalt also perish if thou dare abide
My massy spear, which shall thy pamper'd flesh
Disfigure, and amid the barks of Greece
Falling, thou shalt the vultures with thy bulk
Enormous satiate, and the dogs of Troy.                 1010
 He spake, and led his host ; with clamour loud
They follow'd him, and all the distant rear
Came shouting on.   On the other side the Greeks
Re-echoed shout for shout, all undismay'd,
And waiting firm the bravest of their foes.             1015
Upwent the double roar into the heights
Ethereal, and among the beams of Jove.

# BOOK XIV.

## ARGUMENT.

Agamemnon and the other wounded Chiefs taking Nestor with them, visit
the battle.  Juno having borrowed the Cestus of Venus, first engages
the assistance of Sleep, then hastes to Ida to inveigle Jove.  She prevails.  Jove sleeps; and Neptune takes that opportunity to succour the
Grecians.

NOR was that cry by Nestor unperceived
Though drinking, who in words wing'd with surprise
The son of Æsculapius thus address'd.
   Divine Machaon! think what this may bode.
The cry of our young warriors at the ships          5
Grows louder; sitting here, the sable wine
Quaff thou, while bright-hair'd Hecamede warms
A bath, to cleanse thy crimson stains away.
I from yon eminence will learn the cause.
   So saying, he took a shield radiant with brass    10
There lying in the tent, the shield well-forged
Of valiant Thrasymedes, his own son,
(For he had borne to fight his father's shield)
And arming next his hand with a keen lance
Stood forth before the tent.  Thence soon he saw    15
Foul deeds and strange, the Grecian host confused,
Their broken ranks flying before the host
Of Ilium, and the rampart overthrown.
As when the wide sea, darken'd over all
Its silent flood, forebodes shrill winds to blow,    20
The doubtful waves roll yet to neither side,
Till swept at length by a decisive gale;
So stood the senior, with distressful doubts
Conflicting anxious, whether first to seek
The Grecian host, or Agamemnon's self           25
The sovereign, and at length that course preferr'd.
Meantime with mutual carnage they the field

Spread far and wide, and by spears double-edged
Smitten, and by the sword their corslets rang.
 The royal Chiefs ascending from the fleet,   30
Ulysses, Diomede, and Atreus' son
Imperial Agamemnon, who had each
Bled in the battle, met him on his way.
For from the war remote they had updrawn
Their galleys on the shore of the gray Deep,   35
The foremost to the plain, and at the sterns
Of that exterior line had built the wall.  .
For, spacious though it were, the shore alone
That fleet sufficed not, incommoding much
The people ; wherefore they had ranged the ships  40
Line above line gradual, and the bay
Between both promontories, all was fill'd.
They, therefore, curious to survey the fight,
Came forth together, leaning on the spear,
When Nestor met them ; heavy were their hearts,  45
And at the sight of him still more alarm'd,
Whom royal Agamemnon thus bespake.
 Neleian Nestor, glory of the Greeks !
What moved thee to forsake yon bloody field,
And urged thee hither? Cause I see of fear,   50
Lest furious Hector even now his threat
Among the Trojans publish'd, verify,
That he would never enter Ilium more
Till he had burn'd our fleet, and slain ourselves.
So threaten'd Hector and shall now perform.   55
Alas! alas! the Achaians brazen-greaved
All, like Achilles, have deserted me
Resentful, and decline their fleet's defence.
 To whom Gerenian Nestor thus replied.
Those threats are verified ; nor Jove himself   60
The Thunderer can disappoint them now ;
For our chief strength in which we trusted most
That it should guard impregnably secure
Our navy and ourselves, the wall hath fallen.
Hence all this conflict by our host sustain'd   65
Among the ships ; nor could thy keenest sight
Inform thee where in the Achaian camp
Confusion most prevails, such deaths are dealt

Promiscuous, and the cry ascends to heaven.
But come—consult we on the sum of all,                         70
If counsel yet may profit.   As for you,
Ye shall have exhortation none from me
To seek the fight; the wounded have excuse.
   Whom Agamemnon answer'd, King of men.
Ah Nestor! if beneath our very sterns                          75
The battle rage, if neither trench nor wall
Constructed with such labour, and supposed
Of strength to guard impregnably secure
Our navy and ourselves, avail us aught,
It is because almighty Jove hath will'd                        80
That the Achaian host should perish here
Inglorious, from their country far remote.
When he vouchsafed assistance to the Greeks,
I knew it well; and now, not less I know
That high as the immortal Gods he lifts                        85
Our foes to glory, and depresses us.
Haste therefore all, and act as I advise.
Our ships—all those that nearest skirt the Deep,
Launch we into the sacred flood, and moor
With anchors safely, till o'ershadowing night                 90
(If night itself may save us) shall arrive.
Then may we launch the rest; for I no shame
Account it, even by 'vantage of the night
To fly destruction.   Wiser him I deem
Who 'scapes his foe, than whom his foe enthralls.             95
   But him Ulysses, frowning stern, reproved.
What word, Atrides, now hath pass'd thy lips?
Counsellor of despair! thou should'st command
(And would to heaven thou didst) a different host,
Some dastard race, not ours; whom Jove ordains               100
From youth to hoary age to weave the web
Of toilsome warfare, till we perish all.
Wilt thou the spacious city thus renounce
For which such numerous woes we have endured?
Hush! lest some other hear; it is a word                      105
Which no man qualified by years mature
To speak discreetly, no man bearing rule
O'er such a people as confess thy sway,
Should suffer to contaminate his lips.

I from my soul condemn thee, and condemn          110
Thy counsel, who persuad'st us in the heat
Of battle terrible as this, to launch
Our fleet into the waves, that we may give
Our too successful foes their full desire,
And that our own prepondering scale              115
May plunge us past all hope; for while they draw
Their galleys down, the Grecians shall but ill
Sustain the fight, seaward will cast their eyes
And shun the battle, bent on flight alone.
Then shall they rue thy counsel, King of men!     120
   To whom the imperial leader of the Greeks,
Thy sharp reproof, Ulysses, hath my soul
Pierced deeply.   Yet I gave no such command
That the Achaians should their galleys launch,
Would they, or would they not.   No.   I desire    125
That, young or old, some other may advice
More prudent give, and he shall please me well.
   Then thus the gallant Diomede replied.
That man is near, and may ye but be found
Tractable, our enquiry shall be short.             130
Be patient each, nor chide me or reproach
Because I am of greener years than ye,
For I am sprung from an illustrious Sire,
From Tydeus, who beneath his hill of earth
Lies now entomb'd at Thebes.   Three noble sons    135
Were born to Portheus, who in Pleuro dwelt,
And on the heights of Calydon; the first
Agrius; the second Melas; and the third
Brave Oeneus, father of my father, famed
For virtuous qualities above the rest.             140
Oeneus still dwelt at home; but wandering thence,
My father dwelt in Argos; so the will
Of Jove appointed, and of all the Gods.
There he espoused the daughter of the King
Adrastus, occupied a mansion rich                  145
In all abundance; many a field possess'd
Of wheat, well-planted gardens, numerous flocks,
And was expert in spearmanship esteem'd
Past all the Grecians.   I esteem'd it right
That ye should hear these things, for they are true. 150

Ye will not, therefore, as I were obscure
And of ignoble origin, reject
What I shall well advise.   Expedience bids
That, wounded as we are, we join the host.
We will preserve due distance from the range        155
Of spears and arrows, lest already gall'd,
We suffer worse; but we will others urge
To combat, who have stood too long aloof,
Attentive only to their own repose.
 He spake, whom all approved, and forth they went,   160
Imperial Agamemnon at their head.
 Nor watch'd the glorious Shaker of the shores
In vain, but like a man time-worn approach'd,
And, seizing Agamemnon's better hand,
In accents wing'd the monarch thus address'd.        165
 Atrides! now exults the vengeful heart
Of fierce Achilles, viewing at his ease
The flight and slaughter of Achaia's host;
For he is mad, and let him perish such,
And may his portion from the Gods be shame!          170
But as for thee, not yet the powers of heaven
Thee hate implacable; the Chiefs of Troy
Shall cover yet with cloudy dust the breadth
Of all the plain, and backward from the camp
To Ilium's gates thyself shalt see them driven.      175
 He ceased, and shouting traversed swift the field.
Loud as nine thousand or ten thousand shout
In furious battle mingled, Neptune sent
His voice abroad, force irresistible
Infusing into every Grecian heart,                   180
And thirst of battle not to be assuaged.
 But Juno of the golden throne stood forth
On the Olympian summit, viewing thence
The field, where clear distinguishing the God
Of ocean, her own brother sole engaged              185
Amid the glorious battle, glad was she.
Seeing Jove also on the topmost point
Of spring-fed Ida seated, she conceived
Hatred against him, and thenceforth began
Deliberate how best she might deceive               190
The Thunderer, and thus at last resolved;

Attired with skill celestial to descend
On Ida, with a hope to allure him first
Won by her beauty to a fond embrace,
Then closing fast in balmy sleep profound          195
His eyes, to elude his vigilance, secure.
She sought her chamber; Vulcan her own son
That chamber built.   He framed the solid doors,
And to the posts fast closed them with a key
Mysterious, which, herself except, in heaven        200
None understood.   Entering she secured
The splendid portal.   First, she laved all o'er
Her beauteous body with ambrosial lymph,
Then polish'd it with richest oil divine
Of boundless fragrance; oil that in the courts      205
Eternal only shaken, through the skies
Breathed odours, and through all the distant earth.
Her whole fair body with those sweets bedew'd,
She pass'd the comb through her ambrosial hair,
And braided her bright locks streaming profuse      210
From her immortal brows; with golden studs
She made her gorgeous mantle fast before,
Ethereal texture, labour of the hands
Of Pallas beautified with various art,
And braced it with a zone fringed all around        215
An hundred fold; her pendants triple-gemm'd
Luminous, graceful, in her ears she hung,
And covering all her glories with a veil
Sun-bright, new-woven, bound to her fair feet
Her sandals elegant.   Thus full attired,           220
In all her ornaments, she issued forth,
And beckoning Venus from the other powers
Of heaven apart, the Goddess thus bespake.
    Daughter beloved! shall I obtain my suit,
Or wilt thou thwart me, angry that I aid            225
The Grecians, while thine aid is given to Troy?
    To whom Jove's daughter Venus thus replied.
What would majestic Juno, daughter dread
Of Saturn, sire of Jove? I feel a mind
Disposed to gratify thee, if thou ask               230
Things possible, and possible to me.
    Then thus with wiles veiling her deep design

Imperial Juno.   Give me those desires,
That love-enkindling power by which thou sway'st
Immortal hearts and mortal, all alike ;                     235
For to the green earth's utmost bounds I go,
To visit there the parent of the Gods,
Oceanus, and Tethys his espoused,
Mother of all.   They kindly from the hands
Of Rhea took, and with parental care                        240
Sustain'd and cherish'd me, what time from heaven
The Thunderer hurl'd down Saturn, and beneath
The earth fast bound him and the barren Deep.
Them go I now to visit, and their feuds
Innumerable to compose ; for long                           245
They have from conjugal embrace abstain'd
Through mutual wrath, whom by persuasive speech
Might I restore into each other's arms,
They would for ever love me and revere.
     Her, foam-born Venus then, Goddess of smiles,          250
Thus answer'd.   Thy request, who in the arms
Of Jove reposest the omnipotent,
Nor just it were nor seemly to refuse.
     So saying, the cincture from her breast she loosed
Embroider'd, various, her all-charming zone.               255
It was an ambush of sweet snares, replete
With love, desire, soft intercourse of hearts,
And music of resistless whisper'd sounds
That from the wisest steal their best resolves ;
She placed it in her hands and thus she said.              260
     Take this,—this girdle fraught with every charm.
Hide this within thy bosom, and return,
Whate'er thy purpose, mistress of it all.
     She spake ; imperial Juno smiled, and still
Smiling complacent, bosom'd safe the zone.                 265
Then Venus to her father's court return'd,
And Juno, starting from the Olympian height,
O'erflew Pieria and the lovely plains
Of broad Emathia ; soaring thence she swept
The snow-clad summits of the Thracian hills                270
Steed-famed, nor printed, as she pass'd, the soil.
From Athos o'er the foaming billows borne
She came to Lemnos, city and abode

Of noble Thoas, and there meeting Sleep,
Brother of Death, she press'd his hand, and said,          275
   Sleep, over all, both Gods and men, supreme!
If ever thou hast heard, hear also now
My suit; I will be grateful evermore.
Seal for me fast the radiant eyes of Jove
In the instant of his gratified desire.                   280
Thy recompence shall be a throne of gold,
Bright, incorruptible; my limping son,
Vulcan, shall fashion it himself with art
Laborious, and, beneath, shall place a stool
For thy fair feet, at the convivial board.                285
   Then answer thus the tranquil Sleep return'd.
Great Saturn's daughter, awe-inspiring Queen!
All other of the everlasting Gods
I could with ease make slumber, even the streams
Of Ocean, Sire of all.   Not so the King                  290
The son of Saturn; him, unless himself
Give me command, I dare not lull to rest,
Or even approach him, taught as I have been
Already in the schools of thy commands
That wisdom.   I forget not yet the day                    295
When, Troy laid waste, that valiant son[1] of his
Sail'd homeward: then my influence I diffused
Soft o'er the sovereign intellect of Jove;
While thou, against the Hero plotting harm,
Didst rouse the billows with tempestuous blasts,          300
And separating him from all his friends,
Brought'st him to populous Cos.   Then Jove awoke,
And, hurling in his wrath the Gods about,
Sought chiefly me, whom far below all ken
He had from heaven cast down into the Deep,               305
But Night resistless vanquisher of all,
Both Gods and men, preserved me; for to her
I fled for refuge.   So the Thunderer cool'd,
Though sore displeased, and spared me through a fear
To violate the peaceful sway of Night.                    310
And thou wouldst now embroil me yet again!
   To whom majestic Juno thus replied.
Ah, wherefore, Sleep! should'st thou indulge a fear

---

[1] Hercules.

So groundless? Chase it from thy mind afar.
Think'st thou the Thunderer as intent to serve          315
The Trojans, and as jealous in their cause
As erst for Hercules, his genuine son?
Come then, and I will bless thee with a bride;
One of the younger graces shall be thine,
Pasithea, day by day still thy desire.                  320
    She spake; Sleep heard delighted, and replied.
By the inviolable Stygian flood
Swear to me; lay thy right hand on the glebe
All-teeming, lay thy other on the face
Of the flat sea, that all the Immortal Powers           325
Who compass Saturn in the nether realms
May witness, that thou givest me for a bride
The younger Grace whom thou hast named, divine
Pasithea, day by day still my desire.
    He said, nor beauteous Juno not complied,      330
But sware, by name invoking all the powers
Titanian call'd who in the lowest gulf
Dwell under Tartarus, omitting none.
Her oath with solemn ceremonial sworn,
Together forth they went; Lemnos they left             335
And Imbrus, city of Thrace, and in dark clouds
Mantled, with gliding ease swam through the air
To Ida's mount with rilling waters vein'd,
Parent of savage beasts; at Lectos[2] first
They quitted Ocean, overpassing high                    340
The dry land, while beneath their feet the woods
Their spiry summits waved.   There, unperceived
By Jove, Sleep mounted Ida's loftiest pine
Of growth that pierced the sky, and hidden sat
Secure by its expanded boughs, the bird                 345
Shrill-voiced resembling in the mountains seen,
Chalcis in heaven, on earth Cymindis named.
    But Juno swift to Gargarus the top
Of Ida, soar'd, and there Jove saw his spouse.
—Saw her—and in his breast the same love felt          350
Rekindled vehement, which had of old
Join'd them, when, by their parents unperceived,
They stole aside, and snatch'd their first embrace.
            [2] One of the heads of Ida.

Soon he accosted her, and thus enquired.

Juno! what region seeking hast thou left  355
The Olympian summit, and hast here arrived
With neither steed nor chariot in thy train?

To whom majestic Juno thus replied
Dissembling.  To the green earth's end I go,
To visit there the parent of the Gods  360
Oceanus, and Tethys his espoused,
Mother of all.  They kindly from the hands
Of Rhea took, and with parental care
Sustain'd and cherish'd me; to them I haste
Their feuds innumerable to compose,  365
Who disunited by intestine strife
Long time, from conjugal embrace abstain.
My steeds, that lightly over dank and dry
Shall bear me, at the rooted base I left
Of Ida river-vein'd.  But for thy sake  370
From the Olympian summit I arrive,
Lest journeying remote to the abode
Of Ocean, and with no consent of thine
Entreated first, I should, perchance, offend.

To whom the cloud-assembler God replied.  375
Juno! thy journey thither may be made
Hereafter.  Let us turn to dalliance now.
For never Goddess pour'd, nor woman yet
So full a tide of love into my breast;
I never loved Ixion's consort thus  380
Who bore Pirithoüs, wise as we in heaven;
Nor sweet Acrisian Danäe, from whom
Sprang Perseus, noblest of the race of man;
Nor Phœnix' daughter fair[s], of whom were born
Minos unmatch'd but by the powers above,  385
And Rhadamanthus; nor yet Semele,
Nor yet Alcmena, who in Thebes produced
The valiant Hercules; and though my son
By Semele were Bacchus, joy of man;
Nor Ceres golden-hair'd, nor high-enthroned  390
Latona in the skies, no—nor thyself
As now I love thee, and my soul perceive
O'erwhelm'd with sweetness of intense desire.

[s] Europa.

s. c.—7.  T

Then thus majestic Juno her reply
Framed artful.   Oh unreasonable haste!          395
What speaks the Thunderer?   If on Ida's heights
Where all is open and to view exposed
Thou wilt that we embrace, what must betide,
Should any of the everlasting Gods
Observe us, and declare it to the rest?          400
Never could I, arising, seek again
Thy mansion, so unseemly were the deed.
But if thy inclinations that way tend,
Thou hast a chamber; it is Vulcan's work,
Our son's; he framed and fitted to its posts          405
The solid portal; thither let us hie,
And there repose, since such thy pleasure seems.
    To whom the cloud-assembler Deity.
Fear thou not, Juno, lest the eye of Man
Or of a God discern us; at my word          410
A golden cloud shall fold us so around,
That not the Sun himself shall through that veil
Discover aught, though keenest-eyed of all.
    So spake the son of Saturn, and his spouse
Fast lock'd within his arms.  Beneath them earth          415
With sudden herbage teem'd; at once upsprang
The crocus soft, the lotus bathed in dew,
And the crisp hyacinth with clustering bells;
Thick was their growth, and high above the ground
Upbore them.   On that flowery couch they lay,          420
Invested with a golden cloud that shed
Bright dew-drops all around.   His heart at ease,
There lay the Sire of all, by sleep and love
Vanquish'd on lofty Gargarus, his spouse
Constraining still with amorous embrace.          425
Then, gentle Sleep to the Achaian camp
Sped swift away, with tidings for the ear
Of earth-encircler Neptune charged; him soon
He found, and in wing'd accents thus began.
    Now Neptune, yield the Greeks effectual aid,          430
And, while the moment lasts of Jove's repose,
Make victory theirs; for him in slumbers soft
I have involved, while Juno by deceit
Prevailing, lured him with the bait of love.

He said, and swift departed to his task          435
Among the nations; but his tidings urged
Neptune with still more ardour to assist
The Danaï; he leap'd into the van
Afar, and thus exhorted them aloud.

    Oh Argives! yield we yet again the day          440
To Priameian Hector? Shall he seize
Our ships and make the glory all his own?
Such is his expectation, so he vaunts,          *
For that Achilles leaves not yet his camp,
Resentful; but of him small need, I judge,          445
Should here be felt, could once the rest be roused
To mutual aid.   Act, then, as I advise.
The best and broadest bucklers of the host,
And brightest helmets put we on, and arm'd
With longest spears, advance; myself will lead;          450
And trust me, furious though he be, the son
Of Priam flies.   Ye then who feel your hearts
Undaunted, but are arm'd with smaller shields,
Them give to those who fear, and in exchange
Their stronger shields and broader take yourselves.          455

    So he, whom, unreluctant, all obey'd.
Then, wounded as they were, themselves the Kings,
Tydides, Agamemnon and Ulysses
Marshall'd the warriors, and from rank to rank
Made just exchange of arms, giving the best          460
To the best warriors, to the worse, the worst.
And now in brazen armour all array'd
Refulgent, on they moved, by Neptune led
With firm hand grasping his long-bladed sword
Keen as Jove's bolt; with Him may none contend          465
In dreadful fight; but fear chains every arm.

    Opposite, Priameian Hector ranged
His Trojans; then they stretch'd the bloody cord
Of conflict tight, Neptune cœrulean-hair'd,
And Hector, pride of Ilium; one, the Greeks          470
Supporting firm, and one, the powers of Troy;
A sea-flood dash'd the galleys, and the hosts
Join'd clamorous.   Not so the billows roar
The shores among, when Boreas' roughest blast
Sweeps landward from the main the towering surge;          475

Not so, devouring fire among the trees
That clothe the mountain, when the sheeted flames
Ascending wrap the forest in a blaze ;
Nor howl the winds through leafy boughs of oaks
Upgrown aloft, (though loudest there they rave,)          480
With sounds so aweful as were heard of Greeks
And Trojans shouting when the clash began.
   At Ajax, first, (for face to face they stood,)
Illustrious Hector threw a spear well-aim'd,
But smote him where the belts that bore his shield         485
And faulchion cross'd each other on his breast.
The double guard preserved him unannoy'd.
Indignant that his spear had bootless flown,
Yet fearing death at hand, the Trojan Chief
Toward the phalanx of his friends retired.               490
But, as he went, huge Ajax with a stone
Of those which propp'd the ships, (for numerous such
Lay rolling at the feet of those who fought,)
Assail'd him.   Twirling like a top it pass'd
The shield of Hector, near the neck his breast           495
Struck full, then plough'd circuitous the dust.
As when Jove's arm omnipotent an oak
Prostrates uprooted on the plain, a fume
Rises sulphureous from the riven trunk,
And if, perchance, some traveller nigh at hand           500
See it, he trembles at the bolt of Jove,
So fell the might of Hector, to the earth
Smitten at once.   Down dropp'd his idle spear,
And with his helmet and his shield himself
Also ; loud thunder'd all his gorgeous arms.             505
Swift flew the Grecians shouting to the skies,
And showering darts, to drag his body thence,
But neither spear of theirs nor shaft could harm
The fallen leader, with such instant aid
His princely friends encircled him around,               510
Sarpedon, Lycian Chief, Glaucus the brave,
Polydamas, Æneas, and renown'd
Agenor ; neither tardy were the rest,
But with round shields all shelter'd Hector fallen.
Him soon uplifted from the plain his friends             515
Bore thence, till where his fiery coursers stood,

And splendid chariot in the rear, they came,
Then Troy-ward drove him groaning as he went.
Ere long arriving at the pleasant stream
Of eddied Xanthus, progeny of Jove,　　　　　　　520
They lay'd him on the bank, and on his face
Pour'd water! he, reviving, upward gazed,
And seated on his hams black blood disgorged
Coagulate, but soon relapsing, fell
Supine, his eyes with pitchy darkness veil'd,　　　525
And all his powers still torpid by the blow.
　　Then, seeing Hector borne away, the Greeks
Rush'd fiercer on, all mindful of the fight,
And far before the rest, Ajax the swift,
The Oïlean Chief, with pointed spear　　　　　　530
On Satnius springing, pierced him.　Him a nymph,
A Naiad, bore to Enops, while his herd
Feeding, on Satnio's grassy verge he stray'd.
But Oïliades the spear-renown'd
Approaching, pierced his flank; supine he fell,　535
And fiery contest for the dead arose.
In vengeance of his fall, spear-shaking Chief
The son of Panthus into fight advanced
Polydamas, who Prothöenor pierced
Offspring of Areïlocus, and urged　　　　　　　540
Through his right shoulder sheer the stormy lance.
He prostrate, clench'd the dust, and with loud voice
Polydamas exulted at his fall.
　　Yon spear, methinks, hurl'd from the warlike hand
Of Panthus' noble son, flew not in vain,　　　　545
But some Greek hath it, purposing, I judge,
To lean on it in his descent to hell.
　　So he, whose vaunt the Greeks indignant heard,
But most indignant, Ajax offspring bold
Of Telemon, to whom he nearest fell.　　　　　550
He, quick, at the retiring conqueror cast
His radiant spear; Polydamas the stroke
Shunn'd, starting sideward; but Antenor's son
Archilochus the mortal dint received,
Death-destined by the Gods; where neck and spine　555
Unite, both tendons he dissever'd wide,
And, ere his knees, his nostrils met the ground.

Then Ajax in his turn vaunting aloud
Against renown'd Polydamas, exclaim'd.
Speak now the truth, Polydamas, and weigh            560
My question well.   His life whom I have slain
Makes it not compensation for the loss
Of Prothöenor's life? To me he seems
Nor base himself, nor yet of base descent,
But brother of Antenor steed-renown'd,               565
Or else perchance his son ; for in my eyes
Antenor's lineage he resembles most.
  So he, well knowing him, and sorrow seized
Each Trojan heart.   Then Acamas around
His brother stalking, wounded with his spear         570
Bœotian Promachus, who by the feet
Dragg'd off the slain.   Acamas in his fall
Aloud exulted with a boundless joy.
  Vain-glorious Argives, archers inexpert !
War's toil and trouble are not ours alone,           575
But ye shall perish also ; mark the man,—
How sound he sleeps tamed by my conquering arm,
Your fellow-warrior Promachus ! the debt
Of vengeance on my brother's dear behalf
Demanded quick discharge ; well may the wish         580
Of every dying warrior be to leave
A brother living to avenge his fall.
  He ended, whom the Greeks indignant heard,
But chiefly brave Peneleus ; swift he rush'd
On Acamas ; but from before the force               585
Of King Peneleus Acamus retired,
And, in his stead, Ilioneus he pierced,
Offspring of Phorbas, rich in flocks, and blest
By Mercury with such abundant wealth
As other Trojan none, nor child to him                590
His spouse had borne, Ilioneus except.
Him close beneath the brow to his eye-roots
Piercing, he push'd the pupil from its seat,
And through his eye and through his poll the spear
Urged furious.   He down-sitting on the earth         595
Both hands extended ; but his glittering blade
Forth-drawn, Peneleus through his middle neck
Enforced it ; head and helmet to the ground

He lopp'd together, with the lance infixt
Still in his eye; then like a poppy's head          600
The crimson trophy lifting, in the ears
He vaunted loud of Ilium's host, and cried.
    Go, Trojans! be my messengers! Inform
The parents of Ilioneus the brave
That they may mourn their son through all their house,          605
For so the wife of Alegenor's son
Bœotian Promachus must him bewail,
Nor shall she welcome his return with smiles
Of joy affectionate, when from the shores
Of Troy the fleet shall bear us Grecians home.          610
    He said; fear whiten'd every Trojan cheek,
And every Trojan eye with earnest look
Enquired a refuge from impending fate.
    Say now, ye Muses, blest inhabitants
Of the Olympian realms, what Grecian first          615
Fill'd his victorious hand with armour stript
From slaughter'd Trojans, after Ocean's God
Had, interposing, changed the battle's course?
    First, Telamonian Ajax Hyrtius slew,
Undaunted leader of the Mysian band.          620
Phalces and Mermerus their arms resign'd
To young Antilochus; Hyppotion fell
And Morys by Meriones; the shafts
Right-aim'd of Teucer to the shades dismiss'd
Prothöus and Periphetes, and the prince          625
Of Sparta, Menelaus, in his flank
Pierced Hyperenor; on his entrails prey'd
The hungry steel, and, through the gaping wound
Expell'd, his spirit flew; night veil'd his eyes.
But Ajax Oïliades the swift          630
Slew most; him none could equal in pursuit
Of tremblers scatter'd by the frown of Jove.

# BOOK XV.

---

## ARGUMENT.

Jove, awaking and seeing the Trojans routed, threatens Juno. He sends Iris to admonish Neptune to relinquish the battle, and Apollo to restore health to Hector. Apollo armed with the Ægis, puts to flight the Grecians; they are pursued home to their fleet, and Telamonian Ajax slays twelve Trojans bringing fire to burn it.

But when the flying Trojans had o'erpass'd  
Both stakes and trench, and numerous slaughter'd lay  
By Grecian hands, the remnant halted all  
Beside their chariots, pale, discomfited.  
Then was it that on Ida's summit Jove          5  
At Juno's side awoke; starting, he stood  
At once erect; Trojans and Greeks he saw,  
These broken, those pursuing and led on  
By Neptune; he beheld also remote  
Encircled by his friends, and on the plain     10  
Extended, Hector; there he panting lay,  
Senseless, ejecting blood, bruised by a blow  
From not the feeblest of the sons of Greece.  
Touch'd with compassion at that sight, the Sire  
Of Gods and men, frowning terrific, fix'd     15  
His eyes on Juno, and her thus bespake.  
   No place for doubt remains. Oh, versed in wiles,  
Juno! thy mischief-teeming mind perverse  
Hath plotted this; thou hast contrived the hurt  
Of Hector, and hast driven his host to flight. 20  
I know not but thyself may'st chance to reap  
The first-fruits of thy cunning, scourged[1] by me.

---

[1] The Translator seizes the opportunity afforded to him by this remarkable passage, to assure his readers, who are not readers of the original, that the discipline which Juno is here said to have suffered from the hands of Jove, is not of his own invention. He found it in the

Hast thou forgotten how I once aloft  
Suspended thee, with anvils at thy feet,  
And both thy wrists bound with a golden cord     25  
Indissoluble?    In the clouds of heaven  
I hung thee, while from the Olympian heights  
The Gods look'd mournful on, but of them all  
None could deliver thee, for whom I seized,  
Hurl'd through the gates of heaven on earth he fell,     30  
Half-breathless.    Neither so did I resign  
My hot resentment of the Hero's wrongs  
Immortal Hercules, whom thou by storms  
Call'd from the North, with mischievous intent  
Hadst driven far distant o'er the barren Deep     35  
To populous Cos.    Thence I deliver'd him,  
And after numerous woes severe, he reach'd  
The shores of fruitful Argos, saved by me.  
I thus remind thee now, that thou may'st cease  
Henceforth from artifice, and may'st be taught     40  
How little all the dalliance and the love  
Which, stealing down from heaven, thou hast by fraud  
Obtain'd from me, shall profit thee at last.  
    He ended, whom imperial Juno heard  
Shuddering, and in wing'd accents thus replied.     45  
    Be witness Earth, the boundless Heaven above,  
And Styx beneath, whose stream the blessed Gods  
Even tremble to adjure; be witness too  
Thy sacred life, and our connubial bed,  
Which by a false oath I will never wrong,     50  
That by no art induced or plot of mine  
Neptune, the shaker of the shores, inflicts  
These harms on Hector and the Trojan host  
Aiding the Grecians, but impell'd alone  
By his own heart with pity moved at sight     55  
Of the Achaians at the ships subdued.

original, and considering fidelity as his indispensable duty, has not attempted to soften or to refine away the matter. He begs that this observation may be adverted to as often as any passage shall occur, in which ancient practices or customs, not consonant to our own, either in point of delicacy or humanity, may be either expressed or alluded to.

    He makes this request the rather, because on these occasions Mr. Pope has observed a different conduct, suppressing all such images as he had reason to suppose might be offensive.

But even Him, oh sovereign of the storms !
I am prepared to admonish that he quit
The battle, and retire where thou command'st.
　　So she ; then smiled the Sire of Gods and men,　　　60
And in wing'd accents answer thus return'd.
　　Juno ! wouldst thou on thy celestial throne
Assist my counsels, howsoe'er in heart
He differ now, Neptune should soon his will
Submissive bend to thy desires and mine.　　　65
But if sincerity be in thy words
And truth, repairing to the blest abodes
Send Iris hither, with the archer God
Apollo ; that she, visiting the host
Of Greece, may bid the Sovereign of the Deep　　　70
Renounce the fight, and seek his proper home.
Apollo's part shall be to rouse again
Hector to battle, to inspire his soul
Afresh with courage, and all memory thence
To banish of the pangs which now he feels.　　　75
Apollo also shall again repulse
Achaia's host, which with base panic fill'd,
Shall even to Achilles' ships be driven.
Achilles shall his valiant friend exhort
Patroclus forth ; him under Ilium's walls　　　80
Shall glorious Hector slay ; but many a youth
Shall perish by Patroclus first, with whom,
My noble son Sarpedon.　Peleus' son,
Resentful of Patroclus' death, shall slay
Hector, and I will urge ceaseless myself,　　　85
Thenceforth the routed Trojans back again,
Till by Minerva's aid the Greeks shall take
Ilium's proud city ; till that day arrive
My wrath shall burn, nor will I one permit
Of all the Immortals to assist the Greeks,　　　90
But will perform Achilles' whole desire.
Such was my promise to him at the first,
Ratified by a nod that self-same day
When Thetis clasp'd my knees, begging revenge
And glory for her city-spoiler son.　　　95
　　He ended ; nor his spouse white-arm'd refused
Obedience, but from the Idæan heights

Departing, to the Olympian summit soar'd.
Swift as the traveller's thought, who, many a land
Traversed, deliberates on his future course          100
Uncertain, and his mind sends every way,
So swift updarted Juno to the skies.
Arrived on the Olympian heights, she found
The Gods assembled ; they, at once, their seats
At her approach forsaking, with full cups          105
Her coming hail'd ; heedless of all beside,
She took the cup from blooming Themis' hand,
For she first flew to welcome her, and thus
In accents wing'd of her return enquired.
  Say, Juno, why this sudden re-ascent ?          110
Thou seem'st dismay'd; hath Saturn's son, thy spouse,
Driven thee affrighted to the skies again ?
  To whom the white-arm'd Goddess thus replied.
Themis divine, ask not.   Full well thou know'st
How harshly temper'd is the mind of Jove,          115
And how untractable.   Resume thy seat ;
The banquet calls thee ; at our board preside.
Thou shalt be told, and all in heaven shall hear
What ills he threatens ; such as shall not leave
All minds at ease, I judge, here or on earth,          120
However tranquil some and joyous now.
  So spake the aweful spouse of Jove, and sat.
Then, all alike, the Gods displeasure felt
Throughout the courts of Jove, but she, her lips
Gracing with smiles from which her sable brows          125
Dissented, thus, indignant them address'd.
  Alas ! how vain against the Thunderer's will
Our anger, and the hope to supersede
His purpose, by persuasion or by force !
He solitary sits, all unconcern'd          130
At our resentment, and himself proclaims
Mightiest and most to be revered in heaven.
Be patient, therefore, and let each endure
Such ills as Jove may send him.   Mars, I ween,
Already hath his share ; the warrior God          135
Hath lost Ascalaphus, of all mankind
His most beloved, and whom he calls his own.
  She spake, and with expanded palms his thighs

Smiting, thus, sorrowful, the God exclaim'd.
   Inhabitants of the Olympian heights!          140
Oh bear with me, if to avenge my son
I seek Achaia's fleet, although my doom   .
Be thunder-bolts from Jove, and with the dead
Outstretch'd to lie in carnage and in dust.
   He spake, and bidding Horror and Dismay       145
Lead to the yoke his rapid steeds, put on
His all-refulgent armour.   Then had wrath
More dreadful, some strange vengeance on the Gods
From Jove befallen, had not Minerva, touch'd
With timely fears for all, upstarting sprung      150
From where she sat, right through the vestibule.
She snatch'd the helmet from his brows, the shield
From his broad shoulder, and the brazen spear
Forced from his grasp into its place restored.
Then reprimanding Mars, she thus began.      155
   Frantic, delirious! thou art lost for ever!
Is it in vain that thou hast ears to hear,
And hast thou neither shame nor reason left?
How? hear'st thou not the Goddess? the report
Of white-arm'd Juno from Olympian Jove      160
Return'd this moment? or preferr'st thou rather,
Plagued with a thousand woes, and under force
Of sad necessity to seek again
Olympus, and at thy return to prove
Author of countless miseries to us all?      165
For He at once Grecians and Trojans both
Abandoning, will hither haste prepared
To tempest[2] us in heaven, whom he will seize,
The guilty and the guiltless, all alike.
I bid thee, therefore, patient bear the death     170
Of thy Ascalaphus; braver than he
And abler have, ere now, in battle fallen,
And shall hereafter; arduous were the task
To rescue from the stroke of fate, the race

---

   [2] *To tempest*—κυδοιμήσων—Milton uses *tempest* as a verb.  Speaking
of the fishes, he says

      .  .  .  .  .  .  part, huge of bulk
    Wallowing unwieldy, enormous in their gait,
    *Tempest* the ocean.

Of mortal men, with all their progeny. 175
　So saying, Minerva on his throne replaced
The fiery Mars.　Then, summoning abroad
Apollo from within the hall of Jove,
With Iris, swift embassadress of heaven,
Them in wing'd accents Juno thus bespake. 180
　Jove bids you hence with undelaying speed
To Ida ; in his presence once arrived,
See that ye execute his whole command.
　So saying, the aweful Goddess to her throne
Return'd and sat.　They, cleaving swift the air, 185
Alighted soon on Ida fountain-fed,
Parent of savage kinds.　High on the point
Seated of Gargarus, and wrapt around
With fragrant clouds, they found Saturnian Jove
The Thunderer, and in his presence stood. 190
He, nought displeased that they his high command
Had with such readiness obey'd, his speech
To Iris, first, in accents wing'd address'd.
　Swift Iris, haste—to royal Neptune bear
My charge entire ; falsify not the word. 195
Bid him, relinquishing the fight, withdraw
Either to heaven, or to the boundless Deep.
But should he disobedient prove, and scorn
My message, let him, next, consider well
How he will bear, powerful as he is, 200
My coming.　Me I boast superior far
In force, and elder-born ; yet deems he slight
The danger of comparison with me,
Who am the terror of all heaven beside.
　He spake, nor storm-wing'd Iris disobey'd, 205
But down from the Idæan summit stoop'd
To sacred Ilium.　As when snow or hail
Flies drifted by the cloud-dispelling North,
So swiftly, wing'd with readiness of will,
She shot the gulf between, and standing soon 210
At glorious Neptune's side, him thus address'd.
　To thee, O Neptune azure-hair'd ! I come
With tidings charged from Ægis-bearing Jove.
He bids thee cease from battle, and retire
Either to heaven, or to the boundless Deep. 215

But shouldst thou, disobedient, set at nought
His words, he threatens that himself will ha-te
To fight against thee ; but he bids thee shun
That strife with one superior far to thee,
And elder-born ; yet deem'st thou slight, he saith.                220
The danger of comparison with Him,
Although the terror of all heaven beside.
   Her then the mighty shaker of the shores
Answer'd indignant.  Great as is his power,
Yet he hath spoken proudly, threatening me                        225
With force, high-born and glorious as himself.
We are three brothers ; Saturn is our sire,
And Rhea brought us forth ; first, Jove she bore ;
Me next ; then, Pluto, sovereign of the shades.
By distribution tripart we received                               230
Each his peculiar honours ; me the lots
Made Ruler of the hoary floods, and there
I dwell for ever.  Pluto, for his part,
The regions took of darkness ; and the heavens,
The clouds, and boundless æther, fell to Jove.                    235
The Earth and the Olympian heights alike
Are common to the three.  My life and being
I hold not, therefore, at his will, whose best
And safest course, with all his boasted power,
Were to possess in peace his proper Third.                        240
Let him not seek to terrify with force
Me like a dastard ; let him rather chide
His own-begotten ; with big-sounding words
His sons and daughters govern, who perforce
Obey his voice, and shrink at his commands.                       245
   To whom thus Iris tempest-wing'd replied.
Cœrulean-tress'd Sovereign of the Deep !
Shall I report to Jove, harsh as it is,
Thy speech, or wilt thou soften it ? The wise
Are flexible, and on the Elder-born                               250
Erynnis, with her vengeful sisters, waits.
   Her answer'd then the Shaker of the shores.
Prudent is thy advice, Iris divine !
Discretion in a messenger is good
At all times.  But the cause that fires me thus,                  255
And with resentment my whole heart and mind

Possesses, is the license that he claims
To vex with provocation rude of speech
Me his compeer, and by decree of Fate
Illustrious as himself; yet, though incensed,                    260
And with just cause, I will not now persist.
But hear—for it is treasured in my heart
The threat that my lips utter.   If he still
Resolve to spare proud Ilium in despite
Of me, of Pallas, Goddess of the spoils,                    265
Of Juno, Mercury, and the King of fire,
And will not overturn her lofty towers,
Nor grant immortal glory to the Greeks,
Then tell him thus—Hostility shall burn,
And wrath between us never to be quench'd.                    270
    So saying, the Shaker of the shores forsook
The Grecian host, and plunged into the Deep,
Miss'd by Achaia's heroes.   Then, the cloud-
Assembler God thus to Apollo spake.
    Hence, my Apollo! to the Trojan Chief                    275
Hector; for earth-encircler Neptune, awed
By fear of my displeasure imminent,
Hath sought the sacred Deep.   Else, all the Gods
Who compass Saturn in the nether realms,
Had even there our contest heard, I ween,                    280
And heard it loudly.   But that he retreats
Although at first incensed, shunning my wrath,
Is salutary both for him and me,
Whose difference else had not been heal'd with ease.
Take thou my shaggy Ægis, and with force                    285
Smiting it, terrify the Chiefs of Greece.
As for illustrious Hector, him I give
To thy peculiar care; fail not to rouse
His fiercest courage, till he push the Greeks
To Hellespont, and to their ships again;                    290
Thenceforth to yield to their afflicted host
Some pause from toil, shall be my own concern.
    He ended, nor Apollo disobey'd
His father's voice; from the Idæan heights,
Swift as the swiftest of the fowls of air,                    295
The dove-destroyer falcon, down he flew.
The noble Hector, valiant Priam's son

He found, not now extended on the plain,
But seated; newly, as from death, awaked,
And conscious of his friends; freely he breathed          300
Nor sweated more, by Jove himself revived.
Apollo stood beside him, and began.
  Say, Hector, Priam's son! why sittest here
Feeble and spiritless, and from thy host
Apart? what new disaster hath befall'n?          305
  To whom with difficulty thus replied
The warlike Chief.—But tell me who art Thou,
Divine enquirer! best of powers above!
Know'st not that dauntless Ajax me his friends
Slaughtering at yonder ships, hath with a stone          310
Surceased from fight, smiting me on the breast?
I thought to have beheld, this day, the dead
In Ades, every breath so seem'd my last.
  Then answer thus the Archer God return'd.
Courage this moment! such an helper Jove          315
From Ida sends thee at thy side to war
Continual, Phœbus of the golden sword,
Whose guardian aid both thee and lofty Troy
Hath succour'd many a time.   Therefore arise!
Instant bid drive thy numerous charioteers          320
Their rapid steeds full on the Grecian fleet;
I, marching at their head, will smooth, myself,
The way before them, and will turn again
To flight the Heroes of the host of Greece.
  He said, and with new strength the Chief inspired.          325
As some stall'd horse high-pamper'd, snapping short
His cord, beats under foot the sounding soil,
Accustom'd in smooth-sliding streams to lave
Exulting; high he bears his head, his mane
Wantons around his shoulders; pleased, he eyes          330
His glossy sides, and borne on pliant knees
Soon finds the haunts where all his fellows graze;
So bounded Hector, and his agile joints
Plied lightly, quicken'd by the voice divine,
And gather'd fast his charioteers to battle.          335
But as when hounds and hunters through the woods
Rush in pursuit of stag or of wild goat,
He, in some cave with tangled boughs o'erhung

Lies safe conceal'd, no destined prey of theirs,
Till by their clamours roused, a lion grim       340
Starts forth to meet them ; then, the boldest fly ;
Such hot pursuit the Danaï, with swords
And spears of double edge long time maintain'd,
But seeing Hector in his ranks again
Occupied, felt at once their courage fall'n.       345
     Then, Thoas them, Andræmon's son, address'd,
Foremost of the Ætolians, at the spear
Skilful, in stationary combat bold,
And when the sons of Greece held in dispute
The prize of eloquence, excelled by few.       350
Prudent advising them, he thus began.
     Ye Gods ! what prodigy do I behold ?
Hath Hector, 'scaping death, risen again ?
For him, with confident persuasion all
Believed by Telamonian Ajax slain.       355
But some Divinity hath interposed
To rescue and save Hector, who the joints
Hath stiffen'd of full many a valiant Greek,
As surely now he shall ; for not without
The Thunderer's aid, he flames in front again.       360
But take ye all my counsel.   Send we back
The multitude into the fleet, and first
Let us, who boast ourselves bravest in fight,
Stand, that encountering him with lifted spears,
We may attempt to give his rage a check.       365
To thrust himself into a band like ours
Will, doubtless, even in Hector move a fear.
     He ceased, with whose advice all, glad, complied.
Then Ajax with Idomeneus of Crete.
Teucer, Meriones, and Meges fierce       370
As Mars in battle, summoning aloud
The noblest Greeks, in opposition firm
To Hector and his host their bands prepared,
While others all into the fleet retired.
Troy's crowded host[3] struck first.   With awful strides       375
Came Hector foremost ; him Apollo led,

    [3] Τρῶες δὲ πρότυψαν ἀολλέες. The translation is literal, and affords
one of many instances in which the Greek and English idiom correspond
exactly.
    s. C.—7.                                        U

His shoulders wrapt in clouds, and, on his arm,
The Ægis shagg'd terrific all around,
Tempestuous, dazzling-bright ; it was a gift
To Jove from Vulcan, and design'd to appal,          380
And drive to flight the armies of the earth.
Arm'd with that shield Apollo led them on.
Firm stood the embodied Greeks ; from either host
Shrill cries arose ; the arrows from the nerve
Leap'd, and, by vigorous arms dismiss'd, the spears   385
Flew frequent ; in the flesh some stood infixt
Of warlike youths, but many, ere they reach'd
The mark they coveted, unsated fell
Between the hosts, and rested in the soil.
Long as the God unagitated held                      390
The dreadful disk, so long the vollied darts
Made mutual slaughter, and the people fell ;
But when he look'd the Grecian charioteers
Full in the face and shook it, raising high
Himself the shout of battle, then he quell'd         395
Their spirits, then he struck from every mind
At once all memory of their might in arms.
As when two lions in the still dark night
An herd of beeves scatter or numerous flock
Suddenly, in the absence of the guard,               400
So fled the heartless Greeks, for Phœbus sent
Terrors among them, but renown conferr'd
And triumph proud on Hector and his host.
Then, in that foul disorder of the field,
Man singled man.   Arcesilaüs died                   405
By Hector's arm, and Stichius ; one, a Chief[4]
Of the Bœotians brazen-mail'd, and one,
Menestheus' faithful follower to the fight.
Æneas Medon and Iäsus slew.
Medon was spurious offspring of divine               410
Oïleus Ajax' father, and abode
In Phylace ; for he had slain a Chief
Brother of Eriopis the espoused
Of brave Oïleus ; but Iäsus led
A phalanx of Athenians, and the son                  415
Of Sphelus, son of Bucolus was deem'd.

                    [4] Arcesilaus.

Pierced by Polydamas Mecisteus fell.
Polites, in the van of battle, slew
Echion, and Agenor Clonius;
But Paris, while Deïochus to flight                     420
Turn'd with the routed van, pierced him beneath
His shoulder-blade, and urged the weapon through.
   While them the Trojans spoil'd, meantime the Greeks,
Entangled in the piles of the deep foss,
Fled every way, and through necessity                   425
Repass'd the wall.   Then Hector with a voice
Of loud command bade every Trojan cease
From spoil, and rush impetuous on the fleet.
⁵And whom I find far lingering from the ships
Wherever, there he dies; no funeral fires               430
Brother on him, or sister, shall bestow,
But dogs shall rend him in the sight of Troy.
   So saying, he lash'd the shoulders of his steeds,
And through the ranks vociferating, call'd
His Trojans on; they, clamorous as he,                  435
All lash'd their steeds, and menacing, advanced.
Before them with his feet Apollo push'd
The banks into the foss, bridging the gulf
With pass commodious, both in length and breadth
A lance's flight, for proof of vigour hurl'd.           440
There, phalanx after phalanx, they their host
Pour'd dense along, while Phœbus in the van
Display'd the awful ægis, and the wall
Levell'd with ease divine.   As, on the shore
Some wanton boy with sand builds plaything walls,       445
Then, sportive, spreads them with his feet abroad,
So thou, shaft-arm'd Apollo! that huge work
Laborious of the Greeks didst turn with ease
To ruin, and themselves drovest all to flight.
They, thus enforced into the fleet, again               450
Stood fast, with mutual exhortation each
His friend encouraging, and all the Gods
With lifted hands soliciting aloud.
But, more than all, Gerenian Nestor pray'd
Fervent, Achaia's guardian, and with arms               455

⁵ This abruptness of transition from the third person to the first,
follows the original.

Outstretch'd toward the starry skies, exclaim'd.
　Jove, Father! if in corn-clad Argos, one,
One Greek hath ever, burning at thy shrine
Fat thighs of sheep or oxen, ask'd from thee
A safe return, whom thou hast gracious heard,          460
Olympian King! and promised what he sought,
Now, in remembrance of it, give us help
In this disastrous day, nor thus permit
Their Trojan foes to tread the Grecians down!
　So Nestor pray'd, and Jove thunder'd aloud          465
Responsive to the old Neleïan's prayer.
But when that voice of ægis-bearing Jove
The Trojans heard, more furious on the Greeks
They sprang, all mindful of the fight.　As when
A turgid billow of some spacious sea,                470
While the wind blows that heaves its highest, borne
Sheer o'er the vessel's side, rolls into her,
With such loud roar the Trojans pass'd the wall;
In rush'd the steeds, and at the ships they waged
Fierce battle hand to hand, from chariots, these,      475
With spears of double edge, those, from the decks
Of many a sable bark, with naval poles
Long, ponderous, shod with steel; for every ship
Had such, for conflict maritime prepared.
　While yet the battle raged only without            480
The wall, and from the ships apart, so long
Patroclus quiet in the tent and calm
Sat of Eurypylus, his generous friend
Consoling with sweet converse, and his wound
Sprinkling with drugs assuasive of his pains.         485
But soon as through the broken rampart borne
He saw the Trojans, and the clamour heard
And tumult of the flying Greeks, a voice
Of loud lament uttering, with open palms
His thighs he smote, and, sorrowful, exclaim'd.       490
　Eurypylus! although thy need be great,
No longer may I now sit at thy side,
Such contest hath arisen; thy servant's voice
Must soothe thee now, for I will to the tent
Haste of Achilles, and exhort him forth;              495
Who knows? if such the pleasure of the Gods,

I may prevail; friends rarely plead in vain.
　　So saying, he went.   Meantime the Greeks endured
The Trojan onset, firm, yet from the ships
Repulsed them not, though fewer than themselves,　　　　500
Nor could the host of Troy, breaking the ranks
Of Greece, mix either with the camp or fleet;
But as the line divides the plank aright,
Stretch'd by some naval architect, whose hand
Minerva hath accomplish'd in his art,　　　　　　　　505
So stretched on them the cord of battle lay.
Others at other ships the conflict waged,
But Hector to the ship advanced direct
Of glorious Ajax; for one ship they strove;
Nor Hector, him dislodging thence, could fire　　　　510
The fleet, nor Ajax from the fleet repulse
Hector, conducted thither by the Gods.
Then, noble Ajax with a spear the breast
Pierced of Caletor, son of Clytius, arm'd
With fire to burn his bark; sounding he fell,　　　　515
And from his loosened grasp down dropp'd the brand.
But Hector seeing his own kinsman fallen
Beneath the sable bark, with mighty voice
Call'd on the hosts of Lycia and of Troy.
　　Trojans and Lycians, and close-fighting sons　　520
Of Dardanus, within this narrow pass
Stand firm, retreat not, but redeem the son
Of Clytius, lest the Grecians of his arms
Despoil him slain in battle at the ships.
　　So saying, at Ajax his bright spear he cast.　　　525
Him pierced he not, but Lycophron the son
Of Mastor, a Cytherian, who had left
Cytheræ, fugitive for blood, and dwelt
With Ajax.   Him standing at Ajax' side,
He pierced above his ear; down from the stern　　　530
Supine he fell, and in the dust expired.
Then, shuddering, Ajax to his brother spake.
　　Alas, my Teucer! we have lost our friend;
Mastorides is slain, whom we received
An inmate from Cytheræ, and with love　　　　　　535
And reverence even filial, entertain'd;
By Hector pierced, he dies.   Where are thy shafts

Death-wing'd, and bow, by gift from Phœbus thine?
  He said, whom Teucer hearing, instant ran
With bow and well-stored quiver to his side,      540
Whence soon his arrows sought the Trojan host.
He struck Pisenor's son Clytus, the friend
And charioteer of brave Polydamas,
Offspring of Panthus, toiling with both hands
To rule his fiery steeds ; for more to please      545
The Trojans and their Chief, where stormy most
He saw the battle, thither he had driven.
But sudden mischief, valiant as he was,
Found him, and such as none could waft aside,
For right into his neck the arrow plunged,      550
And down he fell ; his startled coursers shook
Their trappings, and the empty chariot rang.
That sound alarm'd Polydamas ; he turn'd,
And flying to their heads, consign'd them o'er
To Protiaön's son, Astynoüs,      555
Whom he enjoin'd to keep them in his view,
Then, turning, mingled with the van again.
But Teucer still another shaft produced
Design'd for valiant Hector, whose exploits
(Had that shaft reach'd him) at the ships of Greece    560
Had ceased for ever.  But the eye of Jove,
Guardian of Hector's life, slept not ; he took
From Telamonian Teucer that renown,
And while he stood straining the twisted nerve
Against the Trojan, snapp'd it.  Devious flew    565
The steel-charged[6] arrow, and he dropp'd his bow.
Then, shuddering, to his brother thus he spake.
  Ah ! it is evident.  Some Power divine
Makes fruitless all our efforts, who hath struck
My bow out of my hand, and snapt the cord      570
With which I strung it new at dawn of day,
That it might bear the bound of many a shaft.
  To whom the towering son of Telamon.
Leave then thy bow, and let thine arrows rest,
Which envious of the Greeks, some God confounds    575

---

[6] The Translator hopes that his learned readers will pardon him, if sometimes, to avoid an irksome cacophony, he turns brass into steel. In fact, the arrow had not a point of steel, but a brazen one.

That thou may'st fight with spear and buckler arm'd,
And animate the rest.   Such be our deeds
That, should they conquer us, our foes may find
Our ships, at least a prize not lightly won.
　　So Ajax spake ; then Teucer, in his tent          580
The bow.replacing, slung his fourfold shield,
Settled on his illustrious brows his casque
With hair high-crested, waving, as he moved,
Terrible from above, took forth a spear
Tough-grain'd, acuminated sharp with brass,          585
And stood incontinent, at Ajax' side.
Hector perceived the change, and of the cause
Conscious, with echoing voice call'd to his host.
　　Trojans and Lycians and close-fighting sons
Of Dardanus, oh now, my friends, be men,          590
Now, wheresoever through the fleet dispersed,
Call into mind the fury of your might !
For I have seen, myself, Jove rendering vain
The arrows of their mightiest.   Man may know
With ease the hand of interposing Jove,          595
Both whom to glory he ordains, and whom
He weakens and aids not ; so now he leaves
The  Grecians, but propitious smiles on us.
Therefore stand fast, and whosoever gall'd
By arrow or by spear, dies—Let him die ;          600
It shall not shame him that he died to serve
His country, but his children, wife and home,
With all his heritage, shall be secure,
Drive but  the Grecians from the shores of Troy.
　　So saying, he animated each.   Meantime,          605
Ajax his fellow-warriors thus address'd.
　　Shame on you all ! Now, Grecians, either die,
Or save at once your galley and yourselves.
Hope ye, that should your ships become the prize
Of warlike Hector, ye shall yet return          610
On foot ? Or hear ye not the Chief aloud
Summoning all his host, and publishing
His own heart's wish to burn your fleet with fire ?
Not to a dance, believe me, but to fight
He calls them ; therefore wiser course for us          615
Is none, than that we mingle hands with hands

In contest obstinate, and force with force.
Better at once to perish, or at once
To rescue life, than to consume the time
Hour after hour in lingering conflict vain          620
Here at the ships, with an inferior foe.
    He said, and by his words into all hearts
Fresh confidence infused.   Then Hector smote
Schedius, a Chief of the Phocensian powers
And son of Perimedes ; Ajax slew,                   625
Meantime, a Chief of Trojan infantry,
Laodamas, Antenor's noble son,
While by Polydamas, a leader bold
Of the Epeans, and Phylides'[7] friend,
Cyllenian Otus died.   Meges that sight         •   630
Viewing indignant on the conqueror sprang,
But, starting wide, Polydamas escaped,
Saved by Apollo, and his spear transpierced
The breast of Cræsmus ; on his sounding shield
Prostrate he fell, and Meges stripp'd his arms.     635
Him so employ'd Dolops assail'd, brave son
Of Lampus, best of men and bold in fight,
Offspring of King Laomedon ; he stood
Full near, and through his middle buckler struck
The son of Phyleus, but his corslet thick           640
With plates of scaly brass his life secured.
That corslet Phyleus on a time brought home
From Ephyre, where the Selleïs winds,
And it was given him for his life's defence
In furious battle by the King of men,               645
Euphetes.   Many a time had it preserved
Unharm'd the sire, and now it saved the son.
Then Meges, rising with his pointed lance
The bushy crest of Dolops' helmet drove
Sheer from its base ; new tinged with purple bright  650
Entire it fell and mingled with the dust.
While thus they strove, each hoping victory,
Came martial Menelaus to the aid
Of Meges ; spear in hand apart he stood
By Dolops unperceived, through his back drove       655
And through his breast the spear, and far beyond,

[7] Meges.

And down fell Dolops, forehead to the ground.
At once both flew to strip his radiant arms.
Then, Hector summoning his kindred, call'd
Each to his aid, and Melanippus first,   660
Illustrious Hicetaon's son, reproved.
Ere yet the enemies of Troy arrived
He in Percote fed his wandering beeves,
But when the Danaï with all their fleet
Came thither, then returning, he outshone  665
The noblest Trojans, and at Priam's side
Dwelling, was honour'd by him as a son.
Him Hector reprimanding, stern began.
  Are we thus slack? Can Melanippus view
Unmoved a kinsman slain? Seest not the Greeks 670
How busy there with Dolops and his arms?
Come on. It is no time for distant war,
But either our Achaian foes must bleed,
Or Ilium taken, from her topmost height
Must stoop, and all her citizens be slain.  675
  So saying he went, whose steps the godlike Chief
Attended, and the Telamonian, next,
Huge Ajax, animated thus the Greeks.
  Oh friends, be men! Deep treasure in your hearts
An honest shame, and, fighting bravely, fear  680
Each to incur the censure of the rest.
Of men so minded more survive than die,
While dastards forfeit life and glory both.
  So moved he them, themselves already bent
To chase the Trojans; yet his word they bore  685
Faithful in mind, and with a wall of brass
Fenced firm the fleet, while Jove impell'd the foe.
Then Menelaus, brave in fight, approach'd
Antilochus, and thus his courage roused.
  Antilochus! in all the host is none   690
Younger, or swifter, or of stronger limb
Than thou. Make trial, therefore, of thy might,
Spring forth and prove it on some Chief of Troy.
  He ended and retired, but him his praise
Effectual animated; from the van   695
Starting, he cast a wistful eye around
And hurl'd his glittering spear; back fell the ranks

Of Troy appall'd; nor vain his weapon flew,
But Melanippus pierced heroic son
Of Hicetaon, coming forth to fight,                    700
Full in the bosom, and with dreadful sound
Of all his batter'd armour down he fell.
Swift flew Antilochus as flies the hound
Some fawn to seize, which issuing from her lair
The hunter with his lance hath stricken dead,         705
So thee, O Melanippus! to despoil
Of thy bright arms valiant Antilochus
Sprang forth, but not unnoticed by the eye
Of noble Hector, who through all the war
Ran to encounter him; his dread approach              710
Antilochus, although expert in arms,
Stood not, but as some prowler of the wilds,
Conscious of injury that he hath done,
Slaying the watchful herdsman or his dog,
Escapes, ere yet the peasantry arise,                 715
So fled the son of Nestor, after whom
The Trojans clamouring and Hector pour'd
Darts numberless; but at the front arrived
Of his own phalanx, there he turn'd and stood.
Then, eager as voracious lions, rush'd                720
The Trojans on the fleet of Greece, the mind
Of Jove accomplishing who them impell'd
Continual, calling all their courage forth,
While, every Grecian heart he tamed, and took
Their glory from them, strengthening Ilium's host.    725
For Jove's unalter'd purpose was to give
Success to Priameian Hector's arms,
That he might cast into the fleet of Greece
Devouring flames, and that no part might fail
Of Thetis' ruthless prayer; that sight alone          730
He watch'd to see, one galley in a blaze,
Ordaining foul repulse, thenceforth, and flight
To Ilium's host, but glory to the Greeks.
Such was the cause for which, at first, he moved
To that assault Hector, himself prepared              735
And ardent for the task; nor less he raged
Than Mars while fighting, or than flames that seize
Some forest on the mountain-tops; the foam

Hung at his lips, beneath his awful front
His keen eyes glisten'd, and his helmet mark'd          740
The agitation wild with which he fought.
For Jove omnipotent, himself, from heaven
Assisted Hector, and, although alone
With multitudes he strove, gave him to reach
The heights of glory, for that now his life          745
Waned fast, and, urged by Pallas on, his hour
To die by Peleus' mighty son approach'd.
He then, wherever richest arms he saw
And thickest throng, the warrior-ranks essay'd
To break, but broke them not, though fierce resolved,          750
In even square compact so firm they stood.
As some vast rock beside the hoary Deep
The stress endures of many a hollow wind,
And the huge billows tumbling at his base,
So stood the Danaï, nor fled nor fear'd.          755
But He, all-fiery bright in arms, the host
Assail'd on every side, and on the van
Fell, as a wave by wintry blasts upheaved
Falls ponderous on the ship ; white clings the foam
Around her, in her sail shrill howls the storm,          760
And every seaman trembles at the view
Of thousand deaths from which he scarce escapes,
Such anguish rent the bosom of the Greeks.
⁸But He, as leaps a famish'd lion fell
On beeves that graze some marshy meadow's breadth          765
A countless herd, tended by one unskill'd
To cope with savage beasts in their defence,
Beside the foremost kine or with the last
He paces heedless, but the lion, borne
Impetuous on the midmost, one devours          770
And scatters all the rest, ⁸so fled the Greeks,
Terrified from above, before the arm
Of Hector, and before the frown of Jove.
All fled, but of them all alone he slew
The Mycenæan Periphetes, son          775
Of Copreus custom'd messenger of King

⁸ This termination of the period, so little consonant to the beginning
of it, follows the original, where it is esteemed by commentators a great
beauty.

Eurystheus to the might of Hercules.
From such a sire inglorious had arisen
A son far worthier, with all virtue graced,
Swift-footed, valiant, and by none excell'd          780
In wisdom of the Mycenæan name ;
Yet all but served to ennoble Hector more.
For Periphetes, with a backward step
Retiring, on his buckler's border trod,
Which swept his heels ; so check'd, he fell supine,          785
And dreadful rang the helmet on his brows.
Him Hector quick noticing, to his side
Hasted, and, planting in his breast a spear,
Slew him before the phalanx of his friends.
But they, although their fellow-warrior's fate          790
They mourn'd, no succour interposed, or could,
Themselves by noble Hector sore appall'd.
And now behind the ships (all that updrawn
Above the shore, stood foremost of the fleet)
The Greeks retired ; in rush'd a flood of foes ;          795
Then, through necessity, the ships in front
Abandoning, amid the tents they stood
Compact, not disarray'd, for shame and fear
Fast held them, and vociferating each
Aloud, call'd ceaseless on the rest to stand.          800
But earnest more than all, guardian of all,
Gerenian Nestor in their parents' name
Implored them, falling at the knees of each.
    Oh friends ! be men.   Now dearly prize your place
Each in the estimation of the rest.          805
Now call to memory your children, wives,
Possessions, parents ; ye whose parents live,
And ye whose parents are not, all alike !
By them as if here present, I entreat
That ye stand fast,—Oh be not turn'd to flight !          810
    So saying he roused the courage of the Greeks ;
Then, Pallas chased the cloud fall'n from above
On every eye ; great light the plain illumed
On all sides, both toward the fleet, and where
The undiscriminating battle raged.          815
Then might be seen Hector and Hector's host
Distinct, as well the rearmost who the fight

Shared not, as those who waged it at the ships.
To stand aloof where other Grecians stood
No longer now would satisfy the mind     820
Of Ajax, but from deck to deck with strides
Enormous marching, to and fro he swung
With iron studs emboss'd a battle-pole
Unwieldy, twenty and two cubits long.
As one, expert to spring from horse to horse,     825
From many steeds selecting four, toward
Some noble city drives them from the plain
Along the populous road; him many a youth
And many a maiden eyes, while still secure
From steed to steed he vaults; they rapid fly;     830
So Ajax o'er the decks of numerous ships
Stalk'd striding large, and sent his voice to heaven.
Thus, ever clamouring, he bade the Greeks
Stand both for camp and fleet.   Nor could himself
Hector, contented, now, the battle wage     835
Lost in the multitude of Trojans more,
But as the tawny eagle on full wing
Assails the feather'd nations, geese or cranes
Or swans lithe-neck'd grazing the river's verge,
So Hector at a galley sable-prow'd     840
Darted; for, from behind, Jove urged him on
With mighty hand, and his host after him.
And now again the battle at the ships
Grew furious; thou hadst deem'd them of a kind
By toil untameable, so fierce they strove,     845
And, striving, thus they thought. The Grecians judged
Hope vain, and the whole host's destruction sure;
But nought expected every Trojan less
Than to consume the fleet with fire, and leave
Achaia's heroes lifeless on the field.     850
With such persuasion occupied, they fought.
    Then Hector seized the stern of a brave bark
Well-built, sharp-keel'd, and of the swiftest sail,
Which had to Troy Protesiläus brought,
But bore him never thence. For that same ship     855
Contending, Greeks and Trojans hand to hand
Dealt slaughter mutual. Javelins now no more

Might serve them, or the arrow-starting bow,
But close conflicting and of one mind all
With bill and battle-axe, with ponderous swords          860
And with long lances double-edged they fought.
Many a black-hilted faulchion huge of haft
Fell to the ground, some from the grasp, and some
From shoulders of embattled warriors hewn,
And pools of blood soak'd all the sable glebe.          865
Hector that ship once grappled by the stern
Left not, but griping fast her upper edge
With both hands, to his Trojans call'd aloud.
    Fire! Bring me fire! Stand fast and shout to heaven!
Jove gives us now a day worth all the past;          870
The ships are ours which, in the Gods' despite
Steer'd hither, such calamities to us
Have caused, for which our Seniors most I blame
Who me withheld from battle at the fleet
And check'd the people; but if then the hand          875
Of Thunderer Jove our better judgment marr'd,
Himself now urges and commands us—On.
    He ceased; they still more violent assail'd
The Grecians.    Even Ajax could endure,
Whelm'd under weapons numberless, that storm          880
No longer, but expecting death retired
Down from the decks to an inferior stand,
Where still he watch'd, and if a Trojan bore
Fire thither, he repulsed him with his spear,
Roaring continual to the host of Greece.          885
    Friends! Grecian heroes! ministers of Mars!
Be men, my friends! now summon all your might!
Think we that we have thousands at our backs
To succour us, or yet some stronger wall
To guard our warriors from the battle's force?          890
Not so.   No tower'd city is at hand,
None that presents us with a safe retreat
While others occupy our station here,
But from the shores of Argos far remote
Our camp is, where the Trojans arm'd complete          895
Swarm on the plain, and Ocean shuts us in.
Our hands must therefore save us, not our heels.

He said, and furious with his spear again
Press'd them, and whatsoever Trojan came,
Obsequious to the will of Hector, arm'd                    900
With fire to burn the fleet, on his spear's point
Ajax receiving pierced him, till at length
Twelve in close fight fell by his single arm.

# BOOK XVI.

## ARGUMENT.

Achilles, at the suit of Patroclus, grants him his own armour, and permission to lead the Myrmidons to battle. They, sallying, repulse the Trojans. Patroclus slays Sarpedon, and Hector, when Apollo had first stripped off his armour and Euphorbus wounded him, slays Patroclus.

Such contest for that gallant bark they waged.
Meantime Patroclus, standing at the side
Of the illustrious Chief Achilles, wept
Fast as a crystal fountain from the height
Of some rude rock pours down its rapid[1] stream.      5
Divine Achilles with compassion moved
Mark'd him, and in wing'd accents thus began.
    Why weeps Patroclus like an infant girl
Who, running at her mother's side, entreats
To be uplifted in her arms?  She grasps      10
Her mantle, checks her haste, and looking up
With tearful eyes, pleads earnest to be borne ;
So fall, Patroclus ! thy unceasing tears.
Bring'st thou to me or to my people aught
Afflictive?  Hast thou mournful tidings learn'd      15
From Phthia, trusted to thine ear alone ?
Menœtius, son of Actor, as they say,
Still lives ; still lives his Myrmidons among
Peleus Æacides ; whom, were they dead,
With cause sufficient we should both deplore.      20
Or weep'st thou the Achaians at the ships
Perishing, for their outrage done to me ?
Speak.  Name thy trouble.  I would learn the cause.
    To whom, deep-sorrowing, thou didst reply,

---

[1] This translation of δνοφερον is warranted by the Scholiast, who paraphrases it thus :—

      μετα δονησεως φερομενον.      *Iliad per Vill.*

Patroclus! Oh Achilles, Peleus' son!       25
Noblest of all our host! bear with my grief,
Since such distress hath on the Grecians fallen.
The bravest of their ships disabled lie;
Some wounded from afar, some hand to hand.
Diomede, warlike son of Tydeus, bleeds,       30
Gall'd by a shaft; Ulysses, glorious Chief,
And Agamemnon suffer by the spear,
And brave Eurypylus an arrow-point
Bears in his thigh.    These all, are now the care
Of healing hands.    Oh thou art pity-proof,       35
Achilles! be my bosom ever free
From anger such as harbour finds in thine,
Scorning all limits! whom, of men unborn,
Hereafter wilt thou save, from whom avert
Disgrace, if not from the Achaians now?       40
Ah ruthless! neither Peleus thee begat,
Nor Thetis bore, but rugged rocks sublime,
And roaring billows blue gave birth to thee,
Who bear'st a mind that knows not to relent.
But, if some prophecy alarm thy fears,       45
If from thy Goddess-mother thou have aught
Received, and with authority of Jove,
Me send at least, me quickly, and with me
The Myrmidons.    A dawn of cheerful hope
Shall thence, it may be, on the Greeks arise.       50
Grant me thine armour also, that the foe
Thyself supposing present, may abstain
From battle, and the weary Greeks enjoy
Short respite; it is all that war allows.
We, fresh and vigorous, by our shouts alone       55
May easily repulse an army spent
With labour from the camp, and from the fleet.
   Such suit he made, alas! all unforewarn'd
That his own death should be the bitter fruit,
And thus Achilles, sorrowful, replied.       60
   Patroclus, noble friend! what hast thou spoken?
Me neither prophecy that I have heard
Holds in suspense, nor aught that I have learn'd
From Thetis with authority of Jove!
Hence springs, and hence alone, my grief of heart;       65

If one, in nought superior to myself
Save in his office only, should by force
Amerce me of my well-earn'd recompense—
How then ?  There lies the grief that stings my soul.
The virgin chosen for me by the sons                70
Of Greece, my just reward, by my own spear
Obtain'd when I Eëtion's city took,
Her, Agamemnon, leader of the host
From my possession wrung, as I had been
Some alien wretch, unhonour'd and unknown.          75
But let it pass ; anger is not a flame
To feed for ever ; I affirm'd, indeed,
Mine inextinguishable till the shout
Of battle should invade my proper barks ;
But thou put on my glorious arms, lead forth         80
My valiant Myrmidons, since such a cloud,
So dark, of dire hostility surrounds
The fleet, and the Achaians, by the waves
Hemm'd in, are prison'd now in narrow space.
Because the Trojans meet not in the field            85
My dazzling helmet, therefore bolder grown
All Ilium comes abroad ; but had I found
Kindness at royal Agamemnon's hands,
Soon had they fled, and with their bodies chok'd
The streams, from whom ourselves now suffer siege.   90
For in the hands of Diomede his spear
No longer rages rescuing from death
The afflicted Danaï, nor hear I more
The voice of Agamemnon issuing harsh
From his detested throat, but all around              95
The burst[2] of homicidal Hector's cries,
Calling his Trojans on ; they loud insult
The vanquish'd Greeks, and claim the field their own.
Go therefore, my Patroclus ; furious fall
On these assailants, even now preserve               100
From fire the only hope of our return.
But hear the sum of all ; mark well my word ;
So shalt thou glorify me in the eyes
Of all the Danaï, and they shall yield
Briseïs mine, with many a gift beside.               105

[2] περιάγνυται. A word of incomparable force, and that defies translation

The Trojans from the fleet expell'd, return.
Should Juno's awful spouse give thee to win
Victory, be content; seek not to press
The Trojans without me, for thou shalt add
Still more to the disgrace already mine.                    110
Much less, by martial ardour urged, conduct
Thy slaughtering legions to the walls of Troy,
Lest some immortal power on her behalf
Descend, for much the Archer of the skies
Loves Ilium.  No—the fleet once saved, lead back    115
Thy band, and leave the battle to themselves.
For oh, by all the powers of heaven I would
That not one Trojan might escape of all,
Nor yet a Grecian, but that we, from death
Ourselves escaping, might survive to spread           120
Troy's sacred bulwarks on the ground alone.
      Thus they conferr'd.   But Ajax overwhelm'd
Meantime with darts no longer could endure,
Quell'd both by Jupiter and by the spears
Of many a noble Trojan; hideous rang                    125
His batter'd helmet bright, stroke after stroke
Sustaining on all sides, and his left arm
That had so long shifted from side to side
His restless shield, now fail'd; yet could not all
Displace him with united force, or move.               130
Quick pantings heaved his chest, copious the sweat
Trickled from all his limbs, nor found he time,
However short, to breathe again, so close
Evil on evil heap'd hemm'd him around.
      Olympian Muses! now declare, how first        135
The fire was kindled in Achaia's fleet?
      Hector the ashen lance of Ajax smote
With his broad faulchion, at the nether end,
And lopp'd it sheer.   The Telamonian Chief
His mutilated beam brandish'd in vain,                   140
And the bright point shrill-sounding fell remote.
Then Ajax in his noble mind perceived,
Shuddering with awe, the interposing power
Of heaven, and that, propitious to the arms
Of Troy, the Thunderer had ordain'd to mar         145
And frustrate all the counsels of the Greeks.

He left his stand ; they fired the gallant bark ;
Through all her length the conflagration ran
Incontinent, and wrapp'd her stern in flames.
Achilles saw them, smote his thighs, and said,　　　150
　　Patroclus, noble charioteer, arise !
I see the rapid run of hostile fires
Already in the fleet—lest all be lost,
And our return impossible, arm, arm
This moment ; I will call, myself, the band.　　　155
　　Then put Patroclus on his radiant arms.
Around his legs his polish'd greaves he clasp'd,
With argent studs secured ; the hauberk rich
Star-spangled to his breast he bound of swift
Æacides : he slung his brazen sword　　　160
With silver bright emboss'd, and his broad shield
Ponderous ; on his noble head his casque
He settled elegant, whose lofty crest
Waved dreadful o'er his brows, and last he seized
Well fitted to his gripe two sturdy spears.　　　165
Of all Achilles' arms his spear alone
He took not ; that huge beam, of bulk and length
Enormous, none, Æacides except,
In all Achaia's host had power to wield.
It was that Pelian ash which from the top　　　170
Of Pelion hewn that it might prove the death
Of heroes, Chiron had to Peleus given.
He bade Automedon his coursers bind
Speedily to the yoke, for him he loved
Next to Achillès most, as worthiest found　　　175
Of trust, what time the battle loudest roar'd.
Then led Automedon the fiery steeds
Swift as wing'd tempests to the chariot-yoke,
Xanthus and Balius.　Then the harpy bore
Podarge, while in meadows green she fed　　　180
On Ocean's side, to Zephyrus the wind.
To these he added, at their side, a third
The noble Pedasus ; him Peleus' son,
Eëtion's city taken, thence had brought,
Though mortal, yet a match for steeds divine.　　　185
Meantime from every tent Achilles call'd
And arm'd his Myrmidons.　As wolves that gorge

The prey yet panting, terrible in force,
When on the mountains wild they have devour'd
An antler'd stag new-slain, with bloody jaws                190
Troop all at once to some clear fountain, there
To lap with slender tongues the brimming wave ;
No fears have they, but at their ease eject
From full maws flatulent the clotted gore ;
Such seem'd the Myrmidon heroic Chiefs                     195
Assembling fast around the valiant friend
Of swift Æacides.   Amid them stood
Warlike Achilles, the well-shielded ranks
Exhorting, and the steeds, to glorious war.
    The galleys by Achilles dear to Jove                   200
Commanded, when to Ilium's coast he steer'd,
Were fifty ; fifty rowers sat in each,
And five, in whom he trusted, o'er the rest
He captains named, but ruled, himself, supreme.
One band Menestheus swift in battle led,                   205
Offspring of Sperchius heaven-descended stream.
Him Polydora, Peleus' daughter, bore
To ever-flowing Sperchius, compress'd,
Although a mortal woman, by a God.
But his reputed father was the son                         210
Of Perieres, Borus, who with dower
Enrich'd, and made her openly his bride.
Warlike Eudorus led the second band.
Him Polymela, graceful in the dance,
And daughter beautiful of Phylas, bore,                    215
A mother unsuspected of a child.
Her worshipping the golden-shafted Queen
Diana, in full choir, with song and dance,
The valiant Argicide beheld and loved.
Ascending with her to an upper room,                       220
All-bounteous Mercury clandestine there
Embraced her, who a noble son produced
Eudorus, swift to run, and bold in fight.
No sooner Ilithya, arbitress
Of pangs puerperal, had given him birth,                   225
And he beheld the beaming sun, than her
Echechleus, Actor's mighty son, enrich'd
With countless dower, and led her to his home ;

While ancient Phylas, cherishing her boy  
With fond affection, reared him as his own.　230  
The third brave troop warlike Pisander led,  
Offspring of Maimalus; he far excell'd  
In spear-fight every Myrmidon, the friend  
Of Peleus' dauntless son alone except.  
The hoary Phœnix of equestrian fame　235  
The fourth band led to battle, and the fifth  
Laërceus' offspring, bold Alcimedon.  
Thus, all his bands beneath their proper Chiefs  
Marshall'd, Achilles gave them strict command—  
　Myrmidons! all that vengeance now inflict,　240  
Which in this fleet ye ceased not to denounce  
Against the Trojans while my wrath endured.  
Me censuring, ye have proclaim'd me oft  
Obdurate.　Oh Achilles! ye have said,  
Thee not with milk thy mother but with bile　245  
Suckled, who hold'st thy people here in camp  
Thus long imprison'd.　Unrelenting Chief!  
Even let us hence in our sea-skimming barks  
To Phthia, since thou can'st not be appeased—  
Thus in full council have ye spoken oft.　250  
Now, therefore, since a day of glorious toil  
At last appears, such as ye have desired,  
There lies the field—go—give your courage proof.  
　So them he roused, and they, their leader's voice  
Hearing elate, to closest order drew.　255  
As when an architect some palace wall  
With shapely stones upbuilds, cementing close  
A barrier against all the winds of heaven,  
So wedged, the helmets and boss'd bucklers stood;  
Shield, helmet, man, press'd helmet, man, and shield,　260  
And every bright-arm'd warrior's bushy crest  
Its fellow swept, so dense was their array.  
In front of all, two Chiefs their station took,  
Patroclus and Automedon; one mind  
In both prevail'd, to combat in the van　265  
Of all the Myrmidons.　Achilles, then,  
Retiring to his tent, displaced the lid  
Of a capacious chest magnificent  
By silver-footed Thetis stow'd on board

His bark, and fill'd with tunics, mantles warm,  270
And gorgeous arras ; there he also kept
Secure a goblet exquisitely wrought,
Which never lip touch'd save his own, and whence
He offer'd only to the Sire of all.
That cup producing from the chest, he first  275
With sulphur fumed it, then with water rinsed
Pellucid of the running stream, and. last
(His hands clean laved) he charged it high with wine.
And now, advancing to his middle court,
He pour'd libation, and with eyes to heaven  280
Uplifted pray'd, of Jove not unobserved.
 Pelasgian, Dodonæan Jove supreme,
Dwelling remote, who on Dodona's heights
Snow-clad reign'st Sovereign, by thy seers around
Compass'd the Selli, prophets vow-constrain'd  285
To unwash'd feet and slumbers on the ground !
Plain I behold my former prayer perform'd,
Myself exalted, and the Greeks abased.
Now also grant me, Jove, this my desire !
Here, in my fleet, I shall myself abide,  290
But lo ! with all these Myrmidons I send
My friend to battle. Thunder-rolling Jove,
Send glory with him, make his courage firm !
That even Hector may himself be taught,
If my companion have a valiant heart  295
When he goes forth alone, or only then
The noble frenzy feels that Mars inspires
When I rush also to the glorious field.
But when he shall have driven the battle-shout
Once from the fleet, grant him with all his arms,  300
None lost, himself unhurt, and my whole band
Of dauntless warriors with him, safe return !
 Such prayer Achilles offer'd, and his suit
Jove hearing, part confirm'd, and part refused ;
To chase the dreadful battle from the fleet  305
He gave him, but vouchsafed him no return.
Prayer and libation thus perform'd to Jove
The Sire of all, Achilles to his tent
Return'd, replaced the goblet in his chest,
And anxious still that conflict to behold  310

Between the hosts, stood forth before his tent.
 Then rush'd the bands by brave Patroclus led,
Full on the Trojan host.   As wasps forsake
Their home by the way-side, provoked by boys
Disturbing inconsiderate their abode,                               315
Not without nuisance sore to all who pass,
For if, thenceforth, some traveller unaware
Annoy them, issuing one and all they swarm
Around him, fearless in their broods' defence,
So issued from their feet the Myrmidons                             320
Undaunted; clamour infinite arose,
And thus Patroclus loud his host address'd.
 Oh Myrmidons, attendants in the field
On Peleus' son, now be ye men, my friends!
Call now to mind the fury of your might;                            325
That we, close-fighting servants of the Chief
Most excellent in all the camp of Greece,
May glory gain for Him, and that the wide-
Commanding Agamemnon, Atreus' son,
May learn his fault, that he dishonour'd foul                       330
The prince in whom Achaia glories most.
 So saying he fired their hearts, and on the van
Of Troy at once they fell; loud shouted all
The joyful Grecians, and the navy rang.
Then, soon as Ilium's host the valiant son                          335
Saw of Menœtius and his charioteer
In dazzling armour clad, all courage lost,
Their closest ranks gave way, believing sure
That, wrath renounced, and terms of friendship chosen,
Achilles' self was there; thus thinking, each                       340
Look'd every way for refuge from his fate.
 Patroclus first, where thickest throng he saw
Gather'd tumultuous around the bark
Of brave Protesilaüs, hurl'd direct
At the whole multitude his glittering spear.                        345
He smote Pyræchmes; he his horseman band
Pœonian led from Amydon, and from
Broad-flowing Axius.   In his shoulder stood
The spear, and with loud groans supine he fell.
At once fled all his followers, on all sides                        350
With consternation fill'd, seeing their Chief

And their best warrior, by Patroclus slain.
Forth from the fleet he drove them, quench'd the flames,
And rescued half the ship.    Then scatter'd fled
With infinite uproar the host of Troy,                           355
While from between their ships the Danaï
Pour'd after them, and hideous rout ensued.
As when the king of lightnings, Jove, dispels
From some huge eminence a gloomy cloud,
The groves, the mountain-tops, the headland heights           360
Shine all, illumined from the boundless heaven,
So when the Danaï those hostile fires
Had from their fleet expell'd, awhile they breathed,
Yet found short respite, for the battle yet
Ceased not, nor fled the Trojans in all parts                 365
Alike, but still resisted, from the ships
Retiring through necessity alone.
Then, in that scatter'd warfare, every Chief
Slew one.    While Areïlochus his back
Turn'd on Patroclus, sudden with a lance                      370
His thigh he pierced, and urged the weapon through
Shivering the bone ; he headlong smote the ground.
The Hero Menelaus, where he saw
The breast of Thoas by his slanting shield
Unguarded, struck and stretch'd him at his feet.             375
Phylides³, meeting with preventive spear
The furious onset of Amphiclus, gash'd
His leg below the knee, where brawny most
The muscles swell in man ; disparted wide
The tendons shrank, and darkness veil'd his eyes.            380
The two Nestoridæ slew each a Chief.
Of these, Antilochus Atymnius pierced
Right through his flank, and at his feet he fell.
With fierce resentment fired Maris beheld
His brother's fall, and guarding, spear in hand,            385
The slain, impetuous on the conqueror flew ;
But Godlike Thrasymedes⁴ wounded first
Maris, ere he Antilochus ; he pierced
His upper arm, and with the lance's point
Rent off and stript the muscles to the bone.                390

³ Meges.                    ⁴ Brother of Antilochus.

Sounding he fell, and darkness veil'd his eyes.
They thus, two brothers by two brothers slain,
Went down to Erebus, associates both
Of brave Sarpedon, and spear-practised sons
Of Amisodarus ; of him who fed       395
Chimæra[5], monster, by whom many died.
Ajax the swift on Cleobulus sprang,
Whom while he toil'd entangled in the crowd,
He seized alive, but smote him where he stood
With his huge-hafted sword full on the neck ;      400
The blood warm'd all his blade, and ruthless fate
Benighted dark the dying warrior's eyes.
Peneleus into close contention rush'd
And Lycon.  Each had hurl'd his glittering spear,
But each in vain, and now with swords they met.   405
He smote Peneleus on the crested casque,
But snapp'd his faulchion ; him Peneleus smote
Beneath his ear ; the whole blade entering sank
Into his neck, and Lycon with his head
Depending by the skin alone, expired.      410
Meriones o'ertaking Acamas
Ere yet he could ascend his chariot, thrust
A lance into his shoulder ; down he fell
In dreary death's eternal darkness whelm'd.
Idomeneus his ruthless spear enforced     415
Into the mouth of Erymas.  The point
Stay'd not, but gliding close beneath the brain,
Transpierced his spine[6], and started forth beyond.
It wrench'd his teeth, and fill'd his eyes with blood ;
Blood also blowing through his open mouth    420
And nostrils, to the realms of death he passed.
Thus slew these Grecian leaders, each, a foe.
  Sudden as hungry wolves the kids purloin

---

[5] *ἀμαιμακέτην*—is a word which I can find nowhere satisfactorily derived. Perhaps it is expressive of great length, and I am the more inclined to that sense of it, because it is the epithet given to the mast on which Ulysses floated to Charybdis. We must in that case derive it from *ἅμα* and *μῆκος* Doricé, *μᾶκος*—longitudo. In this uncertainty I thought myself free to translate it as I have, by the word—monster.

[6] Apollonius says that the *ὀϛεα λευκα* here mean the *σπονδυλους*, or vertebræ of the neck.—See Villoisson.

Or lambs, which haply some unheeding swain
Hath left to roam at large the mountains wild ;     425
They, seeing, snatch'd them from beside the dams,
And rend incontinent the feeble prey,
So swift the Danaï the host assail'd
Of Ilium ; they, into tumultuous flight
Together driven, all hope, all courage lost.     430
    Huge Ajax ceaseless sought his spear to cast
At Hector brazen-mail'd, who, not untaught
The warrior's art, with bull-hide buckler stood
Sheltering his ample shoulders, while he mark'd
The hiss of flying shafts and crash of spears.     435
Full sure he saw the shifting course of war
Now turn'd, but scorning flight, bent all his thoughts
To rescue yet the remnant of his friends.
    As when the Thunderer spreads a sable storm
O'er ether, late serene, the cloud that wrapp'd     440
Olympus' head escapes into the skies,
So fled the Trojans from the fleet of Greece
Clamouring in their flight, nor pass'd the trench
In fair array ; the coursers fleet indeed
Of Hector, Him bore safe with all his arms     445
Right through, but in the foss entangled foul
He left his host, and struggling to escape.
Then many a chariot-whirling steed, the pole
Broken at its extremity, forsook
His driver, while Patroclus with the shout     450
Of battle calling his Achaians on,
Destruction purposed to the powers of Troy.
They, once dispersed, with clamour and with flight
Fill'd all the ways, the dust beneath the clouds
Hung like a tempest, and the steeds firm-hoof'd     455
Whirl'd off at stretch the chariots to the town.
He, wheresoe'er most troubled he perceived
The routed host, loud-threatening thither drove,
While under his own axle many a Chief
Fell prone, and the o'ertumbled chariots rang.     460
Right o'er the hollow foss the coursers leap'd
Immortal, by the Gods to Peleus given,
Impatient for the plain, nor less desire
Felt he who drove to smite the Trojan Chief,

But him his fiery steeds caught swift away.                      465
  . As when a tempest from autumnal skies
Floats all the fields, what time Jove heaviest pours
Impetuous rain, token of wrath divine
Against perverters of the laws by force,
Who drive forth justice, reckless of the Gods ;                 470
The rivers and the torrents, where they dwell,
Sweep many a green declivity away,
And plunge at length, groaning, into the Deep
From the hills headlong, leaving where they pass'd
No traces of the pleasant works of man,                         475
So, in their flight, loud groan'd the steeds of Troy.
And now, their foremost intercepted all,
Patroclus back again toward the fleet
Drove them precipitate, nor the ascent
Permitted them to Troy for which they strove,                   480
But in the midway space between the ships
The river and the lofty Trojan wall
Pursued them ardent, slaughtering whom he reach'd,
And vengeance took for many a Grecian slain.
First then, with glittering spear the breast he pierced         485
Of Pronöus, undefended by his shield,
And stretch'd him dead ; loud rang his batter'd arms.
The son of Enops, Thestor next he smote.
He on his chariot-seat magnificent
Low-cowering sat, a fear-distracted form,                        490
And from his palsied grasp the reins had fallen.
Then came Patroclus nigh, and through his cheek
His teeth transpiercing, drew him by his lance
Sheer o'er the chariot front.   As when a man
On some projecting rock seated, with line                       495
And splendid hook draws forth a sea-fish huge,
So him wide-gaping from his seat he drew
At his spear-point, then shook him to the ground
Prone on his face, where gasping he expired.
At Eryalus, next, advancing swift                               500
He hurl'd a rock ; full on the middle front
He smote him, and within the ponderous casque
His whole head open'd into equal halves.
With deadliest night surrounded, prone he fell.
Epaltes, Erymas, Amphoterus,                                    505

Echius, Tlepolemus Damastor's son,
Evippus, Ipheus, Pyres, Polymelus,
All these he on the champion, corse on corse
Promiscuous flung. Sarpedon, when he saw
Such havoc made of his uncinctured[7] friends  510
By Menœtiades, with sharp rebuke
His band of godlike Lycians loud address'd.
 Shame on you, Lycians! whither would ye fly?
Now are ye swift indeed! I will oppose
Myself this conqueror, that I may learn  515
Who thus afflicts the Trojan host, of life
Bereaving numerous of their warriors bold.
 He said, and with his arms leap'd to the ground.
On the other side, Patroclus at that sight
Sprang from his chariot. As two vultures clash  520
Bow-beak'd, crook-talon'd, on some lofty rock
Clamouring both, so they together rush'd
With clamours loud; whom when the son observed
Of wily Saturn, with compassion moved
His sister and his spouse he thus bespake.  525
 Alas he falls! my most beloved of men
Sarpedon, vanquish'd by Patroclus falls!
So will the Fates. Yet, doubtful, much I muse
Whether to place him, snatch'd from furious fight,
In Lycia's wealthy realm, or to permit  530
His death by valiant Menœtiades.
 To whom his awful spouse, displeased, replied.
How speaks the terrible Saturnian Jove?
Wouldst thou again from pangs of death exempt
A mortal man, destined long since to die?  535
Do it. But small thy praise shall be in heaven.
Mark thou my words, and in thy inmost breast
Treasure them. If thou send Sarpedon safe
To his own home, how many Gods *their* sons
May also send from battle? Weigh it well.  540
For under yon great city fight no few
Sprung from Immortals whom thou shalt provoke.

---

[7] 'Αμιτροχίτωνας is a word, according to Clarke, descriptive of their peculiar habit. Their corslet, and the mail worn under it, were of a piece, and put on together. To them therefore the cincture or belt of the Greeks was unnecessary.

But if thou love him, and thine heart his lot
Commiserate, leave him by the hands to fall
Of Menœtiades in conflict dire;                                   545
But give command to Death and gentle Sleep
That him of life bereft at once they bear
To Lycia's ample realm, where, with due rites
Funereal, his next kindred and his friends
Shall honour him, a pillar and a tomb                             550
(The dead man's portion) rearing to his name.
    She said, from whom the Sire of Gods and men
Dissented not, but on the earth distill'd
A sanguine shower in honour of a son
Dear to him, whom Patroclus on the field                          555
Of fruitful Troy should slay, far from his home.
    Opposite now, small interval between,
Those heroes stood.   Patroclus at his waist
Pierced Thrasymelus the illustrious friend
Of King Sarpedon, and his charioteer.                             560
Spear'd through the lower bowels, dead he fell.
Then hurl'd Sarpedon in his turn a lance,
But miss'd Patroclus and the shoulder pierced
Of Pedasus the horse; he groaning heaved
His spirit forth, and fallen on the field                         565
In long loud moanings sorrowful expired.
Wide started the immortal pair; the yoke
Creak'd, and entanglement of reins ensued
To both, their fellow slaughtered at their side.
That mischief soon Automedon redress'd.                           570
He rose, and from beside his sturdy thigh
Drawing his faulchion, with effectual stroke
Cut loose the side-horse; then the pair reduced
To order, in their traces stood composed,
And the two heroes fierce engaged again.                          575
    Again his radiant spear Sarpedon hurl'd,
But miss'd Patroclus; the innocuous point,
O'erflying his left shoulder, pass'd beyond.
Then with bright lance Patroclus in his turn
Assail'd Sarpedon, nor with erring course                         580
The weapon sped or vain, but pierced profound
His chest, enclosure of the guarded heart.
As falls an oak, poplar, or lofty pine

With new edged axes on the mountains hewn
Right through, for structure of some gallant bark,　　585
So fell Sarpedon stretch'd his steeds before
And gnash'd his teeth and clutch'd the bloody dust.
And as a lion slays a tawny bull
Leader magnanimous of all the herd ;
Beneath the lion's jaws groaning he dies ;　　590
So, leader of the shielded Lycians groan'd
Indignant, by Patroclus slain, the bold
Sarpedon, and his friend thus, sad, bespake.
　　Glaucus, my friend, among these warring Chiefs
Thyself a Chief illustrious ! thou hast need　　595
Of all thy valour now ; now strenuous fight,
And, if thou bear within thee a brave mind,
Now make the war's calamities thy joy.
First, marching through the host of Lycia, rouse
Our Chiefs to combat for Sarpedon slain,　　600
Then haste, thyself, to battle for thy friend.
For shame and foul dishonour which no time
Shall e'er obliterate, I must prove to thee,
Should the Achaians of my glorious arms
Despoil me in full prospect[8] of the fleet.　　605
Fight, therefore, thou, and others urge to fight.
　　He said, and cover'd by the night of death,
Nor look'd nor breathed again ; for on his chest
Implanting firm his heel, Patroclus drew

[8] Sarpedon certainly was not slain *in the fleet*, neither can the Greek expression νεῶν ἐν ἀγῶνι be with property interpreted—*in certamine de navibus*—as Clarke and M$^{me}$ Dacier are inclined to render it. *Juvenum in certamine*, seems equally an improbable sense of it. Eustathius, indeed, and Terrasson, supposing Sarpedon to assert that he dies in the middle of the fleet, (which was false in fact,) are kind enough to vindicate Homer by pleading in his favour, that Sarpedon, being in the article of death, was delirious, and knew not, in reality, where he died. But Homer, however he may have been charged with now and then a nap, (a crime of which I am persuaded he is never guilty,) certainly does not slumber here, nor needs to be so defended. 'Αγῶν, in the 23d Iliad, means the *whole extensive area* in which the games were exhibited, and may therefore here, without any strain of the expression, be understood to signify the *whole range of shore* on which the ships were stationed. In which case Sarpedon represents the matter as it was, saying that he dies—νεῶν ἐν ἀγῶνι,—that is, in the neighbourhood of the ships, and in full prospect of them.
　　The Translator assumes not to himself the honour of this judicious remark. It belongs to Mr. Fuseli.

The spear enfolded with his vitals forth,        610
Weapon and life at once.   Meantime his steeds
Snorted by Myrmidons detain'd, and, loosed
From their own master's chariot, foam'd to fly.
Terrible was the grief by Glaucus felt
Hearing that charge, and troubled was his heart     615
That all power fail'd him to protect the dead.
Compressing his own arm he stood, with pain
Extreme tormented which the shaft had caused
Of Teucer, who while Glaucus climb'd the wall,
Had pierced him from it in the fleet's defence.     620
Then, thus, to Phœbus, King shaft-arm'd, he pray'd.
    Hear now, O King! For whether in the land
Of wealthy Lycia dwelling, or in Troy,
Thou hear'st in every place alike the prayer
Of the afflicted heart, and such is mine;     625
Behold my wound; it fills my useless hand
With anguish, neither can my blood be stay'd,
And all my shoulder suffers.   I can grasp
A spear, or rush to conflict with the Greeks
No longer now; and we have also lost     630
Our noblest Chief, Sarpedon, son of Jove,
Who guards not his own son.   But thou, O King!
Heal me, assuage my anguish, give me strength,
That I may animate the Lycian host
To fight, and may, myself, defend the dead!     635
    Such prayer he offer'd, whom Apollo heard;
He eased at once his pain, his sable blood
Staunch'd, and his soul with vigour new inspired.
Then Glaucus in his heart that prayer perceived
Granted, and joyful for the sudden aid     640
Vouchsafed to him by Phœbus, first the lines
Of Lycia ranged, summoning every Chief
To fight for slain Sarpedon; striding next
With eager haste into the ranks of Troy,
Renown'd Agenor and the son he call'd     645
Of Panthus, brave Polydamas, with whom
Æneas also, and approaching last
To Hector brazen-mail'd him thus bespake.
    Now, Hector! now, thou hast indeed resign'd
All care of thy allies, who, for thy sake,     650

Lost both to friends and country, on these plains
Perish, unaided and unmiss'd by thee.
Sarpedon breathless lies, who led to fight
Our shielded bands, and from whose just control .
And courage Lycia drew her chief defence.          655
Him brazen Mars hath by the spear subdued
Of Menœtiades.   But stand ye firm !
Let indignation fire you, O my friends !
Lest, stripping him of his resplendent arms,
The Myrmidons with foul dishonour shame          660
His body, through resentment of the deaths
Of numerous Grecians slain by spears of ours.
    He ceased ; then sorrow every Trojan heart
Seized insupportable and that disdain'd
All bounds, for that, although a stranger born,          665
Sarpedon ever had a bulwark proved
To Troy, the leader of a numerous host,
And of that host by none in fight excell'd.
Right on toward the Danaï they moved
Ardent for battle all, and at their head          670
Enraged for slain Sarpedon, Hector came.
Meantime, stout-hearted[9] Chief, Patroclus roused
The Grecians, and exhorting first (themselves
Already prompt) the Ajaces, thus began.
    Heroic pair ! now make it all your joy          675
To chase the Trojan host, and such to prove
As erst, or even bolder, if ye may.
The Chief lies breathless who ascended first
Our wall, Sarpedon.   Let us bear him hence,
Strip and dishonour him, and in the blood          680
Of his protectors drench the ruthless spear.
    So Menœtiades his warriors urged,
Themselves courageous.   Then the Lycian host
And Trojan here, and there the Myrmidons
With all the host of Greece, closing the ranks          685
Rush'd into furious contest for the dead,
Shouting tremendous ; clang'd their brazen arms,
And Jove with Night's pernicious shades o'erhung
The bloody field, so to enhance the more
Their toilsome strife for his own son.   First then          690

    [9] λασιον κηρ.

The Trojans from their place and order shock'd
The bright-eyed Grecians, slaying not the least
Nor worst among the Myrmidons, the brave
Epigeus, from renown'd Agacles sprung.
He, erst, in populous Budeum ruled.                    695
But for a valiant kinsman of his own
Whom there he slew, had thence to Peleus fled
And to his silver-footed spouse divine,
Who with Achilles, phalanx-breaker Chief,
Sent him to fight beneath the walls of Troy.           700
Him seizing fast the body, with a stone
Illustrious Hector smote full on the front,
And his whole scull within the ponderous casque
Split sheer ; he prostrate on the body fell
In shades of soul-divorcing death involved.            705
Patroclus, grieving for his slaughter'd friend,
Rush'd through the foremost warriors.  As the hawk
Swift-wing'd before him starlings drives or daws,
So thou Patroclus, of equestrian fame !
Full on the Lycian ranks and Trojan drov'st            710
Resentful of thy fellow-warrior's fall.
At Stheneläus an huge stone he cast
Son of Ithæmenes, whom on the neck
He smote and burst the tendons ; then the van
Of Ilium's host, with Hector, all retired.             715
Far as the slender javelin cuts the air
Hurl'd with collected force, or in the games,
Or even in battle at a desperate foe,
So far the Greeks repulsed the host of Troy.
Then Glaucus first, Chief of the shielded bands        720
Of Lycia, slew Bathycles, valiant son
Of Calchon ; Hellas was his home, and far
He pass'd in riches all the Myrmidons.
Him chasing Glaucus whom he now attain'd,
The Lycian, turning sudden, with his lance             725
Pierced through the breast, and, sounding, down he fell.
Grief fill'd Achaia's sons for such a Chief
So slain, but joy the Trojans ; thick they throng'd
The conqueror around, nor yet the Greeks
Forgat their force, but resolute advanced.             730
Then, by Meriones a Trojan died

Of noble rank, Laogonus, the son
Undaunted of Onetor great in Troy,
Priest of Idæan Jove. The ear and jaw
Between, he pierced him with a mortal force;        735
Swift flew the life, and darkness veil'd his eyes.
Æneas, in return, his brazen spear
Hurl'd at Meriones with ardent hope
To pierce him, while, with nimble[10] steps and short
Behind his buckler made, he paced the field;        740
But, warn'd of its approach, Meriones
Bow'd low his head, shunning it, and the spear
Behind him pierced the soil; there quivering stood
The weapon, vain, though from a vigorous arm,
Till spent by slow degrees its fury slept.        745

    *     *     *     *     *     *     *
    *     *     *     *     *     *    *[11]

Indignant then Æneas thus exclaim'd.
    Meriones! I sent thee such a spear
As, reaching thee, should have for ever marr'd        750
Thy step, accomplish'd dancer as thou art.
    To whom Meriones spear-famed replied.
Æneas! thou wilt find the labour hard,
How great soe'er thy might, to quell the force
Of all opposers. Thou art also doom'd        755
Thyself to die; and may but spear of mine
Well-aim'd once strike thee full, what strength soe'er
Or magnanimity be thine to boast,
Thy glory in that moment thou resign'st
To me, thy soul to Pluto steed-renown'd.        760

[10] Ὑπασπίδια προβιβῶντος. A similar expression occurs in Book XIII. 158. There we read ὑπασπίδια προποδίζων. Which is explained by the Scholiast in Villoisson to signify—advancing with quick short steps, and at the same time covering the feet with a shield. A practice which, unless they bore the ἀμφιβρότην ἀσπίδα, must necessarily leave the upper parts exposed.

It is not improbable, though the translation is not accommodated to that conjecture, that Æneas, in his following speech to Meriones, calls him, ὀρχησήν, with a view to the agility with which he performed this particular step in battle.

[11] Two lines occurring here in the original which contain only the same matter as the two preceding, and which are found neither in the MSS. used by Barnes nor in the Harleian, the Translator has omitted them in his version as interpolated and superfluous.

sharp reproved.

h in fight

my gallant friend!

h of ours

st first be spilt.                                    765

war decide;

vaunts, we need.

m follow'd close

depth

the mountain's side                              770

l remote,

ple plain

rass

faulchions huge

double-edge.                                       775

st to discern,

from his head

blood and dust

th weapons.   They

As hovel-flies                                       780

he brimming pails

around the dead.

orious eyes

with watchful note

in battle deep                                        785

her Him

on divine

his arms,

s strife prolong.

e most

t the valiant friend                               790

in compel

brazen-mail'd

ous by the way.

y he possess'd                                       795

ng to his seat

d bade his host

purpose[12] changed.

ycia's host

*vis cui cedendum.*—So it is interpreted

—Vide Schaufelbergerus.

*Endured, but all ...*

*Thy sovereign thr...*

*For numerous, while...*

*Held in suspense, had...*

*... once the Grecians ...*

*Despoil'd Sarpedon, wh...*

*By order of Menœtius' va...*

*Bore thence into the fleet.*

*The Thunderer to Apollo th...*

*Phœbus, my son, delay no...*

*I'm hill of weapons drawn cle...*

*Sarpedon's corse; then, bear...*

*Lave him in waters of the run...*

*With oils divine anoint, and i...*

*Immortal clothe him.   Last, t...*

*Swift bearers both, twin-born,...*

*Th' hence to Lycia's opulent ab...*

*They shall transport him quickly...*

*Funereal, his next kindred...*

*Shall honour him, a pillar and h...*

*The dead man's portion) rearing t...*

*He ceased; nor was Apollo slow ...*

*(a father's will, but from the Idæan...*

*Descending swift into the dreadful fiel...*

*Godlike Sarpedon's body from beneath...*

*The hill of weapons drew, which, borne ...*

*With oils ambrosial bathed, and clothed in ...*

*Immortal.   Then to Death and gentle Sleep,...*

*Swift-bearers both, twin-born, he gave the ch...*

*Who placed it soon in Lycia's wealthy realm.*

*Meantime Patroclus, calling to his steeds,...*

*And to Automedon, the Trojans chased...*

*And Lycians, on his own destruction bent...*

*Infatuate; heedless of his charge received...*

*From Peleus' son, which, well perform'd, had sav...*

*Him from his miserable doom.*

*Jove's high purpose evermore prevails...*

*Against the thoughts of man; He turns to flight...*

*The bravest, and the victory takes with ease...*

*Even from the Chief whom he impels t...*

Endured, but all fled scatter'd, seeing pierced                     800
Their sovereign through his heart, and heap'd with dead;
For numerous, while Saturnian Jove the fight
Held in suspense, had on his body fallen.
At once the Grecians of his dazzling arms
Despoil'd Sarpedon, which the Myrmidons                             805
By order of Menœtius' valiant son
Bore thence into the fleet.   Meantime his will
The Thunderer to Apollo thus express'd.
   Phœbus, my son, delay not; from beneath
Yon hill of weapons drawn cleanse from his blood                    810
Sarpedon's corse; then, bearing him remote,
Lave him in waters of the running stream,
With oils divine anoint, and in attire
Immortal clothe him.   Last, to Death and Sleep,
Swift bearers both, twin-born, deliver him;                         815
For hence to Lycia's opulent abodes
They shall transport him quickly, where, with rites
Funereal, his next kindred and his friends
Shall honour him, a pillar and a tomb
(The dead man's portion) rearing to his name.                       820
   He ceased; nor was Apollo slow to hear
His father's will, but from the Idæan heights
Descending swift into the dreadful field,
Godlike Sarpedon's body from beneath
The hill of weapons drew, which, borne remote,                      825
He laved in waters of the running stream,
With oils ambrosial bathed, and clothed in robes
Immortal.   Then to Death and gentle Sleep,
Swift-bearers both, twin-born, he gave the charge,
Who placed it soon in Lycia's wealthy realm.                        830
   Meantime Patroclus, calling to his steeds,
And to Automedon, the Trojans chased
And Lycians, on his own destruction bent
Infatuate; heedless of his charge received
From Peleus' son, which, well perform'd, had saved                  835
The Hero from his miserable doom.
But Jove's high purpose evermore prevails
Against the thoughts of man; He turns to flight
The bravest, and the victory takes with ease
E'en from the Chief whom he impels himself                          840

To battle, as he now this Chief impell'd.
Who, then, Patroclus! first, who last by thee
Fell slain, what time thyself wast call'd to die?
Adrastus first, then Perimus he slew,
Offspring of Megas, then Autonoüs,                     845
Echechlus, Melanippus, and Epistor,
Pylartes, Mulius, Elasus.   All these
He slew, and from the field chased all beside.
Then, doubtless, had Achaia's sons prevail'd
To take proud-gated Troy, such havoc made            850
He with his spear, but that the son of Jove
Apollo, on a tower's conspicuous height
Station'd, devoted him for Ilium's sake.
Thrice on a buttress of the lofty wall
Patroclus mounted, and him thrice the God             855
With hands immortal his resplendent shield
Smiting, struck down again; but when he rush'd
A fourth time, demon-like, to the assault,
The King of radiant shafts him, stern, rebuked.
　　Patroclus, warrior of renown, retire!           860
The fates ordain not that imperial Troy
Stoop to thy spear, nor to the spear itself
Of Peleus' son, though mightier far than thou.
　　He said, and Menœtiades the wrath
Of shaft-arm'd Phœbus shunning, far retired.         865
But in the Scæan gate Hector his steeds
Detain'd, uncertain whether thence to drive
Amid the warring multitude again,
Or, loud commandment issuing, to collect
His host within the walls.   Him musing long         870
Apollo, clad in semblance of a Chief
Youthful and valiant, join'd.   Asius he seem'd
Equestrian Hector's uncle, brother born
Of Hecuba the queen, and Dymas' son,
Who on the Sangar's banks in Phrygia dwelt.          875
Apollo, so disguised, him thus bespake.
　·Why, Hector, hast thou left the fight? this sloth
Not well befits thee.   Oh that I as far
Thee pass'd in force as thou transcendest me,
Then, not unpunish'd long, should'st thou retire;    880
But haste, and with thy coursers solid-hoof'd

Seek out Patroclus, him perchance to slay,
Should Phœbus have decreed that glory thine.
　So saying, Apollo join'd the host again.
Then noble Hector bade his charioteer　　　　　885
Valiant Cebriones his coursers lash
Back into battle, while the God himself
Entering the multitude confounded sore
The Argives, victory conferring proud
And glory on Hector and the host of Troy.　　　890
But Hector, leaving all beside unslain,
Furious impell'd his coursers solid-hoof'd
Against Patroclus; on the other side
Patroclus from his chariot to the ground
Leap'd ardent; in his left a spear he bore,　　　895
And in his right a marble fragment rough,
Large as his grasp.　With full collected might
He hurl'd it; neither was the weapon slow
To find whom he had mark'd, or sent in vain.
He smote the charioteer of Hector, bold　　　　900
Cebriones, King Priam's spurious son,
Full on the forehead, while he sway'd the reins.
The bone that force withstood not, but the rock
With ragged points beset dash'd both his brows
In pieces, and his eyes fell at his feet.　　　　905
He, diver-like, from his exalted stand
Behind the steeds pitch'd headlong, and expired;
O'er whom, Patroclus of equestrian fame!
Thou didst exult with taunting speech severe.
　Ye Gods, with what agility he dives!　　　　910
Ah! it were well if in the fishy Deep
This man were occupied; he might no few
With oysters satisfy, although the waves
Were churlish, plunging headlong from his bark
As easily as from his chariot here.　　　　　915
So then—in Troy, it seems, are divers too!
　So saying, on bold Cebriones he sprang
With all a lion's force, who, while the folds
He ravages, is wounded in the breast,
And, victim of his own fierce courage, dies.　　920
So didst thou spring, Patroclus! to despoil
Cebriones, and Hector opposite

Leap'd also to thè ground.   Then contest such
For dead Cebriones those two between
Arose, as in the lofty mountain-tops                    925
Two lions wage, contending for a deer
New-slain, both hunger-pinch'd and haughty both.
So for Cebriones, alike in arms
Expert, brave Hector and Patroclus strove
To pierce each other with the ruthless spear.          930
First, Hector seized his head, nor loosed his hold,
Patroclus, next, his feet, while all beside
Of either host in furious battle join'd.
    As when the East wind and the South contend
To shake some deep wood on the mountain's side,        935
Or beech, or ash, or rugged cornel old,
With stormy violence the mingled boughs
Smite and snap short each other, crashing loud ;
So, Trojans and Achaians, mingling, slew
Mutual, while neither felt a wish to fly.              940
Around Cebriones stood many a spear,
And many a shaft sent smartly from the nerve
Implanted deep, and many a stone of grasp
Enormous sounded on their batter'd shields
Who fought to gain him.   He, in eddies lost          945
Of sable dust, with his huge trunk huge space
O'erspread, nor steeds nor chariots heeded more.
    While yet the sun ascending climb'd the heavens,
Their darts flew equal, and the people fell ;
But when he westward journey'd, by a change           950
Surpassing hope the Grecians then prevail'd.
They drew Cebriones the Hero forth
From all those weapons, and his armour stripp'd
At leisure, distant from the battle's roar.
Then sprang Patroclus on the Trojan host ;            955
Thrice, like another Mars, he sprang with shouts
Tremendous, and nine warriors thrice he slew.
But when the fourth time, dæmon-like, he rush'd
Against them, then, oh then, too manifest
The consummation of thy days approach'd               960
Patroclus ! whom Apollo terror-clad
Met then in battle.   He the coming God
Through all that multitude knew not, such gloom

Impenetrable him involved around.  
Behind him close he stood, and with his palms       965  
Expanded on the spine and shoulders broad  
Smote him ; his eyes swam dizzy at the stroke.  
Then Phœbus from his head his helmet dash'd  
To earth, sonorous at the feet it roll'd  
Of many a prancing steed, and all the crest       970  
Defilement gather'd gross of dust and blood,  
Then first ; till then, impossible ; for how  
Should dust the tresses of that helmet shame  
With which Achilles fighting fenced his head  
Illustrious, and his graceful brows divine ?       975  
But Jove now made it Hector's ; he awhile  
Bore it, himself to swift perdition doom'd.  
His spear brass-mounted, ponderous, huge and long,  
Fell shiver'd from his grasp.   His shield that swept  
His ancle, with its belt dropp'd from his arm,       980  
And Phœbus loosed the corslet from his breast.  
Confusion seized his brain ; his noble limbs  
Quaked under him, and panic-stunn'd he stood.  
Then came a Dardan Chief, who from behind  
Enforced a pointed lance into his back       985  
Between the shoulders ; Panthus' son was he,  
Euphorbus, famous for equestrian skill,  
For spearmanship, and in the rapid race  
Past all of equal age.   He twenty men  
(Although a learner yet of martial feats,       990  
And by his steeds then first to battle borne)  
Dismounted.   He, Patroclus, mighty Chief !  
First threw a lance at thee, which yet thy life  
Quell'd not ; then snatching hasty from the wound  
His ashen beam, he ran into the crowd,       995  
Nor dared confront in fight even the unarm'd  
Patroclus.   But Patroclus, by the lance,  
And by the stroke of an immortal hand  
Subdued, fell back toward his ranks again.  
Then, soon as Hector the retreat perceived       1000  
Of brave Patroclus wounded, issuing forth  
From his own phalanx, he approach'd and drove  
A spear right through his body at the waist.  
Sounding he fell.   Loud groan'd Achaia's host.

As when the lion and the sturdy boar                    1005
Contend in battle on the mountain-tops
For some scant rivulet, thirst-parch'd alike,
Ere long the lion quells the panting boar ;
So Priameian Hector, spear in hand,
Slew Menœtiades the valiant slayer                      1010
Of multitudes, and thus in accents wing'd,
With fierce delight exulted in his fall.
   It was thy thought, Patroclus, to have laid
Our city waste, and to have wafted hence
Our wives and daughters to thy native land,             1015
Their day of liberty for ever set.
Fool ! for their sakes the feet of Hector's steeds
Fly into battle, and myself excel,
For their sakes, all our bravest of the spear,
That I may turn from them that evil hour               1020
Necessitous.   But thou art vulture's food.
Unhappy youth ! all valiant as he is,
Achilles hath no succour given to thee,
Who when he sent thee forth whither himself
Would not, thus doubtless gave thee oft in charge :    1025
Ah, well beware, Patroclus, glorious Chief !
That thou revisit not these ships again,
Till first on Hero-slaughterer Hector's breast
Thou cleave his bloody corslet.   So he spake,
And with vain words thee credulous beguiled.           1030
   To whom Patroclus, mighty Chief, with breath
Drawn faintly, and dying, thou didst thus reply.
Now Hector, boast ! now glory, for the son
Of Saturn and Apollo, me with ease
Vanquishing, whom they had themselves disarm'd,        1035
Have made the victory thine ; else, twenty such
As thou, had fallen by my victorious spear.
Me Phœbus and my ruthless fate combined
To slay ; these foremost ; but of mortal men
Euphorbus, and thy praise is only third.               1040
I tell thee also, and within thy heart
Repose it deep—Thou shalt not long survive ;
But, even now, fate, and a violent death
Attend thee by Achilles' hands ordain'd
To perish, by Æcides the brave.                        1045

So saying, the shades of death him wrapp'd around.
Down into Ades from his limbs dismiss'd,
His spirit fled sorrowful, of youth's prime
And vigorous manhood suddenly bereft.
Then, him though dead, Hector again bespake.          1050
    Patroclus! these prophetic strains of death
At hand, and fate, why hast thou sung to me?
May not the son of Thetis azure-hair'd,
Achilles, perish first by spear of mine?
    He said; then pressing with his heel the trunk          1055
Supine, and backward thrusting it, he drew
His glittering weapon from the wound, nor stay'd,
But, lance in hand, the godlike charioteer
Pursued of swift Æcides, on fire
To smite Automedon; but him the steeds          1060
Immortal, rapid, by the Gods conferr'd
(A glorious gift) on Peleus, snatch'd away.

# BOOK XVII.

---

## ARGUMENT.

Sharp contest ensues around the body of Patroclus.   Hector puts on the
armour of Achilles.   Menelaus, having dispatched Antilochus to Achilles
with news of the death of Patroclus, returns to the battle, and, together
with Meriones, bears Patroclus off the field, while the Ajaces cover
their retreat.

Nor Menelaus, Atreus' valiant son,
Knew not how Menœtiades had fallen
By Trojan hands in battle ; forth he rush'd
All bright in burnish'd armour through his van,
And as some heifer with maternal fears                              5
Now first acquainted, compasses around
Her young one murmuring, with tender moan,
So moved the Hero of the amber locks
Around Patroclus, before whom his spear
Advancing and broad shield, he death denounced          10
On all opposers ; neither stood the son
Spear-famed of Panthus inattentive long
To slain Patroclus, but approach'd the dead,
And warlike Menelaus thus bespake.
 Prince ! Menelaus ! Atreus' mighty son !               15
Yield.   Leave the body and these gory spoils ;
For of the Trojans or allies of Troy
None sooner made Patroclus bleed than I.
Seek not to rob me, therefore, of my praise
Among the Trojans, lest my spear assail                          20
Thee also, and thou perish premature.
 To whom, indignant, Atreus' son replied.
Self-praise, the Gods do know, is little worth.
But neither lion may in pride compare
Nor panther, nor the savage boar whose heart's          25
High temper flashes in his eyes, with these
The spear-accomplish'd youths of Panthus' house.

Yet Hyperenor of equestrian fame
Lived not his lusty manhood to enjoy,
Who scoffingly defied my force in arms,                    30
And call'd me most contemptible in fight
Of all the Danaï.   But him, I ween,
His feet bore never hence to cheer at home
His wife and parents with his glad return.
So also shall thy courage fierce be tamed,                 35
If thou oppose me.   I command thee, go—
Mix with the multitude; withstand not me,
Lest evil overtake thee!   To be taught
·By sufferings only, is the part of fools.
   He said, but him sway'd not, who thus replied.    40
Now, even now, Atrides! thou shalt rue
My brother's blood which thou hast shed, and makest
His death thy boast.   Thou hast his blooming bride
Widow'd, and thou hast fill'd his parents' hearts
With anguish of unutterable woe;                           45
But bearing hence thy armour and thy head
To Troy, and casting them at Panthus' feet,
And at the feet of Phrontis, his espoused,
I shall console the miserable pair.
Nor will I leave that service unessay'd                    50
Longer, nor will I fail through want of force,
Of courage, or of terrible address.
   He ceased, and smote his shield, nor pierced the disk,
But bent his point against the stubborn brass.
Then Menelaus, prayer preferring first                     55
To Jove, assail'd Euphorbus in his turn,
Whom pacing backward in the throat he struck,
And with both hands and his full force the spear
Impelling, urged it through his neck behind.
Sounding he fell; loud rang his batter'd arms.             60
His locks, which even the Graces might have own'd,
Blood-sullied, and his ringlets wound about
With twine of gold and silver, swept the dust.
As the luxuriant olive by a swain
Rear'd in some solitude where rills abound,                65
Puts forth her buds, and fann'd by genial airs
On all sides, hangs her boughs with whitest flowers,
But by a sudden whirlwind from its trench

Uptorn, it lies extended on the field ;
Such, Panthus' warlike son Euphorbus seem'd,          70
By Menelaus, son of Atreus, slain
Suddenly, and of all his arms despoil'd.
But as the lion on the mountains bred,
Glorious in strength, when he hath seized the best
And fairest of the herd, with savage fangs          75
First breaks her neck, then laps the bloody paunch
Torn wide ; meantime, around him, but remote,
Dogs stand and swains clamouring, yet by fear
Repress'd, annoy him not or dare approach ;
So there all wanted courage to oppose          80
The force of Menelaus, glorious Chief.
Then, easily had Menelaus borne
The armour of the son of Panthus thence,
But that Apollo the illustrious prize
Denied him, who in semblance of the Chief          85
Of the Ciconians, Mentes, prompted forth
Against him Hector terrible as Mars,
Whose spirit thus in accents wing'd he roused.
     Hector ! the chase is vain ; here thou pursuest
The horses of Æacides the brave,          90
Which thou shalt never win, for they are steeds
Of fiery nature, such as ill endure
To draw or carry mortal man, himself
Excépt, whom an immortal mother bore.
Meantime, bold Menelaus, in defence          95
Of dead Patroclus, hath a Trojan slain
Of highest note, Euphorbus, Panthus' son,
And hath his might in arms for ever quell'd.
     So spake the God and to the fight return'd.
But grief intolerable at that word          100
Seized Hector ; darting through the ranks his eye,
He knew at once who stripp'd Euphorbus' arms,
And him knew also lying on the field,
And from his wide wound bleeding copious still.
Then dazzling bright in arms, through all the van          105
He flew, shrill-shouting, fierce as Vulcan's fire
Unquenchable ; nor were his shouts unheard
By Atreus' son, who with his noble mind
Conferring sad, thus to himself began.

Alas! if I forsake these gorgeous spoils,           110
And leave Patroclus for my glory slain,
I fear lest the Achaians at that sight
Incensed, reproach me; and if, urged by shame,
I fight with Hector and his host, alone,
Lest, hemm'd around by multitudes, I fall;          115
For Hector, by his whole imbattled force
Attended, comes.  But whither turn my thoughts?
No man may combat with another fenced
By power divine and whom the Gods exalt,
But he must draw down woe on his own head.          120
Me, therefore, none of all Achaia's host
Will blame indignant, seeing my retreat
From Hector, whom themselves the Gods assist.
But might the battle-shout of Ajax once
Reach me, with force united we would strive,        125
Even in opposition to a God,
To rescue for Achilles' sake, his friend.
Task arduous! but less arduous than this.
    While he thus meditated, swift advanced
The Trojan ranks, with Hector at their head.        130
He then, retiring slow, and turning oft,
Forsook the body.  As by dogs and swains
With clamours loud and spears driven from the stalls
A bearded lion goes, his noble heart
Abhors retreat, and slow he quits the prey;         135
So Menelaus with slow steps forsook
Patroclus, and arrived in front, at length,
Of his own phalanx, stood, with sharpen'd eyes
Seeking vast Ajax, son of Telamon.
Him leftward, soon, of all the field he mark'd      140
Encouraging aloud his band, whose hearts
With terrors irresistible himself
Phœbus had fill'd.  He ran, and at his side
Standing, incontinent, him thus bespake.
    My gallant Ajax, haste—come quickly—strive      145
With me to rescue for Achilles' sake
His friend, though bare, for Hector hath his arms.
    He said, and by his words the noble mind
Of Ajax roused; issuing through the van
He went, and Menelaus at his side.                  150

Hector the body of Patroclus dragg'd,
Stript of his arms, with faulchion keen erelong
Purposing to strike off his head, and cast
His trunk, drawn distant, to the dogs of Troy.
But Ajax, with broad shield tower-like, approach'd.      155
Then Hector, to his bands retreating, sprang
Into his chariot, and to others gave
The splendid arms in charge, who into Troy
Should bear the destined trophy of his praise.
But Ajax with his broad shield guarding stood           160
Slain Menœtiades, as for his whelps
The lion stands; him through some forest drear
Leading his little ones, the hunters meet;
Fire glimmers in his looks, and down he draws
His whole brow into frowns, covering his eyes;          165
So, guarding slain Patroclus, Ajax lour'd.
On the other side, with tender grief oppress'd
Unspeakable, brave Menelaus stood.
But Glaucus, leader of the Lycian band,
Son of Hippolochus, in bitter terms                     170
Indignant, reprimanded Hector thus.
   Ah, Hector, Chieftain of excelling form,
But all unfurnish'd with a warrior's heart!
Unwarranted I deem thy great renown
Who art to flight addicted.  Think, henceforth,         175
How ye shall save city and citadel
Thou and thy people born in Troy, alone.
No Lycian shall, at least, in your defence
Fight with the Grecians, for our ceaseless toil
In arms, hath ever been a thankless task.               180
Inglorious Chief! how wilt thou save a worse
From warring crowds, who hast Sarpedon left
Thy guest, thy friend, to be a spoil, a prey
To yonder Argives?  While he lived he much
Thee and thy city profited, whom dead                   185
Thou fear'st to rescue even from the dogs.
Now, therefore, may but my advice prevail,
Back to your country, Lycians! so, at once,
Shall remediless ruin fall on Troy.
For had the Trojans now a daring heart                  190
Intrepid, such as in the breast resides

Of labourers in their country's dear behalf,
We soon should drag Patroclus into Troy;
And were his body, from the battle drawn,
In Priam's royal city once secured,                               195
As soon, the Argives would in ransom give
Sarpedon's body with his splendid arms
To be conducted safe into the town.
For when Patroclus fell, the friend was slain
Of such a Chief as is not in the fleet                            200
For valour, and his bands are dauntless all.
But thou, at the first glimpse of Ajax' eye
Confounded, hast not dared in arms to face
That warrior bold, superior far to thee.
    To whom brave Hector, frowning stern, replied.               205
Why, Glaucus! should a Chief like thee his tongue
Presume to employ thus haughtily?   My friend!
I thee accounted wisest, once, of all
Who dwell in fruitful Lycia, but thy speech
Now utter'd altogether merits blame,                             210
In which thou tell'st me that I fear to stand
Against vast Ajax.   Know that I from fight
Shrink not, nor yet from sound of prancing steeds;
But Jove's high purpose evermore prevails
Against the thoughts of man; he turns to flight                  215
The bravest, and the victory takes with ease
Even from those whom once he favour'd most.
But hither, friend! stand with me; mark my deed;
Prove me, if I be found, as thou hast said,
An idler all the day, or if by force                             220
I not compel some Grecian to renounce
Patroclus, even the boldest of them all.
    He ceased, and to his host exclaim'd aloud.
Trojans, and Lycians, and close-fighting sons
Of Dardanus, oh be ye men, my friends!                           225
Now summon all your fortitude, while I
Put on the armour of Achilles, won
From the renown'd Patroclus slain by me.
    So saying, illustrious Hector from the clash
Of spears withdrew, and with his swiftest pace                   230
Departing, overtook, not far remote,
The bearers of Achilles' arms to Troy.

s. c.—7.                                    z

Apart from all the horrors of the field
Standing, he changed his armour; gave his own
To be by them to sacred Ilium borne,                           235
And the immortal arms of Peleus' son
Achilles, by the ever-living Gods
To Peleus given, put on.   Those arms the Sire,
Now old himself, had on his son conferr'd,
But in those arms his son grew never old.                      240
   Him, therefore, soon as cloud-assembler Jove
Saw glittering in divine Achilles' arms,
Contemplative he shook his brows, and said.
   Ah hapless Chief! thy death, although at hand,
Nought troubles thee.   Thou wear'st his heavenly arms,        245
Who all excels, terror of Ilium's host.
His friend, though bold yet gentle, thou hast slain,
And hast the brows and bosom of the dead
Unseemly bared: yet, bright success awhile
I give thee; so compensating thy lot,                          250
From whom Andromache shall ne'er receive
Those glorious arms, for thou shalt ne'er return.
   So spake the Thunderer, and his sable brows
Shaking, confirm'd the word.   But Hector found
The armour apt; the God of war his soul                        255
With fury fill'd, he felt his limbs afresh
Invigorated, and with loudest shouts
Return'd to his illustrious allies.
To them he seem'd, clad in those radiant arms,
Himself Achilles; rank by rank he pass'd                       260
Through all the host, exhorting every Chief,
Asteropæus, Mesthles, Phorcys, Medon,
Thersilochus, Deisenor, augur Ennomus,
Chromius, Hippothoüs; all these he roused
To battle, and in accents wing'd began.                        265
   Hear me, ye myriads, neighbours and allies!
For not through fond desire to fill the plain
With multitudes, have I convened you here
Each from his city, but that well-inclined
To Ilium, ye might help to guard our wives                     270
And little ones against the host of Greece.
Therefore it is that forage large and gifts
Providing for you, I exhaust the stores

Of Troy, and drain our people for your sake.
Turn then direct against them, and his life　　　275
Save each, or lose ; it is the course of war.
Him who shall drag, though dead, Patroclus home
Into the host of Troy, and shall repulse
Ajax, I will reward with half the spoils,
And half shall be my own ; glory and praise　　　280
Shall also be his meed, equal to mine.
　　He ended ; they compact with lifted spears
Bore on the Danaï, conceiving each
Warm expectation in his heart to wrest
From Ajax son of Telamon, the dead.　　　285
Vain hope ! he many a lifeless Trojan heap'd
On slain Patroclus, but at length his speech
To warlike Menelaus thus address'd.
　　Ah, Menelaus, valiant friend ! I hope
No longer, now, that even we shall 'scape　　　290
Ourselves from fight ; nor fear I so the loss
Of dead Patroclus, who shall soon the dogs
Of Ilium, and the fowls sate with his flesh,
As for my life I tremble and for thine,
That cloud of battle, Hector, such a gloom　　　295
Sheds all around ; death manifest impends.
Haste—call our best, if even they can hear.
　　He spake, nor Menelaus not complied,
But call'd aloud on all the Chiefs of Greece.
　　Friends, senators, and leaders of the powers　　　300
Of Argos ! who with Agamemnon drink
And Menelaus at the public feast,
Each bearing rule o'er many, by the will
Of Jove advanced to honour and renown !
The task were difficult to single out　　　305
Chief after Chief by name amid the blaze
Of such contention ; but oh come yourselves
Indignant forth, nor let the dogs of Troy
Patroclus rend, and gambol with his bones !
　　He ceased, whom Oïliades the swift　　　310
Hearing incontinent, of all the Chiefs
Ran foremost, after whom Idomeneus
Approach'd, and dread as homicidal Mars
Meriones.　But never mind of man

Could even in silent recollection name                        315
The whole vast multitude who, following these,
Renew'd the battle on the part of Greece.
The Trojans first, with Hector at their head,
Wedged in close phalanx, rush'd to the assault.
   As when within some rapid river's mouth          320
The billows and stream clash, on either shore[1]
Loud sounds the roar[1] of waves ejected wide,
Such seem'd the clamours of the Trojan host.
But the Achaians, one in heart, around
Patroclus stood, bulwark'd with shields of brass,         325
And over all their glittering helmets Jove
Darkness diffused, for he had loved Patroclus
While yet he lived friend of Æacides,
And, now, abhorring that the dogs of Troy
Should eat him, urged the Greeks to his defence.          330
The host of Troy first shook the Grecian host;
The body left, they fled; yet of them all,
The Trojan powers, determined as they were,
Slew none, but dragg'd the body.   Neither stood
The Greeks long time aloof, soon as repulsed               335
Again led on by Ajax, who in form
And in exploits all others far excell'd,
Peerless Æacides alone except.
Right through the foremost combatants he rush'd,
In force resembling most some savage boar                  340
That in the mountains bursting through the brakes,
The swains disperses and their hounds with ease;
Like him, illustrious Ajax, mighty son
Of Telamon, at his assault dispersed
With ease the close imbattled ranks, who fought           345
Around Patroclus' body, strong in hope
To achieve it, and to make the glory theirs.
Hippothoüs, a youth of high renown,
Son of Pelasgian Lethus, by a noose
Around his ancle cast dragg'd through the fight           350
Patroclus, so to gratify the host

---

[1] There is no word in our language expressive of loud sound at all comparable in effect to the Greek *Bo-o-osin*. I have therefore endeavoured by the juxtaposition of two words similar in sound, to palliate in some degree a defect which it was not in my power to cure.

Of Ilium and their Chief; but evil him
Reach'd suddenly, by none of all his friends
(Though numerous wish'd to save him) turn'd aside.
For swift advancing on him through the crowd          355
The son of Telamon pierced, spear in hand,
His helmet brazen-cheek'd; the crested casque,
So smitten, open'd wide, for huge the hand
And ponderous was the spear that gave the blow,
And all around its neck, mingled with blood          360
Gush'd forth the brain.   There, lifeless, down he sank,
Let fall the Hero's foot, and fell himself
Prone on the dead, never to see again
Deep-soil'd Larissa, never to requite
Their kind solicitudes who gave him birth,          '   365
In bloom of life by dauntless Ajax slain.
Then, Hector hurl'd at Ajax his bright spear,
But he, forewarn'd of its approach, escaped
Narrowly, and it pierced Schedius instead,
Brave son of Iphitus; he, noblest Chief             370
Of the Phocensians, over many reign'd,
Dwelling in Panopeus the far-renown'd.
Entering beneath the clavicle[2] the point
Right through his shoulder's summit pass'd behind,
And on his loud-resounding arms he fell.            375
But Ajax at his waist wounded the son
Of Phœnops, valiant Phorcys, while he stood
Guarding Hippothöus; through his hollow mail
Enforced the weapon drank his inmost life,
And in his palm, supine, he clench'd the dust.      380
Then, Hector with the foremost Chiefs of Troy
Fell back; the Argives sent a shout to heaven,
And dragging Phorcys and Hippothöus thence
Stripp'd both.   In that bright moment Ilium's host
Fear-quell'd before Achaia's warlike sons           385
Had Troy re-enter'd, and the host of Greece
By matchless might and fortitude their own
Had snatch'd a victory from the grasp of Fate,
But that, himself, the King of radiant shafts
Æneas roused; Epytis' son he seem'd                 390
Periphas, ancient in the service grown

2 Or collar-bone.

Of old Anchises whom he dearly loved ;
His form assumed, Apollo thus began.
 How could ye save, Æneas, were the Gods
Your enemies, the towers of lofty Troy ?    395
As I have others seen, warriors who would,
Men fill'd with might and valour, firm themselves
And Chiefs of multitudes disdaining fear.
But Jove to us the victory far more
Than to the Grecians wills ; therefore the fault  400
Is yours, who tremble and refuse the fight.
 He ended, whom Æneas marking, knew
At once the glorious Archer of the skies,
And thus to distant Hector call'd aloud.
 Oh, Hector, and ye other Chiefs of Troy   405
And of her brave confederates ! Shame it were
Should we re-enter Ilium, driven to flight
By dastard fear before the host of Greece.
A God assured me even now, that Jove,
Supreme in battle, gives his aid to Troy.   410
Rush, therefore, on the Danaï direct,
Nor let them, safe at least and unannoy'd,
Bear hence Patroclus' body to the fleet.
 He spake, and starting far into the van
Stood foremost forth ; they, wheeling, faced the Greeks. 415
Then, spear in hand, Æneas smote the friend .
Of Lycomedes, brave Leocritus,
Son of Arisbas. Lycomedes saw
Compassionate his death, and drawing nigh
First stood, then hurling his resplendent lance,  420
Right through the liver Apisaon pierced
Offspring of Hippasus, his chest beneath,
And, lifeless, instant, on the field he fell.
He from Pæonia the deep-soil'd to Troy
Came forth, Asteropæus sole except,    425
Bravest of all Pæonia's band in arms.
Asteropæus saw, and to the van
Sprang forth for furious combat well prepared,
But room for fight found none, so thick a fence
Of shields and ported spears fronted secure  430
The phalanx guarding Menœtiades.
For Ajax ranging all the ranks, aloud

Admonish'd them that no man yielding ground
Should leave Patroclus, or advance before
The rest, but all alike fight and stand fast.          435
Such order gave huge Ajax; purple gore
Drench'd all the ground; in slaughter'd heaps they fell,
Trojans and Trojan aids of dauntless hearts
And Grecians; for not even they the fight
Waged bloodless, though with far less cost of blood,          440
Each mindful to avert his fellow's fate.
    Thus burn'd the battle; neither hadst thou deem'd
The sun himself in heaven unquench'd, or moon,
Beneath a cope so dense of darkness strove
Unceasing all the most renown'd in arms          445
For Menœtiades.  Meantime the war,
Wherever else, the bright-arm'd Grecians waged
And Trojans under skies serene.  The sun
On them his radiance darted; not a cloud,
From mountain or from vale rising, allay'd          450
His fervour; there at distance due they fought
And paused by turns, and shunn'd the cruel dart.
But in the middle field not war alone
They suffer'd, but night also; ruthless raged
The iron storm, and all the mightiest bled.          455
Two glorious Chiefs, the while, Antilochus
And Thrasymedes, had no tidings heard
Of brave Patroclus slain, but deem'd him still
Living, and troubling still the host of Troy;
For watchful[3] only to prevent the flight          460
Or slaughter of their fellow-warriors, they
Maintain'd a distant station, so enjoin'd
By Nestor when he sent them to the field.
But fiery conflict arduous employ'd
The rest all day continual; knees and legs,          465
Feet, hands, and eyes of those who fought to guard
The valiant friend of swift Æacides

---

[3] The proper meaning of ἐπιοσσομένω—is not simply *looking on*, but *providing against*. And thus their ignorance of the death of Patroclus is accounted for. They were ordered by Nestor to a post in which they should have little to do themselves, except to superintend others, and were consequently too remote from Patroclus to see him fall, or even to hear that he had fallen.—See Villoisson.

Sweat gather'd foul and dust.   As when a man
An huge ox-hide drunken with slippery lard
Gives to be stretch'd, his servants all around          470
Disposed, just intervals between, the task
Ply strenuous, and while many straining hard
Extend it equal on all sides, it sweats
The moisture out, and drinks the unction in,
So they, in narrow space struggling, the dead          475
Dragg'd every way, warm hope conceiving, these
To drag him thence to Troy, those, to the ships.
Wild tumult raged around him ; neither Mars,
Gatherer of hosts to battle, nor herself
Pallas, however angry, had beheld                       480
That conflict with disdain, Jove to such length
Protracted on that day the bloody toil
Of steeds and men for Menœtiades.
Nor knew divine Achilles or had aught
Heard of Patroclus slain, for from the ships           485
Remote they fought, beneath the walls of Troy.
He, therefore, fear'd not for his death, but hope
Indulged much rather, that, the battle push'd
To Ilium's gates, he should return alive.
For that his friend, unaided by himself                 490
Or even aided, should prevail to lay
Troy waste, he nought supposed ; by Thetis warn'd
In secret conference oft, he better knew
Jove's purpose ; yet not even she had borne
Those dreadful tidings to his ear, the loss            495
Immeasurable of his dearest friend.
    They all around the dead fought spear in hand
With mutual slaughter ceaseless, and amid
Achaia's host thus spake a Chief mail-arm'd.
    Shame were it, Grecians ! should we seek by flight  500
Our galleys now ; yawn earth our feet beneath
And here ingulf us rather !  Better far
Than to permit the steed-famed host of Troy
To drag Patroclus hence into the town,
And make the glory of this conflict theirs.             505
    Thus also of the dauntless Trojans spake
A certain warrior.  Oh, my friends ! although
The fates ordain us, one and all, to die

Around this body, stand! quit not the field.
   So spake the warrior prompting into act      510
The courage of his friends, and such they strove
On both sides; high into the vault of heaven
The iron din pass'd through the desert air.
Meantime the horses of Æacides
From fight withdrawn, soon as they understood    515
Their charioteer fallen in the dust beneath
The arm of homicidal Hector, wept.
Them oft with hasty lash Diores' son
Automedon impatient smote, full oft
He stroked them gently, and as oft he chode[4];    520
Yet neither to the fleet ranged on the shore
Of spacious Hellespont would they return,
Nor with the Grecians seek the fight, but stood
As a sepulchral pillar stands, unmoved
Between their traces; to the earth they hung    525
Their heads, with plenteous tears their driver mourn'd,
And mingled their dishevell'd manes with dust.
Jove saw their grief with pity, and his brows
Shaking, within himself thus, pensive, said.
   Ah hapless pair! Wherefore by gift divine    530
Were ye to Peleus given, a mortal king,
Yourselves immortal and from age exempt?
Was it that ye might share in human woes?
For, of all things that breathe or creep the earth,
No creature lives so mere a wretch as man.    535
Yet shall not Priameian Hector ride
Triumphant, drawn by you. Myself forbid.
Suffice it that he boasts vain-gloriously
Those arms his own. Your spirit and your limbs
I will invigorate, that ye may bear    540
Safe hence Automedon into the fleet.
For I ordain the Trojans still to spread
Carnage around victorious, till they reach
The gallant barks, and till the sun at length
Descending, sacred darkness cover all.    545
   He said, and with new might the steeds inspired.

[4] This is the proper imperfect of the verb *chide*, though modern usage has substituted *chid*, a word of mean and awkward sound, in the place of it.

They, shaking from their hair profuse the dust,
Between the van of either army whirl'd
The rapid chariot.  Fighting as he pass'd,
Though fill'd with sorrow for his slaughter'd friend,          550
Automedon high mounted swept the field
Impetuous as a vulture scattering geese ;
Now would he vanish, and now turn'd again,
Chase through a multitude his trembling foe ;
But whomsoe'er he follow'd, none he slew,                     555
Nor was the task possible to a Chief
Sole in the sacred chariot, both to aim
The spear aright and guide the fiery steeds.
At length Alcimedon, his friend in arms,
Son of Laerceus son of Æmon, him                              560
Observing, from behind the chariot hail'd
The flying warrior, whom he thus bespake.
    What power, Automedon! hath ta'en away
Thy better judgment, and thy breast inspired
With this vain purpose to assail alone                        565
The Trojan van? Thy partner in the fight
Is slain and Hector on his shoulders bears,
Elate, the armour of Æacides.
    Then, answer thus Automedon return'd,
Son of Diores.  Who of all our host                           570
Was ever skill'd, Alcimedon! as thou
To rule the fire of these immortal steeds,
Save only while he lived, peer of the Gods  ·
In that great art, Patroclus, now no more?
Thou, therefore, the resplendent reins receive               575
And scourge, while I, dismounting, wage the fight.
    He ceased ; Alcimedon without delay
The battle-chariot mounting, seized at once
The lash and reins, and from his seat down leap'd
Automedon.  Them noble Hector mark'd,                         580
And to Æneas at his side began.
    Illustrious Chief of Trojans brazen-mail'd
Æneas! I have noticed yonder steeds
Of swift Achilles rushing into fight
Conspicuous, but under sway of hands                          585
Unskilful ; whence arises a fair hope
That we might seize them, wert thou so inclined ;

For never would those two dare to oppose
In battle an assault dreadful as ours.
 He ended, nor the valiant son refused    590
Of old Anchises, but with targets firm
Of season'd hide brass-plated thrown athwart
Their shoulders, both advanced direct, with whom
Of godlike form Aretus also went
And Chromius. Ardent hope they all conceived  595
To slay those Chiefs, and from the field to drive
Achilles' lofty steeds. Vain hope! for them
No bloodless strife awaited with the force
Of brave Automedon; he, prayer to Jove
First offering, felt his angry soul with might  600
Heroic fill'd, and thus his faithful friend
Alcimedon, incontinent, address'd.
 Alcimedon! hold not the steeds remote
But breathing on my back; for I expect
That never Priameïan Hector's rage    605
Shall limit know, or pause, till, slaying us,
He shall himself the coursers ample-maned
Mount of Achilles, and to flight compel
The Argive host, or perish in the van.
 So saying, he call'd aloud on Menelaus  610
With either Ajax. Oh, illustrious Chiefs
Of Argos, Menelaus, and ye bold
Ajaces![5] leaving all your best to cope
With Ilium's powers and to protect the dead,
From friends still living ward the bitter day.  615
For hither borne, two Chiefs, bravest of all
The Trojans, Hector and Æneas rush
Right through the battle. The events of war
Heaven orders; therefore even I will give
My spear its flight, and Jove dispose the rest!  620
 He said, and brandishing his massy spear
Dismiss'd it at Aretus; full he smote
His ample shield, nor stay'd the pointed brass,
But penetrating sheer the disk, his belt
Pierc'd also, and stood planted in his waist.  625
As when some vigorous youth with sharpen'd axe

 [5] The Latin plural of Ajax is sometimes necessary, because the English plural—Ajaxes—would be insupportable.

A pastured bullock smites behind the horns
And hews the muscle through ; he, at the stroke
Springs forth and falls, so sprang Aretus forth,
Then fell supine, and in his bowels stood                    630
The keen-edged lance still quivering till he died.
Then Hector, in return, his radiant spear
Hurl'd at Automedon, who of its flight
Forewarn'd, his body bowing prone, the stroke
Eluded, and the spear piercing the soil                      635
Behind him, shook to its superior end,
Till, spent by slow degrees, its fury slept.
And now, with hand to hilt, for closer war
Both stood prepared, when through the multitude
Advancing at their fellow-warrior's call,                    640
The Ajaces suddenly their combat fierce
Prevented.   Awed at once by their approach
Hector retired, with whom Æneas went
Also and godlike Chromius, leaving there
Aretus with his vitals torn, whose arms,                     645
Fierce as the God of war Automedon
Stripp'd off, and thus exulted o'er the slain.
    My soul some portion of her grief resigns
Consoled, although by slaughter of a worse,
For loss of valiant Menœtiades.                              650
    So saying, within his chariot he disposed
The gory spoils, then mounted it himself
With hands and feet purpled, as from a bull
His bloody prey, some lion newly-gorged.
    And now around Patroclus raged again                     655
Dread strife deplorable ; for from the skies
Descending at the Thunderer's command
Whose purpose now was to assist the Greeks,
Pallas enhanced the fury of the fight.
As when from heaven, in view of mortals, Jove                660
Exhibits bright his bow, a sign ordain'd
Of war, or numbing frost which all the works
Suspends of man and saddens all the flocks ;
So she, all mantled with a radiant cloud
Entering Achaia's host, fired every breast.                  665
But meeting Menelaus first, brave son
Of Atreus, in the form and with the voice

Robust of Phœnix, him she thus bespake.
    Shame, Menelaus, shall to thee redound
For ever, and reproach, should dogs devour          670
The faithful friend of Peleus' noble son
Under Troy's battlements; but stand, thyself,
Undaunted, and encourage all the host.
    To whom the son of Atreus bold in arms.
Ah, Phœnix, friend revered, ancient and sage!       675
Would Pallas give me might and from the dint
Shield me of dart and spear, with willing mind
I would defend Patroclus, for his death
Hath touch'd me deep.   But Hector with the rage
Burns of consuming fire, nor to his spear           680
Gives pause, for him Jove leads to victory.
    He ceased, whom Pallas, Goddess azure-eyed
Hearing, rejoiced that of the heavenly powers
He had invoked *her* foremost to his aid.
His shoulders with new might, and limbs she fill'd,  685
And persevering boldness to his breast
Imparted, such as prompts the fly, which oft
From flesh of man repulsed, her purpose yet
To bite holds fast, resolved on human blood.
His stormy bosom with such courage fill'd           690
By Pallas, to Patroclus he approach'd
And hurl'd, incontinent, his glittering spear.
There was a Trojan Chief, Podes by name,
Son of Eëtion, valorous and rich;
Of all Troy's citizens him Hector most              695
Respected, in convivial pleasures sweet
His chosen companion.   As he sprang to flight,
The hero of the golden locks his belt
Struck with full force and sent the weapon through.
Sounding he fell, and from the Trojan ranks         700
Atrides dragg'd the body to his own.
Then drew Apollo near to Hector's side,
And in the form of Phœnops, Asius' son,
Of all the foreign guests at Hector's board
His favourite most, the hero thus address'd.        705
    What Chief of all  the Grecians shall henceforth
Fear Hector, who from Menelaus shrinks
Once deem'd effeminate, but dragging now

The body of thy valiant friend approved
Whom he hath slain, Podes, Eëtion's son ?                710
   He spake, and at his words grief like a cloud
Involved the mind of Hector dark around ;
Right through the foremost combatants he rush'd
All clad in dazzling brass.   Then, lifting high
His tassel'd ægis radiant, Jove with storms               715
Enveloped Ida ; flash'd his lightnings, roar'd
His thunders, and the mountain shook throughout.
Troy's host he prosper'd, and the Greeks dispersed.
   First fled Peneleus, the Bœotian Chief,
Whom facing firm the foe Polydamas                       720
Struck on his shoulder's summit with a lance
Hurl'd nigh at hand, which slight inscribed the bone.
⁶Leïtus also, son of the renown'd
Alectryon, pierced by Hector in the wrist,
Disabled left the fight ; trembling he fled               725
And peering narrowly around, nor hoped
To lift a spear against the Trojans more.
Hector, pursuing Leïtus, the point
Encounter'd of the brave Idomeneus
Full on his chest ; but in his mail the lance             73.
Snapp'd, and the Trojans shouted to the skies.
He, in his turn, cast at Deucalion's son
Idomeneus, who in that moment gain'd⁷
A chariot-seat ; but him the erring spear
Attain'd not, piercing Cœranus instead                    735
The friend and follower of Meriones
From wealthy Lyctus, and his charioteer.
For when he left, that day, the gallant barks
Idomeneus had sought the field on foot,
And triumph proud, full sure, to Ilium's host             74.
Had yielded now, but that with rapid haste

---

⁶ Leïtus was another Chief of the Bœotians.
⁷ Δίφρῳ ἐφεςαόρος.—Yet we learn soon after that he fought on foot.
But the Scholiast explains the expression thus—νεωςι τῳ διφωῳ ἐπιβαρ-
τος.   The fact was that Idomeneus had left the camp on foot, and was
on foot when Hector prepared to throw at him.   But Cœranus, charioteer
of Meriones, observing his danger, drove instantly to his aid.   Idomeneus
had just time to mount, and the spear designed for him, struck Cœranus.
—For a right understanding of this very intricate and difficult passage, I
am altogether indebted to the Scholiast as quoted by Villoisson.

Cœranus drove to his relief, from him
The fate averting which himself incurr'd
Victim of Hector's homicidal arm.
Him Hector smiting between ear and jaw,           745
Push'd from their sockets with the lance's point
His firm-set teeth, and sever'd sheer his tongue.
Dismounted down he fell, and from his hand
Let slide the flowing reins, which, to the earth
Stooping, Meriones in haste resumed,              750
And briefly thus Idomeneus address'd.
    Now drive, and cease not, to the fleet of Greece !
Thyself see'st victory no longer ours.
    He said ; Idomeneus whom, now, dismay
Seized also, with his lash plying severe          755
The coursers ample-maned, flew to the fleet.
Nor Ajax, dauntless hero, not perceived,
Nor Menelaus, by the sway of Jove
The victory inclining fast to Troy,
And thus the Telamonian Chief began.              760
    Ah ! who can be so blind as not to see
The eternal Father, now, with his own hand
Awarding glory to the Trojan host,
Whose every spear flies, instant, to the mark
Sent forth by brave or base? Jove guides them all ;  765
While, ineffectual, ours fall to the ground.
But haste, devise we of ourselves the means
How likeliest we may bear Patroclus hence,
And gladden, safe returning, all our friends,
Who, hither looking anxious, hope have none       770
That we shall longer check the unconquer'd force
Of hero-slaughtering Hector, but expect
⁸To see him soon amid the fleet of Greece.
Oh for some Grecian now to carry swift
The tidings to Achilles' ear, untaught,           775
As I conjecture, yet, the doleful news
Of his Patroclus slain ! but no such Greek
May I discern, such universal gloom

⁸ The Translator here follows the interpretation preferred by the
Scholiast. The original expression is ambiguous, and may signify, either,
that *we shall perish in the fleet ourselves*, or that Hector will soon be in
the midst of it. Vide Villoisson *in loco*.

Both men and steeds envelops all around.
Father of heaven and earth! deliver thou                          780
Achaia's host from darkness; clear the skies;
Give day; and (since thy sovereign will is such)
Destruction with it—but oh give us day!
   He spake, whose tears Jove saw with pity moved,
And chased the untimely shades; bright beam'd the sun            785
And the whole battle was display'd.  Then spake
The hero thus to Atreus' mighty son.
   Now noble Menelaus! looking forth,
See if Antilochus be yet alive,
Brave son of Nestor, whom exhort to fly                          790
With tidings to Achilles, of the friend
Whom most he loved, of his Patroclus slain.
   He ceased, nor Menelaus, dauntless Chief,
That task refused, but went; yet neither swift
Nor willing.   As a lion leaves the stalls                      795
Wearied himself with harassing the guard,
Who, interdicting him his purposed prey,
Watch all the night; he famish'd, yet again
Comes furious on, but speeds not, kept aloof
By spears from daring hands dismiss'd, but more                 800
By flash of torches which, though fierce, he dreads,
Till at the dawn, sullen he stalks away;
So from Patroclus Menelaus went
Heroic Chief! reluctant; for he fear'd
Lest the Achaians should resign the dead,                       805
Through consternation, to the host of Troy.
Departing, therefore, he admonish'd oft
Meriones and the Ajaces, thus.
   Ye two brave leaders of the Argive host,
And thou, Meriones! now recollect                               810
The gentle manners of Patroclus fallen
Hapless in battle, who by carriage mild
Well understood, while yet he lived, to engage
All hearts, though prisoner now of death and fate.
   So saying, the Hero amber-hair'd his steps                   815
Turn'd thence, the field exploring with an eye
Sharp as the eagle's, of all fowls beneath
The azure heavens for keenest sight renown'd,
Whom, though he soar sublime, the leveret

By broadest leaves conceal'd 'scapes not, but swift          820
Descending, even her he makes his prey;
So, noble Menelaus! were thine eyes
Turn'd into every quarter of the host
In search of Nestor's son, if still he lived.
Him, soon, encouraging his band to fight,          825
He noticed on the left of all the field,
And sudden standing at his side, began.
     Antilochus! oh hear me, noble friend!
And thou shalt learn tidings of such a deed
As best had never been.   Thou know'st, I judge,          830
And hast already seen, how Jove exalts
To victory the Trojan host, and rolls
Distress on ours; but ah! Patroclus lies,
Our chief Achaian, slain, whose loss the Greeks
Fills with regret.   Haste, therefore, to the fleet,          835
Inform Achilles; bid him haste to save,
If save he can, the body of his friend;
He can no more, for Hector hath his arms.
     He ceased.   Antilochus with horror heard
Those tidings; mute long time he stood, his eyes          840
Swam tearful, and his voice, sonorous erst,
Found utterance none.   Yet even so distress'd,
He not the more neglected the command
Of Menelaus.   Setting forth to run,
He gave his armour to his noble friend          845
Laodocus, who thither turn'd his steeds,
And, weeping as he went, on rapid feet
Sped to Achilles with that tale of woe.
     Nor could the noble Menelaus stay
To give the weary Pylian band, bereft          850
Of their beloved Antilochus, his aid,
But leaving them to Thrasymedes' care,
He flew to Menœtiades again,
And the Ajaces, thus, instant bespake.
     He goes.   I have dispatch'd him to the fleet          855
To seek Achilles; but his coming nought
Expect I now, although with rage he burn
Against illustrious Hector; for what fight
Can he, unarm'd, against the Trojans wage?
Deliberating, therefore, frame we means          860

s. c.—7.                                  A A

How best to save Patroclus, and to 'scape
Ourselves unslain from this disastrous field.
   Whom answer'd the vast son of Telamon.
Most noble Menelaus! good is all
Which thou hast spoken.  Lift ye from the earth    865
Thou and Meriones, at once, and bear
The dead Patroclus from the bloody field.
To cope meantime with Hector and his host
Shall be our task, who, one in name, nor less
In spirit one, already have the brunt    870
. Of much sharp conflict, side by side, sustain'd.
   He ended; they enfolding in their arms
The dead, upbore him high above the ground
With force united; after whom the host
Of Troy, seeing the body borne away,    875
Shouted, and with impetuous onset all
Follow'd them.  As the hounds, urged from behind
By youthful hunters, on the wounded boar
Make fierce assault; awhile at utmost speed
They stretch toward him, hungering for the prey,    880
But oft as, turning sudden, the stout brawn
Faces them, scatter'd on all sides escape;
The Trojans so, thick thronging in the rear,
Ceaseless with faulchions and spears double-edged
Annoy'd them sore, but oft as in retreat    885
The dauntless Heroes, the Ajaces turn'd
To face them, deadly wan grew every cheek,
And not a Trojan dared with onset rude
Molest them more in conflict for the dead.
   Thus they, laborious, forth from battle bore    890
Patroclus to the fleet, tempestuous war
Their steps attending, rapid as the flames
Which, kindled suddenly, some city waste;
Consumed amid the blaze house after house
Sinks, and the wind, meantime, roars through the fire;    895
So them a deafening tumult as they went
Pursued, of horses and of men spear-arm'd.
And as two mules with strength for toil endued,
Draw through rough ways down from the distant hills
Huge timber, beam or mast; sweating they go,    900
And overlabour'd to faint weariness;

So they the body bore, while, turning oft,
The Ajaces check'd the Trojans.   As a mound
Planted with trees and stretch'd athwart the mead
Repels an overflow; the torrents loud          905
Baffling, it sends them far away to float
The level land, nor can they with the force
Of all their waters burst a passage through;
So the Ajaces, constant, in the rear
Repress'd the Trojans; but the Trojans them          910
Attended still, of whom Æneas most
Troubled them, and the glorious Chief of Troy.
They as a cloud of starlings or of daws
Fly screaming shrill, warn'd timely of the kite
Or hawk, devourers of the smaller kinds,          915
So they shrill-clamouring toward the fleet,
Hasted before Æneas and the might
Of Hector, nor the battle heeded more.
Much radiant armour round about the foss
Fell of the flying  Grecians, or within          920
Lay scatter'd, and no pause of war they found.

# BOOK XVIII.

## ARGUMENT.

Achilles, by command of Juno, shows himself to the Trojans, who fly at
his appearance ; Vulcan, at the instance of Thetis, forges for him a suit
of armour.

THUS burn'd the battle like devouring fire.
Meantime, Antilochus with rapid steps
Came to Achilles.   Him he found before
His lofty barks, occupied, as he stood,
With boding fears of all that had befall'n.                     5
He groan'd, and to his noble self he said,
   Ah ! woe is me—why falls Achaia's host,
With such disorder foul, back on the fleet ?
I tremble lest the Gods my anxious thoughts
Accomplish and my mother's words, who erst              10
Hath warn'd me, that the bravest and the best
Of all my Myrmidons, while yet I live,
Slain under Troy, must view the sun no more.
Brave Menœtiades is, doubtless, slain.
Unhappy friend ! I bade thee oft, our barks              15
Deliver'd once from hostile fires, not seek
To cope in arms with Hector, but return.
   While musing thus he stood, the son approach'd
Of noble Nestor, and with tears his cheeks
Bedewing copious, his sad message told.                   20
   Oh son of warlike Peleus! thou shalt hear
Tidings of deeds which best had never been.
Patroclus is no more.   The Grecians fight
For his bare corse, and Hector hath his arms.
   Then clouds of sorrow fell on Peleus' son,        25
And, grasping with both hands the ashes, down
He pour'd them on his head, his graceful brows
Dishonouring, and thick the sooty shower
Descending settled on his fragrant vest.

Then, stretch'd in ashes, at the vast extent              30
Of his whole length he lay, disordering wild
With his own hands, and rending off his hair.
The maidens, captived by himself in war
And by Patroclus, shrieking from the tent
Ran forth, and hemm'd the glorious Chief around.          35
All smote their bosoms, and all, fainting, fell.
On the other side, Antilochus the hands
Held of Achilles, mourning and deep groans
Uttering from his noble heart, through fear
Lest Peleus' son should perish self-destroy'd.            40
Loud groan'd the Hero, whose loud groans within
The gulfs of ocean, where she sat beside
Her ancient Sire, his Goddess-mother heard,
And hearing shriek'd; around, her at the voice
Assembled all the Nereids of the Deep.                    45
Cymodoce, Thalia, Glauca came,
Nisæa, Spio, Thoa, and with eyes
Protuberant beauteous Halia; came with these
Cymothöe, and Actæ, and the nymph
Of marshes, Limnorea, nor delay'd                         50
Agave, nor Amphithöe the swift,
Iæra, Doto, Melita, nor thence
Was absent Proto or Dynamene,
Callianira, Doris, Panope,
Pherusa or Amphinome, or fair                             55
Dexamene, or Galatea praised
For matchless form divine; Nemertes pure
Came also, with Apseudes chrystal-bright,
Callianassa, Mæra, Clymene,
Janeira and Janassa, sister pair,                         60
And Orithya, and with azure locks
Luxuriant, Amathea; nor alone
Came these, but every ocean-nymph beside.
The silver cave was fill'd; each smote her breast,
And Thetis, loud lamenting, thus began.                   65
    Ye sister Nereids, hear! that ye may all
From my own lips my boundless sorrow learn.
Ah me forlorn! ah me, parent in vain
Of an illustrious birth! who, having borne
A noble son magnanimous, the chief                        70

Of Heroes, saw him like a thriving plant
Shoot vigorous under my maternal care,
And sent him early in his gallant fleet
Embark'd, to combat with the sons of Troy.
But him from fight return'd I shall receive          75
Beneath the roof of Peleus, never more;
And while he lives, and on the sun his eyes
Opens, he mourns, nor, going, can I aught
Assist him; yet I go, that I may see
My darling son, and from his lips be taught          80
What grief hath now befallen him, who close
Abiding in his tent shares not the war.
   So saying she left the cave, whom all her nymphs
Attended weeping, and where'er they pass'd
The breaking billows open'd wide a way.              85
At fruitful Troy arrived, in order fair
They climb'd the beach, where by his numerous barks
Encompass'd, swift Achilles sighing lay.
Then, drawing nigh to her afflicted son,
The Goddess-mother press'd between her palms  ·      90
His temples, and in accents wing'd enquired.
   Why weeps my son? what sorrow wrings thy soul?
Speak, hide it not.   Jove hath fulfill'd the prayer
Which erst with lifted hands thou didst prefer,
That all Achaia's host, wanting thy aid,             95
Might be compell'd into the fleet, and foul
Disgrace incur, there prison'd for thy sake.
   To whom Achilles, groaning deep, replied.
My mother! it is true; Olympian Jove
That prayer fulfils; but thence, what joy to me,    100
Patroclus slain? the friend of all my friends
Whom most I loved, dear to me as my life—
Him I have lost.   Slain and despoil'd he lies
By Hector of his glorious armour bright
The wonder of all eyes, a matchless gift            105
Given by the Gods to Peleus on that day
When thee they doom'd into a mortal's arms.
Oh that with these thy deathless ocean-nymphs
Dwelling content, thou hadst my father left
To espouse a mortal bride, so hadst thou 'scaped    110
Pangs numberless which thou must now endure

For thy son's death, whom thou shalt never meet
From Troy return'd, in Peleus' mansion more!
For life I covet not, nor longer wish
To mix with human kind, unless my spear                    115
May find out Hector, and atonement take
By slaying Him, for my Patroclus slain.
   To whom, with streaming tears, Thetis replied.
Swift comes thy destiny as thou hast said,
For after Hector's death thine next ensues.                120
   Then answer, thus, indignant he return'd.
Death seize me now! since when my friend was slain,
My doom was, not to succour him.   He died
From home remote, and wanting me to save him.
Now, therefore, since I neither visit more                 125
My native land, nor, present here, have aught
Avail'd Patroclus or my many friends
Whom noble Hector hath in battle slain,
But here I sit unprofitable grown,
Earth's burden, though of such heroic note,                130
If not in council foremost (for I yield
That prize to others) yet in feats of arms,
Such as none other in Achaia's host,
May fierce contention from among the Gods
Perish, and from among the human race,                     135
With wrath, which sets the wisest hearts on fire;
Sweeter than dropping honey to the taste,
But in the bosom of mankind, a smoke!
Such was my wrath which Agamemnon roused,
The king of men.   But since the past is fled              140
Irrevocable, howsoe'er distress'd,
Renounce we now vain musings on the past,
Content through sad necessity.   I go
In quest of noble Hector, who hath slain
My loved Patroclus, and such death will take,              145
As Jove ordains me and the Powers of Heaven
At their own season, send it when they may.
For neither might the force of Hercules,
Although high-favour'd of Saturnian Jove,
From death escape, but Fate and the revenge                150
Restless of Juno vanquish'd even Him.
I also, if a destiny like his

Await me, shall, like him, find rest in death ;
But glory calls me now ; now will I make
Some Trojan wife or Dardan with both hands　　155
Wipe her soft cheeks, and utter many a groan.
Long time have I been absent from the field,
And they shall know it.　Love me as thou may'st,
Yet thwart me not, for I am fixt to go.
　　Whom Thetis answer'd, Goddess of the Deep.　　160
Thou hast well said, my son ! it is no blame
To save from threaten'd death our suffering friends.
But thy magnificent and dazzling arms
Are now in Trojan hands ; them Hector wears
Exulting, but ordain'd not long to exult,　　165
So habited ; his death is also nigh.
But thou with yonder warring multitudes
Mix not, till thou behold me here again ;
For with the rising sun I will return
To-morrow, and will bring thee glorious arms,　　170
By Vulcan forged himself, the king of fire.
　　She said, and turning from her son aside,
The sisterhood of Ocean thus address'd.
　　Plunge ye again into the briny Deep,
And to the hoary Sovereign of the floods　　175
Report as ye have heard.　I to the heights
Olympian haste, that I may there obtain
From Vulcan, glorious artist of the skies,
Arms of excelling beauty for my son.
　　She said ; they plunged into the waves again,　　180
And silver-footed Thetis, to the heights
Olympian soaring swiftly to obtain
Arms for renown'd Achilles, disappear'd.
Meantime, with infinite uproar the Greeks
From Hector's hero-slaying arm had fled　　185
Home to their galleys station'd on the banks
Of Hellespont.　Nor yet Achaia's sons
Had borne the body of Patroclus clear
From flight of darts away, but still again
The multitude of warriors and of steeds　　190
Came on, by Priameian Hector led
Rapid as fire.　Thrice, noble Hector seized
His ancles from behind, ardent to drag

She said; they plung'd into the waves again,
And silver footed Thetis, to the heights
Olympian soaring swiftly, to obtain
Arms for renown'd Achilles, disappear'd.

Patroclus, calling to his host the while ;
But thrice, the two Ajaces, clothed with might,          195
Shock'd and repulsed him reeling.   He with force
Fill'd indefatigable, through his ranks
Issuing, by turns assail'd them, and by turns
Stood clamouring, yet not a step retired :
But as the hinds deter not from his prey          200
A tawny lion by keen hunger urged,
So could not both Ajaces, warriors bold,
Intimidate and from the body drive
Hector ; and he had dragg'd him thence and won
Immortal glory, but that Iris, sent          205
Unseen by Jove and by the Powers of heaven,
From Juno, to Achilles brought command
That he should show himself.  Full near she drew,
And in wing'd accents thus the Chief address'd.
    Hero ! most terrible of men, arise !          210
Protect Patroclus, for whose sake the war
Stands at the fleet of Greece.   Mutual prevails
The slaughter, these the dead defending, those
Resolute hence to drag him to the gates
Of wind-swept Ilium.   But beyond them all          215
Illustrious Hector obstinate is bent
To win him, purposing to lop his head,
And to exhibit it impaled on high.
Thou then arise, nor longer on the ground
Lie stretch'd inactive ; let the thought with shame          220
Touch thee, of thy Patroclus made the sport
Of Trojan dogs, whose corse, if it return
Dishonour'd home, brings with it thy reproach.
    To whom Achilles, matchless in the race.
Iris divine ! of all the Gods who sent thee ?          225
    Then, thus, the swift ambassadress of heaven.
By Juno sent I come, consort of Jove.
Nor knows Saturnian Jove high-throned, himself,
My flight, or any of the Immortal Powers,
Tenants of the Olympian heights snow-crown'd.          230
    Her answer'd then Pelides, glorious Chief.
How shall I seek the fight ? they have my arms.
My mother charged me also to abstain
From battle, till she bring me armour new

Which she hath promised me from Vulcan's hand.　　235
Meantime, whose armour else might serve my need
I know not, save perhaps alone the shield
Of Telamonian Ajax, whom I deem
Himself now busied in the stormy van,
Slaying the Trojans in my friend's defence.　　240
　　To whom the swift-wing'd messenger of heaven.
Full well we know thine armour Hector's prize.
Yet, issuing to the margin of the foss,
Show thyself only.　Panic-seized, perchance,
The Trojans shall from fight desist, and yield　　245
To the o'ertoil'd though dauntless sons of Greece
Short respite ; it is all that war allows.
　　So saying, the storm-wing'd Iris disappear'd.
Then rose at once Achilles dear to Jove,
Athwart whose shoulders broad Minerva cast　　250
Her Ægis fringed terrific, and his brows
Encircled with a golden cloud that shot
Fires insupportable to sight abroad.
As when some island, situate afar
On the wide waves, invested all the day　　255
By cruel foes from their own city pour'd,
Upsends a smoke to heaven, and torches shows
On all her turrets at the close of eve
Which flash against the clouds, kindled in hope
Of aid from neighbour maritime allies,　　260
So from Achilles' head light flash'd to heaven.
Issuing through the wall, beside the foss
He stood, but mix'd not with Achaia's host,
Obedient to his mother's wise command.
He stood and shouted ; Pallas also raised　　265
A dreadful shout, and tumult infinite
Excited throughout all the host of Troy.
Clear as the trumpet's note when it proclaims
A numerous host approaching to invest
Some city close around, so clear the voice　　270
Rang of Æacides, and tumult-toss'd
Was every soul that heard the brazen tone.
With swift recoil the long-maned coursers thrust
The chariots back, all boding woe at hand,
And every charioteer astonish'd saw　　275

Fires, that fail'd not, illumining the brows
Of Peleus' son, by Pallas kindled there.
Thrice, o'er the trench Achilles sent his voice
Sonorous, and confusion at the sound
Thrice seized the Trojans, and their famed allies.          280
Twelve, in that moment of their noblest died
By their own spears and chariots, and with joy
The Grecians from beneath an hill of darts
Dragging Patroclus, placed him on his bier.
Around him throng'd his fellow-warriors bold,              285
All weeping, after whom Achilles went
Fast-weeping also at the doleful sight
Of his true friend on his funereal bed
Extended, gash'd with many a mortal wound,
Whom he had sent into the fight with steeds                290
And chariot, but received him thence no more.
    And now majestic Juno sent the sun,
Unwearied minister of light, although
Reluctant, down into the Ocean stream.
So the sun sank, and the Achaians ceased                   295
From the all-wasting labours of the war.
On the other side, the Trojans, from the fight
Retiring, loosed their steeds, but ere they took
Thought of refreshment, in full council met.
It was a council at which no man sat,                      300
Or dared ; all stood ; such terror had on all
Fallen, for that Achilles had appear'd,
After long pause from battle's arduous toil.
First rose Polydamas the prudent son
Of Panthus, above all the Trojans skill'd                  305
Both in futurity and in the past.
He was the friend of Hector, and one night
Gave birth to both.   In council one excell'd,
And one still more in feats of high renown.
Thus then, admonishing them, he began.                     310
    My friends ! weigh well the occasion.   Back to Troy
By my advice, nor wait the sacred morn
Here, on the plain, from Ilium's walls remote.
So long as yet the anger of this Chief
'Gainst noble Agamemnon burn'd, so long                    315
We found the Greeks less formidable foes,

And I rejoiced, myself, spending the night
Beside their oary barks, for that I hoped
To seize them; but I now tremble at thought
Of Peleus' rapid son again in arms.                        320
A spirit proud as his will scorn to fight
Here, on the plain, where Greeks and Trojans take
Their common share of danger and of toil,
And will at once strike at your citadel,
Impatient till he make your wives his prey.                325
Haste—let us home—else thus shall it befall;
Night's balmy influence in his tent detains
Achilles now, but rushing arm'd abroad
To-morrow, should he find us lingering here,
None shall mistake him then; happy the man                330
Who soonest, then, shall scape to sacred Troy!
Then, dogs shall make and vultures on our flesh
Plenteous repast.   Oh spare mine ears the tale!
But if, though troubled, ye can yet receive
My counsel, thus assembled we will keep                   335
Strict guard to-night; meantime, her gates and towers
With all their mass of solid timbers, smooth
And cramp'd with bolts of steel, will keep the town.
But early on the morrow we will stand
All arm'd on Ilium's towers. Then, if he choose,          340
His galleys left, to compass Troy about,
He shall be task'd enough; his lofty steeds
Shall have their fill of coursing to and fro
Beneath, and gladly shall to camp return.
But waste the town he shall not, nor attempt              345
With all the utmost valour that he boasts
To force a pass; dogs shall devour him first.
   To whom brave Hector louring, and in wrath.
Polydamas, I like not thy advice
Who bidd'st us in our city skulk, again                   350
Imprison'd there.   Are ye not yet content?
Wish ye for durance still in your own towers?
Time was, when in all regions under heaven
Men praised the wealth of Priam's city stored
With gold and brass; but all our houses now              355
Stand emptied of their hidden treasures rare.
Jove in his wrath hath scatter'd them; our wealth

Is marketted, and Phrygia hath a part
Purchased, and part Mæonia's lovely land.
But since the son of wily Saturn old                    360
Hath given me glory now, and to enclose
The Grecians in their fleet hemm'd by the sea,
Fool! taint not with such talk the public mind.
For not a Trojan here will thy advice
Follow, or shall; it hath not my consent.              365
But thus I counsel.   Let us, band by band,
Throughout the host take supper, and let each,
Guarded against nocturnal danger, watch.
And if a Trojan here be rack'd in mind
Lest his possessions perish, let him cast              370
His golden heaps into the public maw,[1]
Far better so consumed than by the Greeks.
Then, with the morrow's dawn, all fair array'd
In battle, we will give them at their fleet
Sharp onset, and if Peleus' noble son                 375
Have risen indeed to conflict for the ships,
The worse for him.   I shall not for his sake
Avoid the deep-toned battle, but will firm
Oppose his utmost.   Either he shall gain
Or I, great glory.   Mars his favours deals           380
Impartial, and the slayer oft is slain.
    So counsell'd Hector, whom with shouts of praise
The Trojans answer'd :—fools, and by the power
Of Pallas of all sober thought bereft!
For all applauded Hector, who had given               385
Advice pernicious, and Polydamas,
Whose counsel was discreet and wholesome, none.
So then they took repast.   But all night long
The Grecians o'er Patroclus wept aloud,
While, standing in the midst, Pelides led             390
The lamentation, heaving many a groan,
And on the bosom of his breathless friend
Imposing, sad, his homicidal hands.
As the grim lion, from whose gloomy lair
Among thick trees the hunter hath his whelps          395
Purloin'd, too late returning mourns his loss,
Then, up and down, the length of many a vale

_____
[1] Καταδημοβορῆσαι.

Courses, exploring fierce the robber's foot,
Incensed as he, and with a sigh deep-drawn
Thus to his Myrmidons Achilles spake.                        400
   How vain, alas! my word spoken that day
At random, when to soothe the Hero's fears
Menœtius, then our guest, I promised him
His noble son at Opoeis again,
Living and laden with the spoils of Troy!                    405
But Jove performs not all the thoughts of man,
For we were both destined to tinge the soil
Of Ilium with our blood, nor I shall see,
Myself, my father in his mansion more
Or Thetis, but must find·my burial here.                     410
Yet, my Patroclus! since the earth expects.
Me next, I will not thy funereal rights
Finish, till I shall bring both head and arms
Of that bold Chief who slew thee, to my tent.
I also will smite off, before thy pile,                      415
The heads of twelve illustrious sons of Troy,
Resentful of thy death.   Meantime, among
My lofty galleys thou shalt lie, with tears
Mourn'd day and night by Trojan captives fair
And Dardan compassing thy bier around,                       420
Whom we, at price of labour hard, ourselves
With massy spears toiling in battle took
From many an opulent city, now no more.
   So saying, he bade his train surround with fire
A tripod huge, that they might quickly cleanse              425
Patroclus from all stain of clotted gore.
They on the blazing hearth a tripod placed
Capacious, fill'd with water its wide womb,
And thrust dry wood beneath, till, fierce, the flames
Embraced it round, and warm'd the flood within.            430
Soon as the water in the singing brass
Simmer'd, they bathed him, and with limpid oil
Anointed; filling, next, his ruddy wounds
With unguent mellow'd by nine circling years,
They stretch'd him on his bed, then cover'd him             435
From head to feet with linen texture light,
And with a wide unsullied mantle, last.
All night the Myrmidons around the swift

Achilles stood, deploring loud his friend,
And Jove his spouse and sister thus bespake.　　　440
　　So then, Imperial Juno! not in vain
Thou hast the swift Achilles sought to rouse
Again to battle; the Achaians, sure,
Are thy own children, thou hast borne them all.
　　To whom the aweful Goddess ample-eyed.　　　445
What word hath pass'd thy lips, Jove, most severe?
A man, though mortal merely, and to me
Inferior in device, might have achieved
That labour easily.　Can I who boast
Myself the Chief of Goddesses, and such　　　450
Not by birth only, but as thine espoused,
Who art thyself Sovereign of all the Gods,
Can I with anger burn against the house
Of Priam, and want means of just revenge?
　　Thus they in heaven their mutual conference held.　　455
Meantime, the silver-footed Thetis reach'd
The starr'd abode eternal, brazen-wall'd
Of Vulcan, by the builder lame himself
Uprear'd, a wonder even in eyes divine.
She found him sweating, at his bellows huge　　　460
Toiling industrious; tripods bright he form'd
Twenty at once, his palace-wall to grace
Ranged in harmonious order.　Under each
Two golden wheels he set, on which (a sight
Marvellous!) into council they should roll　　　465
Self-moved, and to his house, self-moved, return.
Thus far the work was finish'd, but not yet
Their ears of exquisite design affixt,
For them he stood fashioning, and prepared
The rivets.　While he thus his matchless skill　　　470
Employ'd laborious, to his palace-gate
The silver-footed Thetis now advanced,
Whom Charis, Vulcan's well-attired spouse,
Beholding from the palace portal, flew
To seize the Goddess' hand, and thus enquired.　　　475
　　Why, Thetis! worthy of all reverence
And of all love, comest thou to our abode,
Unfrequent here? But enter, and accept
Such welcome as to such a guest is due.

So saying, she introduced and to a seat                                    480
Led her with argent studs border'd around
And foot-stool'd sumptuously; then, calling forth
Her spouse, the glorious artist, thus she said.
    Haste, Vulcan! Thetis wants thee; linger not.
To whom the artist of the skies replied.                                   485
    A Goddess then, whom with much cause I love
And venerate is here, who when I fell
Saved me, what time my shameless mother sought
To cast me, because lame, out of all sight;
Then had I been indeed forlorn, had not                                    490
Eurynome the daughter of the Deep
And Thetis in their laps received me fallen.
Nine years with them residing, for their use
I form'd nice trinkets, clasps, rings, pipes, and chains,
While loud around our hollow cavern roar'd                                 495
The surge of the vast Deep, nor God nor man,
Save Thetis and Eurynome, my life's
Preservers, knew where I was kept conceal'd.
Since, therefore, she is come, I cannot less
Than recompense to Thetis amber-hair'd                                     500
With readiness the boon of life preserved.
Haste, then, and hospitably spread the board
For her regale, while with my best dispatch
I lay my bellows and my tools aside.
    He spake, and vast in bulk and hot with toil                          505
Rose limping from beside his anvil-stock
Upborne with pain on legs tortuous and weak.
First, from the forge dislodged he thrust apart
His bellows, and his tools collecting all
Bestow'd them, careful, in a silver chest,                                 510
Then all around with a wet sponge he wiped
His visage, and his arms and brawny neck
Purified, and his shaggy breast from smutch;
Last, putting on his vest, he took in hand
His sturdy staff, and shuffled through the door.                           515
Beside the King of fire two golden forms
Majestic moved, that served him in the place
Of handmaids; young they seem'd, and seem'd alive,
Nor want they intellect, or speech, or force,
Or prompt dexterity by the Gods inspired.                                  520

These his supporters were, and at his side
Attended diligent, while He, with gait
Uncouth, approaching Thetis where she sat
On a bright throne, seized fast her hand and said.

　　Why, Thetis! worthy as thou art of love　　　　525
And of all reverence, hast thou arrived,
Unfrequent here? Speak—tell me thy desire,
Nor doubt my services, if thou demand
Things possible, and possible to me.

　　Then Thetis, weeping plenteously, replied.　　　　530
Oh Vulcan! Is there on Olympus' heights
A Goddess with such load of sorrow oppress'd
As, in peculiar, Jove assigns to me?
Me only, of all ocean-nymphs, he made
Spouse to a man, Peleus Æacides,　　　　535
Whose bed, although reluctant and perforce,
I yet endured to share.　He now, the prey
Of cheerless age, decrepid lies, and Jove
Still other woes heaps on my wretched head.
He gave me to bring forth, gave me to rear　　　　540
A son illustrious, valiant, and the chief
Of heroes; he, like a luxuriant plant
Upran[2] to manhood, while his lusty growth
I nourish'd as the husbandman his vine
Set in a fruitful field, and being grown　　　　545
I sent him early in his gallant fleet
Embark'd, to combat with the sons of Troy;
But him from fight return'd I shall receive,
Beneath the roof of Peleus, never more,
And while he lives and on the sun his eyes　　　　550
Opens, affliction is his certain doom,
Nor aid resides or remedy in me.
The virgin, his own portion of the spoils,
Allotted to him by the Grecians—Her
Atrides, King of Men, resumed, and grief　　　　555
Devour'd Achilles' spirit for her sake.
Meantime, the Trojans shutting close within
Their camp the Grecians, have forbidden them
All egress, and the senators of Greece
Have sought with splendid gifts to soothe my son.　　　　560

　　　　　　　　[2] 'Ανέδραμε.

s. c.—7.　　　　　　　　　　　　　　B B

He, indisposed to rescue them himself
From ruin, sent, instead, Patroclus forth
Clad in his own resplendent armour, Chief
Of the whole host of Myrmidons.   Before
The Scæan gate from morn to eve they fought,          565
And on that self-same day had Ilium fallen,
But that Apollo, to advance the fame
Of Hector, slew Menœtius' noble son
Full-flush'd with victory.   Therefore at thy knees
Suppliant I fall, imploring from thine art          570
A shield and helmet, greaves of shapely form
With clasps secured, and corslet for my son.
For those, once his, his faithful friend hath lost,
Slain by the Trojans, and Achilles lies,
Himself, extended mournful on the ground.          575
   Her answer'd then the artist of the skies.
Courage ! Perplex not with these cares thy soul.
I would that when his fatal hour shall come,
I could as sure secrete him from the stroke
Of destiny, as he shall soon have arms          580
Illustrious, such as each particular man
Of thousands, seeing them, shall wish his own.
   He said, and to his bellows quick repair'd,
Which turning to the fire he bade them heave.
Full twenty bellows working all at once          585
Breathed on the furnace, blowing easy and free
The managed winds, now forcible, as best
Suited dispatch, now gentle, if the will
Of Vulcan and his labour so required.
Impenetrable brass, tin, silver, gold,          590
He cast into the forge, then, settling firm
His ponderous anvil on the block, one hand
With his huge hammer fill'd, one with the tongs.
   He fashion'd first a shield massy and broad
Of labour exquisite, for which he form'd          595
A triple border beauteous, dazzling bright,
And loop'd it with a silver brace behind.
The shield itself with five strong folds he forged,
And with devices multiform the disk
Capacious charged, toiling with skill divine..          600
   There he described the earth, the heaven, the sea,

The sun that rests not, and the moon full-orb'd.
There also, all the stars which round about
As with a radiant frontlet bind the skies,
The Pleiads and the Hyads, and the might                605
Of huge Orion, with Him Ursa call'd,
Known also by his popular name, the Wain,
That spins around the pole looking toward
Orion, only star of these denied
To slake his beams in Ocean's briny baths.              610
    Two splendid cities also there he form'd
Such as men build.   In one were to be seen
Rites matrimonial solemnized with pomp
Of sumptuous banquets; from their chambers forth
Leading the brides they usher'd them along             615
With torches through the streets, and sweet was heard
The voice around of Hymenæal song.
Here striplings danced in circles to the sound
Of pipe and harp, while in the portals stood
Women, admiring, all, the gallant show.                620
Elsewhere was to be seen in council met
The close-throng'd multitude.   There strife arose.
Two citizens contended for a mulct
The price of blood.   This man affirm'd the fine
All paid, haranguing vehement the crowd,               625
That man denied that he had aught received,
And to the judges each made his appeal
Eager for their reward.   Meantime the people,
As favour sway'd them, clamour'd loud for each.
The heralds quell'd the tumult; reverend sat           630
On polish'd stones the Elders in a ring,
Each with an herald's sceptre in his hand,
Which holding they arose, and all in turn
Gave sentence.   In the midst two talents lay
Of gold, his destined recompense whose voice           635
Decisive should pronounce the best award.
    The other city by two glittering hosts
Invested stood, and a dispute arose
Between the hosts, whether to burn the town
And lay all waste, or to divide the spoil.             640
Meantime, the citizens, still undismay'd,
Surrender'd not the town, but taking arms

B B 2

Secretly, set the ambush in array,
And on the walls their wives and children kept
Vigilant guard, with all the ancient men.          645
They sallied; at their head Pallas and Mars
Both golden and in golden vests attired
Advanced, proportion each showing divine,
Large, prominent, and such as Gods beseem'd.
Not such the people, but of humbler size.          650
Arriving at the spot for ambush chosen,
A river's side, where cattle of each kind
Drank, down they sat, all arm'd in dazzling brass.
Apart from all the rest sat also down
Two spies, both looking for the flocks and herds.   655
Soon they appear'd, and at their side were seen
Two shepherd swains, each playing on his pipe
Careless, and of the danger nought apprized.
Swift ran the spies, perceiving their approach,
And intercepting suddenly the herds               660
And flocks of silver fleece, slew also those
Who fed them.   The besiegers, at that time
In council, by the sound alarm'd, their steeds
Mounted, and hasted, instant, to the place;
Then, standing on the river's brink they fought    665
And push'd each other with the brazen lance.
There Discord raged, there Tumult, and the force
Of ruthless Destiny; she now a Chief
Seized newly wounded, and now captive held
Another yet unhurt, and now a third               670
Dragg'd breathless through the battle by his feet,
And all her garb was dappled thick with blood.
Like living men they traversed and they strove,
And dragg'd by turns the bodies of the slain.
    He also graved on it a fallow field           675
Rich, spacious, and well till'd.   Ploughers not few,
There driving to and fro their sturdy teams,
Labour'd the land; and oft as in their course
They came to the field's bourn, so oft a man
Met them, who in their hands a goblet placed       680
Charged with delicious wine.   They, turning, wrought
Each his own furrow, and impatient seem'd
To reach the border of the tilth, which black

Appear'd behind them as a glebe new-turn'd,
Though golden.   Sight to be admired by all!      685
   There too he form'd the likeness of a field
Crowded with corn, in which the reapers toil'd
Each with a sharp-tooth'd sickle in his hand.
Along the furrow here, the harvest fell
In frequent handfulls, there, they bound the sheaves.     690
Three binders of the sheaves their sultry task
All plied industrious, and behind them boys
Attended, filling with the corn their arms
And offering still their bundles to be bound.
Amid them, staff in hand, the master stood      695
Silent exulting, while beneath an oak
Apart, his heralds busily prepared
The banquet, dressing a well-thriven ox
New slain, and the attendant maidens mix'd
Large supper for the hinds of whitest flour.      700
   There also, laden with its fruit he form'd
A vineyard all of gold ; purple he made
The clusters, and the vines supported stood
By poles of silver set in even rows.
The trench he colour'd sable, and around      705
Fenced it with tin.   One only path it show'd
By which the gatherers when they stripp'd the vines
Pass'd and repass'd.   There, youths and maidens blithe
In frails of wicker bore the luscious fruit,
While in the midst, a boy on his shrill harp      710
Harmonious play'd, still as he struck the chord
Carolling to it with a slender voice.
They smote the ground together, and with song
And sprightly reed came dancing on behind.
   There too an herd he fashion'd of tall beeves      715
Part gold, part tin.   They, lowing, from the stalls
Rush'd forth to pasture by a river-side
Rapid, sonorous, fringed with whispering reeds.
Four golden herdsmen drove the kine a-field
By nine swift dogs attended.   Dreadful sprang      720
Two lions forth, and of the foremost herd
Seized fast a bull.   Him bellowing they dragg'd,
While dogs and peasants all flew to his aid.
The lions tore the hide of the huge prey

And lapped his entrails and his blood.  Meantime     725
The herdsmen, troubling them in vain, their hounds
Encouraged ; but no tooth for lions' flesh
Found they, and  therefore stood aside and bark'd.
   There also, the illustrious smith divine
Amidst a pleasant grove a pasture form'd     730
Spacious, and sprinkled o'er with silver sheep
Numerous, and stalls and huts and shepherds' tents.
   To these the glorious Artist added next,
With various skill delineated exact,
A labyrinth for the dance, such as of old     735
In Crete's broad island Dædalus composed
For bright-hair'd Ariadne.   There the youths
And youth-alluring maidens, hand in hand,
Danced jocund, every maiden, neat-attired
In finest linen, and the youths in vests     740
Well-woven, glossy as the glaze of oil.
These all wore garlands, and bright faulchions, those,
Of burnish'd gold in silver trappings hung :——
They with well-tutor'd step, now, nimbly ran
The circle, swift, as when, before his wheel     745
Seated, the potter twirls it with both hands
For trial of its speed, now crossing quick
They pass'd at once into each other's place.
On either side spectators numerous stood
Delighted, and two tumblers roll'd themselves     750
Between the dancers, singing as they roll'd.
   Last, with the might of Ocean's boundless flood
He fill'd the border of the wonderous shield.
   When thus the massy shield magnificent
He had accomplish'd, for the hero next     755
He forged, more ardent than the blaze of fire,
A corslet ; then, a ponderous helmet bright
Well fitted to his brows, crested with gold,
And with laborious art divine adorn'd.
He also made him greaves of molten tin.     760
   The armour finish'd, bearing in his hand
The whole, he set it down at Thetis' feet.
She, like a falcon, from the snowy top
Stoop'd of Olympus, bearing to the earth
The dazzling wonder fresh from Vulcan's hand.     765

# BOOK XIX.

## ARGUMENT

Achilles is reconciled to Agamemnon, and clothed in new armour forged
by Vulcan, leads out the Myrmidons to battle.

Now rose the morn in saffron vest attired
From Ocean, with new day for Gods and men,
When Thetis at the fleet of Greece arrived,
Bearing that gift divine.   She found her son
All tears, and close enfolding in his arms        5
Patroclus, while his Myrmidons around
Wept also ; she amid them, graceful stood,
And seizing fast his hand, him thus bespake.
    Although our loss be great, yet, oh my son !
Leave we Patroclus lying on the bier              10
To which the Gods ordain'd him from the first.
Receive from Vulcan's hands these glorious arms,
Such as no mortal shoulders ever bore.
    So saying, she placed the armour on the ground
Before him, and the whole bright treasure rang.    15
A tremor shook the Myrmidons ; none dared
Look on it, but all fled.   Not so himself.
In him fresh vengeance kindled at the view,
And, while he gazed, a splendour as of fire
Flash'd from his eyes.   Delighted, in his hand     20
He held the glorious bounty of the God,
And, wondering at those strokes of art divine,
His eager speech thus to his mother turn'd.
    The God, my mother ! hath bestow'd in truth
Such armour on me as demanded skill                25
Like his, surpassing far all power of man.
Now, therefore, I will arm.   But anxious fears
Trouble me, lest intrusive flies, meantime,
Breed worms within the spear-inflicted wounds
Of Menœtiades, and fill with taint                 30

Of putrefaction his whole breathless form.
   But him the silver-footed Goddess fair
Thus answer'd.  Oh, my son! chase from thy mind
All such concern.  I will myself, essay
To drive the noisome swarms which on the slain     35
In battle feed voracious.  Should he lie
The year complete, his flesh shall yet be found
Untainted, and, it may be, fragrant too.
But thou the Heroes of Achaia's host
Convening, in their ears thy wrath renounce     40
Against the King of men, then, instant, arm
For battle, and put on thy glorious might.
   So saying, the Goddess raised his courage high.
Then, through the nostrils of the dead she pour'd
Ambrosia, and the ruddy juice divine     45
Of nectar, antidotes against decay.
   And now forth went Achilles by the side
Of Ocean, calling with a dreadful shout
To council all the Heroes of the host.
Then, even they who in the fleet before     50
Constant abode, helmsmen and those who held
In stewardship the food and public stores,
All flock'd to council, for that now at length
After long abstinence from dread exploits
Of war, Achilles had once more appear'd.     55
Two went together, halting on the spear,
(For still they felt the anguish of their wounds)
Noble Ulysses and brave Diomede,
And took an early seat; whom follow'd last
The King of men, by Coön in the field     60
Of furious battle wounded with a lance.
The Grecians all assembled, in the midst
Upstood the swift Achilles, and began.
   Atrides! we had doubtless better sped
Both thou and I, thus doing, when at first     65
With cruel rage we burn'd, a girl the cause.
I would that Dian's shaft had in the fleet
Slain her that self-same day when I destroy'd
Lyrnessus, and by conquest made her mine!
Then had not many a Grecian lifeless now,     70
Clench'd with his teeth the ground, victim, alas!

Of my revenge ; whence triumph hath accrued
To Hector and his host, while ours have cause
For long remembrance of our mutual strife.
But evils past let pass, yielding perforce                    75
To sad necessity.   My wrath shall cease
Now ; I resign it ; it hath burn'd too long.
Thou therefore summon forth the host to fight,
That I may learn, meeting them in the field,
If still the Trojans purpose at our fleet                     80
To watch us this night also.   But I judge
That driven by my spear to rapid flight,
They shall escape with weary limbs[1] at least.

   He ended, and the Grecians brazen-greaved
Rejoiced that Peleus' mighty son had cast                     85
His wrath aside.   Then not into the midst
Proceeding, but at his own seat, upstood
King Agamemnon, and them thus bespake.

   Friends ! Grecian  Heroes ! Ministers of Mars !
Arise who may to speak, he claims your ear ;                  90
All interruption wrongs him, and distracts,
Howe'er expert the speaker.   Who can hear
Amid the roar of tumult, or who speak ?
The clearest voice, best utterance, both are vain.
I shall address Achilles.   Hear my speech                    95
Ye Argives, and with understanding mark.
I hear not now the voice of your reproach[2]
First ; ye have oft condemn'd me.   Yet the blame
Rests not with me ; Jove, Destiny, and she
Who roams the shades, Erynnis, caused the offence.           100
She fill'd my soul with fury on that day
In council, when I seized Achilles' prize.
For what could I ? All things obey the Gods.
Ate, pernicious Power, daughter of Jove,
By whom all suffer, challenges from all                       105
Reverence and fear.   Delicate are her feet
Which scorn the ground, and over human heads
She glides, injurious to the race of man,

---

[1] Ἀσπασιως γονυ καμψειν—Shall be glad to bend their knee, i. e. to sit
and repose themselves.

[2] Τᵿτον μυθον.—He seems to intend the reproaches sounded in his ear
from all quarters, and which he had repeatedly heard before.

Of Two who strive, at least entangling One.
She injured, on a day, dread Jove himself　　　　110
Most excellent of all in earth or heaven,
When Juno, although female, him deceived,
What time Alcmena should have brought to light
In bulwark'd Thebes the force of Hercules.
Then Jove, among the gods glorying, spake.　　　115
　　Hear all! both Gods and Goddesses, attend!
That I may make my purpose known.　This day
Birth-pang-dispensing Ilithya brings
An Hero forth to light, who, sprung from those
That sprang from me, his empire shall extend　　120
Over all kingdoms bordering on his own.
　　To whom, designing fraud, Juno replied.
Thou wilt be found false, and this word of thine
Shall want performance.　But Olympian Jove!
Swear now the inviolable oath, that He　　　　125
Who shall, this day, fall from between the feet
Of woman, drawing his descent from thee,
Shall rule all kingdoms bordering on his own.
　　She said, and Jove, suspecting nought her wiles,
The great oath swore, to his own grief and wrong.　130
At once from the Olympian summit flew
Juno, and to Achaian Argos borne,
There sought the noble wife[3] of Sthenelus,
Offspring of Perseus.　Pregnant with a son
Six months, she now the seventh saw at hand,　135
But him the Goddess premature produced,
And check'd Alcmena's pangs already due.
Then joyful to have so prevail'd, she bore
Herself the tidings to Saturnian Jove.
　　Lord of the candent lightnings! Sire of all!　140
I bring thee tidings.　The great prince, ordain'd
To rule the Argive race, this day is born,
Eurystheus, son of Sthenelus, the son
Of Perseus; therefore he derives from thee,
Nor shall the throne of Argos shame his birth.　145
　　She spake; then anguish stung the heart of Jove
Deeply, and seizing by her glossy locks
The Goddess Ate, in his wrath he swore

　　　　[3] By some called Antibia, by others, Nicippe.

That never to the starry skies again
And the Olympian heights he would permit          150
The universal mischief to return.
Then, whirling her around, he cast her down
To earth.   She, mingling with all works of men,
Caused many a pang to Jove, who saw his son
Laborious tasks servile, and of his birth          155
Unworthy, at Eurystheus' will enjoin'd.
     So when the Hero Hector at our ships
Slew us, I then regretted my offence
Which Ate first impell'd me to commit.
But since, infatuated by the Gods          160
I err'd, behold me ready to appease
With gifts of price immense whom I have wrong'd.
Thou, then, arise to battle, and the host
Rouse also.   Not a promise yesternight
Was made thee by Ulysses in thy tent          165
On my behalf, but shall be well perform'd.
Or if it please thee, though impatient, wait
Short season, and my train shall bring the gifts
Even now; that thou may'st understand and know
That my peace-offerings are indeed sincere.          170
     To whom Achilles, swiftest of the swift.
Atrides! Agamemnon! passing all
In glory! King of men! recompense just
By gifts to make me, or to make me none,
That rests with thee.   But let us to the fight          175
Incontinent.   It is no time to play
The game of rhetoric, and to waste the hours
In speeches.   Much remains yet unperform'd.
Achilles must go forth.   He must be seen
Once more in front of battle, wasting wide          180
With brazen spear, the crowded ranks of Troy.
Mark Him—and as He fights, fight also ye.
     To whom Ulysses ever-wise replied.
Nay—Urge not, valiant as thou art thyself,
Achaia's sons up to the battlements          185
Of Ilium, by repast yet unrefresh'd,
Godlike Achilles!—For when phalanx once
Shall clash with phalanx, and the Gods with rage
Both hosts inspire, the contest shall not then

Prove short.   Bid rather the Achaians take                    190
Both food and wine, for they are strength and might.
To stand all day till sunset to a foe
Opposed in battle, fasting, were a task
Might foil the best ; for though his will be prompt
To combat, yet the power must by degrees                       195
Forsake him ; thirst and hunger he must feel,
And his limbs failing him at every step.
But he who hath his vigour to the full
Fed with due nourishment, although he fight
All day, yet feels his courage unimpair'd,                     200
Nor weariness perceives till all retire.
Come then—dismiss the people with command
That each prepare replenishment.   Meantime
Let Agamemnon, King of men, his gifts
In presence here of the assembled Greeks                       205
Produce, that all may view them, and that thou
May'st feel thine own heart gladden'd at the sight.
Let the King also, standing in the midst,
Swear to thee, that he renders back the maid
A virgin still, and strange to his embrace,                    210
And let thy own composure prove, the while,
That thou art satisfied.   Last, let him spread
A princely banquet for thee in his tent,
That thou may'st want no part of just amends.
Thou too, Atrides, shalt hereafter prove                       215
More just to others ; for himself, a King,
Stoops not too low, soothing whom he hath wrong'd.
     Him Agamemnon answer'd King of men.
Thou hast arranged wisely the whole concern,
O Laertiades, and I have heard                                 220
Thy speech, both words and method with delight.
Willing I am, yea more, I wish to swear
As thou hast said, for by the Gods I can
Most truly.   Let Achilles, though of pause
Impatient, suffer yet a short delay                            225
With all assembled here, till from my tent
The gifts arrive, and oaths of peace be sworn.
To thee I give it in peculiar charge
That choosing forth the most illustrious youths
Of all Achaia, thou produce the gifts                          230

From my own ship, all those which yesternight
We promised, nor the women leave behind.
And let Talthybius throughout all the camp
Of the Achaians, instant, seek a boar
For sacrifice to Jove and to the Sun.                235
    Then thus Achilles matchless in the race.
Atrides! most illustrious! King of men!
Expedience bids us to these cares attend
Hereafter, when some pause, perchance, of fight
Shall happen, and the martial rage which fires      240
My bosom now, shall somewhat less be felt.
Our friends by Priameian Hector slain,
Now strew the field mangled, for him hath Jove
Exalted high, and given him great renown.
But haste, now take refreshment; though, in truth,  245
Might I direct, the host should by all means
Unfed to battle, and at set of sun
All sup together, this affront revenged.
But as for me, no drop shall pass my lips
Or morsel, whose companion lies with feet           250
Turn'd to the vestibule, pierced by the spear,
And compass'd by my weeping train around.
No want of food feel I.   My wishes call
For carnage, blood, and agonies and groans.
    But Him, excelling in all wisdom, thus          255
Ulysses answer'd.   Oh Achilles! son
Of Peleus! bravest far of all our host!
Me, in no scanty measure, thou excell'st
Wielding the spear, and thee in prudence, I
Not less.   For I am elder, and have learn'd        260
What thou hast yet to learn.   Bid then thine heart
Endure with patience to be taught by me.
Men, satiate soon with battle, loathe the field
On which the most abundant harvest falls,
Reap'd by the sword; and when the hand of Jove,     265
Dispenser of the great events of war,
Turns once the scale, then, farewell every hope
Of more than scanty gleanings.   Shall the Greeks
Abstain from sustenance for all who die?
That were indeed severe, since day by day           270
No few expire, and respite could be none.

The dead, die whoso may, should be inhumed.
This, duty bids, but bids us also deem
One day sufficient for our sighs and tears.
Ourselves, all we who still survive the war,                    275
Have need of sustenance, that we may bear
The lengthen'd conflict with recruited might,
Cased in enduring brass.—Ye all have heard
Your call to battle; let none lingering stand
In expectation of a farther call,                              280
Which if it sound, shall thunder prove to him
Who lurks among the ships.   No.   Rush we all
Together forth, for contest sharp, prepared,
And persevering with the host of Troy.
    So saying, the sons of Nestor, glorious Chief,             285
He chose, with Meges Phyleus' noble son,
Thoas, Meriones, and Melanippus
And Lycomedes.   These, together, sought
The tent of Agamemnon, King of men.
They ask'd, and they received.   Soon they produced            290
The seven promised tripods from the tent,
Twice ten bright cauldrons, twelve high-mettled steeds,
Seven lovely captives skilled alike in arts
Domestic, of unblemish'd beauty rare,
And last, Briseïs with the blooming cheeks.                    295
Before them went Ulysses, bearing weigh'd
Ten golden talents, whom the chosen Greeks
Attended laden with the remnant gifts.
Full in the midst they placed them.   Then arose
King Agamemnon, and Talthybius                                 300
The herald, clear in utterance as a God,
Beside him stood, holding the victim boar.
Atrides, drawing forth his dagger bright,
Appendant ever to his sword's huge sheath,
Sever'd the bristly forelock of the boar,                      305
A previous offering.   Next, with lifted hands
To Jove he pray'd, while, all around, the Greeks
Sat listening silent to the Sovereign's voice.
He look'd to the wide heaven, and thus he pray'd.
    First, Jove be witness! of all Powers above                310
Best and supreme; Earth next, and next the Sun!
And last, who under earth the guilt avenge
Of oaths sworn falsely, let the Furies hear!

For no respect of amorous desire
Or other purpose, have I laid mine hand                    315
On fair Brisëis, but within my tent
Untouch'd, immaculate she hath remain'd.
And if I falsely swear, then may the Gods
The many woes with which they mark the crime
Of men forsworn, pour also down on me!                    320
   So saying, he pierced the victim in his throat,
And, whirling him around, Talthybius, next,
Cast him into the ocean, fishes' food.
Then, in the centre of Achaia's sons
Uprose Achilles, and thus spake again.                    325
   Jove! Father! dire calamities, effects
Of thy appointment, fall on human-kind.
Never had Agamemnon in my breast
Such anger kindled, never had he seized,
Blinded by wrath, and torn my prize away,                 330
But that the slaughter of our numerous friends
Which thence ensued, thou hadst, thyself, ordain'd.
Now go, ye Grecians, eat, and then to battle.
   So saying, Achilles suddenly dissolved
The hasty council, and all flew dispersed                 335
To their own ships.   Then took the Myrmidons
Those splendid gifts which in the tent they lodged
Of swift Achilles, and the damsels led
Each to a seat, while others of his train
Drove forth the steeds to pasture with his herd.         340
But when Brisëis, bright as Venus, saw
Patroclus lying mangled by the spear,
Enfolding him around, she shriek'd and tore
Her bosom, her smooth neck and beauteous cheeks.
Then thus, divinely fair, with tears she said.           345
   Ah, my Patroclus! dearest friend of all
To hapless me, departing from this tent
I left thee living, and now, generous Chief!
Restored to it again, here find thee dead.
How rapid in succession are my woes!                      350
I saw, myself, the valiant prince to whom
My parents had betroth'd me, slain before
Our city walls; and my three brothers, sons
Of my own mother, whom with long regret

I mourn, fell also in that dreadful field.          355
But when the swift Achilles slew the prince
Design'd my spouse, and the fair city sack'd
Of noble Mynes, thou by every art
Of tender friendship didst forbid my tears,
Promising oft that thou would'st make me bride          360
Of Peleus' godlike son, that thy own ship
Should waft me hence to Phthia, and that thyself
Would'st furnish forth among the Myrmidons
Our nuptial feast.   Therefore thy death I mourn
Ceaseless, for thou wast ever kind to me.          365
 She spake, and all her fellow-captives heaved
Responsive sighs, deploring each, in show,
The dead Patroclus, but, in truth, herself.
Then the Achaian Chiefs gather'd around
Achilles, wooing him to eat, but He          370
Groan'd, and still resolute, their suit refused—
 If I have here a friend on whom by prayers
I may prevail, I pray that ye desist,
Nor longer press me, mourner as I am,
To eat or drink, for till the sun go down          375
I am inflexible, and *will* abstain.
 So saying, the other princes he dismiss'd
Impatient, but the sons of Atreus both
Ulysses, Nestor, and Idomeneus,
With Phœnix, hoary warrior, in his tent          380
Abiding still, with cheerful converse kind
Essay'd to soothe him, whose afflicted soul
All soothing scorn'd till he should once again
Rush on the ravening edge of bloody war.
Then, mindful of his friend, groaning he said.          385
 Time was, unhappiest, dearest of my friends!
When even thou, with diligent dispatch,
Thyself, hast spread a table in my tent,
The hour of battle drawing nigh between
The Greeks and warlike Trojans.   But there lies          390
Thy body now, gored by the ruthless steel,
And for thy sake I neither eat nor drink,
Though dearth be none, conscious that other woe
Surpassing this I can have none to fear.
No, not if tidings of my father's death          395

Should reach me, who, this moment, weeps, perhaps,
In Phthia tears of tenderest regret
For such a son ; while I, remote from home,
Fight for detested Helen under Troy.
Nor even were *He* dead, whom, if he live, 400
I rear in Scyros, my own darling son,
My Neoptolemus of form divine.
For still this hope I cherish'd in my breast
Till now, that, of us two, myself alone
Should fall at Ilium, and that thou, restored 405
To Phthia, should'st have wafted o'er the waves
My son from Scyros to his native home,
That thou might'st show him all his heritage,
My train of menials, and my fair abode.
For either dead already I account 410
Peleus, or doubt not that his residue
Of miserable life shall soon be spent,
Through stress of age and expectation sad
That tidings of my death shall, next, arrive.
　　So spake Achilles weeping, around whom 415
The Chiefs all sigh'd, each with remembrance pain'd
Of some loved object left at home.　Meantime
Jove, with compassion moved, their sorrow saw,
And in wing'd accents thus to Pallas spake.
　　Daughter! thou hast abandon'd, as it seems, 420
Yon virtuous Chief for ever ; shall no care
Thy mind engage of brave Achilles more?
Before his gallant fleet mourning he sits
His friend, disconsolate ; the other Greeks
Eat and are satisfied ; he only fasts. 425
Go, then—instil nectar into his breast,
And sweets ambrosial, that he hunger not.
　　So saying, he urged Minerva prompt before.
In form a shrill-voiced harpy of long wing
Through ether down she darted, while the Greeks 430
In all their camp for instant battle arm'd.
Ambrosial sweets and nectar she instill'd
Into his breast, lest he should suffer loss
Of strength through abstinence, then soar'd again
To her great Sire's unperishing abode. 435
And now the Grecians from their gallant fleet

All pour'd themselves abroad.   As when thick snow
From Jove descends, driven by impetuous gusts
Of the cloud-scattering North, so frequent shone
Issuing from the fleet the dazzling casques,          440
Boss'd bucklers, hauberks strong, and ashen spears.
Upwent the flash to heaven ; wide all around
The champaign laugh'd with beamy brass illumed,
And tramplings of the warriors on all sides
Resounded, amidst whom Achilles arm'd.                445
He gnash'd his teeth, fire glimmer'd in his eyes,
Anguish intolerable wrung his heart
And fury against Troy, while he put on
His glorious arms, the labour of a God.
First, to his legs his polish'd greaves he clasp'd    450
Studded with silver, then his corslet bright
Braced to his bosom, his huge sword of brass
Athwart his shoulder slung, and his broad shield
Uplifted last, luminous as the moon.
Such as to mariners a fire appears,                   455
Kindled by shepherds on the distant top
Of some lone hill ; they, driven by stormy winds,
Reluctant roam far off the fishy Deep,
Such from Achilles' burning shield divine
A lustre struck the skies ; his ponderous helm        460
He lifted to his brows ; starlike it shone,
And shook its curling crest of bushy gold,
By Vulcan taught to wave profuse around.
So clad, godlike Achilles trial made
If his arms fitted him, and gave free scope           465
To his proportion'd limbs ; buoyant they proved
As wings, and high upbore his airy tread.
He drew his father's spear forth from its case,
Heavy and huge and long.   That spear, of all
Achaia's sons, none else had power to wield ;         470
Achilles only could the Pelian spear
Brandish, by Chiron for his father hewn
From Pelion's top for slaughter of the brave.
His coursers, then, Automedon prepared
And Alcimus, adjusting diligent                        475
The fair caparisons ; they thrust the bits
Into their mouths, and to the chariot seat

Extended and made fast the reins behind.
The splendid scourge commodious to the grasp
Seizing, at once Automedon upsprang                    480
Into his place ; behind him, arm'd complete
Achilles mounted, as the orient sun
All dazzling, and with aweful tone his speech
Directed to the coursers of his Sire.
   Xanthus, and Balius of Podarges' blood           485
Illustrious ! see ye that, the battle done,
Ye bring whom now ye bear back to the host
Of the Achaians in far other sort,
Nor leave him, as ye left Patroclus, dead.
   Him then his steed unconquer'd in the race,       490
Xanthus, thus answer'd from beneath his yoke,
But, hanging low his head, and with his mane
Dishevell'd all, and streaming to the ground.
Him Juno vocal made, Goddess white-arm'd.
   And doubtless so we will.   This day at least      495
We bear thee safe from battle, stormy Chief !
But thee the hour of thy destruction swift
Approaches, hasten'd by no fault of ours,
But by the force of fate and power divine.
For not through sloth or tardiness on us                500
Aught chargeable, have Ilium's sons thine arms
Stript from Patroclus' shoulders, but a God
Matchless in battle, offspring of bright-hair'd
Latona, him contending in the van
Slew, for the glory of the Chief of Troy.               505
We, Zephyrus himself, though by report
Swiftest of all the winds of heaven, in speed
Could equal, but the Fates thee also doom
By human hands to fall, and hands divine.
   The interposing Furies at that word               510
Suppress'd his utterance, and indignant, thus,
Achilles, swiftest of the swift, replied.
   Why, Xanthus, prophesiest thou my death ?
It ill beseems thee.  I already know
That from my parents far remote my doom                 515
Appoints me here to die ; yet not the more
Cease I from feats of arms, till Ilium's host
Shall have received, at length, their fill of war.
   He said, and with a shout drove forth to battle.

# BOOK XX.

---

### ARGUMENT.

By permission of Jupiter the Gods descend into the battle, and range themselves on either side respectively. Neptune rescues Æneas from death by the hand of Achilles, from whom Apollo, soon after, rescues Hector. Achilles slays many Trojans.

THE Grecians, thus, before their lofty ships
Stood arm'd around Achilles, glorious Chief
Insatiable with war, and opposite
The Trojans on the rising-ground appear'd.
Meantime, Jove order'd Themis, from the head        5
Of the deep-fork'd Olympian to convene
The Gods in council.  She to every part
Proceeding, bade them to the courts of Jove.
Nor of the Floods was any absent thence
Oceanus except, or of the Nymphs        10
Who haunt the pleasant groves, or dwell beside
Stream-feeding fountains, or in meadows green.
Within the courts of cloud-assembler Jove
Arrived, on pillar'd thrones radiant they sat,
With ingenuity divine contrived        15
By Vulcan for the mighty Sire of all.
Thus they within the Thunderer's palace sat
Assembled ; nor was Neptune slow to hear
The voice of Themis, but (the billows left)
Came also ; in the midst his seat he took,        20
And ask'd, incontinent, the mind of Jove.
    King of the lightnings ! wherefore hast thou call'd
The Gods to council ? Hast thou aught at heart
Important to the hosts of Greece and Troy ?
For on the battle's fiery edge they stand.        25
    To whom replied Jove, Sovereign of the storms.
Thou know'st my counsel, Shaker of the shores !
And wherefore ye are call'd.  Although ordain'd

So soon to die, they interest me still.
Myself, here seated on Olympus' top,                    30
With contemplation will my mind indulge
Of yon great spectacle; but ye, the rest,
Descend into the field, Trojan or Greek
Each to assist, as each shall most incline.
For should Achilles in the field no foe                 35
Find save the Trojans, quickly should they fly
Before the rapid force of Peleus' son.
They trembled ever at his look, and since
Such fury for his friend hath fired his heart,
I fear lest he anticipate the will                      40
Of Fate, and Ilium perish premature.
    So spake the son of Saturn, kindling war
Inevitable, and the Gods to fight
'Gan move with minds discordant.   Juno sought
And Pallas, with the earth-encircling Power             45
Neptune, the Grecian fleet, with whom were join'd
Mercury, teacher of all useful arts,
And Vulcan, rolling on all sides his eyes
Tremendous, but on disproportion'd legs,
Not without labour hard, halting uncouth.               50
Mars, warrior-God, on Ilium's part appear'd
With Phœbus never-shorn, Dian shaft-arm'd,
Xanthus, Latona, and the Queen of smiles,
Venus.   So long as the Immortal Gods
Mix'd not with either host, Achaia's sons               55
Exulted, seeing, after tedious pause,
Achilles in the field, and terror shook
The knees of every Trojan, at the sight
Of swift Achilles like another Mars
Panting for blood, and bright in arms again.            60
But when the Olympian Powers had enter'd once
The multitude, then Discord, at whose voice
The million maddens, vehement arose;
Then, Pallas at the trench without the wall
By turns stood shouting, and by turns a shout           65
Sent terrible along the sounding shore.
While, gloomy as a tempest, opposite,
Mars from the lofty citadel of Troy
Now yell'd aloud, now running o'er the hill

Callicolone, on the Simois' side.                           70
   Thus the Immortals, ever-blest, impell'd
Both hosts to battle, and dire inroad caused
Of strife among them.   Sudden from on high
The Sire of Gods and men thunder'd; meantime,
Neptune the earth and the high mountains shook;            75
Through all her base and to her topmost peak
Ida spring-fed the agitation felt
Reeling, all Ilium and the fleet of Greece.
Upstarted from his throne, appall'd, the King
Of Erebus, and with a cry his fears                        80
Through hell proclaim'd, lest Neptune, o'er his head
Shattering the vaulted earth, should wide disclose
To mortal and immortal eyes his realm
Terrible, squalid, to the Gods themselves
A dreaded spectacle; with such a sound                     85
The Powers eternal into battle rush'd.
Opposed to Neptune, King of the vast Deep,
Apollo stood with his wing'd arrows arm'd;
Pallas to Mars; Diana shaft-expert,
Sister of Phœbus, in her golden bow                        90
Rejoicing, with whose shouts the forests ring,
To Juno; Mercury, for useful arts
Famed, to Latona; and to Vulcan's force
The eddied River broad by mortal men
Scamander call'd, but Xanthus by the Gods.                 95
   So Gods encounter'd Gods.   But most desire
Achilles felt, breaking the ranks, to rush
On Priameian Hector, with whose blood
Chiefly his fury prompted him to sate
The indefatigable God of war.                              100
But, the encourager of Ilium's host
Apollo, urged Æneas to assail
The son of Peleus, with heroic might
Inspiring his bold heart.   He feign'd the voice
Of Priam's son Lycaon, and his form                        105
Assuming, thus the Trojan Chief address'd.
   Æneas! Trojan leader! where are now
Thy vaunts, which, banquetting erewhile among
Our princes, o'er thy brimming cups thou mad'st,
That thou would'st fight, thyself, with Peleus' son?       110

To whom Æneas answer thus returned.
Offspring of Priam! why enjoin'st thou me
Not so inclined, that arduous task, to cope
With the unmatch'd Achilles? I have proved
His force already, when he chased me down          115
From Ida with his spear, what time he made
Seizure of all our cattle, and destroy'd
Pedasus and Lyrnessus; but I 'scaped
Unslain, by Jove himself empower'd to fly.
Else had I fallen by Achilles' hand,              120
And by the hand of Pallas, who his steps
Conducted, and exhorted him to slay
Us and the Leleges.   Vain, therefore, proves
All mortal force to Peleus' son opposed;
For one, at least, of the Immortals stands        125
Ever beside him, guardian of his life,
And, of himself, he hath an arm that sends
His rapid spear unerring to the mark.
Yet, would the Gods more equal sway the scales
Of battle, not with ease should he subdue         130
Me, though he boast a panoply of brass.
    Him, then, Apollo answer'd, son of Jove.
Hero! prefer to the Immortal Gods
Thy prayer, for thee men rumour Venus' son,
Daughter of Jove, and Peleus' son his birth       135
Drew from a Goddess of inferior note.
Thy mother is from Jove; the offspring, his,
Less noble of the hoary Ocean old.
Go, therefore, and thy conquering spear uplift
Against him, nor let aught his sounding words      140
Appal thee, or his threats turn thee away.
    So saying, with martial force the chief he fill'd,
Who through the foremost combatants advanced
Radiant in arms.   Nor pass'd Anchises' son
Unseen of Juno, through the crowded ranks         145
Seeking Achilles, but the Powers of heaven
Convened by her command, she thus address'd.
    Neptune, and thou, Minerva! with mature
Deliberation, ponder the event.
Yon Chief, Æneas, dazzling bright in arms,        150
Goes to withstand Achilles, and he goes

Sent by Apollo; in despite of whom
Be it our task to give him quick repulse,
Or, of ourselves, let some propitious Power
Strengthen Achilles with a mind exempt                    155
From terror, and with force invincible.
So shall he know that of the Gods above
The mightiest are his friends, with whom compared
The favourers of Ilium in time past,
Who stood her guardians in the bloody strife,             160
Are empty boasters all, and nothing worth.
For therefore came we down, that we may share
This fight, and that Achilles suffer nought
Fatal to-day, though suffer all he must
Hereafter, with his thread of life entwined               165
By Destiny, the day when he was born.
But should Achilles unapprized remain
Of such advantage by a voice divine,
When he shall meet some Deity in the field,
Fear then will seize him, for celestial forms             170
Unveil'd are terrible to mortal eyes.
  To whom replied the Shaker of the shores.
Juno! thy hot impatience needs control;
It ill befits thee.   No desire I feel
To force into contention with ourselves                   175
Gods, our inferiors.   No.   Let us, retired
To yonder hill, distant from all resort,
There sit, while these the battle wage alone.
But if Apollo, or if Mars the fight
Entering, begin, themselves, to interfere                 180
Against Achilles, then will we at once
To battle also; and, I much misdeem,
Or glad they shall be soon to mix again
Among the Gods on the Olympian heights,
By strong coercion of our arms subdued.                   185
  So saying, the God of Ocean azure-hair'd
Moved foremost to the lofty mound earth-built
Of noble Hercules, by Pallas raised
And by the Trojans for his safe escape,
What time the monster of the Deep pursued                 190
The Hero from the sea-bank o'er the plain.
There Neptune sat, and his confederate Gods,

Their shoulders with impenetrable clouds
O'ermantled, while the city-spoiler Mars
Sat with Apollo opposite on the hill                          195
Callicolone, with their aids divine.
So, Gods to Gods in opposite aspect
Sat ruminating, and alike the work
All fearing to begin of arduous war,
While from his seat sublime Jove urged them on.              200
The champaign all was fill'd, and with the blaze
Illumined wide of men and steeds brass-arm'd,
And the incumber'd earth jarr'd under foot
Of the encountering hosts.   Then, two, the rest
Surpassing far, into the midst advanced                      205
Impatient for the fight, Anchises' son .
Æneas, and Achilles, glorious Chief!
Æneas first, under his ponderous casque
Nodding and menacing, advanced ; before
His breast he held the well-conducted orb          .         210
Of his broad shield, and shook his brazen spear.
On the other side, Achilles to the fight
Flew like a ravening lion, on whose death
Resolved the peasants from all quarters meet ;
He, viewing with disdain the foremost, stalks                215
Right on, but smitten by some dauntless youth
Writhes himself, and discloses his huge fangs
Hung with white foam ; then, growling for revenge,
Lashes himself to battle with his tail,
Till with a burning eye and a bold heart                     220
He springs to slaughter, or himself is slain ;
So, by his valour and his noble mind
Impell'd, renown'd Achilles moved toward
Æneas, and, small interval between,
Thus spake the Hero matchless in the race.                   225
   Why stand'st thou here, Æneas! thy own band
Left at such distance ? Is it that thine heart
Glows with ambition to contend with me
In hope of Priam's honours, and to fill
His throne hereafter in Troy steed-renown'd ?                230
But shouldst thou slay me, not for that exploit
Would Priam such large recompense bestow,
For he hath sons, and hath, beside, a mind

And disposition not so lightly changed.
Or have the Trojans of their richest soil　　　　235
For vineyard apt or plough assign'd thee part
If thou shalt slay me? Difficult, I hope,
At least, thou shalt experience that emprize.
For, as I think, I have already chased
Thee with my spear.　Forgettest thou the day　　　240
When, finding thee alone, I drove thee down
Headlong from Ida, and, thy cattle left
Afar, thou didst not dare in all thy flight
Turn once, till at Lyrnessus safe arrived,
Which city by Jove's aid and by the aid　　　　245
Of Pallas I destroy'd, and captive led
Their women? Thee, indeed, the Gods preserved,
But they shall not preserve thee, as thou dream'st,
Now also.　Back into thy host again;
Hence, I command thee, nor oppose in fight　　　250
My force, lest evil find thee.　To be taught
By sufferings only is the part of fools.
　　To whom Æneas answer thus return'd.
Pelides! hope not, as I were a boy,
With words to scare me.　I have also taunts　　　255
At my command, and could be sharp as thou.
By such report as from the lips of men
We oft have heard, each other's birth we know
And parents; but my parents to behold
Was ne'er thy lot, nor have I thine beheld.　　　260
Thee men proclaim from noble Peleus sprung
And Thetis, bright-hair'd Goddess of the Deep;
I boast myself of lovely Venus born
To brave Anchises, and his son this day
In battle slain thy Sire shall mourn, or mine;　　　265
For I expect not that we shall depart
Like children, satisfied with words alone.
But if it please thee more at large to learn
My lineage (thousands can attest it true)
Know this. Jove, Sovereign of the storms, begat　　　270
Dardanus, and ere yet the sacred walls
Of Ilium rose, the glory of this plain,
He built Dardania; for at Ida's foot
Dwelt our progenitors in ancient days.

Dardanus was the father of a son,                            275
King Ericthonius, wealthiest of mankind.
Three thousand mares of his the marish grazed,
Each suckling with delight her tender foal.
Boreas, enamour'd of no few of these,
The pasture sought, and covered them in form        280
Of a steed azure-maned.  They, pregnant thence,
Twelve foals produced, and all so light of foot,
That when they wanton'd in the fruitful field
They swept, and snapp'd it not, the golden ear,
And when they wanton'd on the boundless Deep,      285
They skimm'd the green wave's frothy ridge, secure.
From Ericthonius sprang Tros, King of Troy,
And Tros was father of three famous sons,
Ilus, Assaracus, and Ganymede
Loveliest of human-kind, whom for his charms        290
The Gods caught up to heaven, there to abide
With the Immortals, cup-bearer of Jove.
Ilus begat Laomedon, and he
Five sons, Tithonus, Priam, Clytius,
Lampus, and Hicetaon, branch of Mars.                 295
Assaracus a son begat, by name
Capys, and Capys in due time his son
Warlike Anchises, and Anchises me.
But Priam is the noble Hector's sire.
Such is my lineage, and such blood I boast ;          300
But valour is from Jove ;  He, as he wills,
Increases or reduces it in man,
For He is Lord of all.   Therefore enough—
Too long like children we have stood, the time
Consuming here, while battle roars around.           305
Reproach is cheap.   Easily might we cast
Gibes at each other, till a ship that asks
An hundred oars should sink beneath the load.
The tongue of man is voluble, hath words
For every theme, nor wants wide field and long,     310
And as he speaks so shall he hear again.
But we—why should we wrangle, and with taunts
Assail each other, as the practice is
Of women, who with heart-devouring strife
On fire, start forth into the public way               315

To mock each other, uttering, as may chance,
Much truth, much falsehood, as their anger bids ?
The ardour of my courage will not slack
For all thy speeches; we must combat first ;
Now, therefore, without more delay, begin,                320
That we may taste each other's force in arms.
    So spake Æneas, and his brazen lance
Hurl'd with full force against the dreadful shield.
Loud roar'd its ample concave at the blow.
Not unalarm'd Pelides his broad disk                      325
Thrust farther from him, deeming that the force
Of such an arm should pierce his guard with ease.
Vain fear ! he recollected not that arms
Glorious as his, gifts of the Immortal Gods,
Yield not so quickly to the force of man.                 330
The stormy spear by brave Æneas sent,
No passage found ; the golden plate divine
Repress'd its vehemence ; two folds it pierced,
But three were still behind, for with five folds
Vulcan had fortified it ; two were brass ;                335
The two interior, tin ; the midmost gold ;
And at the golden one the weapon stood[1].
Achilles, next, hurl'd his long shadow'd spear,
And struck Æneas on the utmost verge
Of his broad shield, where thinnest lay the brass,        340
And thinnest the ox-hide.   The Pelian ash
Started right through the buckler, and it rang.
Æneas crouch'd terrified, and his shield
Thrust farther from him ; but the rapid beam
Bursting both borders of the ample disk,                  345
Glanced o'er his back, and plunged into the soil.
He 'scaped it, and he stood ; but, as he stood,
With horror infinite the weapon saw

---

[1] Some commentators, supposing the golden plate the outermost as the
most ornamental, have perplexed themselves much with this passage, for
how, say they, could two folds be pierced and the spear be stopped by
the gold, if the gold lay on the surface ? But to avoid the difficulty, we
need only suppose that the gold was inserted between the two plates of
brass and the two of tin, Vulcan, in this particular, having attended less
to ornament than to security.
    See the Scholiast in Villoisson, who argues at large in favour of this
opinion.

Planted so near him. Then, Achilles drew
His faulchion keen, and with a deafening shout   350
Sprang on him; but Æneas seized a stone
Heavy and huge, a weight to overcharge
Two men (such men as are accounted strong
Now), but He wielded it with ease, alone.
Then had Æneas, as Achilles came    355
Impetuous on, smitten, although in vain,
His helmet or his shield, and Peleus' son
Had with his faulchion him stretch'd at his feet,
But that the God of Ocean quick perceived
His peril, and the Immortals thus bespake.   360
 I pity brave Æneas, who shall soon,
Slain by Achilles, see the realms below,
By smooth suggestions of Apollo lured
To danger, such as He can ne'er avert.
But wherefore should the Chief, guiltless himself,  365
Die for the fault of others? at no time
His gifts have fail'd, grateful to all in heaven.
Come, therefore, and let us from death ourselves
Rescue Him, lest if by Achilles' arm
This Hero perish, Jove himself be wroth;   370
For he is destined to survive, lest all
The house of Dardanus (whom Jove beyond
All others loved, his sons of woman born)
Fail with Æneas, and be found no more.
Saturnian Jove hath hated now long time   375
The family of Priam, and henceforth
Æneas and his son, and his sons' sons,
Shall sway the sceptre o'er the race of Troy.
 To whom, majestic thus the spouse of Jove.
Neptune! deliberate thyself, and choose   380
Whether to save Æneas, or to leave
The Hero victim of Achilles' ire.
For Pallas and myself ofttimes have sworn
In full assembly of the Gods, to aid
Troy never, never to avert the day    385
Of her distress, not even when the flames
Kindled by the heroic sons of Greece
Shall climb with fury to her topmost towers.
 She spake; then Neptune, instant, through the throng

Of battle flying, and the clash of spears,     390
Came where Achilles and Æneas fought.
At once with shadows dim he blurr'd the sight
Of Peleus' son, and from the shield, himself,
Of brave Æneas the bright-pointed ash
Retracting, placed it at Achilles' feet.     395
Then, lifting high Æneas from the ground,
He heaved him far remote; o'er many a rank
Of Heroes and of bounding steeds he flew,
Launch'd into air from the expanded palm
Of Neptune, and alighted in the rear     400
Of all the battle where the Caucons stood.
Neptune approach'd him there, and at his side
Standing, in accents wing'd, him thus bespake.
    What God, Æneas! tempted thee to cope
Thus inconsiderately with the son     405
Of Peleus, both more excellent in fight
Than thou, and more the favourite of the skies?
From him retire hereafter, or expect
A premature descent into the shades.
But when Achilles shall have once fulfill'd     410
His destiny, in battle slain, then fight
Fearless, for thou canst fall by none beside.
    So saying, he left the well-admonish'd Chief,
And from Achilles' eyes scatter'd the gloom
Shed o'er them by himself. The Hero saw     415
Clearly, and with his noble heart, incensed
By disappointment, thus conferring, said.
    Gods! I behold a prodigy. My spear
Lies at my foot, and He at whom I cast
The weapon with such deadly force, is gone!     420
Æneas therefore, as it seems, himself
Interests the Immortal Gods, although
I deem'd his boast of their protection vain.
I reck not. Let him go. So gladly 'scaped
From slaughter now, he shall not soon again     425
Feel an ambition to contend with me.
Now will I rouse the Danaï, and prove
The force in fight of many a Trojan more.
    He said, and sprang to battle with loud voice,
Calling the Grecians after him.—Ye sons     430

Of the Achaians! stand not now aloof,
My noble friends! but foot to foot let each
Fall on courageous, and desire the fight.
The task were difficult for me alone,
Brave as I boast myself, to chase a foe       435
So numerous, and to combat with them all.
Not Mars himself, immortal though he be,
Nor Pallas, could with all the ranks contend
Of this vast multitude, and drive the whole.
With hands, with feet, with spirit and with might,       440
All that I can I will; right through I go,
And not a Trojan who shall chance within
Spear's reach of me, shall, as I judge, rejoice.
    Thus he the Greeks exhorted. Opposite,
Meantime, illustrious Hector to his host       445
Vociferated, his design to oppose
Achilles publishing in every ear.
    Fear not, ye valiant men of Troy! fear not
The son of Peleus. In a war of words
I could, myself, cope even with the Gods;       450
But not with spears; there they excel us all.
Nor shall Achilles full performance give
To all his vaunts, but, if he some fulfil,
Shall others leave mutilate in the midst.
I will encounter him, though his hands be fire,       455
Though fire his hands, and his heart hammer'd steel.
    So spake he them exhorting. At his word
Uprose the Trojan spears, thick intermixt
The battle join'd, and clamour loud began.
Then thus, approaching Hector, Phœbus spake.       460
Henceforth, advance not Hector! in the front
Seeking Achilles, but retired within
The stormy multitude his coming wait,
Lest his spear reach thee, or his glittering sword.
    He said, and Hector far into his host       465
Withdrew, admonish'd by the voice divine.
Then, shouting terrible, and clothed with might,
Achilles sprang to battle. First, he slew
The valiant Chief Iphition, whom a band
Numerous obey'd. Otrynteus was his Sire.       470
Him to Otrynteus, city-waster Chief,

A Naiad under snowy Tmolus bore
In fruitful Hyda.   Right into his front
As he advanced, Achilles drove his spear,
And rived his skull; with thundering sound he fell,            475
And thus the conqueror gloried in his fall.
   Ah Otryntides! thou art slain.   Here lies
The terrible in arms, who born beside
The broad Gygæan lake, where Hyllus flows
And Hermus, call'd the fertile soil his own.                    480
   Thus gloried he.   Meantime the shades of death
Cover'd Iphition, and Achaian wheels
And horses ground his body in the van.
Demoleon next, Antenor's son, a brave
Defender of the walls of Troy, he slew.                         485
Into his temples through his brazen casque
He thrust the Pelian ash, nor could the brass
Such force resist, but the huge weapon drove
The shatter'd bone into his inmost brain,
And his fierce onset at a stroke repress'd.                     490
Hippodamas his weapon next received
Within his spine, while with a leap he left
His steeds and fled.   He, panting forth his life,
Moan'd like a bull, by consecrated youths
Dragg'd round the Heliconian King[2], who views               495
That victim with delight.   So, with loud moans
The noble warrior sigh'd his soul away.
Then, spear in hand, against the godlike son
Of Priam, Polydorus, he advanced.
Not yet his father had to him indulged                          500
A warrior's place, for that of all his sons
He was the youngest-born, his hoary Sire's
Chief darling, and in speed surpass'd them all.
Then also, in the vanity of youth,
For show of nimbleness, he started oft                          505
Into the vaward, till at last he fell.
Him gliding swiftly by, swifter than he
Achilles with a javelin reached; he struck
His belt behind him, where the golden clasps

---

[2] Neptune.   So called, either because he was worshipped of Helicon, a
mountain of Bœotia, or from Helice, an island of Achaia, where he had
a temple.

Met, and the double hauberk interposed.                     510
The point transpierced his bowels, and sprang through
His navel ; screaming, on his knees he fell,
Death-shadows dimm'd his eyes, and with both hands,
Stooping, he press'd his gather'd bowels back.
But noble Hector, soon as he beheld                          515
His brother Polydorus to the earth
Inclined, and with his bowels in his hands,
Sightless well-nigh with anguish could endure
No longer to remain aloof ; flame-like
He burst abroad, and shaking his sharp spear,               520
Advanced to meet Achilles, whose approach
Seeing, Achilles bounded with delight,
And thus, exulting, to himself he said.
    Ah ! he approaches, who hath stung my soul
Deepest, the slayer of whom most I loved !                  525
Behold, we meet ! Caution is at an end,
And timid skulking in the walks of war.
    He ceased, and with a brow knit into frowns,
Call'd to illustrious Hector.   Haste, approach,
That I may quick dispatch thee to the shades.               530
    Whom answer'd warlike Hector nought appall'd.
Pelides ! hope not, as I were a boy,
With words to scare me.   I have also taunts
At my command, and can be sharp as thou.
I know thee valiant, and myself I know                      535
Inferior far ; yet, whether thou shalt slay
Me, or, inferior as I am, be slain
By me, is at the pleasure of the Gods,
For I wield also not a pointless beam.
    He said, and, brandishing it, hurl'd his spear,   540
Which Pallas, breathing softly, wafted back
From the renown'd Achilles, and it fell
Successless at illustrious Hector's feet.
Then, all on fire to slay him, with a shout
That rent the air Achilles rapid flew                       545
Toward him, but him wrapt in clouds opaque
Apollo caught with ease divine away.
Thrice, swift Achilles sprang to the assault
Impetuous, thrice the pitchy cloud he smote,
And at his fourth assault, godlike in act,                  550

   s. c.—7.                                      D D

And terrible in utterance, thus exclaim'd.

Dog! thou art safe, and hast escaped again;
But narrowly, and by the aid once more
Of Phœbus, without previous suit to whom
Thou venturest never where the javelin sings.          555
But when we next encounter, then expect,
If one of all in heaven aid also me,
To close thy proud career.   Meantime I seek
Some other, and assail e'en whom I may.

So saying, he pierced the neck of Dryops through,      560
And at his feet he fell.   Him there he left,
And turning on a valiant warrior huge,
Philetor's son, Demuchus, in the knee
Pierced, and detain'd him by the planted spear,
Till with his sword he smote him, and he died.         565
Laogonus and Dardanus he next
Assaulted, sons of Bias; to the ground
Dismounting both, one with his spear he slew,
The other with his faulchion at a blow.
Tros too, Alastor's son—He suppliant clasp'd           570
Achilles' knees, and for his pity sued,
Pleading equality of years, in hope
That he would spare, and send him thence alive.
Ah dreamer! ignorant how much in vain
That suit he urged; for not of milky mind,             575
Or placable in temper was the Chief
To whom he sued, but fiery.   With both hands
His knees he clasp'd importunate, and he
Fast by the liver gash'd him with his sword.
His liver falling forth, with sable blood              580
His bosom fill'd, and darkness veil'd his eyes.
Then, drawing close to Mulius, in his ear
He set the pointed brass, and at a thrust
Sent it, next moment, through his ear beyond.
Then, through the forehead of Agenor's son             585
Echechlus, his huge-hafted blade he drove,
And death and fate for ever veil'd his eyes.
Next, where the tendons of the elbow meet,
Striking Deucalion, through his wrist he urged
The brazen point; he all defenceless stood,            590
Expecting death; down came Achilles' blade

Full on his neck : away went head and casque
Together ; from his spine the marrow sprang,
And at his length outstretch'd he press'd the plain.
From him to Rhigmus, Pireus' noble son,      595
He flew, a warrior from the fields of Thrace.
Him through the loins he pierced, and with the beam
Fixt in his bowels, to the earth he fell ;
Then piercing, as he turn'd to flight, the spine   ·
Of Areïthöus his charioteer,      600
He thrust him from his seat ; wild with dismay
Back flew the fiery coursers at his fall.
As a devouring fire within the glens
Of some dry mountain ravages the trees,
While, blown around, the flames roll to all sides,   ·605
So, on all sides, terrible as a God,
Achilles drove the death-devoted host
Of Ilium, and the champaign ran with blood.
As when the peasant his yoked steers employs
To tread his barley, the broad-fronted pair     610
With ponderous hoofs trample it out with ease,
So, by magnanimous Achilles driven,
His coursers solid-hoof'd stamp'd as they ran
The shields, at once, and bodies of the slain ;
Blood spatter'd all his axle, and with blood     615
From the horse-hoofs and from the fellied wheels
His chariot redden'd, while himself, athirst
For glory, his unconquerable hands
Defiled with mingled carnage, sweat, and dust.

# BOOK XXI.

---

### ARGUMENT.

Achilles having separated the Trojans, and driven one part of them to the city and the other into the Scamander, takes twelve young men alive, his intended victims to the manes of Patroclus. The river overflowing his banks with purpose to overwhelm him, is opposed by Vulcan, and gladly relinquishes the attempt. The battle of the Gods ensues. Apollo, in the form of Agenor, decoys Achilles from the town, which in the mean time the Trojans enter and shut the gates against him.

BUT when they came, at length, where Xanthus winds
His stream vortiginous from Jove derived,
There, separating Ilium's host, he drove
Part o'er the plain to Troy in the same road
By which the Grecians had so lately fled                    5
The fury of illustrious Hector's arm.
That way they fled pouring themselves along
Flood-like, and Juno, to retard them, threw
Darkness as night before them.   Other part,
Push'd down the sides of Xanthus, headlong plunged          10
With dashing sound into his dizzy stream,
And all his banks re-echoed loud the roar.
They, struggling, shriek'd in silver eddies whirl'd.
As when, by violence of fire expell'd,
Locusts uplifted on the wing escape                         15
To some broad river, swift the sudden blaze
Pursues them, they, astonish'd, strew the flood,
So, by Achilles driven, a mingled throng
Of horses and of warriors overspread
Xanthus, and glutted all his sounding course.               20
He, chief of heroes, leaving on the bank
His spear against a tamarisk reclined,
Plunged like a God, with faulchion arm'd alone,
But fill'd with thoughts of havoc.   On all sides
Down came his edge; groans follow'd dread to hear           25

Of warriors smitten by the sword, and all
The waters as they ran redden'd with blood.
As smaller fishes, flying the pursuit
Of some huge dolphin, terrified, the creeks
And secret hollows of a haven fill,                        30
For none of all that he can seize he spares,
So lurk'd the trembling Trojans in the caves
Of Xanthus' awful flood.   But He (his hands
Wearied at length with slaughter) from the rest
Twelve youths selected whom to death he doom'd,           35
In vengeance for his loved Patroclus slain.
Them stupified with dread like fawns he drove
Forth from the river, manacling their hands
Behind them fast with their own tunic-strings,.
And gave them to his warrior train in charge.             40
Then, ardent still for blood, rushing again
Toward the stream, Dardanian Priam's son
He met, Lycaon, as he climb'd the bank.
Him erst by night, in his own father's field
Finding him, he had led captive away.                     45
Lycaon was employ'd cutting green shoots
Of the wild-fig for chariot-rings, when lo !
Terrible, unforeseen, Achilles came.
He seized and sent him in a ship afar
To Lemnos ; there the son of Jason paid                   50
His price, and, at great cost, Eëtion
The guest of Jason, thence redeeming him,
Sent him to fair Arisba ; but he 'scaped
Thence also, and regain'd his father's house.
Eleven days, at his return, he gave                       55
To recreation joyous with his friends,
And on the twelfth his fate cast him again
Into Achilles' hands, who to the shades
Now doom'd him, howsoever loth to go.
Soon as Achilles swiftest of the swift                    60
Him naked saw (for neither spear had he
Nor shield nor helmet, but, when he emerged,
Weary and faint had cast them all away)
Indignant to his mighty self he said.
   Gods ! I behold a miracle ! Ere long                   65
The valiant Trojans whom myself have slain

Shall rise from Erebus, for he is here,
The self-same warrior whom I lately sold
At Lemnos, free, and in the field again.
The hoary Deep is prison strong enough　　　　70
For most, but not for him.　Now shall he taste
The point of this my spear, that I may learn
By sure experience, whether hell itself
That holds the strongest fast, can him detain,
Or whether he shall thence also escape.　　　　75
　　While musing thus he stood, stunn'd with dismay
The youth approach'd, eager to clasp his knees,
For vehement he felt the dread of death
Working within him; with his Pelian ash
Uplifted high noble Achilles stood　　　　80
Ardent to smite him; he with body bent
Ran under it, and to his knees adhered;
The weapon, missing him, implanted stood
Close at his back, when, seizing with one hand
Achilles' knees, he with the other grasp'd　　　　85
The dreadful beam, resolute through despair,
And in wing'd accents suppliant thus began.
　　Oh spare me! pity me! Behold I clasp
Thy knees, Achilles! Ah, illustrious Chief!
Reject not with disdain a suppliant's prayer.　　　　90
I am thy guest also, who at thy own board
Have eaten bread, and did partake the gift
Of Ceres with thee on the very day
When thou didst send me in yon field surprised
For sale to sacred Lemnos, far remote,　　　　95
And for my price receiv'dst an hundred beeves.
Loose me, and I will yield thee now that sum
Thrice told.　Alas! this morn is but the twelfth
Since, after numerous hardships, I arrived
Once more in Troy, and now my ruthless lot　　　　100
Hath given me into thy hands again.
Jove cannot less than hate me, who hath twice
Made me thy prisoner, and my doom was death,
Death in my prime, the day when I was born
Son of Laothöe from Alta sprung,　　　　105
From Alta, whom the Leleges obey
On Satnio's banks in lofty Pedasus.

His daughter to his other numerous wives
King Priam added, and two sons she bore
Only to be deprived by thee of both.      110
My brother hath already died, in front
Of Ilium's infantry, by thy bright spear,
The godlike Polydorus ; and like doom
Shall now be mine, for I despair to escape
Thine hands, to which the Gods yield me again.    115
But hear and mark me well.   My birth was not
From the same womb as Hector's, who hath slain
Thy valiant friend for clemency renown'd.
 Such supplication the illustrious son
Of Priam made, but answer harsh received.     120
 Fool ! speak'st of ransom ? Name it not to me.
For till my friend his miserable fate
Accomplish'd, I was somewhat given to spare,
And numerous, whom I seized alive, I sold.
But now, of all the Trojans whom the Gods     125
Deliver to me, none shall death escape,
'Specially of the house of Priam, none.
Die, therefore, even thou, my friend ! What mean
Thy tears unreasonably shed and vain ?
Died not Patroclus, braver far than thou ?     130
And look on me,—see'st not to what an height
My stature towers, and what a bulk I boast ?
A King begat me, and a Goddess bore.
What then ! A death by violence awaits
Me also, and at morn, or eve, or noon,      135
I perish, whensoe'er the destined spear
Shall reach me, or the arrow from the nerve.
 He ceased, and where the suppliant kneel'd, he died.
Quitting the spear, with both hands spread abroad
He sat, but swift Achilles with his sword     140
'Twixt neck and key-bone smote him, and his blade
Of double edge sank all into the wound.
He prone extended on the champaign lay
Bedewing with his sable blood the glebe,
Till, by the foot, Achilles cast him far      145
Into the stream, and, as he floated down,
Thus in wing'd accents, glorying, exclaim'd.
 Lie there, and feed the fishes, which shall lick

Thy blood secure.   Thy mother ne'er shall place
Thee on thy bier, nor on thy body weep,                          150
But swift Scamander on his giddy tide
Shall bear thee to the bosom of the sea.
There, many a fish shall through the crystal flood
Ascending to the rippled surface, find
Lycaon's pamper'd flesh delicious fare.                          155
Die Trojans! till we reach your city, you
Fleeing, and slaughtering, I.   This pleasant stream
Of dimpling silver which ye worship oft
With victim bulls, and sate with living steeds
His rapid whirlpools, shall avail you nought,                    160
But ye shall die, die terribly, till all
Shall have requited me with just amends
For my Patroclus, and for other Greeks
Slain at the ships while I declined the war.
    He ended, at whose words still more incensed                 165
Scamander means devised, thenceforth to check
Achilles, and avert the doom of Troy.
Meantime the son of Peleus, his huge spear
Grasping, assail'd Asteropæus son
Of Pelegon, on fire to take his life.                            170
Fair Peribœa, daughter eldest-born
Of Acessamenus, his father bore
To broad-stream'd Axius, who had clasp'd the nymph
In his embrace.   On him Achilles sprang.
He newly risen from the river, stood                             175
Armed with two lances opposite, for him
Xanthus embolden'd, at the deaths incensed
Of many a youth whom, mercy none vouchsafed,
Achilles had in all his current slain.
And now small distance interposed, they faced                   180
Each other, when Achilles thus began.
    Who art and whence, who dar'st encounter me?
Hapless the sires whose sons my force defy.
    To whom the noble son of Pelegon.
Pelides, mighty Chief! Why hast thou ask'd                       185
My derivation? from the land I come
Of mellow-soil'd Pœonia far remote,
Chief leader of Pœonia's host spear-arm'd;
This day hath also the eleventh risen

Since I at Troy arrived.   For my descent,                190
It is from Axius river wide-diffused,
From Axius, fairest stream that waters earth,
Sire of bold Pelegon whom men report
My sire.   Let this suffice.   Now fight, Achilles!
    So spake he threatening, and Achilles raised         195
Dauntless the Pelian ash.   At once two spears
The hero bold, Asteropæus threw,
With both hands apt for battle.   One his shield
Struck but pierced not, impeded by the gold,
Gift of a God, the other as it flew                      200
Grazed his right elbow ; sprang the sable blood ;
But, overflying him, the spear in earth
Stood planted deep, still hungering for the prey.
Then full at the Pœonian Peleus' son
Hurl'd forth his weapon with unsparing force             205
But vain ; he struck the sloping river-bank,
And mid-length deep stood plunged the ashen beam.
Then, with his faulchion drawn, Achilles flew
To smite him ; he in vain, meantime, assay'd
To pluck the rooted spear forth from the bank ;          210
Thrice with full force he shook the beam, and thrice,
Although reluctant, left it ; at his fourth
Last effort, bending it he sought to break
The ashen spear-beam of Æacides,
But perish'd by his keen-edged faulchion first ;         215
For on the belly at his navel's side
He smote him ; to the ground effused fell all
His bowels, death's dim shadows veil'd his eyes.
Achilles ardent on his bosom fix'd
His foot, despoil'd him, and exulting cried.             220
    Lie there ; though River-sprung thou find'st it hard
To cope with sons of Jove omnipotent.
Thou said'st, a mighty River is my sire—
But my descent from mightier Jove I boast ;
My father, whom the Myrmidons obey,                      225
Is son of Æacus, and he of Jove.
As Jove all streams excels that seek the sea,
So, Jove's descendants nobler are than theirs.
Behold a River at thy side—Let Him
Afford thee, if he can, some succour—No—                 230

He may not fight against Saturnian Jove.
Therefore, not kingly Acheloïus,
Nor yet the strength of Ocean's vast profound,
Although from Him all rivers and all seas
All fountains and all wells proceed, may boast     235
Comparison with Jove, but even He
Astonish'd trembles at his fiery bolt,
And his dread thunders rattling in the sky.

    He said, and drawing from the bank his spear,
Asteropæus left stretch'd on the sands,     240
Where, while the clear wave dashed him, eels his flanks
And ravening fishes numerous nibbled bare.
The horsed Pœonians next he fierce assail'd,
Who seeing their brave Chief slain by the sword
And forceful arm of Peleus' son, beside     245
The eddy-whirling stream fled all dispersed.
Thersilochus and Mydon then he slew,
Thrasius, Astypylus and Ophelestes,
Ænius and Mnesus ; nor had these sufficed
Achilles, but Pœonians more had fallen,     250
Had not the angry River from within
His circling gulfs in semblance of a man
Call'd to him, interrupting thus his rage.

    Oh both in courage and injurious deeds
Unmatch'd, Achilles ! whom themselves the Gods     255
Cease not to aid, if Saturn's son have doom'd
All Ilium's race to perish by thine arm,
Expel them, first, from me, ere thou achieve
That dread exploit ; for, cumber'd as I am
With bodies, I can pour my pleasant stream     260
No longer down into the sacred Deep ;
All vanish where thou comest. But oh desist
Dread Chief ! Amazement fills me at thy deeds.

    To whom Achilles, matchless in the race.
River divine ! hereafter be it so.     265
But not from slaughter of this faithless host
I cease, till I shall shut them fast in Troy
And trial make of Hector, if his arm
In single fight shall strongest prove, or mine.

    He said, and like a God, furious, again.     270
Assail'd the Trojans ; then the circling Flood

To Phœbus thus his loud complaint address'd.
　Ah son of Jove, God of the silver bow!
The mandate of the son of Saturn ill
Hast thou perform'd, who, earnest, bade thee aid　　275
The Trojans, till (the sun sunk in the West)
Night's shadow dim should veil the fruitful field.
　He ended, and Achilles spear-renown'd
Plunged from the bank into the middle stream.
Then, turbulent, the River all his tide　　280
Stirr'd from the bottom, landward heaving off
The numerous bodies that his current chok'd
Slain by Achilles; them, as with the roar
Of bulls, he cast aground, but deep within
His oozy gulfs the living safe conceal'd.　　285
Terrible all around Achilles stood
The curling wave, then, falling on his shield
Dash'd him, nor found his footsteps where to rest.
An elm of massy trunk he seized and branch
Luxuriant, but it fell torn from the root　　290
And drew the whole bank after it; immersed
It damm'd the current with its ample boughs,
And join'd as with a bridge the distant shores.
Upsprang Achilles from the gulf and turn'd
His feet, now wing'd for flight, into the plain　　295
Astonish'd; but the God, not so appeased,
Arose against him with a darker curl,[1]
That he might quell him and deliver Troy.
Back flew Achilles with a bound, the length
Of a spear's cast, for such a spring he own'd　　300
As bears the black-plumed eagle on her prey
Strongest and swiftest of the fowls of air.
Like Her he sprang, and dreadful on his chest
Clang'd his bright armour.　Then, with course oblique
He fled his fierce pursuer, but the flood,　　305
Fly where he might, came thundering in his rear.
As when the peasant with his spade a rill
Conducts from some pure fountain through his grove
Or garden, clearing the obstructed course,
The pebbles, as it runs, all ring beneath,　　310

---

[1] 'Ακροκελαινιόων.—The beauty and force of this word are wonderful;
I have in vain endeavoured to do it justice.

And, as the slope still deepens, swifter still
It runs, and, murmuring, outstrips the guide,
So Him, though swift, the River always reach'd
Still swifter ; who can cope with power divine ?
Oft as the noble Chief, turning, essay'd                    315
Resistance, and to learn if all the Gods
Alike rush'd after him, so oft the flood,
Jove's offspring, laved his shoulders.   Upward then
He sprang distress'd, but with a sidelong sweep
Assailing him, and from beneath his steps                    320
Wasting the soil, the Stream his force subdued.
Then looking to the skies, aloud he mourn'd.
    Eternal Sire ! forsaken by the Gods
I sink, none deigns to save me from the flood,
From which once saved, I would no death decline.            325
Yet blame I none of all the Powers of heaven
As Thetis ; she with falsehood sooth'd my soul,
She promised me a death by Phœbus' shafts
Swift-wing'd, beneath the battlements of Troy.
I would that Hector, noblest of his race,                    330
Had slain me, I had then bravely expired
And a brave man had stripp'd me of my arms.
But Fate now dooms me to a death abhorr'd
Whelm'd in deep waters, like a swine-herd's boy
Drown'd in wet weather while he fords a brook.              335
    So spake Achilles ; then, in human form,
Minerva stood and Neptune at his side ;       •
Each seized his hand confirming him, and thus
The mighty Shaker of the shores began.
    Achilles ! moderate thy dismay, fear nought.            340
In us behold, in Pallas and in me,
Effectual aids, and with consent of Jove ;
For to be vanquish'd by a River's force
Is not thy doom.   This foe shall soon be quell'd ;
Thine eyes shall see it.   Let our counsel rule             345
Thy deed, and all is well.   Cease not from war
Till fast within proud Ilium's walls her host
Again be prison'd, all who shall escape ;
Then (Hector slain) to the Achaian fleet
Return ; we make the glorious victory thine.                350
    So they, and both departing sought the skies.

Then, animated by the voice divine,
He moved toward the plain now all o'erspread
By the vast flood on which the bodies swam
And shields of many a youth in battle slain.      355
He leap'd, he waded, and the current stemm'd
Right onward, by the flood in vain opposed,
With such might Pallas fill'd him.    Nor his rage
Scamander aught repress'd, but still the more
Incensed against Achilles, curl'd aloft      360
His waters, and on Simoïs call'd aloud.
    Brother! oh let us with united force
Check, if we may, this warrior; he shall else
Soon lay the lofty towers of Priam low,
Whose host, appall'd, defend them now no more.      365
Haste—succour me—Thy channel fill with streams
From all thy fountains; call thy torrents down;
Lift high the waters; mingle trees and stones
With uproar wild, that we may quell the force
Of this dread Chief triumphant now, and fill'd      370
With projects that might more beseem a God.
But vain shall be his strength, his beauty nought
Shall profit him or his resplendent arms,
For I will bury them in slime and ooze,
And I will overwhelm himself with soil,      375
Sands heaping o'er him and around him sands
Infinite, that no Greek shall find his bones
For ever, in my bottom deep immersed.
There shall his tomb be piled, nor other earth,
At his last rites, his friends shall need for Him.      380
   He said, and lifting high his angry tide
Vortiginous, against Achilles hurl'd,
Roaring, the foam, the bodies, and the blood;
Then all his sable waves divine again
Accumulating, bore him swift along.      385
Shriek'd Juno at that sight, terrified lest
Achilles in the whirling deluge sunk
Should perish, and to Vulcan quick exclaim'd.
   Vulcan, my son, arise; for we account
Xanthus well able to contend with thee.      390
Give instant succour; show forth all thy fires.
Myself will haste to call the rapid South

And Zephyrus, that tempests from the sea
Blowing, thou may'st both arms and dead consume
With hideous conflagration.  Burn along          395
The banks of Xanthus, fire his trees and Him
Seize also.   Let him by no specious guile
Of flattery soothe thee, or by threats appal,
Nor slack thy furious fires 'till with a shout
I give command, then bid them cease to blaze.    400
     She spake, and Vulcan at her word his fires
Shot dreadful forth ; first, kindling on the field,
He burn'd the bodies strew'd numerous around
Slain by Achilles ; arid grew the earth
And the flood ceased.  As when a sprightly breeze   405
Autumnal blowing from the North, at once
Dries the new-water'd garden,² gladdening him
Who tills the soil, so was the champaign dried ;
The dead consumed, against the River, next,
He turn'd the fierceness of his glittering fires.    410
Willows and tamarisks and elms he burn'd,
Burn'd lotus, rushes, reeds ; all plants and herbs
That clothed profuse the margin of his flood.
His eels and fishes, whether wont to dwell
In gulfs beneath, or tumble in the stream,           415
All languish'd while the Artist of the skies
Breath'd on them ; even Xanthus lost, himself,
All force, and, suppliant, Vulcan thus address'd.
     Oh Vulcan ! none in heaven itself may cope
With thee.   I yield to thy consuming fires.         420
Cease, cease.   I reck not if Achilles drive
Her citizens, this moment, forth from Troy,
For what are war and war's concerns to me ?
     So spake he scorch'd, and all his waters boil'd.
As some huge cauldron hisses urged by force          425
Of circling fires and fill'd with melted lard,
The unctuous fluid overbubbling³ streams
On all sides, while the dry wood flames beneath,
So Xanthus bubbled and his pleasant flood

---

² The reason given in the Scholium is, that the surface being hardened
by the wind the moisture remains unexhaled from beneath, and has
time to saturate the roots.—See Villoisson.
   ³ 'Αμβολάδην.

Hiss'd in the fire, nor could he longer flow 430
But check'd his current, with hot steams annoy'd
By Vulcan raised. His supplication, then,
Importunate to Juno thus he turn'd.

Ah Juno! why assails thy son my streams,
Hostile to me alone? Of all who aid 435
The Trojans I am surely least to blame,
Yet even I desist if thou command;
And let thy son cease also; for I swear
That never will I from the Trojans turn
Their evil day, not even when the host 440
Of Greece shall set all Ilium in a blaze.

He said, and by his oath pacified, thus
The white-arm'd Deity to Vulcan spake.

Peace, glorious son! we may not in behalf
Of mortal man thus longer vex a God. 445

Then Vulcan his tremendous fires repress'd,
And down into his gulfy channel rush'd
The refluent flood; for when the force was once
Subdued of Xanthus, Juno interposed,
Although incensed, herself to quell the strife. 450

But contest vehement the other Gods
Now waged, each breathing discord; loud they rush'd
And fierce to battle, while the boundless earth
Quaked under them, and, all around, the heavens
Sang them together with a trumpet's voice. 455
Jove listening, on the Olympian summit sat
Well-pleased, and, in his heart laughing for joy,
Beheld the Powers of heaven in battle join'd.
Not long aloof they stood. Shield-piercer Mars
His brazen spear grasp'd, and began the fight 460
Rushing on Pallas, whom he thus reproach'd.

Wasp! front of impudence, and past all bounds
Audacious! Why impellest thou the Gods
To fight? Thy own proud spirit is the cause.
Remember'st not, how, urged by thee, the son 465
Of Tydeus, Diomede, myself assail'd,
When thou, the radiant spear with thy own hand
Guiding, didst rend my body? Now, I ween,
The hour is come in which I shall exact
Vengeance for all thy malice shown to me. 470

So saying, her shield he smote tassell'd around
Terrific, proof against the bolts of Jove ;
That shield gore-tainted Mars with fury smote.
But she, retiring, with strong grasp upheaved
A rugged stone, black, ponderous, from the plain,          475
A land-mark fix'd by men of ancient times,
Which hurling at the neck of stormy Mars
She smote him.   Down he fell.   Seven acres, stretch'd,
He overspread, his ringlets in the dust
Polluted lay, and dreadful rang his arms.                  480
The Goddess laugh'd, and thus in accents wing'd
With exultation, as he lay, exclaim'd.
    Fool! Art thou still to learn how far my force
Surpasses thine, and darest thou cope with me ?
Now feel the furies of thy mother's ire                    485
Who hates thee for thy treachery to the Greeks,
And for thy succour given to faithless Troy.
    She said, and turn'd from Mars her glorious eyes.
But him deep-groaning and his torpid powers
Recovering slow, Venus conducted thence                    490
Daughter of Jove, whom soon as Juno mark'd,
In accents wing'd to Pallas thus she spake.
    Daughter invincible of glorious Jove !
Haste—follow her—Ah shameless ! how she leads
Gore-tainted Mars through all the host of heaven.          495
    So she, whom Pallas with delight obey'd ;
To Venus swift she flew, and on the breast
With such force smote her that of sense bereft
The fainting Goddess fell.   There Venus lay
And Mars extended on the fruitful glebe,                   500
And Pallas thus in accents wing'd exclaim'd.
    I would that all who on the part of Troy
Oppose in fight Achaia's valiant sons,
Were firm and bold as Venus in defence
Of Mars, for whom she dared my power defy !                505
So had dissension (Ilium overthrown
And desolated) ceased long since in heaven.
    So Pallas, and approving Juno smiled.
Then the Imperial Shaker of the shores
Thus to Apollo.   Phœbus ! wherefore stand                 510
*We* thus aloof ? Since others have begun,

Begin we also ; shame it were to both
Should we, no combat waged, ascend again
Olympus and the brass-built hall of Jove.
Begin, for thou art younger ; me whose years          515
Alike and knowledge thine surpass so far,
It suits not.   Oh stupidity ! how gross
Art thou and senseless ! Are no traces left
In thy remembrance of our numerous wrongs
Sustain'd at Ilium, when, of all the Gods             520
Ourselves alone, by Jove's commandment, served
For stipulated hire, a year complete,
Our task-master the proud Laomedon ?
Myself a bulwark'd town, spacious, secure
Against assault, and beautiful as strong              525
Built for the Trojans, and thine office was
To feed for King Laomedon his herds
Among the groves of Ida many-valed.
But when the gladsome hours the season brought
Of payment, then the unjust King of Troy              530
Dismiss'd us of our whole reward amerced
By violence, and added threats beside.
Thee into distant isles, bound hand and foot,
To sell he threaten'd, and to amputate
The ears of both ; we, therefore, hasted thence       535
Resenting deep our promised hire withheld.
Aid'st thou for this the Trojans ?   Canst thou less
Than seek, with us, to exterminate the whole
Perfidious race, wives, children, husbands, all ?

    To whom the King of radiant shafts Apollo.        540
Me, Neptune, thou wouldst deem, thyself, unwise
Contending for the sake of mortal men
With thee ; a wretched race, who like the leaves
Now flourish rank, by fruits of earth sustain'd,
Now sapless fall.   Here, therefore, us between       545
Let all strife cease, far better left to Them.

    He said, and turn'd away, fearing to lift
His hand against the brother of his sire.
But him Diana of the woods with sharp
Rebuke, his huntress sister, thus reproved.           550

    Fly'st thou, Apollo ! and to Neptune yield'st
An unearn'd victory, the prize of fame

s. o.—7.                                              E E

Resigning patient and with no dispute?
Fool! wherefore bearest thou the bow in vain?
Ah, let me never in my father's courts                    555
Hear thee among the Immortals vaunting more
That thou would'st Neptune's self confront in arms.
  So she, to whom Apollo nought replied.
But thus the consort of the Thunderer, fired
With wrath, reproved the Archeress of heaven.             560
  How hast thou dared, impudent, to oppose
My will? Bow-practised as thou art, the task
To match my force were difficult to thee.
Is it, because by ordinance of Jove
Thou art a lioness to womankind,                          565
Killing them at thy pleasure? Ah beware,—
Far easier is it, on the mountain-heights
To slay wild beasts and chase the roving hind,
Than to conflict with mightier than ourselves.
But, if thou wish a lesson on that theme,                 570
Approach—Thou shalt be taught with good effect
How far my force in combat passes thine.
  She said, and with her left hand seizing both
Diana's wrists, snatch'd suddenly the bow
Suspended on her shoulder with the right,                 575
And, smiling, smote her with it on the ears.
She, writhing oft and struggling, to the ground
Shook forth her rapid shafts, then, weeping, fled
As to her cavern in some hollow rock
The dove, not destined to his talons, flies               580
The hawk's pursuit, and left her arms behind.
  Then, messenger of heaven, the Argicide
Address'd Latona.  Combat none with thee,
Latona, will I wage.  Unsafe it were
To cope in battle with a spouse of Jove.                  585
Go, therefore, loudly as thou wilt, proclaim
To all the Gods that thou hast vanquish'd me.
  Collecting, then, the bow and arrows fallen
In wild disorder on the dusty plain,
Latona with the sacred charge withdrew                    590
Following her daughter; she, in the abode
Brass-built arriving of Olympian Jove,
Sat on his knees, weeping till all her robe

Ambrosial shook.   The mighty Father smiled,
And to his bosom straining her, enquired.                    595
    Daughter beloved ! who, which of all the Gods
Hath raised his hand, presumptuous, against Thee,
As if convicted of some open wrong?
    To whom the clear-voiced Huntress crescent-crown'd.
My Father ! Juno, thy own consort fair                    600
My sorrow caused, from whom dispute and strife
Perpetual, threaten the Immortal Powers.
    Thus they in heaven mutual conferr'd.   Meantime
Apollo into sacred Troy return'd
Mindful to guard her bulwarks, lest the Greeks                    605
Too soon for Fate should desolate the town.
The other Gods, some angry, some elate
With victory, the Olympian heights regain'd,
And sat beside the Thunderer.   But the son
Of Peleus—He both Trojans slew and steeds.                    610
As when in volumes slow smoke climbs the skies
From some great city which the Gods have fired
Vindictive, sorrow thence to many ensues
With mischief, and to all labour severe,
So caused Achilles labour, on that day,                    615
Severe, and mischief to the men of Troy.
    But ancient Priam from a sacred tower
Stood looking forth, whence soon he noticed vast
Achilles, before whom the Trojans fled,
All courage lost.   Descending from the tower                    620
With mournful cries and hasting to the wall
He thus enjoin'd the keepers of the gates.
    Hold wide the portals till the flying host
Re-enter, for himself is nigh, himself
Achilles drives them home.  Now, woe to Troy !                    625
But soon as safe within the walls received
They breathe again, shut fast the ponderous gates
At once, lest that destroyer also pass.
    He said ; they, shooting back the bars, threw wide
The gates and saved the people, whom to aid                    630
Apollo also sprang into the field.
They, parch'd with drought and whiten'd all with dust,
Flew right toward the town, while, spear in hand,
Achilles press'd them, vengeance in his heart

                                        E E 2

And all on fire for glory.   Then, full sure,          635
Ilium, the city of lofty gates, had fallen
Won by the Grecians, had not Phœbus roused
Antenor's valiant son, the noble Chief
Agenor ; him with dauntless might he fill'd,
And shielding him against the stroke of fate          640
Beside him, stood himself, by the broad beech
Cover'd and wrapt in clouds.   Agenor, then,
Seeing the city-waster hero nigh
Achilles, stood, but standing, felt his mind
Troubled with doubts ; he groan'd, and thus he mused.  645
    Alas ! if following the tumultuous flight
Of these, I shun Achilles, swifter far
He soon will lop my ignominious head.
But if, these leaving to be thus dispersed
Before him, from the city-wall I fly                   650
Across the plain of Troy into the groves
Of Ida, and in Ida's thickets lurk,
I may, at evening, to the town return
Bathed and refreshed.   But whither tend my thoughts ?
Should he my flight into the plain observe,            655
And swift pursuing seize me, then, farewell
All hope to 'scape a miserable death,
For he hath strength passing the strength of man.
How then—shall I withstand him here before
The city ?   He hath also flesh to steal              660
Pervious, within it but a single life,
And men report him mortal, howsoe'er
Saturnian Jove lift him to glory now.
So saying, he turn'd and stood, his dauntless heart
Beating for battle.   As the pard springs forth        665
To meet the hunter from her gloomy lair,
Nor, hearing loud the hounds, fears or retires,
But whether from afar or nigh at hand
He pierce her first, although transfixt, the fight
Still tries, and combats desperate till she fall,      670
So, brave Antenor's son fled not, or shrank,
Till he had proved Achilles, but his breast
O'ershadowing with his buckler, and his spear
Aiming well-poised against him, loud exclaim'd.
    Renown'd Achilles ! Thou art high in hope           675

Doubtless, that thou shalt this day overthrow
The city of the glorious sons of Troy.
Fool! ye must labour yet ere she be won,
For numerous are her citizens and bold,
And we will guard her for our parents' sake                    680
Our wives and little ones.   But here thou diest
Terrible Chief and dauntless as thou art.
    He said, and with full force hurling his lance
Smote, and err'd not, his greave beneath the knee.
The glittering tin, forged newly, at the stroke                685
Tremendous rang, but quick recoiled and vain
The weapon, weak against that guard divine.
Then sprang Achilles in his turn to assail
Godlike Agenor, but Apollo took
That glory from him, snatching wrapt in clouds.                690
Agenor thence, whom calm he sent away.
    Then Phœbus from pursuit of Ilium's host
By art averted Peleus' son; the form
Assuming of Agenor, swift he fled
Before him, and Achilles swift pursued.                        695
While Him Apollo thus lured to the chase
Wide o'er the fruitful plain, inclining still
Toward Scamander's dizzy stream his course
Nor flying far before, but with false hope
Always beguiling him, the scatter'd host                       700
Meantime, in joyful throngs, regained the town.
They fill'd and shut it fast, nor dared to wait
Each other in the field, or to enquire
Who lived and who had fallen, but all, whom flight
Had rescued, like a flood pour'd into Troy.                    705

# BOOK XXII.

---

### ARGUMENT.

#### Achilles slays Hector.

THUS they, throughout all Troy, like hunted fawns
Dispersed, their trickling limbs at leisure cool'd,
And, drinking, slaked their fiery thirst, reclined
Against the battlements.   Meantime, the Greeks
Sloping their shields, approach'd the walls of Troy,          5
And Hector, by his adverse fate ensnared,
Still stood exposed before the Scæan gate.
Then spake Apollo thus to Peleus' son.
　　Wherefore, thyself mortal, pursuest thou me
Immortal ? oh Achilles ! blind with rage,                   10
Thou know'st not yet, that thou pursuest a God.
Unmindful of thy proper task, to press
The flying Trojans, thou hast hither turn'd
Devious, and they are all now safe in Troy ;
Yet hope not me to slay ; I cannot die.                     15
　　To whom Achilles swifest of the swift,
Indignant.   Oh, of all the Powers above
To me most adverse, Archer of the skies !
Thou hast beguiled me, leading me away
From Ilium far, whence intercepted, else,                   20
No few had at this moment gnaw'd the glebe.
Thou hast defrauded me of great renown,
And, safe thyself, hast rescued *them* with ease.
Ah—had I power, I would requite thee well.
　　So saying, incensed he turn'd toward the town            25
His rapid course, like some victorious steed
That whirls, at stretch, a chariot to the goal.
Such seem'd Achilles, coursing light the field.
　　Him, first, the ancient King of Troy perceived
Scouring the plain, resplendent as the star                 30

Autumnal, of all stars in dead of night
Conspicuous most, and named Orion's dog;
Brightest it shines, but ominous, and dire
Disease portends to miserable man;
So beam'd Achilles' armour as he flew.                    35
Loud wail'd the hoary King; with lifted hands
His head he smote, and, uttering doleful cries
Of supplication, sued to his own son.
He, fix'd before the gate, desirous stood
Of combat with Achilles, when his Sire                    40
With arms outstretch'd toward him, thus began.
    My Hector! wait not, oh my son! the approach
Of this dread Chief, alone, lest premature
Thou die, this moment by Achilles slain,
For he is strongest far.   Oh that the Gods               45
Him loved as I! then, soon should vultures rend
And dogs his carcase, and my grief should cease.
He hath unchilded me of many a son,
All valiant youths, whom he hath slain or sold
To distant isles, and even now, I miss                    50
Two sons, whom since the shutting of the gates
I find not, Polydorus and Lycaon,
My children by Laothöe the fair.
If they survive prisoners in yonder camp,
I will redeem them with the gold and brass                55
By noble Eltes to his daughter given,
Large store, and still reserved.   But should they both,
Already slain, have journey'd to the shades,
We, then, from whom they sprang have cause to mourn
And mourn them long, but shorter shall the grief          60
Of Ilium prove, if thou escape and live.
Come then, my son! enter the city-gate
That thou may'st save us all, nor in thy bloom
Of life cut off, enhance Achilles' fame.
Commiserate also thy unhappy Sire                         65
Ere yet distracted, whom Saturnian Jove
Ordains to a sad death, and ere I die
To woes innumerable; to behold
Sons slaughter'd, daughters ravish'd, torn and stripp'd
The matrimonial chamber, infants dash'd                   70
Against the ground in dire hostility,

And matrons dragg'd by ruthless Grecian hands.
Me, haply, last of all, dogs shall devour
In my own vestibule, when once the spear
Or faulchion of some Greek hath laid me low.                    75
The very dogs fed at my table-side,
My portal-guards, drinking their master's blood
To drunkenness, shall wallow in my courts.
Fair falls the warlike youth in battle slain,
And when he lies torn by the pointed steel;                     80
His death becomes him well; he is secure,
Though dead, from shame, whatever next befalls:
But when the silver locks and silver beard
Of an old man slain by the sword, from dogs
Receive dishonour, of all ills that wait                        85
On miserable man, that sure is worst.
   So spake the ancient King, and his grey hairs
Pluck'd with both hands, but Hector firm endured.
On the other side all tears his mother stood,
And lamentation; with one hand she bared,                       90
And with the other hand produced her breast,
Then in wing'd accents, weeping, him bespake.
   My Hector! reverence This, and pity me.
If ever, drawing forth this breast, thy griefs
Of infancy I soothed, oh now, my son!                           95
Acknowledge it, and from within the walls
Repulse this enemy; stand not abroad
To cope with *Him*, for he is savage-fierce,
And should he slay thee, neither shall myself
Who bore thee, nor thy noble spouse weep o'er                  100
Thy body, but, where we can never come,
Dogs shall devour it in the fleet of Greece.
   So they with prayers importuned, and with tears
Their son, but him sway'd not; unmoved he stood,
Expecting vast Achilles now at hand.                           105
As some fell serpent in his cave expects
The traveller's approach, batten'd with herbs
Of baneful juice to fury, forth he looks
Hideous, and lies coil'd all around his den,
So Hector, fill'd with confidence untamed,                     110
Fled not, but placing his bright shield against
A buttress, with his noble heart conferr'd.

Alas for me! should I repass the gate,
Polydamas would be the first to heap
Reproaches on me, for he bade me lead       115
The Trojans back this last calamitous night
In which Achilles rose to arms again.
But I refused, although to have complied,
Had proved more profitable far; since then
By rash resolves of mine I have destroy'd       120
The people, how can I escape the blame
Of all in Troy? The meanest there will say—
By his self-will he hath destroy'd us all.
So shall they speak, and then shall I regret
That I return'd ere I had slain in fight       125
Achilles, or that, by Achilles slain,
I died not nobly in defence of Troy.
But shall I thus? Lay down my bossy shield,
Put off my helmet, and my spear recline
Against the city wall, then go myself       130
To meet the brave Achilles, and at once
Promise him Helen, for whose sake we strive,
With all the wealth that Paris in his fleet
Brought home, to be restored to Atreus' sons,
And to distribute to the Greeks at large       135
All hidden treasures of the town, an oath
Taking beside from every senator,
That he will nought conceal, but will produce
And share in just equality what stores
Soever our fair city still includes?       140
Ah, airy speculations, questions vain!
I may not sue to Him; compassion none
Will he vouchsafe me, or my suit respect,
But, seeing me unarm'd, will sate at once
His rage, and womanlike I shall be slain.       145
It is no time from oak or hollow rock
With Him to parley, as a nymph and swain,
A nymph and swain[1] soft parley mutual hold,
But rather to engage in combat fierce

---

[1] The repetition follows the Original, and the Scholiast is of opinion
that Homer uses it here that he may express more emphatically the length
to which such conferences are apt to proceed.—Διά την πολυλογιαν τη
ἀναληψιι ἐχρησατο.

Incontinent; so shall we soonest learn                    150
Whom Jove will make victorious, Him or me.
   Thus pondering he stood; meantime approach'd
Achilles, terrible as fiery Mars,
Crest-tossing God, and brandish'd as he came
O'er his right shoulder high the Pelian spear.            155
Like lightning, or like flame, or like the sun
Ascending, beam'd his armour.    At that sight
Trembled the Trojan Chief, nor dared expect
His nearer step, but flying left the gates
Far distant, and Achilles swift pursued.                  160
As in the mountains, fleetest fowl of air,
The hawk darts eager at the dove; she scuds
Aslant, he, screaming, springs and springs again
To seize her, all impatient for the prey,
So flew Achilles constant to the track                    165
Of Hector, who with dreadful haste beneath
The Trojan bulwarks plied his agile limbs.
Passing the prospect-mount where high in air
The wild-fig waved², they rush'd along the road,
Declining never from the wall of Troy.                    170
And now they reach'd the running rivulets clear,
Where from Scamander's dizzy flood arise
Two fountains, tepid one, from which a smoke
Issues voluminous as from a fire,
The other, even in summer heats, like hail                175
For cold, or snow, or chrystal-stream frost-bound.
Beside them may be seen the broad canals
Of marble scoop'd, in which the wives of Troy
And all her daughters fair were wont to lave
Their costly raiment, while the land had rest,            180
And ere the warlike sons of Greece arrived.
By these they ran, one fleeing, one in chase.
Valiant was he who fled, but valiant far
Beyond him He who urged the swift pursuit;
Nor ran they for a vulgar prize, a beast                  185
For sacrifice, or for the hide of such,
The swift foot-racer's customary meed,
But for the noble Hector's life they ran.
As when two steeds, oft conquerors, trim the goal

² It grew near to the tomb of Ilus.

For some illustrious prize, a tripod bright                    190
Or beauteous virgin, at a funeral game,
So they with nimble feet the city thrice
Of Priam compass'd.   All the Gods look'd on,
And thus the Sire of Gods and men began.
    Ah—I behold a warrior dear to me                          195
Around the walls of Ilium driven, and grieve
For Hector, who the thighs of fatted bulls
On yonder heights of Ida many-valed
Burn'd oft to me, and in the heights of Troy:
But Him Achilles, glorious Chief, around                      200
The city-walls of Priam now pursues.
Consider this, ye Gods! weigh the event.
Shall we from death save Hector? or, at length,
Leave him, although in battle high-renown'd,
To perish by the might of Peleus' son?                        205 ·
    Whom answer'd thus Pallas cœrulean-eyed.
Dread Sovereign of the storms! what hast thou said?
Wouldst thou deliver from the stroke of fate
A mortal man death-destined from of old?
Do it; but small thy praise shall be in heaven.              210
    Then answer thus, cloud-gatherer Jove return'd.
Fear not, Tritonia, daughter dear! that word
Spake not my purpose; me thou shalt perceive
Always to thee indulgent.   What thou wilt
That execute, and use thou no delay.                         215
    So roused he Pallas of herself prepared,
And from the heights Olympian down she flew.
With unremitting speed Achilles still
Urged Hector.   As among the mountain-heights
The hound pursues, roused newly from her lair                220
The flying fawn through many a vale and grove;
And though she trembling skulk the shrubs beneath,
Tracks her continual, till he find the prey,
So 'scaped not Hector, Peleus' rapid son.
Oft as toward the Dardan gates he sprang                      225
Direct, and to the bulwarks firm of Troy,
Hoping some aid by volleys from the wall,
So oft, outstripping him, Achilles thence
Enforced him to the field, who, as he might,
Still ever stretch'd toward the walls again.                 230

As, in a dream,[3] pursuit hesitates oft,
This hath no power to fly, that to pursue,
So these—One fled, and one pursued in vain.
How, then, had Hector his impending fate
Eluded. had not Phœbus, at his last,                     235
Last effort meeting him, his strength restored,
And wing'd for flight his agile limbs anew?
The son of Peleus, as he ran, his brows
Shaking, forbad the people to dismiss
A dart at Hector, lest a meaner hand                     240
Piercing him, should usurp the foremost praise.
But when the fourth time to those rivulets
They came, then lifting high his golden scales,
Two lots the everlasting Father placed
Within them, for Achilles one, and one                   245
For Hector, balancing the doom of both.
Grasping it in the midst, he raised the beam.
Down went the fatal day of Hector, down
To Ades, and Apollo left his side.
Then blue-eyed Pallas hasting to the son                 250
Of Peleus, in wing'd accents him address'd.
    Now, dear to Jove, Achilles famed in arms!
I hope that, fierce in combat though he be,
We shall, at last, slay Hector, and return
Crown'd with great glory to the fleet of Greece.         255
No fear of his deliverance now remains,
Not even should the King of radiant shafts
Apollo toil in supplication, roll'd
And roll'd again[4] before the Thunderer's feet.
But stand, recover breath; myself, the while,            260
Shall urge him to oppose thee face to face.
    So Pallas spake, whom joyful he obey'd,
And on his spear brass-pointed lean'd.  But she,
(Achilles left) to noble Hector pass'd,
And in the form, and with the voice loud-toned           265
Approaching of Deiphobus, his ear
In accents, as of pity, thus address'd.
    Ah brother! thou art overtask'd, around

---

[3] The numbers in the original are so constructed as to express the
painful struggle that characterizes such a dream.
[4] προπροκυλινδόμενος.

The walls of Troy by swift Achilles driven;
But stand, that we may chase him in his turn.          270
  To whom crest-tossing Hector huge replied.
Deiphobus! of all my father's sons
Brought forth by Hecuba, I ever loved
Thee most, but more than ever love thee now,
Who hast not fear'd, seeing me, for my sake          275
To quit the town, where others rest content.
  To whom the Goddess, thus, cœrulean-eyed.
Brother! our parents with much earnest suit
Clasping my knees, and all my friends implored me
To stay in Troy, (such fear hath seized on all)          280
But grief for thee prey'd on my inmost soul.
Come—fight we bravely—spare we now our spears
No longer; now for proof if Peleus' son
Slaying us both, shall bear into the fleet
Our arms gore-stain'd, or perish slain by thee.          285
  So saying, the wily Goddess led the way.
They soon, approaching each the other, stood
Opposite, and huge Hector thus began.
  Pelides! I will fly thee now no more.
Thrice I have compass'd Priam's spacious walls          290
A fugitive, and have not dared abide
Thy onset, but my heart now bids me stand
Dauntless, and I will slay, or will be slain.
But come.  We will attest the Gods; for they
Are fittest both to witness and to guard          295
Our covenant.  If Jove to me vouchsafe
The hard-earn'd victory, and to take thy life,
I will not with dishonour foul insult
Thy body, but, thine armour stripp'd, will give
Thee to thy friends, as thou shalt me to mine.          300
  To whom Achilles, louring dark, replied.
Hector! my bitterest foe! speak not to me
Of covenants! as concord can be none
Lions and men between, nor wolves and lambs
Can be unanimous, but hate perforce          305
Each other by a law not to be changed,
So cannot amity subsist between
Thee and myself; nor league make I with thee
Or compact, till thy blood in battle shed

Or mine, shall gratify the fiery Mars. 310
Rouse all thy virtue, thou hast utmost need
Of valour now, and of address in arms.
Escape me more thou canst not, Pallas' hand
By mine subdues thee ; now will I avenge
At once the agonies of every Greek 315
In thy unsparing fury slain by thee.
   He said, and, brandishing the Pelian ash,
Dismiss'd it ; but illustrious Hector warn'd,
Couch'd low, and, overflying him, it pierced
The soil beyond, whence Pallas plucking it 320
Unseen, restored it to Achilles' hand,
And Hector to his godlike foe replied.
   Godlike Achilles ! thou hast err'd, nor know'st
At all my doom from Jove, as thou pretend'st,
But seek'st, by subtlety and wind of words, 325
All empty sounds, to rob me of my might.
Yet stand I firm.   Think not to pierce my back.
Behold my bosom ! if the Gods permit,
Meet me advancing, and transpierce me there.
Meantime avoid my glittering spear, but oh 330
May'st thou receive it all ! since lighter far
To Ilium should the toils of battle prove,
Wert thou once slain, fiercest of her foes.
   He said, and hurling his long spear with aim
Unerring, smote the centre of the shield 335
Of Peleus' son, but his spear glanced away.
He, angry to have sent it forth in vain,
(For he had other none) with eyes downcast
Stood motionless awhile, then with loud voice
Sought from Deiphobus, white-shielded Chief, 340
A second ; but Deiphobus was gone.
Then Hector understood his doom, and said.
   Ah, it is plain ; this is mine hour to die.
I thought Deiphobus at hand, but me
Pallas beguiled, and he is still in Troy. 345
A bitter death threatens me, it is nigh,
And there is no escape ; Jove, and Jove's son
Apollo, from the first, although awhile
My prompt deliverers, chose this lot for me,
And now it finds me.   But I will not fall 350

Inglorious; I will act some great exploit
That shall be celebrated ages hence.
    So saying, his keen faulchion from his side
He drew, well-temper'd, ponderous, and rush'd
At once to combat.   As the eagle darts          355
Right downward through a sullen cloud to seize
Weak lamb or timorous hare, so brandishing
His splendid faulchion, Hector rush'd to fight.
Achilles, opposite, with fellest ire
Full-fraught came on; his shield with various art          360
Celestial form'd, o'erspread his ample chest,
And on his radiant casque terrific waved
The bushy gold of his resplendent crest,
By Vulcan spun, and pour'd profuse around.
Bright as, among the stars, the star of all          365
Most radiant, Hesperus, at midnight moves,
So, in the right-hand of Achilles beam'd
His brandish'd spear, while, meditating woe
To Hector, he explored his noble form,
Seeking where he was vulnerable most.          370
But every part, his dazzling armour torn
From brave Patroclus' body, well secured,
Save where the circling key-bone from the neck
Disjoins the shoulder; there his throat appear'd,
Whence injured life with swiftest flight escapes;          375
Achilles, plunging in that part his spear,
Impell'd it through the yielding flesh beyond.
The ashen beam his power of utterance left
Still unimpair'd, but in the dust he fell,
And the exulting conqueror exclaim'd.          380
    But Hector! thou hadst once far other hopes,
And, stripping slain Patroclus, thought'st thee safe,
Nor caredst for absent me.   Fond dream and vain!
I was not distant far; in yonder fleet
He left one able to avenge his death,          385
And he hath slain thee.   Thee the dogs shall rend
Dishonourably, and the fowls of air,
But all Achaia's host shall him entomb.
    To whom the Trojan Chief languid replied.
By thy own life, by theirs who gave thee birth,          390

And by thy knees[5], oh let not Grecian dogs
Rend and devour me, but in gold accept
And brass a ransom at my father's hands,
And at my mother's, an illustrious price;
Send home my body, grant me burial rites          395
Among the daughters and the sons of Troy.
 To whom with aspect stern Achilles thus.
Dog! neither knees nor parents name to me.
I would my fierceness of revenge were such,
That I could carve and eat thee, to whose arms     400
Such griefs I owe; so true it is and sure,
That none shall save thy carcase from the dogs.
No, trust me, would thy parents bring me weigh'd
Ten—twenty ransoms, and engage on oath
To add still more; would thy Dardanian Sire        405
Priam, redeem thee with thy weight in gold,
Not even at that price would I consent
That she who bare should place thee on thy bier
With lamentation; dogs and ravening fowls
Shall rend thy body while a scrap remains.          410
 Then, dying, warlike Hector thus replied.
Full well I knew before, how suit of mine
Should speed preferr'd to thee.   Thy heart is steel.
But oh, while yet thou livest, think, lest the Gods
Requite thee on that day, when pierced thyself      415
By Paris and Apollo, thou shalt fall,
Brave as thou art, before the Scæan gate.
 He ceased, and death involved him dark around.
His spirit, from his limbs dismiss'd, the house
Of Ades sought, mourning in her descent            420
Youth's prime and vigour lost, disastrous doom!
But Him though dead, Achilles thus bespake.
 Die thou.   My death shall find me at what hour
Jove gives commandment, and the Gods above.
 He spake, and from the dead drawing away         425
His brazen spear, placed it apart, then stripp'd
His arms gore-stain'd.   Meantime the other sons
Of the Achaians, gathering fast around,
The bulk admired, and the proportion just

---

[5] The knees of the conqueror were a kind of sanctuary to which the
vanquished fled for refuge.

Of Hector, neither stood a Grecian there        430
Who pierced him not, and thus the soldier spake.
   Ye Gods! how far more patient of the touch
Is Hector now, than when he fired the fleet!
   Thus would they speak, then give him each a stab.
And now, the body stripp'd, their noble Chief     435
The swift Achilles standing in the midst,
The Grecians in wing'd accents thus address'd.
   Friends, Chiefs and Senators of Argos' host!
Since, by the will of heaven, this man is slain
Who harm'd us more than all our foes beside,     440
Essay we next the city, so to learn
The Trojan purpose, whether (Hector slain)
They will forsake the citadel, or still
Defend it, even though of Him deprived.
But wherefore speak I thus? still undeplored,     445
Unburied in my fleet Patroclus lies;
Him never, while alive myself, I mix
With living men and move, will I forget.
In Ades, haply, they forget the dead,
Yet will not I Patroclus, even there.     450
Now chaunting pæans, ye Achaian youths
Return we to the fleet with this our prize;
We have achieved great glory[6], we have slain
Illustrious Hector, him whom Ilium praised
In all her gates, and as a God revered.     455
   He said; then purposing dishonour foul
To noble Hector, both his feet he bored
From heel to ancle, and, inserting thongs,
Them tied behind his chariot, but his head
Left unsustain'd to trail along the ground.     460
Ascending next, the armour at his side
He placed, then lash'd the steeds; they willing flew.
Thick dust around the body dragg'd arose,
His sable locks all swept the plain, and all
His head, so graceful once, now track'd the dust,     465
For Jove had given it into hostile hands
That they might shame it in his native soil.

---

[6] The lines of which these three are a translation, are supposed by some to have been designed for the Επινικιον, or song of victory sung by the whole army.

Thus, whelm'd in dust, it went.  The mother Queen
Her son beholding, pluck'd her hair away,
Cast far aside her lucid veil, and fill'd          470
With shrieks the air.   His father wept aloud,
And, all around, long long complaints were heard
And lamentations in the streets of Troy,
Not fewer or less piercing, than if flames
Had wrapt all Ilium to her topmost towers.          475
His people scarce detain'd the ancient King
Grief-stung, and resolute to issue forth
Through the Dardanian gates; to all he kneel'd
In turn, then roll'd himself in dust, and each
By name solicited to give him way.          480
   Stand off, my fellow mourners! I would pass
The gates, would seek, alone, the Grecian fleet.
I go to supplicate the bloody man,
Yon ravager; he may respect, perchance,
My years, may feel some pity of my age;          485
For, such as I am, his own father is,
Peleus, who rear'd him for a curse to Troy,
But chiefly rear'd him to myself a curse,
So numerous have my sons in prime of youth
Fall'n by his hand, all whom I less deplore          490
(Through mourning all) than one ; my agonies
For Hector, soon shall send me to the shades.
Oh had he but within these arms expired,
The hapless Queen who bore him, and myself
Had wept him, then, till sorrow could no more !          495
   So spake he weeping, and the citizens
All sigh'd around; next, Hecuba began
Amid the women, thus, her sad complaint.
   Ah wherefore, oh my son! wretch that I am,
Breathe I forlorn of thee? Thou, night and day,          500
My glory wast in Ilium, thee her sons
And daughters, both, hail'd as their guardian God,
Conscious of benefits from thee received,
Whose life prolong'd should have advanced them all
To high renown.  Vain boast! thou art no more.          505
   So mourn'd the Queen.   But fair Andromache
Nought yet had heard, nor knew by sure report
Hector's delay without the city-gates.

She in a closet of her palace sat,
A twofold web weaving magnificent,                    510
With sprinkled flowers inwrought of various hues,
And to her maidens had commandment given
Through all her house, that compassing with fire
An ample tripod, they should warm a bath
For noble Hector from the fight return'd.             515
Tenderness ill-inform'd! she little knew
That in the field, from such refreshments far,
Pallas had slain him by Achilles' hand.
She heard a cry of sorrow from the tower;
Her limbs shook under her, her shuttle fell,          520
And to her bright-hair'd train, alarm'd, she cried.
    Attend me two of you, that I may learn
What hath befallen.   I have heard the voice
Of the Queen-mother; my rebounding heart
Chokes me, and I seem fetter'd by a frost.            525
Some mischief sure o'er Priam's sons impends.
Far be such tidings from me! but I fear
Horribly, lest Achilles, cutting off
My dauntless Hector from the gates alone,
Enforce him to the field, and quell perhaps           530
The might, this moment, of that dreadful arm
His hinderance long; for Hector ne'er was wont
To seek his safety in the ranks, but flew
First into battle, yielding place to none.
    So saying, she rush'd with palpitating heart      535
And frantic air abroad, by her two maids
Attended; soon arriving at the tower,
And at the throng of men, awhile she stood
Down-looking wistful from the city-wall,
And, seeing him in front of Ilium, dragg'd            540
So cruelly toward the fleet of Greece,
O'erwhelm'd with sudden darkness at the view
Fell backward, with a sigh heard all around.
Far distant flew dispersed her head-attire,
Twist, frontlet, diadem, and even the veil            545
By golden Venus given her on the day
When Hector led her from Eëtion's house
Enrich'd with nuptial presents to his home.
Around her throng'd her sisters of the house

F F 2

Of Priam, numerous, who within their arms 550
Fast held her[7] loathing life; but she, her breath
At length and sense recovering, her complaint
Broken with sighs amid them thus began.

Hector! I am undone; we both were born
To misery, thou in Priam's house in Troy, 555
And I in Hypoplacian Thebes wood-crown'd
Beneath Eëtion's roof. He, doom'd himself
To sorrow, me more sorrowfully doom'd,
Sustain'd in helpless infancy, whom oh
That he had ne'er begotten! thou descend'st 560
To Pluto's subterraneous dwelling drear,
Leaving myself destitute, and thy boy,
Fruit of our hapless loves, an infant yet,
Never to be hereafter thy delight,
Nor love of thine to share or kindness more. 565
For should he safe survive this cruel war,
With the Achaians penury and toil
Must be his lot, since strangers will remove
At will his landmarks, and possess his fields.
Thee lost, he loses all, of father, both, 570
And equal playmate in one day deprived,
To sad looks doom'd, and never-ceasing tears.
He seeks, necessitous his father's friends,
One by his mantle pulls, one by his vest,
Whose utmost pity yields to his parch'd lips 575
A thirst-provoking drop, and grudges more;
Some happier child, as yet untaught to mourn
A parent's loss, shoves rudely from the board
My son, and, smiting him, reproachful cries—
Away—Thy father is no guest of ours— 580
Then, weeping, to his widow'd mother comes
Astyanax, who on his father's lap
Ate marrow only, once, and fat of lambs,
And when sleep took him, and his crying fit
Had ceased, slept ever on the softest bed, 585
Warm in his nurse's arms, fed to his fill

---

[7] It is an observation of the Scholiast, that two more affecting spectacles cannot be imagined, than Priam struggling to escape into the field, and Andromache to cast herself from the wall; for so he understands ἀτυζομένην ἀπολεσθαι.

With delicacies, and his heart at rest.
But now, Astyanax (so named in Troy
For thy sake, guardian of her gates and towers)
His father lost, must many a pang endure.                          590
And as for thee, cast naked forth among
Yon galleys, where no parent's eye of thine
Shall find thee, when the dogs have torn thee once
Till they are sated, worms shall eat thee next.
Meantime, thy graceful raiment rich, prepared                      595
By our own maidens, in thy palace lies ;
But I will burn it, burn it all, because
Useless to thee, who never, so adorn'd,
Shalt slumber more ; yet every eye in Troy
Shall see, how glorious once was thy attire.                       600
    So, weeping, she ; to whom the multitude
Of Trojan dames responsive sigh'd around.

# BOOK XXIII.

### ARGUMENT.

The body of Patroclus is burned, and the funeral games ensue.

SUCH mourning was in Troy; meantime the Greeks
Their galleys and the shores of Hellespont
Regaining, each to his own ship retired.
But not the Myrmidons; Achilles them
Close rank'd in martial order still detain'd,                  5
And thus his fellow-warriors brave address'd.
　　Ye swift-horsed Myrmidons, associates dear!
Release not from your chariots yet your steeds
Firm-hoof'd, but, steeds and chariots driving near,
Bewail Patroclus, as the rites demand                          10
Of burial; then, satiate with grief and tears,
We will release our steeds, and take repast.
　　He ended, and, himself leading the way,
His numerous band all mourn'd at once the dead.
Around the body thrice their glossy steeds,                    15
Mourning they drove, while Thetis in their hearts
The thirst of sorrow kindled; they with tears
The sands bedew'd, with tears their radiant arms,
Such deep regret of one so brave they felt.
Then, placing on the bosom of his friend                       20
His homicidal hands, Achilles thus
The shade of his Patroclus, sad, bespake.
　　Hail, oh Patroclus, even in Ades hail!
For I will now accomplish to the full
My promise pledged to thee, that I would give                  25
Hector dragg'd hither to be torn by dogs
Piecemeal, and would before thy funeral pile
The necks dissever of twelve Trojan youths
Of noblest rank, resentful of thy death.
　　He said, and meditating foul disgrace                       30
To noble Hector, stretch'd him prone in dust

Beside the bier of Menœtiades.
Then all the Myrmidons their radiant arms
Put off, and their shrill-neighing steeds released.
A numerous band beside the bark they sat                    35
Of swift Æacides, who furnish'd forth
Himself a feast funereal for them all.
Many a white ox under the ruthless steel
Lay bleeding, many a sheep and blatant goat,
With many a saginated boar bright-tusk'd,                   40
Amid fierce flames Vulcanian stretch'd to roast.
Copious the blood ran all around the dead.
   And now the Kings of Greece conducted thence
To Agamemnon's tent the royal son
Of Peleus, loth to go, and won at last                      45
With difficulty, such his anger was
And deep resentment of his slaughter'd friend.
Soon then as Agamemnon's tent they reach'd,
The Sovereign bade his heralds kindle fire
Around an ample vase, with purpose kind                     50
Moving Achilles from his limbs to cleanse
The stains of battle; but he firm refused
That suit, and bound refusal with an oath—·
   No; by the Highest and the best of all,
By Jove I will not.  Never may it be                        55
That brazen bath approach this head of mine,
Till I shall first Patroclus' body give
To his last fires, till I shall pile his tomb,
And sheer my locks in honour of my friend;
For, like to this, no second woe shall e'er                 60
My heart invade, while vital breath I draw.
But, all unwelcome as it is, repast
Now calls us.  Agamemnon, King of men!
Give thou command that at the dawn they bring
Wood hither, such large portion as beseems                  65
The dead, descending to the shades, to share,
That hungry flames consuming out of sight
His body soon, the host may war again.
   He spake; they, hearing, readily obey'd.
Then, each his food preparing with dispatch,                70
They ate, nor wanted any of the guests
Due portion, and their appetite sufficed

To food and wine, all to their tents repair'd
Seeking repose; but on the sands beside
The billowy deep Achilles groaning lay                    75
Amidst his Myrmidons, where space he found
With blood unstain'd beside the dashing wave.
There, soon as sleep, deliverer of the mind,
Wrapp'd him around (for much his noble limbs
With chase of Hector round the battlements                80
Of wind-swept Ilium wearied were and spent)
The soul came to him of his hapless friend,
In bulk resembling, in expressive eyes
And voice Patroclus, and so clad as he.
Him, hovering o'er his head, the form address'd.          85
    Sleep'st thou, Achilles! of thy friend become
Heedless? Him living thou didst not neglect
Whom thou neglectest dead.   Give me a tomb
Instant, that I may pass the infernal gates.
For now, the shades and spirits of the dead               90
Drive me afar, denying me my wish
To mingle with them on the farthest shore,
And in wide-portal'd Ades sole I roam.
Give me thine hand, I pray thee, for the earth
I visit never more, once burnt with fire;                 95
We never shall again close council hold
As we were wont, for me my fate severe,
Mine even from my birth, hath deep absorb'd.
And oh Achilles, semblance of the Gods!
Thou too predestined art beneath the wall                 100
To perish of the high-born Trojan race.
But hear my last injunction! ah, my friend!
My bones sepulchre not from thine apart,
But as, together we were nourish'd both
Beneath thy roof, (what time from Opoëis                  105
Menœtius led me to thy father's house,
Although a child, yet fugitive for blood,
Which, in a quarrel at the dice, I spilt,
Killing my playmate by a casual blow,
The offspring of Amphidamas, when, like                   110
A father, Peleus with all tenderness
Received and cherish'd me, and call'd me thine)
So, let one vase inclose, at last, our bones,

The golden vase, thy Goddess mother's gift.
　To whom Achilles, matchless in the race.　　115
Ah, loved and honour'd! wherefore hast thou come?
Why thus enjoin'd me? I will all perform
With diligence that thou hast now desired.
But nearer stand, that we may mutual clasp
Each other, though but with a short embrace,　　120
And sad satiety of grief enjoy.
　He said, and stretch'd his arms toward the shade,
But him seized not; shrill-clamouring and light.
As smoke, the spirit pass'd into the earth.
Amazed, upsprang Achilles, clash'd aloud　　125
His palms together, and thus, sad, exclaim'd.
　Ah then, ye Gods! there doubtless are below
The soul and semblance both, but empty forms;
For all night long, mourning, disconsolate,
The soul of my Patroclus, hapless friend!　　130
Hath hover'd o'er me, giving me in charge
His last requests, just image of himself.
　So saying, he call'd anew their sorrow forth,
And rosy-palm'd Aurora found them all
Mourning afresh the pitiable dead.　　135
Then royal Agamemnon call'd abroad
Mules and mule-drivers from the tents in haste
To gather wood.　Uprose a valiant man,
Friend of the virtuous Chief Idomeneus,
Meriones, who led them to the task.　　140
They, bearing each in hand his sharpen'd axe
And twisted cord, thence journey'd forth, the mules
Driving before them; much uneven space
They measured, hill and dale, right onward now,
And now circuitous; but at the groves　　145
Arrived, at length, of Ida fountain-fed,
Their keen-edged axes to the towering oaks
Dispatchful they applied; down fell the trees
With crash sonorous.　Splitting, next, the trunks,
They bound them on the mules; they, with firm hoofs　　150
The hill-side stamping, through the thickets rush'd,
Desirous of the plain.　Each man his log
(For so the armour-bearer of the King
Of Crete, Meriones, had them enjoin'd)

Bore after them, and each his burthen cast          155
Down on the beach regular, where a tomb
Of ample size Achilles for his friend
Patroclus had, and for himself, design'd.
   Much fuel thrown together, side by side
There down they sat, and his command at once       160
Achilles issued to his warriors bold,
That all should gird their armour, and the steeds
Join to their chariots; undelaying each
Complied, and in bright arms stood soon array'd.
Then mounted combatants and charioteers.           165
First, moved the chariots, next, the infantry
Proceeded numerous, amid whom his friends,
Bearing the body of Patroclus, went.
They poll'd their heads, and cover'd him with hair
Shower'd over all his body, while behind            170
Noble Achilles march'd the Hero's head
Sustaining sorrowful, for to the realms
Of Ades a distinguish'd friend he sent.
   And now, arriving on the ground erewhile
Mark'd by Achilles, setting down the dead,          175
They heap'd the fuel quick, a lofty pile.
But Peleus' son, on other thoughts intent,
Retiring from the funeral pile, shore off
His amber ringlets, whose exuberant growth
Sacred to Sperchius he had kept unshorn,            180
And looking o'er the gloomy Deep, he said.
   Sperchius! in vain Peleus my father vow'd
That, hence returning to my native land,
These ringlets shorn I should present to thee
With a whole hecatomb, and should, beside,          185
Rams offer fifty at thy fountain head
In thy own field, at thy own fragrant shrine.
So vow'd the hoary Chief, whose wishes thou
Leavest unperform'd.   Since, therefore, never more
I see my native home, the Hero these               190
Patroclus takes down with him to the shades.
   He said, and filling with his hair the hand
Of his dead friend, the sorrows of his train
Waken'd afresh.   And now the lamp of day
Westering[1] apace, had left them still in tears,   195

       [1] Westering wheel.  MILTON.

Had not Achilles suddenly address'd
King Agamemnon, standing at his side.
　　Atrides! (for Achaia's sons thy word
Will readiest execute,) we may with grief
Satiate ourselves hereafter; but, the host                    200
Dispersing from the pile, now give command
That they prepare repast; ourselves,[2] to whom
These labours in peculiar appertain
Will finish them; but bid the Chiefs abide.
　　Which when imperial Agamemnon heard,          205
He scatter'd instant to their several ships
The people; but the burial-dressers thence
Went not; they, still abiding, heap'd the pile.
An hundred feet of breadth from side to side
They gave to it, and on the summit placed           210
With sorrowing hearts the body of the dead.
Many a fat sheep, with many an ox full-horn'd
They flay'd before the pile, busy their task
Administering, and Peleus' son the fat
Taking from every victim, overspread                215
Complete the body with it of his friend
Patroclus, and the flay'd beasts heap'd around.
Then, placing flagons on the pile, replete
With oil and honey, he inclined their mouths
Toward the bier, and slew and added next,           220
Deep-groaning and in haste, four martial steeds.
Nine dogs the Hero at his table fed,
Of which beheading two, their carcases
He added also.　Last, twelve gallant sons
Of noble Trojans slaying, (for his heart               225
Teem'd with great vengeance,) he applied the force
Of hungry flames that should devour the whole,
Then, mourning loud, by name his friend invoked.
　　Rejoice, Patroclus! even in the shades.
Behold my promise to thee all fulfill'd!                230
Twelve gallant sons of Trojans famed in arms,
Together with thyself, are all become
Food for these fires: but fire shall never feed
On Hector; him I destine to the dogs.
　　So threaten'd he; but Him no dogs devour'd;      235

　　　　　　　[2] Himself and the Myrmidons.

Them, day and night, Jove's daughter Venus chased
Afar, and smooth'd the Hero o'er with oils
Of rosy scent ambrosial, lest his corse,
Behind Achilles' chariot dragg'd along
So rudely, should be torn, and Phœbus hung                240
A veil of sable clouds from heaven to earth,
O'ershadowing broad the space where Hector lay,
Lest parching suns intense should stiffen him.
 But the pile kindled not. Then, Peleus' son
Seeking a place apart, two Winds in prayer                245
Boreas invoked and Zephyrus, to each
Vowing large sacrifice. With earnest suit
(Libation pouring from a golden cup)
Their coming he implored, that so the flames
Kindling, incontinent might burn the dead.                250
Iris, his supplications hearing, swift
Convey'd them to the Winds; they, in the hall
Banquetting of the heavy-blowing West,
Sat frequent. Iris, sudden at the gate
Appear'd; they, at the sight upstarting all,               255
Invited each the Goddess to himself.
But she refused a seat and thus she spake.
 I sit not here. Borne over Ocean's stream
Again, to Æthiopia's land I go
Where hecatombs are offer'd to the Gods,                  260
Which, with the rest, I also wish to share.
But Peleus' son, earnest, the aid implores
Of Boreas and of Zephyrus the loud,
Vowing large sacrifice if ye will fan
Briskly the pile on which Patroclus lies                  265
By all Achaia's warriors deep deplored.
 She said, and went. Then suddenly arose
The Winds, and, roaring, swept the clouds along.
First, on the sea they blew; big rose the waves
Beneath the blast. At fruitful Troy arrived           270
Vehement on the pile they fell, and dread
On all sides soon a crackling blaze ensued.
All night, together blowing shrill, they drove
The sheeted flames wide from the funereal pile,
And all night long, a goblet in his hand                  275
From golden beakers fill'd, Achilles stood

With large libations soaking deep the soil,
And calling on the spirit of his friend.
As some fond father mourns, burning the bones
Of his own son, who, dying on the eve                          280
Of his glad nuptials, hath his parents left
O'erwhelm'd with inconsolable distress,
So mourn'd Achilles, his companion's bones
Burning, and pacing to and fro the field
Beside the pile with many a sigh profound.                     285
But when the star, day's harbinger, arose,
Soon after whom, in saffron vest attired
The morn her beams diffuses o'er the sea,
The pile, then wasted, ceased to flame, and then
Back flew the Winds over the Thracian deep                     290
Rolling the flood before them as they pass'd.
And now Pelides lying down apart
From the funereal pile, slept, but not long,
Though weary; waken'd by the stir and din
Of Agamemnon's train.   He sat erect,                          295
And thus the leaders of the host address'd.
      Atrides, and ye potentates who rule
The whole Achaian host! first quench the pile
Throughout with generous wine, where'er the fire
Hath seized it.   We will then the bones collect              300
Of Menœtiades, which shall with ease
Be known, though many bones lie scatter'd near,
Since in the middle pile Patroclus lay,
But wide apart and on its verge we burn'd
The steeds and Trojans, a promiscuous heap.                    305
Them so collected in a golden vase
We will dispose, lined with a double caul,
Till I shall, also, to my home below.
I wish not now a tomb of amplest bounds
But such as may suffice, which yet in height                   310
The Grecians and in breadth shall much augment
Hereafter, who, survivors of my fate,
Shall still remain in the Achaian fleet.
      So spake Pelides, and the Chiefs complied.
Where'er the pile had blazed, with generous wine              315
They quench'd it, and the hills of ashes sank.
Then, weeping, to a golden vase, with lard

Twice lined, they gave their gentle comrade's bones
Fire-bleach'd, and lodging safely in his tent
The relics, overspread them with a veil.                        320
Designing, next, the compass of the tomb
They mark'd its boundary with stones, then fill'd
The wide enclosure hastily with earth,
And, having heap'd it to its height, return'd.
But all the people, by Achilles still·                          325
Detain'd, there sitting, form'd a spacious ring,
And he the destined prizes from his fleet
Produced, capacious cauldrons, tripods bright,
Steeds, mules, tall oxen, women at the breast
Close-cinctured elegant, and unwrought³ iron.                   330
First, to the chariot-drivers he proposed
A noble prize ; a beauteous maiden versed
In arts domestic, with a tripod ear'd,
Of twenty and two measures.   These he made
The conqueror's meed.   The second should a mare               335
Obtain, unbroken yet, six years her age,
Pregnant, and bearing in her womb a mule.
A cauldron of four measures, never smirch'd
By smoke or flame, but fresh as from the forge
The third awaited ; to the fourth he gave                       340
Two golden talents, and, unsullied yet
By use, a twin-ear'd phial⁴ to the fifth.
He stood erect, and to the Greeks he cried.
     Atrides, and ye Chiefs of all the host !
These prizes, in the circus placed, attend                      345
The charioteers.   Held we the present games
In honour of some other Grecian dead,
I would myself bear hence the foremost prize ;
For ye are all witnesses well-inform'd
Of the superior virtue of my steeds.                            350
They are immortal ; Neptune on my sire
Peleus conferr'd them, and my sire on me.
But neither I this contest share myself,
Nor shall my steeds ; for they would miss the force

³ Such it appears to have been in the sequel.
⁴ Φιάλη—a vessel, as Athenæus describes it, made for the purpose of
warming water.  It was formed of brass, and expanded somewhat in
the shape of a broad leaf.

And guidance of a charioteer so kind 355
As they have lost, who many a time hath cleansed
Their manes with water of the crystal brook,
And made them sleek, himself, with limpid oil.
Him, therefore, mourning, motionless they stand
With hair dishevell'd, streaming to the ground. 360
But ye, whoever of the host profess
Superior skill, and glory in your steeds
And well-built chariots, for the strife prepare!
　　So spake Pelides, and the charioteers,
For speed renown'd, arose.　Long ere the rest 365
Eumelus, King of men, Admetus' son
Arose, accomplish'd in equestrian arts.
Next, Tydeus' son, brave Diomede, arose;
He yoked the Trojan coursers by himself
In battle from Æneas won what time 370
Apollo saved their master.　Third, upstood
The son of Atreus with the golden locks,
Who to his chariot Agamemnon's mare
Swift Æthe and his own Podargus join'd.
Her Echepolus from Anchises sprung 375
To Agamemnon gave; she was the price
At which he purchased leave to dwell at home
Excused attendance on the King at Troy;
For, by the gift of Jove, he had acquired
Great riches, and in wide-spread Sicyon dwelt. 380
Her wing'd with ardour, Menelaus yoked.
Antilochus, arising fourth, his steeds
Bright-maned prepared, son of the valiant King
Of Pylus, Nestor Neleïades.
Of Pylian breed were they, and thus his sire, 385
With kind intent approaching to his side,
Advised him, of himself not uninform'd.
　　Antilochus! Thou art, I know, beloved
By Jove and Neptune both, from whom, though young,
Thou hast received knowledge of every art 390
Equestrian, and hast little need to learn.
Thou know'st already how to trim the goal
With nicest skill, yet wondrous slow of foot
Thy coursers are, whence evil may ensue.
But though their steeds be swifter, I account 395

Thee wise, at least, as they.   Now is the time
For counsel, furnish now thy mind with all
Precaution, that the prize escape thee not.
The feller of huge trees by skill prevails
More than by strength ; by skill the pilot guides     400
His flying bark rock'd by tempestuous winds,
And more by skill than speed the race is won.
But He who in his chariot and his steeds
Trusts only, wanders here and wanders there
Unsteady, while his coursers loosely rein'd     405
Roam wide the field ; not so the charioteer
Of sound intelligence ; he though he drive
Inferior steeds, looks ever to the goal
Which close he clips, not ignorant to check
His coursers at the first, but with tight rein     410
Ruling his own, and watching those before.
Now mark ; I will describe so plain the goal
That thou shalt know it surely.   A dry stump
Extant above the ground an ell in height
Stands yonder ; either oak it is, or pine     415
More likely, which the weather least impairs.
Two stones, both white, flank it on either hand.
The way is narrow there, but smooth the course
On both sides.   It is either, as I think,
A monument of one long since deceased,     420
Or was, perchance, in ancient days design'd,
As now by Peleus' mighty son, a goal.
That mark in view, thy steeds and chariot push
Near to it as thou may'st ; then, in thy seat
Inclining gently to the left, prick smart     425
Thy right-hand horse challenging him aloud,
And give him rein ; but let thy left-hand horse
Bear on the goal so closely, that the nave
And felly[5] of thy wheel may seem to meet.
Yet fear to strike the stone, lest foul disgrace     430
Of broken chariot and of crippled steeds

---

[5] This could not happen unless the felly of the wheel were nearly
horizontal to the eye of the spectator, in which case the chariot must be
infallibly overturned.—There is an obscurity in the passage which none
of the commentators explain.  The Scholiast, as quoted by Clarke, attempts an explanation, but, I think, not successfully.

Ensue, and thou become the public jest.
My boy beloved! use caution; for if once
Thou turn the goal at speed, no man thenceforth
Shall reach, or if he reach, shall pass thee by,     435
Although Arion in thy rear he drove
Adrastus' rapid horse of race divine,
Or those, Troy's boast, bred by Laomedon.
   So Nestor spake, inculcating with care
On his son's mind these lessons in the art,     440
And to his place retiring, sat again.
Meriones his coursers glossy-maned
Made ready last.   Then to his chariot-seat
Each mounted, and the lots were thrown; himself
Achilles shook them.   First, forth leap'd the lot     445
Of Nestor's son Antilochus, after whom
The king Eumelus took his destined place.
The third was Menelaus spear-renown'd;
Meriones the fourth; and last of all
Bravest of all, heroic Diomede     450
The son of Tydeus took his lot to drive.
So ranged they stood; Achilles show'd the goal
Far on the champaign, nigh to which he placed
The godlike Phœnix servant of his sire,
To mark the race and make a true report.     455
   All raised the lash at once, and with the reins
At once all smote their steeds, urging them on
Vociferous; they, sudden, left the fleet
Far, far behind them, scouring swift the plain.
Dark, like a stormy cloud, uprose the dust     460
Their chests beneath, and scatter'd in the wind
Their manes all floated; now the chariots swept
The low declivity unseen, and now
Emerging started into view; erect
The drivers stood; emulous, every heart     465
Beat double; each encouraged loud his steeds;
They, flying, fill'd with dust the darken'd air.
But when returning to the hoary deep
They ran their last career, then each display'd
Brightest his charioteership, and the race     470
Lay stretch'd, at once, into its utmost speed.

Then, soon the mares of Pheretiades[6]
Pass'd all, but Diomede behind him came,
Borne by his unemasculated steeds
Of Trojan pedigree; they not remote,                        475
But close pursued him; and at every pace
Seem'd entering both, the chariot at their head;
For blowing warm into Eumelus' neck
Behind, and on his shoulders broad, they went,
And their chins rested on him as they flew.                  480
Then had Tydides pass'd him, or had made
Decision dubious, but Apollo struck,
Resentful[7], from his hand the glittering scourge.
Fast roll'd the tears indignant down his cheeks,
For he beheld the mares with double speed,                   485
Flying, and of the spur deprived, his own
Retarded steeds continual thrown behind.
But not unnoticed by Minerva pass'd
The art by Phœbus practised to impede
The son of Tydeus, whom with winged haste                    490
Following, she gave to him his scourge again,
And with new force his lagging steeds inspired.
Eumelus, next, the angry Goddess, swift
Pursuing, snapt his yoke; wide flew the mares
Asunder, and the pole fell to the ground.                    495
Himself, roll'd from his seat, fast by the wheel
With lacerated elbows, nostrils, mouth,
And batter'd brows lay prone; sorrow his eyes
Deluged, and disappointment choak'd his voice.
Then, far outstripping all, Tydides push'd                   500
His steeds beyond, which Pallas fill'd with power
That she might make the glorious prize his own.
Him follow'd Menelaus amber-hair'd,
The son of Atreus, and his father's steeds
Encouraging, thus spake Antilochus.                          505
    Away—now stretch ye forward to the goal.
I bid you not to an unequal strife
With those of Diomede, for Pallas them
Quickens that he may conquer, and the Chief
So far advanced makes competition vain.                      510

[6] Eumelus.
[7] Resentful of the attack made on him by Diomede in the fifth Book.

But reach the son of Atreus, fly to reach
His steeds, incontinent ; ah, be not shamed
For ever, foil'd by Æthe, by a mare !
Why fall ye thus behind, my noblest steeds ?
I tell you both, and ye shall prove me true,      515
No favour shall ye find at Nestor's hands,
My valiant Sire, but he will thrust his spear
Right through you, should we lose, for sloth of yours,
Or by your negligence, the nobler prize.
Haste then—pursue him—reach the royal Chief—      520
And how to pass him in yon narrow way
Shall be my care, and not my care in vain.
     He ended ; they, awhile, awed by his voice,
With more exertion ran, and Nestor's son
Now saw the hollow straight mark'd by his Sire.      525
It was a chasm abrupt, where winter-floods,
Wearing the soil, had gullied deep the way.
Thither Atrides, anxious to avoid
A clash of chariots drove, and thither drove
Also, but somewhat devious from his track,      530
Antilochus. Then Menelaus fear'd,
And with loud voice the son of Nestor hail'd.
     Antilochus, at what a madman's rate
Drivest thou ! stop—check thy steeds,—the way is here
Too straight, but widening soon, will give thee scope      535
To pass me by ; beware, lest chariot close
To chariot driven, thou maim thyself and me.
     He said ; but still more rapid and the scourge
Plying continual, as he had not heard,
Antilochus came on. Far as the quoit      540
By some broad-shoulder'd youth for trial hurl'd
Of manhood flies, so far Antilochus
Shot forward ; but the coursers fell behind
Of Atreus' son, who now abated much
By choice his driving, lest the steeds of both      545
Justling, should overturn with sudden shock
Both chariots, and themselves in dust be roll'd,
Through hot ambition of the foremost prize.
Him then the Hero golden-hair'd reproved.
     Antilochus ! the man lives not on earth      550
Like thee for love of mischief. Go, extoll'd

For wisdom falsely by the sons of Greece.
Yet, trust me, not without an oath, the prize
Thus foully sought shall even now be thine.

 He said, and to his coursers call'd aloud.    555
Ah be not tardy ; stand not sorrow-check'd ;
Their feet will fail them sooner far than yours,
For years have pass'd since they had youth to boast.

 So He ; and springing at his voice, his steeds
Regain'd apace the vantage lost.  Meantime    560
The Grecians, in full circus seated, mark'd
The steeds ; they flying, fill'd with dust the air.
Then, ere the rest, Idomeneus discern'd
The foremost pair ; for, on a rising ground
Exalted, he without the circus sat,    565
And hearing, though remote, the driver's voice
Chiding his steeds, knew it, and knew beside
The leader horse distinguish'd by his hue,
Chestnut throughout, save that his forehead bore
A splendid blazon white, round as the moon.    570

 He stood erect, and to the Greeks he cried.
Friends !  Chiefs and senators of Argos' host !
Discern I sole the steeds, or also ye ?
The horses, foremost now, to me appear
Other than erst, and I descry at hand    575
A different charioteer ; the mares of late
Victorious, somewhere distant in the race
Are hurt ; I plainly saw them at the first
Turning the goal, but see them now no more ;
And yet with eyes inquisitive I range    580
From side to side the whole broad plain of Troy.
Either the charioteer hath slipp'd the reins,
Or rounded not successfully the goal
Through want of guidance.  Thrown, as it should seem,
Forth from his seat, he hath his chariot maim'd,    585
And his ungovern'd steeds have roam'd away.
Arise and look ye forth yourselves, for I
With doubtful ken behold him ; yet the man
Seems, in my view, Ætolian by descent,
A Chief of prime renown in Argos' host,    590
The Hero Tydeus' son, brave Diomede.

 But Ajax Oïliades the swift

Him sharp reproved.   Why art thou always given
To prate, Idomeneus? thou seest the mares,
Remote indeed, but posting to the goal.                    595
Thou art not youngest of the Argives here
So much, nor from beneath thy brows look forth
Quick-sighted more than ours, thine eyes abroad,
Yet still thou pratest, although silence more
Should suit thee, among wiser far than thou.               600
The mares which led, lead still, and he who drives
Eumelus, is the same who drove before.
   To whom the Cretan Chief, angry, replied.
Ajax! whom none in wrangling can excel
Or rudeness, though in all beside thou fall                605
Below the Argives, being boorish-rough,
Come now—a tripod let us wager each,
Or cauldron, and let Agamemnon judge
Whose horses lead, that, losing, thou may'st learn.
He said; then sudden from his seat upsprang               610
Swift Ajax Oïliades, prepared
For harsh retort, nor had the contest ceased
Between them, but had grown from ill to worse,
Had not himself, Achilles, interposed.
Ajax—Idomeneus—abstain ye both                            615
From bitter speech offensive, and such terms
As ill become you.   Ye would feel, yourselves,
Resentment, should another act as ye,
Survey the course, peaceable, from your seats;
The charioteers, by competition wing'd,                   620
Will soon themselves arrive, then shall ye know
Distinctly, both who follows and who leads.
   He scarce had said, when nigh at hand appear'd
Tydides, lashing, as he came, his steeds
Continual; they with hoofs uplifted high                  625
Their yet remaining ground shorten'd apace,
Sprinkling with dusty drops at every stroke
Their charioteer, while close upon their heels
Radiant with tin and gold the chariot ran,
Scarce tracking light the dust, so swift they flew.       630
He stood in the mid-circus; there the sweat
Rain'd under them from neck and chest profuse,
And Diomede from his resplendent seat

Leaping, reclined his scourge against the yoke.
Nor was his friend brave Sthenelus remiss,               635
But, seizing with alacrity the prize,
Consign'd the tripod and the virgin, first,
To his own band in charge; then loosed the steeds.
Next came, by stratagem, not speed advanced
To that distinction, Nestor's son, whom yet              640
The Hero Menelaus close pursued.
Near as the wheel runs to a courser's heels,
Drawing his master at full speed; his tail
With its extremest hairs the felly sweeps
That close attends him o'er the spacious plain,          645
So near had Menelaus now approach'd
Antilochus; for though at first he fell
A full quoit's cast behind, he soon retrieved
That loss, with such increasing speed the mare
Bright-maned of Agamemnon, Æthe, ran;                    650
She, had the course few paces more to both
Afforded, should have clearly shot beyond
Antilochus, nor dubious left the prize.
But noble Menelaus threw behind
Meriones, companion in the field,                        655
Of King Idomeneus, a lance's flight,
For slowest were his steeds, and he, to rule
The chariot in the race, least skill'd of all.
Last came Eumelus drawing to the goal,
Himself, his splendid chariot, and his mares             660
Driving before him.   Peleus' rapid son
Beheld him with compassion, and, amid
The Argives, in wing'd accents thus he spake.
    Here comes the most expert, driving his steeds
Before him.   Just it were that he received             665
The second prize; Tydides claims the first.
    He said, and all applauded the award.
Then had Achilles to Eumelus given
The mare (for such the pleasure seem'd of all)
Had not the son of mighty Nestor risen,                  670
Antilochus, who pleaded thus his right.
   .Achilles! acting as thou hast proposed,
Thou shalt offend me much, for thou shalt take
The prize from me, because the Gods, his steeds

And chariot-yoke disabling, render'd vain          675
His efforts, and no failure of his own.
It was his duty to have sought the Gods
In prayer, then had he not, following on foot
His coursers, hindmost of us all arrived.
But if thou pity him, and deem it good,          680
Thou hast much gold, much brass, and many sheep
In thy pavilion; thou hast maidens fair,
And coursers also.   Of thy proper stores
Hereafter give to him a richer prize
Than this, or give it now, so shall the Greeks          685
Applaud thee; but this mare yield I to none;
Stand forth  the Grecian who desires to win
That recompense, and let him fight·with me.
    He ended, and Achilles, godlike Chief,
Smiled on him, gratulating his success,          690
Whom much he loved; then, ardent, thus replied.
    Antilochus! if thou wouldst wish me give
Eumelus of my own, even so I will.
I will present to him my corslet bright
Won from Asteropæus, edged around          695
With glittering tin; a precious gift, and rare.
    So saying, he bade Automedon his friend
Produce it from the tent; he at his word
Departing, to Achilles brought the spoil,
Which at his hands Eumelus glad received.          700
Then, stung with grief, and with resentment fired
Immeasurable, Menelaus rose
To charge Antilochus.   His herald gave
The sceptre to his hand, and (silence bidden
To all) the godlike Hero thus began.          705
    Antilochus! oh heretofore discreet!
What hast thou done? Thou hast dishonour'd foul
My skill, and wrong'd my coursers, throwing thine,
Although inferior far, by fraud before them.
Ye Chiefs and Senators of Argos' host!          710
Impartial judge between us, lest of these,
Some say hereafter, Menelaus bore
Antilochus by falsehood down, and led
The mare away, because, although his steeds
Were worse, his arm was mightier, and prevail'd.          715

Yet hold—myself will judge, and will to all
Contentment give, for I will judge aright.
Hither, Antilochus, illustrious youth !
And, as the law prescribes, standing before
Thy steeds and chariot, holding too the scourge          720
With which thou drovest, lay hand on both thy steeds,
And swear by Neptune, circler of the earth,
That neither wilfully, nor yet by fraud
Thou didst impede my chariot in its course.
 Then, prudent, thus Antilochus replied.          725
Oh royal Menelaus ! patient bear
The fault of one thy junior far, in years
Alike unequal and in worth to thee.
Thou know'st how rash is youth, and how propense
To pass the bounds by decency prescribed,          730
Quick, but not wise.   Lay, then, thy wrath aside ;
The mare now given me I will myself
Deliver to thee, and if thou require
A larger recompense, will rather yield
A larger much than from thy favour fall          735
Deservedly for ever, mighty Prince !
And sin so heinously against the Gods.
 So saying, the son of valiant Nestor led
The mare, himself, to Menelaus' hand,
Who with heart-freshening joy the prize received.          740
As on the ears of growing corn the dews
Fall grateful, while the spiry grain erect
Bristles the fields, so, Menelaus, felt
Thy inmost soul a soothing pleasure sweet !
Then answer thus the Hero quick return'd.          745
 Antilochus ! exasperate though I were,
Now, such no longer, I relinquish glad
All strife with thee, for that at other times
Thou never inconsiderate wast or light,
Although by youthful heat misled to-day.          750
Yet safer is it not to over-reach
Superiors, for no other Grecian here
Had my extreme displeasure calm'd so soon ;
But thou hast suffer'd much, and much hast toil'd,
As thy good father and thy brother have,          755
On my behalf; I, therefore, yield, subdued

By thy entreaties, and the mare, though mine,
Will also give thee, that these Grecians all
May know me neither proud nor hard to appease.
    So saying, the mare he to Noëmon gave,      760
Friend of Antilochus, and, well-content,
The polish'd cauldron for *his* prize received.
The fourth awarded lot (for he had fourth
Arrived) Meriones asserted next,
The golden talents ; but the phial still      765
Left unappropriated Achilles bore
Across the circus in his hand, a gift
To ancient Nestor, whom he thus bespake.
    Thou also, oh my father ! this accept,
Which, in remembrance of the funeral rites      770
Of my Patroclus, keep, for him thou seest
Among the Greeks no more.   Receive a prize,
Thine by gratuity ; for thou shalt wield
The cæstus, wrestle, at the spear contend,
Or in the foot-race (fallen as thou art      775
Into the wane of life) never again.
    He said, and placed it in his hands.   He, glad,
Receiving it, in accents wing'd replied.
    True, oh my son ! is all which thou hast spoken.
These limbs, these hands, young friend ! (their vigour lost) 780
No longer, darted from the shoulder, spring
At once to battle.   Ah that I could grow
Young yet again, could feel again such force
Athletic, as when in Buprasium erst
The Epeans with sepulchral pomp entomb'd      785
King Amarynceus, where his sons ordain'd
Funereal games in honour of their Sire !
Epean none or even Pylian there
Could cope with me, or yet Ætolian bold.
Boxing, I vanquish'd Clytomedes, son      790
Of Enops ; wrestling, the Pleuronian Chief
Ancæus ; in the foot-race Iphiclus,
Though a fleet runner ; and I over-pitch'd
Phyleus and Polydorus at the spear.
The sons of Actor in the chariot-race      795
Alone surpass'd me, being two for one,

And jealous both lest I should also win
That prize, for to the victor charioteer
They had assign'd the noblest prize of all.
They were twin-brothers, and one ruled the steeds,                    800
The steeds one ruled[8], the other lash'd them on.
Such once was I; but now, these sports I leave
To younger; me submission most befits
To withering age, who then outshone the best.
But go.   The funeral of thy friend with games                        805
Proceed to celebrate; I accept thy gift
With pleasure; and my heart is also glad
That thou art mindful evermore of one
Who loves thee, and such honour in the sight
Yield'st me of all the Greeks, as is my due.                          810
May the Gods bless thee for it more and more!
    He spake, and Peleus' son, when he had heard
At large his commendation from the lips
Of Nestor, through the assembled Greeks return'd.
He next proposed, not lightly to be won,                              815
The boxer's prize.   He tether'd down a mule,
Untamed and hard to tame, but strong to toil,
And in her prime of vigour, in the midst;
A goblet to the vanquish'd he assign'd,
Then stood erect, and to the Greeks exclaim'd.                        820
    Atridæ! and ye Argives brazen-greaved!
I call for two bold combatants expert
To wage fierce strife for these, with lifted fists
Smiting each other.   He, who by the aid
Of Phœbus shall o'ercome, and whom the Greeks                         825
Shall all pronounce victorious, leads the mule
Hence to his tent; the vanquish'd takes the cup.
    He spake, and at his word a Greek arose
Big, bold, and skilful in the boxer's art,
Epeüs, son of Panopeus; his hand                                      830
He on the mule imposed, and thus he said.
    Approach the man ambitious of the cup!
For no Achaian here shall with his fist
 Te foiling, win the mule.   I boast myself
    all superior.   May it not suffice                                835
    t I to no pre-eminence pretend

                    [8] The repetition follows the Original.

In battle? To attain to foremost praise
Alike in every art is not for one.
But this I promise, and will well perform—
My blows shall lay him open, split him, crush          840
His bones to splinters, and let all his friends,
Attendant on him, wait to bear him hence,
Vanquish'd by my superior force in fight.
    He ended, and his speech found no reply.
One godlike Chief alone, Euryalus,                     845
Son of the King Mecisteus, who, himself,
Sprang from Talaion, opposite arose.
He, on the death of Oedipus, at Thebes
Contending in the games held at his tomb,
Had overcome the whole Cadmean race.                   850
Him Diomede spear-famed for fight prepared,
Giving him all encouragement, for much
He wish'd him victory.   First then he threw[9]
His cincture to him ; next, he gave him thongs[10]
Cut from the hide of a wild buffalo.                   855
Both girt around, into the midst they moved.
Then, lifting high their brawny arms, and fists
Mingling with fists, to furious fight they fell ;
Dire was the crash of jaws, and the sweat stream'd
From every limb.   Epeüs fierce advanced,              860
And while Euryalus with cautious eye
Watch'd his advantage, pash'd him on the cheek.
He stood no longer, but, his shapely limbs,
Unequal to his weight, sinking, he fell.
As by the rising North-wind driven ashore              865
An huge fish flounces on the weedy beach,
Which soon the sable flood covers again,
So, beaten down, he bounded.   But Epeüs,
Heroic Chief, upraised him by his hand,
And his own comrades from the circus forth             870
Led him, step dragging after step, the blood
Ejecting grumous, and at every pace
Rolling his head languid from side to side.
They placed him all unconscious on his seat
In his own band, then fetch'd his prize, the cup.      875

[9] παρακάββαλε.
[10] With which they bound on the cæstus.

Still other prizes, then, Achilles placed
In view of all, the sturdy wrestler's meed.
A large hearth-tripod, valued by the Greeks
At twice six beeves, should pay the victor's toil;
But for the vanquish'd, in the midst he set                    880
A damsel in variety expert
Of arts domestic, valued at four beeves.
He rose erect, and to the Greeks he cried.
  Arise ye, now, who shall this prize dispute.
So spake the son of Peleus; then arose                         885
Huge Telamonian Ajax, and upstood
Ulysses also, in all wiles adept.
Both girt around, into the midst they moved.
With vigorous gripe each lock'd the other fast,
Like rafters, standing, of some mansion built                  890
By a prime artist, proof against all winds.
Their backs, tugg'd vehemently, creak'd[11], the sweat
Trickled, and on their flanks and shoulders, red
The whelks arose; they bearing still in mind
The tripod, ceased not struggling for the prize.               895
Nor could Ulysses from his station move
And cast down Ajax, nor could Ajax him
Unsettle, fixt so firm Ulysses stood.
But when, long time expectant, all the Greeks
Grew weary, then, huge Ajax him bespake.                       900
  Laertes' noble son, for wiles renown'd!
Lift, or be lifted, and let Jove decide.
  He said, and heaved Ulysses.  Then, his wiles
Forgat not He, but on the ham behind
Chopp'd him; the limbs of Ajax at the stroke                   905
Disabled sank; he fell supine, and bore
Ulysses close adhering to his chest
Down with him.  Wonder rivetted all eyes.
Then brave Ulysses from the ground awhile
Him lifted in his turn, but ere he stood,                      910
Inserting his own knee the knees between[12]

[11] τετρίγει.—It is a circumstance on which the Scholiast observes that
it denotes in a wrestler the greatest possible bodily strength and firmness
of position.—See Villoisson.

[12] I have given what seems to me the most probable interpretation, and
such a one as to any person who has ever witnessed a wrestling-match,
vill, I presume, appear intelligible.

Of Ajax, threw him.　To the earth they fell
Both, and with dust defiled lay side by side.
And now, arising to a third essay,
They should have wrestled yet again, had not　　915
Achilles, interfering, them restrain'd.
　　Strive not together more; cease to exhaust
Each other's force; ye both have earn'd the prize.
Depart alike requited, and give place
To other Grecians who shall next contend.　　920
　　He spake; they glad complied, and wiping off
The dust, put on their tunics.　Then again
Achilles other prizes yet proposed,
The rapid runner's meed.　First, he produced
A silver goblet of six measures; earth　　925
.Own'd not its like for elegance of form.
Skilful Sidonian artists had around
Embellish'd it, and o'er the sable Deep
Phœnician merchants into Lemnos' port
Had borne it, and the boon to Thoas[13] given;　　930
But Jason's son, Euneüs, in exchange
For Priam's son Lycaon, to the hand
Had pass'd it of Patroclus famed in arms.
Achilles this, in honour of his friend,
Set forth, the swiftest runner's recompense.　　935
The second should a fatted ox receive
Of largest size, and he assign'd of gold
A just half-talent to the worst and last.
He stood erect, and to the Greeks he cried.
　　Now stand ye forth who shall this prize dispute.　　940
He said, and at his word instant arose
Swift Ajax Oïliades; upsprang
The shrewd Ulysses next, and after him
Brave Nestor's son Antilochus, with whom
None vied in speed of all the youths of Greece.　　945
They stood prepared.　Achilles show'd the goal.
At once all started.　Oïliades
Led swift the course, and closely at his heels
Ulysses ran.　Near as some cinctured maid
Industrious holds the distaff to her breast,　　950

---

[13] King of Lemnos.

While to and fro with practised finger neat
She tends the flax drawing it to a thread,
So near Ulysses follow'd him, and press'd
His footsteps, ere the dust fill'd them again,
Pouring his breath into his neck behind,          955
And never slackening pace.   His ardent thirst
Of victory with universal shouts
All seconded, and, eager, bade him On.
And now, the contest shortening to a close,
Ulysses his request silent and brief          960
To azure-eyed Minerva thus preferr'd.
    Oh Goddess hear, prosper me in the race !
Such was his prayer, with which Minerva pleased,
Freshen'd his limbs, and made him light to run.
And now, when in one moment they should both          965
Have darted on the prize, then Ajax' foot
Sliding, he fell ; for where the dung of beeves
Slain by Achilles for his friend, had spread
The soil, there[14] Pallas tripp'd him.   Ordure foul
His mouth, and ordure foul his nostrils fill'd.          970
Then brave Ulysses, first arriving, seized
The cup, and Ajax took his prize, the ox.
He grasp'd his horn, and sputtering as he stood
The ordure forth, the Argives thus bespake.
    Ah—Pallas tripp'd my footsteps ; she attends          975
Ulysses ever with a mother's care.
    Loud laugh'd the Grecians.   Then, the remnant prize
Antilochus receiving, smiled and said.
    Ye need not, fellow-warriors, to be taught
That now as ever, the immortal Gods          980
Honour on seniority bestow.
Ajax is elder, yet not much, than I.
But Laertiades was born in times
Long past, a Chief coeval with our Sires,
Not young, but vigorous ; and, of the Greeks,          985
Achilles may alone with Him contend.
    So saying, the merit of superior speed
To Peleus' son he gave, who thus replied.
    Antilochus ! thy praise of me shall prove

---

[14] That is to say, Ulysses; who, from the first intending it, had run
close behind him.

Nor vain nor unproductive to thyself,                 990
For the half-talent doubled shall be thine.
 He spake, and, doubling it, the talent placed
Whole in his hand.   He glad the gift received.
Achilles, then, Sarpedon's arms produced,
Stripp'd from him by Patroclus, his long spear,      995
Helmet and shield, which in the midst he placed.
He stood erect, and to the Greeks he cried.
 I call for two brave warriors arm'd to prove
Each other's skill with weapons keen, this prize
Disputing, next, in presence of us all.              1000
Who first shall through his armour reach the skin
Of his antagonist, and shall draw his blood,
To Him this silver-studded faulchion bright
I give ; the blade is Thracian, and of late
Asteropæus wore it, whom I slew.                     1005
These other arms shall be their common meed,
And I will banquet both within my tent.
 He said, then Telamonian Ajax huge·
Arose, and opposite the son arose
Of warlike Tydeus, Diomede the brave.                1010
Apart from all the people each put on
His arms, then moved into the middle space,
Louring terrific, and on fire to fight.
The host look'd on amazed.   Approaching each
The other, thrice they sprang to the assault,        1015
And thrice struck hand to hand.   Ajax the shield
Pierced of his adversary, but the flesh
Attain'd not, baffled by his mail within.
Then Tydeus' son, sheer o'er the ample disk
Of Ajax, thrust a lance home to his neck,            1020
And the Achaians for the life appall'd
Of Ajax, bade them, ceasing, share the prize.
But the huge faulchion with its sheath and belt—
Achilles them on Diomede bestow'd.
 The Hero, next, an iron clod produced            1025
Rough from the forge, and wont to task the might
Of King Eëtion ; but, when him he slew,
Pelides, glorious Chief, with other spoils
From Thebes convey'd it in his fleet to Troy.
He stood erect, and to the Greeks he cried.          1030

Come forth who also shall this prize dispute !
How far soe'er remote the winner's fields,
This lump shall serve his wants five circling years ;
His shepherd shall not, or his plougher, need
In quest of iron book the distant town,                       1035
But hence he shall himself their wants supply.
 Then Polypœtes brave in fight arose,
Arose Leonteus also, godlike Chief,
With Ajax son of Telamon. Each took
His station, and Epeüs seized the clod.                       1040
He swung, he cast it, and the Grecians laugh'd.
Leonteus, branch of Mars, quoited it next.
Huge Telamonian Ajax with strong arm
Dismiss'd it third, and overpitch'd them both.
But when brave Polypœtes seized the mass                      1045
Far as the vigorous herdsman flings his staff
That twirling flies his numerous beeves between,
So far his cast outmeasured all beside,
And the host shouted. · Then the friends arose
Of Polypœtes valiant Chief, and bore                          1050
His ponderous acquisition to the ships.
 The archers' prize Achilles next proposed,
Ten double and ten single axes, form'd
Of steel convertible to arrow points.
He fix'd, far distant on the sands, the mast                  1055
Of a brave bark cœrulean-prow'd, to which
With small cord fasten'd by the foot he tied
A timorous dove, their mark at which to aim.
[15]Who strikes the dove, he conquers, and shall bear
These double axes all into his tent.                          1060
But who the cord alone, missing the bird,
Successful less, he wins the single blades.
 The might of royal Teucer then arose,
And, fellow-warrior of the King of Crete,
Valiant Meriones. A brazen casque                        1065
Received the lots ; they shook them, and the lot
Fell first to Teucer. He, at once, a shaft
Sent smartly forth, but vow'd not to the King[16]

[15] The transition from narrative to dramatic follows the Original.
[16] Apollo ; frequently by Homer called the King without any addition.

An hecatomb, all firstlings of the flock.
He therefore (for Apollo greater praise       1070
Denied him) miss'd the dove, but struck the cord
That tied her, at small distance from the knot,
And with his arrow sever'd it.    Upsprang
The bird into the air, and to the ground
Depending fell the cord.    Shouts rent the skies.       1075
Then, all in haste, Meriones the bow
Caught from his hand holding a shaft the while
Already aim'd, and to Apollo vow'd
An hecatomb, all firstlings of the flock.
He eyed the dove aloft, under a cloud,       1080
And, while she wheel'd around, struck her beneath
The pinion; through her and beyond her pass'd
The arrow, and, returning, pierced the soil
Fast by the foot of brave Meriones.
She, perching on the mast again, her head       1085
Reclined, and hung her wide-unfolded wing,
But, soon expiring, dropp'd and fell remote.
Amazement seized the people.    To his tent
Meriones the ten best axes bore,
And Teucer the inferior ten to his.       1090
    Then, last, Achilles in the circus placed
A ponderous spear and cauldron yet unfired,
Emboss'd with flowers around, its worth an ox.
Upstood the spear-expert; Atrides first,
Wide-ruling Agamemnon, King of men,       1095
And next, brave fellow-warrior of the King
Of Crete, Meriones; when thus his speech
Achilles to the royal Chief address'd.
    Atrides! (for we know thy skill and force
Matchless! that none can hurl the spear as thou)       1100
This prize is thine, order it to thy ship;
And if it please thee, as I would it might,
Let brave Meriones the spear receive.
    He said; nor Agamemnon not complied,
But to Meriones the brazen spear       1105
Presenting, to Talthybius gave in charge
The cauldron, next, his own illustrious prize.

# BOOK XXIV.

---

### ARGUMENT.

Priam, by command of Jupiter, and under conduct of Mercury, seeks
Achilles in his tent, who admonished previously by Thetis, consents
to accept ransom for the body of Hector. Hector is mourned, and the
manner of his funeral, circumstantially described, concludes the poem.

THE games all closed, the people went dispersed
Each to his ship ; they mindful of repast,
And to enjoy repose ; but other thoughts
Achilles' mind employ'd ; he still deplored
With tears his loved Patroclus, nor the force     5
Felt of all-conquering sleep, but turn'd and turn'd
Restless from side to side, mourning the loss
Of such a friend, so manly, and so brave.
Their fellowship in toil ; their hardships oft
Sustain'd in fight laborious, or o'ercome     10
With difficulty on the perilous Deep—
Remembrance busily retracing themes
Like these, drew down his cheeks continual tears.
Now on his side he lay, now lay supine,
Now prone ; then starting from his couch he roam'd     15
Forlorn the beach, nor did the rising morn
On seas and shores escape his watchful eye,
But joining to his chariot his swift steeds,
He fasten'd Hector to be dragg'd behind.
Around the tomb of Menœtiades     20
Him thrice he dragg'd ; then rested in his tent,
Leaving him at his length stretch'd in the dust.
Meantime Apollo with compassion touch'd
Even of the lifeless Hector, from all taint
Saved him, and with the golden ægis broad     25
Covering, preserved him, although dragg'd, untorn.
    While he, indulging thus his wrath, disgraced
Brave Hector, the Immortals, at that sight

With pity moved, exhorted Mercury  
The watchful Argicide, to steal him thence.     30  
That counsel pleased the rest, but neither pleased  
Juno, nor Neptune, nor the blue-eyed maid.  
They still, as at the first, held fast their hate  
Of sacred Troy, detested Priam still,  
And still his people, mindful of the crime     35  
Of Paris, who when to his rural hut  
They came, those Goddesses affronting, praise  
And admiration gave to Her alone  
Who with vile lusts his preference repaid.  
But when the twelfth ensuing morn arose,     40  
Apollo, then, the Immortals thus address'd.  
   Ye Gods, your dealings now injurious seem  
And cruel.   Was not Hector wont to burn  
Thighs of fat goats and bullocks at your shrines ?  
Whom now, though dead, ye cannot yet endure     45  
To rescue, that Andromache once more  
Might view him, his own mother, his own son,  
His father and the people, who would soon  
Yield him his just demand, a funereal fire.  
But, oh ye Gods ! your pleasure is alone     50  
To please Achilles, that pernicious Chief,  
Who neither right regards, nor owns a mind  
That can relent, but as the lion, urged  
By his own dauntless heart and savage force,  
Invades without remorse the rights of man,     55  
That he may banquet on his herds and flocks,  
So Peleus' son all pity from his breast  
Hath driven, and shame, man's blessing[1] or his curse[1].  
For whosoever hath a loss sustain'd  
Still dearer, whether of his brother born     60  
From the same womb, or even of his son,  
When he hath once bewail'd him, weeps no more,  
For fate itself gives man a patient mind.  
Yet Peleus' son, not so contented, slays  
Illustrious Hector first, then drags his corse     65  
In cruel triumph at his chariot-wheels  
Around Patroclus' tomb ; but neither well  

---

[1] His blessing, if he is properly influenced by it ; his curse in its con-  
sequences if he is deaf to its dictates.

He acts, nor honourably to himself,
Who may, perchance, brave though he be, incur
Our anger, while to gratify revenge                           70
He pours dishonour thus on senseless clay.
   To whom, incensed, Juno white-arm'd replied.
And be it so; stand fast this word of thine,
God of the Silver bow ! if ye account
Only such honour to Achilles due                              75
As Hector claims; but Hector was by birth
Mere man, and suckled at a woman's breast.
Not such Achilles; him a Goddess bore,
Whom I myself nourish'd, and on my lap
Fondled, and in due time to Peleus gave                       80
In marriage, to a Chief beloved in heaven
Peculiarly; ye were yourselves, ye Gods !
Partakers of the nuptial feast, and thou
Wast present also with thine harp in hand,
Thou comrade of the vile ! thou faithless ever !             85
   Then answer thus cloud-gatherer Jove return'd.
Juno, forbear.   Indulge not always wrath
Against the Gods.   They shall not share alike,
And in the same proportion our regards.
Yet even Hector was the man in Troy                           90
Most favour'd by the Gods, and him no less
I also loved, for punctual were his gifts
To us; mine altar never miss'd from him
Libation, or the steam of sacrifice,
The meed allotted to us from of old.                          95
But steal him not, since by Achilles' eye
Unseen ye cannot, who both day and night
Watches[2] him, as a mother tends her son.
But call ye Thetis hither, I would give
The Goddess counsel, that, at Priam's hands                   100
Accepting gifts, Achilles loose the dead.
   He ceased.   Then Iris tempest-wing'd arose.
Samos between, and Imbrus rock-begirt,
She plunged into the gloomy flood; loud groan'd
The briny pool, while sudden down she rush'd,                 105

   [2] This is the sense preferred by the Scholiast, for it is not true that
Thetis was always present with Achilles, as is proved by the passage immediately ensuing.

As sinks the bull's[3] horn with its leaden weight,
Death bearing to the raveners of the Deep.
Within her vaulted cave Thetis she found
By every nymph of Ocean round about
Encompass'd; she, amid them all, the fate      110
Wept of her noble son ordain'd to death
At fertile Troy, from Phthia far remote.
Then, Iris, drawing near, her thus address'd.
     Arise, O Thetis! Jove, the author dread
Of everlasting counsels, calls for thee.      115
     To whom the Goddess of the Silver feet.
Why calls the mighty Thunderer me? I fear,
Oppress'd with countless sorrows as I am,
To mingle with the Gods.—Yet I obey—
No word of his can prove an empty sound.      120
     So saying, the Goddess took her sable veil,
(Eye ne'er beheld a darker,) and began
Her progress, by the storm-wing'd Iris led,
On either hand the billows open'd wide
A pass before them; they, ascending soon      125
The shore, updarted swift into the skies.
They found loud-voiced Saturnian Jove around
Environ'd by the ever blessed Gods
Convened in full assembly; she beside
Her Father Jove (Pallas retiring) sat.      130
Then, Juno, with consolatory speech,
Presented to her hand a golden cup,
Of which she drank, then gave it back again,
And thus the Sire of Gods and men began.
     Goddess of ocean, Thetis! thou hast sought      135
Olympus, bearing in thy bosom grief
Never to be assuaged, as well I know.
Yet shalt thou learn, afflicted as thou art,
Why I have summoned thee. Nine days the Gods,
Concerning Hector's body and thy own      140
Brave city-spoiler son, have held dispute,
And some have urged ofttimes the Argicide
Keen-sighted Mercury, to steal the dead.
But I forbad it for Achilles' sake,

---

[3] The angler's custom was, in those days, to guard his line above the hook from the fishes' bite, by passing it through a pipe of horn.

Whom I exalt, the better to insure          145
Thy reverence and thy friendship evermore.
Haste, therefore, seek thy son, and tell him thus.
The Gods resent it, say (but most of all
Myself am angry) that he still detains
Amid his fleet, through fury of revenge,          150
Unransom'd Hector; so shall he, at length,
Through fear of me, perchance, release the slain.
Myself to generous Priam will, the while,
Send Iris, who shall bid him to the fleet
Of Greece, such ransom bearing as may soothe          155
Achilles, for redemption of his son.
   So spake the God, nor Thetis not complied.
Descending swift from the Olympian heights
She reach'd Achilles' tent.　Him there she found
Groaning disconsolate, while others ran          160
To and fro, occupied around a sheep
New-slaughter'd, large, and of exuberant fleece.
She sitting close beside him, softly stroak'd
His cheek, and thus, affectionate, began.
   How long, my son! sorrowing and mourning here,          165
Wilt thou consume thy soul, nor give one thought
Either to food or love? Yet love is good,
And woman grief's best cure; for length of days
Is not thy doom, but, even now, thy death
And ruthless destiny are on the wing.          170
Mark me,—I come a lieger sent from Jove.
The Gods, he saith, resent it, but himself
More deeply than the rest, that thou detain'st
Amid thy fleet, through fury of revenge,
Unransom'd Hector.　Be advised, accept          175
Ransom, and to his friends resign the dead.
   To whom Achilles, swiftest of the swift.
Come then the ransomer, and take him hence;
If Jove himself command it,—Be it so.
   So they, among the ships, conferring sat          180
On various themes, the Goddess and her son;
Meantime Saturnian Jove commanded down
His swift ambassadress to sacred Troy.
   Hence, rapid Iris, leave the Olympian heights,
And, finding noble Priam, bid him haste          185

Into Achaia's fleet, bearing such gifts
As may assuage Achilles, and prevail
To liberate the body of his son.
Alone, he must ; no Trojan of them all
May company the senior thither, save                    190
An ancient herald to direct his mules
And his wheel'd litter, and to bring the dead
Back into Ilium, whom Achilles slew.
Let neither fear of death nor other fear
Trouble him aught, so safe a guard and sure            195
We give him ; Mercury shall be his guide
Into Achilles' presence in his tent.
Nor will himself Achilles slay him there,
Or even permit his death, but will forbid
All violence ; for he is not unwise                    200
Nor heedless, no—nor wilful to offend,
But will his suppliant with much grace receive.[4]
   He ceased ; then Iris tempest-wing'd arose,
Jove's messenger, and, at the gates arrived
Of Priam, woe and wailing found within.                205
Around their father, in the hall, his sons
Their robes with tears water'd, while them amidst
The hoary king sat mantled, muffled close,
And on his venerable head and neck
Much dust was spread, which, rolling on the earth,     210
He had shower'd on them with unsparing hands.
The palace echoed to his daughters' cries,
And to the cries of matrons calling fresh
Into remembrance many a valiant Chief
Now stretch'd in dust by Argive hands destroy'd.       215
The messenger of Jove at Priam's side
Standing, with whisper'd accents low his ear
Saluted, but he trembled at the sound.
   Courage, Dardanian Priam ! fear thou nought ;
To thee no prophetess of ill, I come ;                 220
But with kind purpose : Jove's ambassadress
Am I, who though remote, yet entertains
Much pity, and much tender care for thee.

   [4] Jupiter justifies him against Apollo's charge, affirming him to be free
from those mental defects which chiefly betray men into sin, folly, im-
providence, and perverseness.

Olympian Jove commands thee to redeem
The noble Hector, with an offering large 225
Of gifts that may Achilles' wrath appease.
Alone, thou must; no Trojan of them all
Hath leave to attend thy journey thither, save
An ancient herald to direct thy mules
And thy wheel'd litter, and to bring the dead 230
Back into Ilium, whom Achilles slew.
Let neither fear of death nor other fear
Trouble thee aught, so safe a guard and sure
He gives thee; Mercury shall be thy guide
Even to Achilles' presence in his tent. 235
Nor will himself Achilles slay thee there,
Or even permit thy death, but will forbid
All violence; for he is not unwise
Nor heedless, no—nor wilful to offend,
But will his suppliant with much grace receive. 240
    So spake the swift ambassadress, and went.
Then, calling to his sons, he bade them bring
His litter forth, and bind the coffer on,
While to his fragrant chamber he repair'd
Himself, with cedar lined and lofty roof'd, 245
A treasury of wonders, into which
The Queen he summon'd, whom he thus bespake.
    Hecuba! the ambassadress of Jove
Hath come, who bids me to the Grecian fleet,
Bearing such presents thither as may soothe 250
Achilles, for redemption of my son.
But say, what seems this enterprize to thee?
Myself am much inclined to it, I feel
My courage prompting me amain toward
The fleet, and into the Achaian camp. 255
    Then wept the Queen aloud, and thus replied.
Ah! whither is thy wisdom fled, for which
Both strangers once, and Trojans honour'd *thee?*
How canst thou wish to penetrate alone
The Grecian fleet, and to appear before 260
His face by whom so many valiant sons
Of thine have fallen? Thou hast an iron heart!
For should that savage man and faithless once
Seize and discover thee, no pity expect

Or reverence at his hands.   Come—let us weep     265
Together, here sequester'd ; for the thread
Spun for him by his destiny severe
When he was born, ordain'd our son remote
From us his parents to be food for hounds
In that Chief's tent.   Oh ! clinging to his side,     270
How I could tear him with my teeth ! His deeds,
Disgraceful to my son, then should not want
Retaliation ; for he slew not him
Skulking, but standing boldly for the wives,
The daughters fair, and citizens of Troy,          275
Guiltless of flight[5], and of the wish to fly.
   Whom Godlike Priam answer'd, ancient King.
Impede me not who willing am to·go,
Nor be, thyself, a bird of ominous note
To terrify me under my own roof,                   280
For thou shalt not prevail.   Had mortal man
Enjoin'd me this attempt, prophet, or priest,
Or soothsayer, I had pronounced him false
And fear'd it but the more.   But, since I saw
The Goddess with these eyes, and heard, myself,    285
The voice divine, I go ; that word shall stand ;
And, if my doom be in the fleet of Greece
To perish, be it so ; Achilles' arm
Shall give me speedy death, and I shall die
Folding my son, and satisfied with tears.          290
   So saying, he open'd wide the elegant lids
Of numerous chests, whence mantles twelve he took
Of texture beautiful ; twelve single cloaks ;
As many carpets, with as many robes,
To which he added vests, an equal store.           295
He also took ten talents forth of gold,
All weigh'd, two splendid tripods, cauldrons four,
And after these a cup of matchless worth
Given to him when ambassador in Thrace ;
A noble gift, which yet the hoary King             300
Spared not, such fervour of desire he felt
To loose his son.   Then from his portico,

---

    [5] But, at first, he did fly.  It is therefore spoken, as the Scholiast
observes, φιλοσοργῶς, and must be understood as the language of strong
maternal affection.

With angry taunts he drove the gather'd crowds.
    Away! away! ye dregs of earth, away;
Ye shame of human kind! Have ye no griefs          305
At home, that ye come hither troubling *me*?
Deem ye it little that Saturnian Jove
Afflicts me thus, and of my very best,
Best boy deprives me? Ah! ye shall be taught
Yourselves that loss, far easier to be slain        310
By the Achaians now, since he is dead.
But I, ere yet the city I behold
Taken and pillaged, with these aged eyes,
Shall find safe hiding in the shades below.
    He said, and chased them with his staff; they left   315
In haste the doors, by the old King expell'd.
Then, chiding them aloud, his sons he call'd,
Helenus, Paris, noble Agathon,
Pammon, Antiphonus, and bold in fight
Polites, Dios of illustrious fame,         320
Hippothoüs and Deiphobus—all nine
He call'd, thus issuing, angry, his commands,
    Quick! quick! ye slothful in your father's cause,
Ye worthless brood! would that in Hector's stead
Ye all had perish'd in the fleet of Greece!     325
Oh altogether wretched! in all Troy
No man had sons to boast valiant as mine,
And I have lost them all.   Nestor is gone
The godlike, Troilus the steed-renown'd,
And Hector, who with other men compared    330
Seem'd a Divinity, whom none had deem'd
From mortal man derived, but from a God.
These Mars hath taken, and hath left me none
But scandals of my house, void of all truth,
Dancers, exact step-measurers[6], a band     335
Of public robbers, thieves of kids and lambs.
Will ye not bring my litter to the gate
This moment, and with all this package quick
Charge it, that we may hence without delay?
    He said, and by his chiding awed, his sons    340
Drew forth the royal litter, neat, new-built,
And following swift the draught, on which they bound

       [6] κοροιτυπιῇσιν ἄριϛοι.

The coffer; next, they lower'd from the wall
The sculptured boxen yoke with its two rings[7];
And with the yoke its furniture, in length       345
Nine cubits; this to the extremest end
Adjusting of the pole, they cast the ring
Over the ring-bolt; then, thrice through the yoke
They drew the brace on both sides, made it fast
With even knots, and tuck'd[8] the dangling ends.     350
Producing, next, the glorious ransom-price
Of Hector's body, on the litter's floor
They heap'd it all, then yoked the sturdy mules,
A gift illustrious by the Mysians erst
Conferred on Priam; to the chariot, last,       355
They led forth Priam's steeds, which the old King
(In person serving them) with freshest corn
Constant supplied; meantime, himself within
The palace, and his herald, were employ'd
Girding[9] themselves, to go; wise each and good.    360
And now came mournful Hecuba, with wine
Delicious charged, which in a golden cup
She brought, that not without libation due
First made, they might depart. Before the steeds
Her steps she stay'd, and Priam thus address'd.     365
    Take this, and to the Sire of all perform
Libation, praying him a safe return
From hostile hands, since thou art urged to seek
The Grecian camp, though not by my desire.
Pray also to Idæan Jove cloud-girt,        370
Who oversees all Ilium, that he send
His messenger, or ere thou go, the bird
His favourite most, surpassing all in strength,
At thy right-hand; him seeing, thou shalt tend

---

[7] Through which the reins were passed.

[8] The yoke being flat at bottom, and the pole round, there would of course be a small aperture between the band and the pole on both sides, through which, according to the Scholium in Villoisson, they thrust the ends of the tackle lest they should dangle.

[9] The text here is extremely intricate; as it stands now, the sons are, first, said to yoke the horses, then Priam and Idæus are said to do it, and in the palace too. I have therefore adopted an alteration suggested by Clarke, who with very little violence to the copy, proposes instead of ζευγνύσθην to read—ζωννύσθην.

With better hope toward the fleet of Greece. 375
But should loud-thundering Jove his lieger swift
Withhold, from me far be it to advise
This journey, howsoe'er thou wish to go.
   To whom the godlike Priam thus replied.
This exhortation will I not refuse, 380
O Queen ! for, lifting to the Gods his hands
In prayer for their compassion, none can err.
   So saying, he bade the maiden o'er the rest,
Chief in authority, pour on his hands
Pure water, for the maiden at his side 385
With ewer charged and laver, stood prepared.
He laved his hands ; then, taking from the Queen
The goblet, in his middle area stood
Pouring libation with his eyes upturn'd
Heaven-ward devout, and thus his prayer preferr'd. 390
   Jove, great and glorious above all, who rulest,
On Ida's summit seated, all below !
Grant me arrived within Achilles' tent
Kindness to meet and pity, and oh send
Thy messenger or ere I go, the bird 395
Thy favourite most, surpassing all in strength,
At my right hand, which seeing, I shall tend
With better hope toward the fleet of Greece.
   He ended, at whose prayer, incontinent,
Jove sent his eagle, surest of all signs, 400
The black-plumed bird voracious, Morphnos[10] named,
And Percnos.[10]  Wide as the well-guarded door
Of some rich potentate his vans he spread
On either side ; they saw him on the right,
Skimming the towers of Troy ; glad they beheld 405
That omen, and all felt their hearts consoled.
   Delay'd not then the hoary King, but quick
Ascending to his seat, his coursers urged
Through vestibule and sounding porch abroad.
The four-wheel'd litter led, drawn by the mules 410
Which sage Idæus managed, behind whom
Went Priam, plying with the scourge his steeds
Continual through the town, while all his friends,
Following their sovereign with dejected hearts,

         [10] The words both signify—sable.

Lamented him as going to his death.                       415
But when from Ilium's gate into the plain
They had descended, then the sons-in-law
Of Priam, and his sons, to Troy return'd.
Nor they, now traversing the plain, the note
Escaped of Jove the Thunderer; he beheld         420
Compassionate the venerable King,
And thus his own son Mercury bespake.
    Mercury! (for above all others thou
Delightest to associate with mankind
Familiar, whom thou wilt winning with ease        425
To converse free,) go thou, and so conduct
Priam into the Grecian camp, that none
Of all the numerous Danaï may see
Or mark him, till he reach Achilles' tent.
    He spake, nor the ambassador of heaven        430
The Argicide delay'd, but bound in haste
His undecaying sandals to his feet,
Golden, divine, which waft him o'er the floods
Swift as the wind, and o'er the boundless earth.
He took his rod with which he charms to sleep      435
All eyes, and theirs who sleep opens again.
Arm'd with that rod, forth flew the Argicide.
At Ilium and the Hellespontic shores
Arriving sudden, a King's son he seem'd,
Now clothing first his ruddy cheek with down,      440
Which is youth's loveliest season; so disguised,
His progress he began.   They now (the tomb
Magnificent of Ilus past) beside
The river stay'd the mules and steeds to drink,
For twilight dimm'd the fields.   Idæus first       445
Perceived him near, and Priam thus bespake.
    Think, son of Dardanus! for we have need
Of our best thought.   I see a warrior.   Now,
Now we shall die; I know it.   Turn we quick
Our steeds to flight; or let us clasp his knees    450
And his compassion suppliant essay.
    Terror and consternation at that sound
The mind of Priam felt; erect the hair
Bristled his limbs, and with amaze he stood
Motionless.  But the God, meantime, approach'd,    455

And, seizing ancient Priam's hand, enquired.
   Whither, my father! in the dewy night
Drivest thou thy mules and steeds, while others sleep?
And fear'st thou not the fiery host of Greece,
Thy foes implacable, so nigh at hand?        460
Of whom should any, through the shadow dun
Of flitting night, discern thee bearing forth
So rich a charge, then what wouldst thou expect?
Thou art not young thyself, nor with the aid
Of this thine ancient servant, strong enough     465
Force to repulse, should any threaten force.
But injury fear none or harm from me;
I rather much from harm by other hands
Would save thee, thou resemblest so my sire.
   Whom answer'd godlike Priam, hoar with age.  470
My son! well spoken.  Thou hast judged aright.
Yet even me some Deity protects
Thus far; to whom I owe it that I meet
So seasonably one like thee, in form
So admirable, and in mind discreet        475
As thou art beautiful.  Blest parents, thine!
   To whom the messenger of heaven again,
The Argicide.  Oh ancient and revered!
Thou hast well spoken all.  Yet this declare,
And with sincerity; bear'st thou away     480
Into some foreign country, for the sake
Of safer custody, this precious charge?
Or, urged by fear, forsake ye all alike
Troy's sacred towers? since he whom thou hast lost,
Thy noble son, was of excelling worth     485
In arms, and nought inferior to the Greeks.
   Then thus the godlike Priam, hoary King.
But tell me first, who *Thou* art, and from whom
Descended, loveliest youth! who hast the fate
So well of my unhappy son rehearsed?    490
   To whom the herald Mercury replied.
Thy questions, venerable Sire! proposed
Concerning noble Hector, are design'd
To prove me.  Him, not seldom, with these eyes
In man-ennobling fight I have beheld    495
Most active; saw him when he thinn'd the Greeks

With his sharp spear, and drove them to the ships.
Amazed we stood to notice him ; for us,
Incensed against the ruler of our host,
Achilles suffer'd not to share the fight.                    500
I serve Achilles ; the same gallant bark
Brought us, and of the Myrmidons am I,
Son of Polyctor ; wealthy is my Sire,
And such in years as thou ; six sons he hath,
Beside myself the seventh, and, (the lots cast            505
Among us all,) mine sent me to the wars.
That I have left the ships, seeking the plain,
The cause is this ; the Greeks, at break of day,
Will compass, arm'd, the city, for they loathe
To sit inactive, neither can the chiefs                    510
Restrain the hot impatience of the host.
  Then godlike Priam answer thus return'd.
If of the band thou be of Peleus' son,
Achilles, tell me undisguised the truth.
My son, subsists he still, or hath thy Chief              515
Limb after limb given him to his dogs ?
  Him answer'd then the herald of the skies.
Oh venerable Sir ! him neither dogs
Have eaten yet, nor fowls, but at the ships
His body, and within Achilles' tent                        520
Neglected lies.   Twelve days he so hath lain ;
Yet neither worm which diets on the brave
In battle fallen, hath eaten him, or taint
Invaded.   He around Patroclus' tomb
Drags him indeed pitiless, oft as day                      525
Reddens the East, yet safe from blemish still
His corse remains.   Thou would'st, thyself, admire,
Seeing how fresh the dew-drops, as he lies,
Rest on him, and his blood is cleansed away
That not a stain is left.   Even his wounds                530
(For many a wound they gave him) all are closed,
Such care the blessed Gods have of thy son,
Dead as he is, whom living much they loved.
  So he ; then, glad, the ancient King replied.
Good is it, oh my son ! to yield the Gods                  535
Their just demands.   My boy, while yet he lived,
Lived not unmindful of the worship due

To the Olympian powers, who, therefore, him
Remember, even in the bands of death.
Come then—this beauteous cup take at my hand—     540
Be thou my guard, and, if the Gods permit,
My guide, till to Achilles' tent I come.
    Whom answer'd then the messenger of heaven.
Sir! thou perceivest me young, and art disposed
To try my virtue; but it shall not fail.     545
Thou bidd'st me at thine hand a gift accept,
Whereof Achilles knows not; but I fear
Achilles, and on no account should dare
Defraud him, lest some evil find me next.
But Thee I would with pleasure hence conduct     550
Even to glorious Argos, over sea
Or over land, nor any, through contempt
Of such a guard, should dare to do thee wrong.
    So Mercury, and to the chariot seat
Upspringing, seized at once the lash and reins,     555
And with fresh vigour mules and steeds inspired.
Arriving at the foss and towers, they found
The guard preparing now their evening cheer,
All whom the Argicide with sudden sleep
Oppress'd, then oped the gates, thrust back the bars, .     560
And introduced, with all his litter-load
Of costly gifts, the venerable King.
But when they reach'd the tent for Peleus' son
Raised by the Myrmidons (with trunks of pine
They built it, lopping smooth the boughs away,     565
Then spread with shaggy mowings of the mead
Its lofty roof, and with a spacious court
Surrounded it, all fenced with driven stakes;
One bar alone of pine secured the door,
Which ask'd three Grecians with united force     570
To thrust it to its place, and three again
To thrust it back, although Achilles oft
Would heave it to the door himself alone;)
Then Hermes, benefactor of mankind,
That bar displacing for the King of Troy,     575
Gave entrance to himself and to his gifts
For Peleus' son design'd, and from the seat
Alighting, thus his speech to Priam turn'd.

Oh ancient Priam! an immortal God
Attends thee; I am Hermes, by command          580
Of Jove my father thy appointed guide.
But I return.   I will not, entering here,
Stand in Achilles' sight; immortal Powers
May not so unreservedly indulge
Creatures of mortal kind.   But enter thou,     585
Embrace his knees, and by his father both
And by his Goddess mother sue to him,
And by his son, that his whole heart may melt.
   So Hermes spake, and to the skies again
Ascended.   Then leap'd Priam to the ground,    590
Leaving Idæus; he, the mules and steeds
Watch'd, while the ancient King into the tent
Proceeded of Achilles dear to Jove.
Him there he found, and sitting found apart
His fellow-warriors, of whom two alone          595
Served at his side, Alcimus, branch of Mars,
And brave Automedon; he had himself
Supp'd newly, and the board stood unremoved.
Unseen of all huge Priam enter'd, stood
Near to Achilles, clasp'd his knees, and kiss'd  600
Those terrible and homicidal hands
That had destroy'd so many of his sons.
As when a fugitive for blood the house
Of some Chief enters in a foreign land,
All gaze, astonish'd at the sudden guest,         605
So gazed Achilles, seeing Priam there,
And so stood all astonish'd, each his eyes
In silence fastening on his fellow's face.
But Priam kneel'd, and suppliant thus began.
   Think, oh Achilles, semblance of the Gods!   610
On thy own father full of days like me,
And trembling on the gloomy verge of life.
Some neighbour Chief, it may be, even now,
Oppresses him, and there is none at hand,
No friend to succour him in his distress.          615
Yet, doubtless, hearing that Achilles lives,
He still rejoices, hoping day by day,
That one day he shall see the face again

Of his own son from distant Troy return'd.
But me no comfort cheers, whose bravest sons,          620
So late the flower of Ilium, all are slain.
When Greece came hither, I had fifty sons ;
Nineteen were children of one bed, the rest
Born of my concubines.   A numerous house !
But fiery Mars hath thinn'd it.   One I had,          625
One, more than all my sons the strength of Troy,
Whom standing for his country thou hast slain—
Hector—His body to redeem I come
Into Achaia's fleet, bringing, myself,
Ransom inestimable to thy tent.          630
Reverence the Gods, Achilles ! recollect
Thy father ; for his sake compassion show
To me more pitiable still, who draw
Home to my lips, (humiliation yet
Unseen on earth) his hand who slew my son.          635
      So saying, he waken'd in his soul regret
Of his own Sire ; softly he placed his hand
On Priam's hand, and push'd him gently away.
Remembrance melted both.   Rolling before
Achilles' feet, Priam his son deplored          640
Wide-slaughtering Hector, and Achilles wept
By turns his father, and by turns his friend
Patroclus ; sounds of sorrow fill'd the tent.
But when, at length satiate, Achilles felt
His heart from grief, and all his frame relieved,          645
Upstarting from his seat, with pity moved
Of Priam's silver locks and silver beard,
He raised the ancient father by his hand,
Whom in wing'd accents kind he thus bespake.
      Wretched indeed ! ah what must thou have felt !          650
How hast thou dared to seek alone the fleet
Of the Achaians, and his face by whom
So many of thy valiant sons have fallen ?
Thou hast an heart of iron, terror-proof.
Come—sit beside me—Let us, if we may,          655
Great mourners both, bid sorrow sleep awhile.
There is no profit of our sighs and tears ;
For thus, exempt from care themselves, the Gods

Ordain man's miserable race to mourn.
Fast by the threshold of Jove's courts are placed          660
Two casks, one stored with evil, one with good,
From which the God dispenses as he wills.
For whom the glorious Thunderer mingles both,
He leads a life checker'd with good and ill
Alternate; but to whom he gives unmix'd          665
The bitter cup, he makes that man a curse,
His name becomes a by-word of reproach,
His strength is hunger-bitten, and he walks
The blessed earth, unblest, go where he may.
So was my father Peleus at his birth          670
Nobly endow'd with plenty and with wealth
Distinguish'd by the Gods past all mankind,
Lord of the Myrmidons, and, though a man,
Yet match'd from heaven with an immortal bride.
But even him the Gods afflict, a son          675
Refusing him, who might possess his throne
Hereafter; for myself, his only heir,
Pass as a dream, and while I live, instead
Of solacing his age, here sit, before
Your distant walls, the scourge of thee and thine.          680
Thee also, ancient Priam, we have heard
Reported, once possessor of such wealth
As neither Lesbos, seat of Macar, owns,
Nor Eastern Phrygia, nor yet all the ports
Of Hellespont, but thou didst pass them all          685
In riches, and in number of thy sons.
But since the Powers of Heaven brought on thy land
This fatal war, battle and deeds of death
Always surround the city where thou reign'st.
Cease, therefore, from unprofitable tears,          690
Which, ere they raise thy son to life again,
Shall, doubtless, find fresh cause for which to flow.
    To whom the ancient king godlike replied.
Hero, forbear.   No seat is here for me,
While Hector lies unburied in your camp.          695
Loose him, and loose him now, that with these eyes
I may behold my son; accept a price
Magnificent, which may'st thou long enjoy,

And, since my life was precious in thy sight,
May'st thou revisit safe thy native shore !  700
   To whom Achilles, louring, and in wrath[11].
Urge me no longer, at a time like this,
With that harsh note ; I am already inclined
To loose him.  Thetis, my own mother came
Herself on that same errand, sent from Jove.  705
Priam ! I understand thee well.  I know
That, by some God conducted, thou hast reach'd
Achaia's fleet ; for, without aid divine,
No mortal even in his prime of youth,
Had dared the attempt ; guards vigilant as ours  710
He should not easily elude, such gates,
So massy, should not easily unbar.
Thou, therefore, vex me not in my distress,
Lest I abhor to see thee in my tent,
And, borne beyond all limits, set at nought  715
Thee, and thy prayer, and the command of Jove.
   He said ; the old King trembled, and obey'd.
Then sprang Pelides like a lion forth,
Not sole, but with his two attendant friends
Alcimus and Automedon the brave,  720
For them (Patroclus slain) he honour'd most
Of all the Myrmidons.  They from the yoke
Released both steeds and mules, then introduced
And placed the herald of the hoary King.
They lighten'd next the litter of its charge  725
Inestimable, leaving yet behind
Two mantles and a vest, that, not unveil'd
The body might be borne back into Troy.
Then, calling forth his women, them he bade
Lave and anoint the body, but apart,  730
Lest haply Priam, noticing his son,
Through stress of grief should give resentment scope,
And irritate by some affront himself
To slay him, in despite of Jove's commands.

[11] Mortified to see his generosity, after so much kindness shown to Priam, still distrusted, and that the impatience of the old king threatened to deprive him of all opportunity to do gracefully what he could not be expected to do willingly.

They, thereforo, laving and anointing first                    735
The body, cover'd it with cloak and vest ;
Then, Peleus' son disposed it on the bier,
Lifting it from the ground, and his two friends
Together heaved it to the Royal wain.
Achilles, last, groaning, his friend invoked.                  740
  Patroclus! should the tidings reach thine ear,
Although in Ades, that I have released
The noble Hector at his father's suit,
Resent it not ; nor sordid gifts have paid
His ransom-price, which thou shalt also share.                 745
  So saying, Achilles to his tent return'd,
And on the splendid couch whence he had risen
Again reclined, opposite to the seat
Of Priam, whom the Hero thus bespake.
  Priam! at thy request thy son is loosed,           750
And lying on his bier ; at dawn of day
Thou shalt both see him and convey him hence
Thyself to Troy.   But take we now repast;
For even bright-hair'd Niobe her food
Forgat not, though of children twelve bereft,                  755
Of daughters six, and of six blooming sons.
Apollo these struck from his silver bow,
And those shaft-arm'd Diana, both incensed
That oft Latona's children and her own
Numbering, she scorn'd the Goddess who had borne               760
Two only, while herself had twelve to boast.
Vain boast! those two sufficed to slay them all.
Nine days they welter'd in their blood, no man
Was found to bury them, for Jove had changed
To stone the people ; but themselves, at last,                 765
The Powers of Heaven entomb'd them on the tenth.
Yet even she, once satisfied with tears,
Remember'd food ; and now, the rocks among
And pathless solitudes of Sipylus,
The rumour'd cradle of the nymphs who dance                    770
On Acheloüs' banks, although to stone
Transform'd, she broods her heaven-inflicted woes.
Come, then, my venerable guest! take we
Refreshment also ; once arrived in Troy

With thy dear son, thou shalt have time to weep 775
Sufficient, nor without most weighty cause.
　So spake Achilles, and, upstarting, slew
A sheep white-fleeced, which his attendants flay'd,
And busily and with much skill their task
Administering, first scored the viands well, 780
Then pierced them with the spits, and when the roast
Was finish'd, drew them from the spits again.
And now, Automedon dispensed around
The polish'd board bread in neat baskets piled,
Which done, Achilles portion'd out to each 785
His share, and all assail'd the ready feast.
But when nor hunger more nor thirst they felt,
Dardanian Priam, wond'ring at his bulk
And beauty, (for he seem'd some God from heaven)
Gazed on Achilles, while Achilles held 790
Not less in admiration of his looks
Benign, and of his gentle converse wise,
Gazed on Dardanian Priam, and, at length,
(The eyes of each gratified to the full)
The ancient King thus to Achilles spake. 795
　Hero! dismiss us now each to our bed,
That there at ease reclined, we may enjoy
Sweet sleep; for never have these eyelids closed
Since Hector fell and died, but without cease
I mourn, and nourishing unnumber'd woes, 800
Have roll'd me in the ashes of my courts.
But I have now both tasted food, and given
Wine to my lips, untasted till with thee.
　So he, and at his word Achilles bade
His train beneath his portico prepare 805
With all dispatch two couches, purple rugs,
And arras, and warm mantles over all.
Forth went the women bearing lights, and spread
A couch for each, when feigning needful fear[12],

---

[12] Ἐπικερτομέων. Clarke renders the word in this place *falso metû ludens*, and Eustathius says that Achilles suggested such cause of fear to Priam, to excuse his lodging him in an exterior part of the tent. The general import of the Greek word is sarcastic, but here it signifies rather —to intimidate. See also Dacier.

Achilles thus his speech to Priam turn'd.                                810
   My aged guest beloved! sleep thou without;
Lest some Achaian Chief (for such are wont
Oftimes, here sitting, to consult with me)
Hither repair; of whom should any chance
To spy thee through the gloom, he would at once         815
Convey the tale to Agamemnon's ear,
Whence hindrance might arise, and the release
Haply of Hector's body be delay'd.
But answer me with truth.   How many days
Would'st thou assign to the funereal rites               820
Of noble Hector, for so long I mean
Myself to rest, and keep the host at home?
   Then thus the ancient King godlike replied.
If thou indeed be willing that we give
Burial to noble Hector, by an act                        825
So generous, O Achilles! me thou shalt
Much gratify; for we are shut, thou know'st,
In Ilium close, and fuel must procure
From Ida's side remote; fear, too, hath seized
On all our people.   Therefore thus I say.               830
Nine days we wish to mourn him in the house;
To his interment we would give the tenth,
And to the public banquet; the eleventh
Shall see us build his tomb; and on the twelfth
(If war we must) we will to war again.                   835
   To whom Achilles, matchless in the race.
So be it, ancient Priam! I will curb
Twelve days the rage of war, at thy desire.
   He spake, and at his wrist the right hand grasp'd
Of the old Sovereign, to dispel his fear.                .840
Then in the vestibule the herald slept
And Priam, prudent both, but Peleus' son
In the interior tent, and at his side
Briseïs, with transcendent beauty adorn'd.
Now all, all night, by gentle sleep subdued,             845
Both Gods and chariot-ruling warriors lay,
But not the benefactor of mankind,
Hermes; him sleep seized not, but deep he mused
How likeliest from amid the Grecian fleet

He might deliver by the guard unseen                                    850
The King of Ilium; at his head he stood
In vision, and the senior thus bespake.
     Ah heedless and secure! hast thou no dread
Of mischief, ancient King, that thus by foes
Thou sleep'st surrounded, lull'd by the consent              855
And sufferance of Achilles? Thou hast given
Much for redemption of thy darling son,
But thrice that sum thy sons who still survive
Must give to Agamemnon and the Greeks
For *thy* redemption, should they know thee here.            860
     He ended; at the sound alarm'd upsprang
The King, and roused his herald.   Hermes yoked
Himself both mules and steeds, and through the camp
Drove them incontinent, by all unseen.
     Soon as the windings of the stream they reach'd,         865
Deep-eddied Xanthus, progeny of Jove,
Mercury the Olympian summit sought,
And saffron-vested morn o'erspread the earth.
They, loud lamenting, to the city drove
Their steeds; the mules close follow'd with the dead.        870
Nor warrior yet, nor cinctured matron knew
Of all in Ilium aught of their approach,
Cassandra sole except.   She, beautiful
As golden Venus, mounted on the height
Of Pergamus, her father first discern'd,                     875
Borne on his chariot-seat erect, and knew
The herald heard so oft in echoing Troy;
Him also on his bier outstretch'd she mark'd,
Whom the mules drew.  Then, shrieking through the streets
She ran of Troy, and loud proclaim'd the sight.              880
     Ye sons of Ilium and ye daughters, haste,
Haste all to look on Hector, if ye e'er
With joy beheld him, while he yet survived,
From fight returning; for all Ilium erst
In him, and all her citizens rejoiced.                       885
     She spake.   Then neither male nor female more
In Troy remain'd, such sorrow seized on all.
Issuing from the city-gate, they met
Priam conducting, sad, the body home,

And, foremost of them all, the mother flew                    890
And wife of Hector to the bier, on    hich
Their torn-off tresses with unsparing hands
They shower'd, while all the people wept around.
All day, and to the going down of day
They thus had mourn'd the dead before the gates,              895
Had not their Sovereign from his chariot-seat
Thus spoken to the multitude around.
    Fall back on either side, and let the mules
Pass on ; the body in my palace once
Deposited, ye then may weep your fill.                        900
    He said ; they, opening, gave the litter way.
Arrived within the royal house, they stretch'd
The breathless Hector on a sumptuous bed,
And singers placed beside him, who should chaunt
The strain funereal ; they with many a groan                 905
The dirge began, and still, at every close,
The female train with many a groan replied.
Then, in the midst, Andromache white-arm'd
Between her palms the dreadful Hector's head
Pressing, her lamentation thus began.                        910
    My Hero ! thou hast fallen in prime of life,
Me leaving here desolate, and the fruit
Of our ill-fated loves, an helpless child;
Whom grown to manhood I despair to see.
For ere that day arrive, down from her height                915
Precipitated shall this city fall,
Since thou hast perish'd once her sure defence,
Faithful protector of her spotless wives,
And all their little ones.   Those wives shall soon
In Grecian barks capacious hence be borne,                   920
And I among the rest.   But thee, my child !
Either thy fate shall with thy mother send
Captive into a land where thou shalt serve
In sordid drudgery some cruel lord,
Or haply some Achaian here, thy hand                         925
Seizing, shall hurl thee from a turret-top
To a sad death, avenging brother, son,
Or father by the hands of Hector slain ;
For He made many a Grecian bite the ground.

Thy father, boy, bore never into fight          930
A milky mind, and for that self-same cause
Is now bewailed in every house of Troy.
Sorrow unutterable thou hast caused
Thy parents, Hector! but to me hast left
Largest bequest of misery, to whom,          935
Dying, thou neither didst thy arms extend
Forth from thy bed, nor gavest me precious word
To be remember'd day and night with tears.
 So spake she weeping, whom her maidens all
With sighs accompanied, and her complaint          940
Mingled with sobs Hecuba next began.
 Ah Hector! dearest to thy mother's heart
Of all her sons, much must the Gods have loved
Thee living, whom, though dead, they thus preserve.
What son soever of our house beside          945
Achilles took, over the barren Deep
To Samos, Imbrus, or to Lemnos girt
With rocks inhospitable, him he sold;
But thee, by his dread spear of life deprived,
He dragg'd and dragg'd around Patroclus' tomb,          950
As if to raise again his friend to life
Whom thou hadst vanquish'd; yet he raised him not.
But as for thee, thou liest here with dew
Besprinkled, fresh as a young plant[13], and more
Resemblest some fair youth by gentle shafts          955
Of Phœbus pierced, than one in battle slain.
 So spake the Queen, exciting in all hearts
Sorrow immeasurable, after whom
Thus Helen, third, her lamentation pour'd.
 Ah, dearer far than all my brothers else          960
Of Priam's house! for being Paris' spouse,
Who brought me (would I had first died!) to Troy,
I call thy brothers mine; since forth I came
From Sparta, it is now the twentieth year,
Yet never heard I once hard speech from thee,          965
Or taunt morose, but if it ever chanced,
That of thy father's house female or male

[13] This, according to the Scholiast, is a probable sense of προσφατες.—
He derives it απο των νεωστι πεφασμενων εκ γης φυτων.—See Villoisson.

Blamed me, and even if herself the Queen,
(For in the King, whate'er befell, I found
Always a father,) thou hast interposed                    970
Thy gentle temper and thy gentle speech
To soothe them ; therefore, with the same sad drops
Thy fate, oh Hector ! and my own I weep ;
For other friend within the ample bounds
Of Ilium have I none, nor hope to hear                    975
Kind word again, with horror view'd by all.
    So Helen spake weeping, to whom with groans
The countless multitude replied, and thus
Their ancient Sovereign next his people charged.
    Ye Trojans, now bring fuel home, nor fear             980
Close ambush of the Greeks ; Achilles' self
Gave me, at my dismission from his fleet,
Assurance, that from hostile force secure
We shall remain, till the twelfth dawn arise.
    All, then, their mules and oxen to the wains          985
Join'd speedily, and under Ilium's walls
Assembled numerous ; nine whole days they toil'd,
Bringing much fuel home, and when the tenth
Bright morn, with light for human kind arose,
Then bearing noble Hector forth with tears               990
Shed copious, on the summit of the pile
They placed him, and the fuel fired beneath.
    But when Aurora, daughter of the Dawn,
Redden'd the East, then, thronging forth, all Troy
Encompass'd noble Hector's pile around.                   995
The whole vast multitude convened, with wine
They quench'd the pile throughout, leaving no part
Unvisited, on which the fire had seized.
His brothers, next, collected, and his friends,
His white bones, mourning and with tears profuse         1000
Watering their cheeks ; then in a golden urn
They placed them, which with mantles soft they veil'd
Mæonian-hued, and, delving, buried it,
And overspread with stones the spot adust.
Lastly, short time allowing to the task,                 1005
They heap'd his tomb, while, posted on all sides,
Suspicious of assault, spies watch'd the Greeks.

The tomb once heap'd, assembling all again
Within the palace, they a banquet shared
Magnificent, by godlike Priam given.                    1010

Such burial the illustrious Hector found[14].

[14] Ὡς ὁιγ' αμφιεπον ταφον Ἑκτορος ἱπποδαμοιο.

I cannot take my leave of this noble poem, without expressing how much I am struck with this plain conclusion of it. It is like the exit of a great man out of company whom he has entertained magnificently; neither pompous nor familiar; not contemptuous, yet without much ceremony. I recollect nothing, among the works of mere man, that exemplifies so strongly the true style of great antiquity.

END OF THE ILIAD.

J. BILLING,
PRINTER AND STEREOTYPER,
WOKING, SURREY.

Lightning Source UK Ltd.
Milton Keynes UK
UKHW030634270223
417728UK00009B/832